Teaching
Reading
in Adult
Basic
Education

Fay F. Bowren
Illinois State University

Miles V. Zintz
University of New Mexico

Teaching Reading
in Adult
Basic
Education

wcb

William C. Brown Company Publishers

Dubuque, Iowa

To
Russell A. Bowren
and
Mary Hatley Zintz

I returned and saw under the sun that
the race is not to the swift nor the
battle to the strong. . . .
Ecclesiastes 9:11

Contents

Preface, xi

Part 1: The Adult as a Learner

1. Introduction: Three Case Studies   3
   Steve—A Broken Engagement, 3
   Laura Wants to Know: Can She Ever Learn to Read? 4
   Tom Wonders About His Future, 5
   Prediction, 7

2. A Profile of the Undereducated Adult   8
   Differences in Instructional Needs, 9
   Considerations of Adults as Learners, 10
   Hostility Toward the School World, 19
   Summary, 21

3. Physical Factors Related to Adult Learning   22
   Neurological Factors Involved in the Reading Process, 23
   Auditory Factors Involved in the Reading Process, 25
   Visual Factors Involved in the Reading Process, 26
   Motor Factors Related to Adult Learning, 28
   Provisions for Physical Needs in Adult Learning, 29
   Summary, 30

4. Sociological and Environmental Factors   31
   The Different Value Structure: A Pragmatic One, 31
   Other Poverty-related Factors in Adult Learning, 32
   Family Maintenance Problems Related to Adult Learning, 34
   Summary, 37

5. Psychological Considerations in Teaching Undereducated Adults   38
   Psychological Consequences of Illiteracy, 38
   "Face-Saving" Psychological Defenses in Adult Learning, 39
   The Challenge of Empathy—Not Sympathy, 40
   The Dynamics of Fear and Anxiety in Adult Learning, 41
   Summary, 51

6. The Learning Ability of Adults   52

Adult Intelligence, 52
Changes in Adult Intellectual Functioning, 55
Memory and Retention in Adult Learning, 59
The Relation of Verbal Ability to Intelligence, 60
Correlates of Adult Learning Ability, 61
Summary, 66

Part 2: Developing Reading Skills for the Adult Learner

7. Teaching Reading in Adult Basic Education: An Overview   69

The Nature of the Reading Process, 69
An Operational Model of the Reading Process, 72
Summary, 76

8. Teaching Reading as a Developmental Process   77

Readiness for Reading, 77
The Sequence of Language Development, 78
Summary, 87

9. Learning Theory Applied to Adult Reading Instruction   88

Basic Principles of Learning, 88
The Use of Behavioral Objectives, 94
Summary, 94

10. Orienting Beginning Reading Experiences to Adult Learners   95

Problems in Selecting an Approach to Beginning Reading, 96
The Laubach System to Beginning Reading, 112
The Use of a Language-Experience Approach, 116
Building Sight Vocabulary Systematically, 118
Learning the Alphabet, 119
Developing Word Identification Readiness, 121
Developing Structural and Phonic Analysis Competency, 124
Summary, 129

11. Achieving Independence in Word Identification   130

Twenty General Principles of Teaching Word Identification, 131
Expanding Language Experiences, 134
Summary, 145

12. Comprehension Skills in Reading   147

Finding Information, 148
Comprehension Exercises, 156
Learning to Anticipate Meaning, 167

Extending Vocabulary, 169
Readability, 177
Remembering What You Read, 179
Summary, 180

13. Integrating Handwriting Experience with Reading Instruction   181

Filling in Forms, 183
Writing Dictation Exercises, 194
Summary, 197

14. Teaching Reading to Adults from Non-English Speaking or
Nonstandard Dialect Origins   199

Cultural Awareness, 199
Nonstandard English, 203
Black English, 205
Teaching English as a Second Language, 209
Summary, 223

Part 3: Assessing Reading Needs in Adult Basic Education

15. Resources for Assessment of Reading Needs   227

Basic Considerations for Gathering Diagnostic Data, 227
Observation and Case Study as an Assessment Tool, 230
The Importance of Rapport, 236
Plan for Assessment, 237
Summary, 238

16. Informally Determining Reading Levels   239

Identifying Reading Levels, 239
Quick Assessment Through Word Lists, 241
Teacher-made Informal Reading Inventories, 244
Commercially Prepared Informal Reading Inventories, 246
Cloze Exercises Used for Evaluation, 246
Summary, 248

17. Standardized Evaluation of Reading Achievement   249

Oral Reading Tests, 249
Silent Reading Tests, 250
Summary, 275

18. Looking at Specifics in Analyzing Reading   276

Separating the Strands of the Reading Problem, 276
Learning Style Diagnosis, 281
Summary, 285

19. Assessment of Reading and Learning Potential   287

Assessment Through Listening Comprehension, 287
Assessment Through Measurement of Learning Ability, 289
Summary, 299

20. Guiding Adults in Decision Making   300

The Educational Ladder Is Accessible, 300
Decision Making Can Change Behavior, 304
Common Types of Family Problems, 308
Benjamin: An Illustrative Case Study, 311
Summary, 312

Appendixes
    1. The Fernald Kinesthetic Tracing Technique   313
    2. Selected Sources of Materials for Teaching Reading   315
    3. A Selected List of Tesol Text Materials   320
    4. Evaluation Form   322
    5. Common Prefixes and Suffixes   324
    6. Generalizations About Consonants and Vowels   326
    7. Syllabication Generalizations   329
    8. Word Accent (Stress) Generalizations   330
    9. List of Important Prepositional Phrases   333
   10. The Fry Readability Graph   335
   11. The Flesch Readability Formula   336
   12. The Fog Index—A Quick Estimate of Readability   339
   13. Wilson's Essential Vocabulary List   340
   14. Adult Basic Education Curriculum Guide Vocabulary List   342
   15. A List of Basic Sight Words for Older Disabled Readers   343
   16. Slosson Oral Reading Test (SORT)   344
   17. The Graded Word List: Quick Gauge of Reading Ability   348
   18. Botel Reading Inventory   351
   19. Brief Individual Instant Word Oral Reading Test   355
   20. Model for an Informal Reading Inventory   361
   21. Cloze Exercise   363
   22. Reading Diagnosis Sheet   365
   23. Wepman Auditory Discrimination Test   366
   24. List of Easily Confused Words   370
   25. Boyd Test of Phonetic Skills   371
   26. Compound Words Test   376
   27. Strength-Weakness Spectrum for Wechsler Tests   377

Bibliography, 381
Index, 399

Preface

Teaching Reading in Adult Basic Education was never intended to join the ranks of general basic texts on the pedagogy of reading. Instead, it was written to provide a particular kind of sorely needed material. Therefore, this volume is directed toward several *specific* audiences.

First, *Teaching Reading in Adult Basic Education* was written to serve as a textbook for teacher education programs and for various inservice programs in the specific training of teachers for adult basic education, rather than for the training of reading teachers in general. To insure the greatest usefulness, we have attempted to synthesize the thinking of many outstanding theorists and practitioners in this field with the ideas and thoughts gleaned from our own expertise and experience with adult education programs. Special attention has been paid to documentation and to bibliographies, so that students with scholarly intent can further pursue these topics.

Secondly, *Teaching Reading in Adult Basic Education* is intended to be profitable for that vast segment of adult basic education teachers whose primary professional training or interest has been the education of either children or teenagers. Often, dedicated teachers who work very effectively with child and adolescent learners feel frustrated in coping with some particular needs of adults. This book offers specific suggestions for bridging these gaps.

Thirdly, *Teaching Reading in Adult Basic Education* is addressed to the present teachers of reading in all adult basic education programs, regardless of type or sponsoring agency. Many of these teachers have not been specifically trained in reading methods and are looking for help. We address ourselves to these instructional concerns rather than to administrative problems, and suggest many ways in which present adult basic education programs can be strengthened.

Fourth, *Teaching Reading in Adult Basic Education* is written for the volunteer lay tutor who is conscientiously endeavoring to teach an adult to read. In all probability, whatever specific materials the tutor elects to use in teaching reading, the publisher has provided a sufficient manual (or cookbook) that, if followed, will usually enable the tutor to achieve positive results. However, few manuals attempt to expand the tutor's horizons beyond such specifics into the actual field of reading, such that if the learner is experiencing less than optimum success in learning to read, the tutor can knowledgeably consider alternatives. This book is concerned with this need, which has been voiced by volunteer tutors. In order to be readable to our audience, we have tried when possible to avoid the usage of educational jargon. Where it has been necessary to use terminology that may not be familiar to the lay tutor, the first usage of the term appears in italics with its explanation in the page footnote.

Teaching Reading in Adult Basic Education also has a point of view. Being a complex individual, the adult learner has diverse needs, most of which have some bearing on the reading difficulty. Such needs of a fellow human being may in some respects be as relevant to the teaching of reading as phonics! Therefore, successful reading instruction in adult education is humanistic. It reckons with individual needs, considers the whole person, and provides structure and security.

Throughout the text, the reader will undoubtedly notice the pronoun *he* used in reference to both the learner and the teacher. Masculine pronouns have been employed for succinctness and are intended to refer to females and males.

Teaching Reading in Adult Basic Education is not complete. There seems to be no end to the areas that need to be covered in a book such as this. As each chapter was finished, we were plagued by "I wish we had included. . . ." "Don't you think we should also add. . . ." and "We really ought to go into more depth on. . . ." Finally, being pushed by publication deadlines, we brought it to an end, with the promise that when time came for revision, we would further attempt to build the perfect text!

Acknowledgments

Without the ideas and critiques of the hundreds of adult basic education teachers and their learners throughout the nation, this book would not have been written. They expressed their concerns and needs; let us in on their feelings; and freely shared ideas about those strategies that are effective with adults, and those that do not work. Many read and critiqued the chapters of this book. It is to these people that the authors are truly indebted.

Part 1

The Adult
as a Learner

1.
Introduction:
Three Case
Studies

*The Declaration of Independence—
one of the greatest documents ever
written. Yet, after 200 years, there are
still 21 million Americans who can't
read it. Or a ballot. Or a help-wanted
ad. Or a job application form (U.S.
News and World Report 1975, p. 4).*

A democracy can only survive if its citizens are able to participate in its operation. How is this possible for at least 21 million adults who are unable to read a ballot, much less a newspaper?

A democracy can only survive if its citizens are free to exercise their guaranteed right to the pursuit of happiness. In this space age with its accompanying explosion of knowledge, how can this happen for the 21 million adults who cannot fill out a job application, much less all the other complex forms that are a part of our society, such as social security, income tax, and credit applications?

There are twenty-one million functional illiterates in one of the most literate nations in the world (Harris 1970, 1971). Consider the cases of three of these people.

Steve—A Broken Engagement

Steve is nineteen years old and a nonreader. Despite his fourteen years of attendance in the public school and an average intelligence, he has not learned to read. He now works for his father as a construction worker, and until recently was engaged to be married. This is Steve's own story.

> From the very beginning I had trouble with reading. I repeated the first grade but that didn't help. I was big for my age, so I was never held back, except for that one time in first grade. Each year I was passed to the next grade even though I couldn't read a word. No one seemed to care except my mother. She tried to teach me at home, but that was awful! I don't even want to talk about it; it was that bad! There was just one person at school who ever tried to help me, and that was my eleventh-grade art teacher. But she didn't know how to teach reading and so that was another failure. Finally everyone gave up, and they handed me my diploma.
>
> I'm ashamed of my inability to read, and I manage to hide it from most people. But recently my reading problem blew all my plans for the future sky-high. Joan and I had been engaged for several months. She knew I didn't read much and couldn't read very well, but I guess she hadn't realized how bad my reading really was. Well, on my last

birthday my friends had a party for me. After everyone left, I asked Joan to read the birthday cards to me. What a mistake that was, because it really hit her then that I couldn't read. For several months she tried to teach me to read, but I couldn't learn a thing. Finally, she broke off the engagement, convinced that I was dumb and would make a poor husband.[1]

Laura Wants to Know: Can She Ever Learn to Read?

At age twenty-four, Laura tells her own story of how she failed to learn to read.

I knew from the beginning that I wasn't learning. My parents and two sisters soon became aware of it too. They were all very kind and tried to be helpful, but they kept hoping for a little miracle that would turn my school failure into success! My family never did feel that I was stupid; they just didn't know how to help me. They explained things over and over, but I just didn't understand.

My mother had worried about my not being able to read and had hired elementary school teachers to tutor me. But they always expected me to read from books that were too hard.

By the time I finished eighth grade, one of my sisters had moved to a large city in another state. My family decided that it might be best if I went there and lived with my sister and went to high school, since there was a reading program there. But in spite of the reading program, by the end of the tenth grade, I knew I wasn't learning to read, so I went back home to my parents. By this time, I was eighteen years old, so I got a job as a waitress in one of the restaurants where I could remember each patron's order without writing anything down except the price.

My sisters have never stopped looking for a possible way to find someone who can help me learn to read. There are so many things that I can do better than they can—like baking an apple pie or serving dinner guests, or organizing the three of us efficiently to get the work done— so they know I am not just too stupid to learn.

My sister learned about a reading center in a university town not too far from where we lived. She asked them to find out if I could learn to read.[2]

When Laura appeared for her first interview, she was extremely anxious about how well she could perform. However, as she talked with the read-

---

1. This is an actual case study reported to the authors. Names have been changed and sources not identified to protect the identity of the individuals involved.

2. This is an actual case study reported to the authors. Names have been changed and sources not identified to protect the identity of the individuals involved.

ing clinician, and was able to understand their working relationship as a positive, friendly one, she relaxed enough to explain, "I was really just afraid that you were going to tell me that I *never* could learn how to read."[3]

On the *Gilmore Oral Reading Test* (1968) her reading accuracy score was grade 3.0, with good comprehension.

On a standard spelling test that required the correct spelling of six words for beginning second grade, Laura wrote only five correctly. On a *Gates Reading Survey Test* (1958), she made a grade equivalent score of 2.4 in comprehension and 2.5 on vocabulary. Since these scores more nearly represent frustration than instructional level of reading, she needed easy reading practice at the first-grade level.

When the psychologist administered the *Wechsler Adult Intelligence Scale* (1955), he found that Laura earned her highest score reproducing graphic symbols (sequencing and copying); normal scores on reproducing block designs and arranging pictures to tell a story; and near normal scores on assembling puzzles and explaining similarities. Her *low* scores were on vocabulary, giving factual information, and solving arithmetic problems. In view of her inability to read, and her anxiety about it, it seemed completely logical that the high scores would be those least dependent on learning in school, and the low scores would be those specifically dependent upon having factual information usually learned in school.

In her initial attempt at writing, both reversals and inability to discriminate sounds were noted.

As a result of the initial examination, the staff agreed that Laura really should be able to learn to read. Certainly a hearing evaluation would be needed. If, as the tutoring progresses, other disabilities arise, there may be need for further testing. Since Laura is now wearing well-fitted contact lenses, there is a possibility that she had visual problems during her childhood that went undetected.

With such techniques as a great deal of practice in writing, in spelling word families, and in easy reading practice, Laura should develop literacy skills.

Tom Wonders About His Future

Tom and his wife, Alice, came to the literacy center early in the fall. Embarrassment spoke louder than their words as they asked how Tom might be enrolled in the reading class. The friendly, soft-spoken teacher invited them to have a cup of coffee as she filled out Tom's enrollment card. Soon,

3. Ibid.

both Tom and Alice felt that they were among friends. For this first night, Tom was introduced to his classmates. They told him what they were doing to improve their reading. Then, while Alice was talking to some of the other people, the teacher took Tom aside and asked him to read a list of words to her. It was obvious that Tom's reading instruction needed to start at the beginning levels. The teacher started him with *New Streamlined English, Book 1* (Laubach 1968). As they were working, Alice sat down beside her husband. This is Tom's story.

I never was really interested in school. My family moved frequently. I have never been able to read. We always thought that perhaps the teacher in the next school would be able to teach me, but that never happened. I do remember when I was little, I just couldn't sit still. Teachers were always trying to make me sit down. One teacher tied me to the chair!

Seems like I spent as much time in the principal's office as I did in the classroom. But, I couldn't get anything from the books, and I had to do something—so I pestered people and aggravated the teacher.

I could always do okay with things that I did not have to read— such as arguing a point in a discussion, fixing a motor, or figuring money and interest. I was good at organizing things. People would do what I told them to, so I was put in charge of raising money for things, and getting people to do things. I graduated from high school—finally— but just never did learn to read.

I got this job downtown parking cars at the parking garage. I met Alice. She was a secretary at a business next door to the garage. I fell for her like a ton of bricks! Guess the feeling was mutual, because we started dating and then were married in a few months. While we were dating, I found out that she had graduated from college, so I never told her I couldn't read.

After we were married, I became the manager of the parking garage. I listened to the news on the radio all the time, so I would know what was going on. When I got home at night, I would ask Alice to get me the newspaper. Then I would talk about the news I had heard on the radio. She never knew I couldn't read a word!

I thought I was getting by with it for three years. One day, Alice was baking a cake when I got home in the evening. The newspaper was laying open on the kitchen table. She asked me to read her the rest of the article she had started on page 2 while she finished frosting the cake for dinner. I fumbled around and told her that I had an awful headache and would do it later—hoping she would forget. But she insisted. I told her I had to go outside and mow the grass. But she thought I was being selfish and unfeeling. Finally, nothing would do but I had to tell her I couldn't read.

Well, she says she loves me but wants me to learn to read. She was awfully hurt. If I don't succeed, will she still love me? I wonder if I will lose her. I really need to learn.[4]

Prediction

There are enough case studies in the literature to indicate that adults, even though each case must be decided on its own merits, should be given opportunities to learn at whatever age they become motivated. The following are illustrative cases.

1. David's success in a Job Corps Center Program, reported by Robert D. Johnson (1970), "Reading: A Case Study," in *Reading and Revolution: The Role of Reading in Today's Society,* edited by Dorothy M. Dietrich and Virginia H. Matthews.
2. Benjamin's success in overcoming both severe economic disadvantage and illiteracy in *Benjamin: Reading and Beyond* by Thom Hawkins.
3. The cases of four children clinically taught, followed up in their late teens are reported by Madeline I. Hardy (1969), "Follow-up of Four Who Failed," in *Journal of Reading.*
4. Virginia H. Matthews (1973) writes:

   Recent writing by young black men like Malcolm X, whose homes could not give them a reading start, gives powerful testimony that an adult reading model and a reading atmosphere can come later than early childhood and still make reading a powerful force in one's life. Claude Brown, in *Manchild in the Promised Land* tells of meeting his adult reading model, a middle-aged foreign woman, a refugee whose background could hardly have been more different from his. She believed in his intellect, talked books with him, encouraged him to become a reader, and later, a writer (p. 172).

There is ample evidence that Steve, Laura, Tom, and others like them *can* be taught to read. Their guaranteed right to the pursuit of happiness need not be frustrated simply because they are unable to cope with the reading threshold that could open up so much for them. They *can* and *must* be given functional literacy skills.

---

4. This is an actual case study reported to the authors. Names have been changed and sources not identified to protect the identity of the individuals involved.

2.
A Profile of the Undereducated Adult

Illiteracy is not the same thing as stupidity. We need to give them a chance to join the human race (Source unknown).

It is easy for teachers who themselves are products of the American middle-class culture to feel that disadvantaged adults are by nature lazy, vulgar, and perverse. People characterized in such a way quickly sense these attitudes of educators toward them, and react against such intolerance or condescension with hostility, absenteeism, or failure.

Instead of stereotyping the educationally disadvantaged adults by their shortcomings, the teacher must concentrate on the fact that, despite their handicaps, it is sometimes remarkable that they succeed as well as they do (Warren 1964). There are many familiar rationalizations for these inadequacies, yet refuge to these solves nothing. In describing the disadvantaged adult, it has often been said,

He's just lazy!
He won't try!
He's dull and stupid!
He's not motivated!
I taught it, so it's not my fault if he doesn't learn!

Simply denying responsibility for the problem seldom accomplishes anything constructive.

People who have little understanding of the disadvantaged and of the culture of poverty frequently make such generalizations as,

The poor are always with us.
If they worked as hard as I have had to work, they could have taken care of themselves.
As long as they are happy in their ignorance, why disturb them at all.
They don't care!
They don't do anything to help themselves!
I notice that they have a Cadillac parked beside their shack!

Rather than to categorically condemn those whom we do not really understand and who do not appear to be "pulling their own weight" in our society, it is far more profitable for educators to expend their energies creatively, devising strategies to give these people the literacy skills necessary to break the cycle of poverty.

Jones (1962) has pointed out that there are four steps to take in order to improve the educational potential of anyone not achieving as he should. These four steps are:

1. Measure the extent and degree of unreadiness to learn.
2. Admit it.
3. Determine the whys.
4. Do what needs to be done to remove the unreadiness (p. 83).

Differences in Instructional Needs

> *The toughest part about startin' in this class was listenin' to my friends telling me, "You're too old to learn anything in books and besides, school is for kids!" Now that I'm in school, they don't say anything; they just look at me and grin (Barnes 1966, p. 19).*

Although the specific reading needs of the adult may be very similar to those of the young child in the public school classroom, it is never possible to teach an adult to read in the same manner that a child is taught. According to many administrators, the single most potent contributor to the high drop-out rate in adult basic education is the teacher's lack of ability to "shift gears" from the habits and attitudes that have characterized his teaching patterns in the public schools to those that radiate the dynamic sensitivity required to guide highly anxious adults toward successful learning experiences.

It is seldom productive for an adult learner to have an instructor who becomes a "buddy" to him in the classroom, but he does need an understanding friend. He will seldom learn under an overly stern, "battle-ax" authoritarian teacher, but must be directed by a firm, but empathic, never discouraged guide (Wallace 1965). Neither will adult learners long tolerate being patronized, pitied, or taught in a child-oriented way, as though they were merely "big children." This treatment soon produces behaviors of defensiveness and resistance toward all approaches to learning. The importance of the adult educator's recognition of the differences in the sociological and psychological dynamics in learning from those of children cannot be overemphasized, since without this, there can be little long-lasting success.

Considerations of Adults as Learners

We are never too old for magic—and that is what reading is!
(Source unknown)

There are sociopsychological forces affecting learning that are constantly interacting both externally within the cultural milieu of the adult learner and internally within the individual.

Individuality of Student Personalities

The public school teacher has often been told that there is no such thing as an average student. This timeworn cliché is equally applicable to the widely differing adult learners.

This group will be comprised of both married and unmarried men and women of differing ages. Ethnically, a teacher of adult basic education may expect participants of all races—black, white, red, brown, or yellow. These learners will be products of all economic and sociocultural backgrounds, although the number from the lower socioeconomic levels will probably outweigh the number from other levels. Undereducated adults may be found in all geographic areas, although the majority appear to

Adult learners are people of all ages. (Courtesy of Venice-Lincoln Technical Center, Venice, Illinois.)

be in the inner city. As far as learning potential is concerned, participants in basic reading classes may vary from slow learners to geniuses, with achievement ranging from no schooling whatsoever to high school graduates. Job experiences may be equally diverse.

Needs of Different Age Groups

Adult learners will also be motivated by diverse purposes and objectives. They can be expected to be very different in terms of life goals, and in stages of emotional, physiological, and psychological maturity (Winter and Nuss 1969). But they have *one* thing in common—they want to learn to read, and they want something better out of life for themselves (Cass 1956).

Hertert (1965) has highlighted some of the critical problems in the various age groups of adults who enroll in literacy classes. If the span of working years is categorized as adolescent school dropouts, young adults, middle-aged adults, adults in later years, and adults approaching retirement, certain problems persist in the basic education population. The variation from the "norm" through an adult life span is presented graphically in figure 2.1.

All of the characteristics should not be viewed as liabilities. When undereducated adults present themselves at school for literacy training, they all possess positive values, or assets. Some of these assets are:

1. A greater reservoir of experience, which they have acquired first-hand, enabling them to relate to learning situations.
2. An ability to persevere at a task for long periods of concentration, when they are achieving successfully.
3. An ability to comprehend and remember common formal learnings that have been a part of their practical experience for a long time.

When adults have a genuine desire for self-improvement, they may be most anxious to take advantage of this "last chance" opportunity.

Motivations for Adult Participation in Literacy Training

Regardless of the impression given, the adult learner believes that he has made an important decision by going back to school. No matter what type of course is chosen, he believes that it will help him. Whatever incentive existed to return this individual to school, the teacher needs to be aware of it so that it can be utilized during instructional assistance (Koehler 1968).

	YOUNG ADULTHOOD	MIDDLE ADULTHOOD	OLDER ADULTHOOD
CA*	15 20 25	30 35 40 45	50 55 60 65 70
LIFE TASKS	• Initiating healthy heterosexual contacts. • Completing formal education. • Courtship and marriage. • Career development. • Child rearing. • Financial stresses.	*Normal Patterns* • Career patterns more fixed. • Parents often do things alone. • Still financial stress. • Career established. • Parenthood patterns established. • More freedom for new interests. • Less financial pressures.	• Children establishing own homes. • Closer relationship with mate. • More association with older adults. • Anticipation of retirement and settling into retirement. • Acceptance of senior citizen role.

Physical Factors Related to Adult Basic Education

• Have greater reservoir of experience to bring to learning situations related to first-hand activity; can concentrate better than children; surpass children in ability to memorize immediately.

• Vision changes begin and continue from 35-50. Physical changes begin to appear.

• Memory may begin to decline—passive activity rather than active endeavors.

PHYSIOLOGICAL	• Reaching physical peak—decline begins—motor reactions decline—rate of learning declines—spatial perceptions and arithmetic skills decline.		

Variations from the "Norm" During Life Span

	YOUNG ADULTHOOD	MIDDLE ADULTHOOD	OLDER ADULTHOOD
NONLEARNING PROBLEMS OFTEN AFFECTING ABE STUDENT	• Adolescent school dropouts. • Major crisis period. • Shift from school pattern to pattern of responsibility. • Breakdown in marriage; one parent-family responsibility. Carousing, hotrodding, traffic violations, disturbing peace, unpaid fines, car trouble; narcotics; alcoholism, jail, probation.	• Much folklore in philosophy. • Trouble with school age children. • Sense of "togetherness" in basic education classes. • Trouble with spouse—problems of jealousy. • Glasses—Teeth—Dental care—Denture problems—Physicals—Acute needs for medical care. • Recognition of a "last chance opportunity and genuine desire for self-improvement.	• Physical limitations in vocational choices. • Chronic low-back pain. • Resort to avoidance of reality through drugs and alcohol. • Major crisis period: moving away from full family life and work responsibilities.

Poverty   Poverty   Poverty   Poverty

*CA = Chronological Age

The adult learner believes he has made an important decision by going back to school. (Courtesy of Chicago Urban Skills Institute and City Colleges of Chicago. Photo by V. Bacon.)

There may be many reasons that prod the undereducated adult toward the classroom. Often motives are complex, but are usually directed toward some practical objectives, either for expansion or as a defense against some real or feared loss.

Vocationally Oriented Motivational Forces

Vocationally oriented motivational forces assume two directions: job seeking or job improvement. Of those who have never been employed, it has been observed that these are primarily teenage dropouts who have either never been able to find employment or have been unable to keep steady employment. An equally prominent group are women who, for a number of reasons, felt it necessary to go to work. A few of the reasons most often cited for this decision include:

1. A change in marital status resulting from the death of a husband, divorce, or separation.
2. Either the husband being out of work or a need to supplement the family income because of increased expenses.

3. A desire to get off the welfare rolls.
4. A need for activity after the children are no longer dependent on mother being at home (Barnes 1966, pp. 21-23).

Of those who had previously been employed, but are presently seeking jobs, the majority are males from highly industrialized areas who had been employed as unskilled or semiskilled workers and were then displaced by automation, or by employment cutbacks brought on by economic recession. Some participate so that they can be retrained for a skilled job for which there will be openings within their own community (Barnes 1966).

Many of the employed undereducated male adults who return to school for job improvement do so at their employer's insistence. Most have normal general intelligence. In the majority of cases, the basic drive for an increase in reading ability among these persons is for job security, although some participate in order to master the literacy skills to such a level that they will be eligible to enter another specific vocational training program.

Therefore, in teaching these adults to read, motivation to master the skills may be strengthened by the use of vocationally oriented teaching materials. These learners must become proficient at filling out forms, as well as recognizing the technical vocabulary of their trades. They must become skillful in many reading areas relating to their employment, and will learn most readily when the relevance of these skills to their specific vocational needs is established (Barnes 1966).

Self-improvement Motivational Forces

According to one study (Adult Education Council of Greater Chicago 1965), it was observed that a large proportion of the learners in literacy programs were mothers who might never be gainfully employed, but who could make a real contribution in breaking the poverty cycle through an awareness of their own worth and an ability to provide physical, emotional, and verbal child care. These people appeared to be aware of the fact that in some cases governmental agencies had sometimes coerced them into participating in literacy classes with the hope of removing them from the public assistance rolls. Thus, motivation to learn to read sometimes lacked sufficient strength.

Some adults of both sexes, however, do return to school in order to improve their "parent image." They feel that if their children found out that they could not read or write, it would destroy, or at least decrease, their children's desire to finish school. Sometimes they feel that they

Parents are motivated to learn so that they will be able to read to their children. (Courtesy of Venice-Lincoln Technical Center, Venice, Illinois.)

would lose the respect of their children. They fear also that their own illiteracy might cause their children's circle of friends to be limited. Others are interested only in being able to help their children with schoolwork. Such motivational factors extend not only to parents, but also to grandparents.

Many undereducated adults feel compelled to return to school in order to maintain or to improve their own social status. This is frequently the reason listed by black participants who comment, "It looks like my people are finally getting some breaks. It is up to us to get as much education as we can (Barnes 1966, p. 23)." It would also appear that to the low income whites, there is a growing recognition of the fact that, with the passage and implementation of equal rights, they must improve themselves just in order to maintain the present social status that they now enjoy (Barnes 1966).

For some undereducated adults, the return to school is a social outlet. This type of motivation is found mostly among those persons who are either receiving welfare payments or whose family income is extremely low. As one individual said, "I come to this class because it is the only chance I have to get away from the kids and the old man (Barnes 1966, p. 23)." They want to be a part of a group and to increase their ability to talk to or visit with their friends, neighbors, and people in general. Illiteracy has caused self-degradation, such that they report, "I feel uncomfortable talking with people. They will know I haven't been to school just as soon as I open my mouth (Barnes 1966, p. 23)." Once at ease in adult reading classes, these people become quite gregarious. They like group talk, street-corner or "barbershop" conversation, and have a tendency to visit too much within the classroom—a tendency that sometimes must be tactfully curbed.

Other undereducated adults enroll in reading classes so that they might learn to read the Bible. According to Chapman (1965), most of these are older people in Southern states, the underprivileged who are reached in goodwill centers, or Spanish and Indian populations of various geographical localities. Because the ability to read the Bible has long been considered a prerequisite to an understanding of Christianity, many churches and mission boards sponsor ministries to the illiterates.

A few undereducated adults are motivated to return to school solely for mental stimulation, or to fill in the gaps between their past schooling, if any, and the present. Mostly housewives comprise this group, and such activity really becomes a type of therapy.

A large number of people enroll in classes for the acquisition of citizenship prerequisites, or in order to gain the literacy skills necessary to pass the General Educational Development (GED) examination or the newer Adult Performance Level Test (APL), which is oriented toward adult life situations (Northcutt 1974) rather than the broader academic areas tested by the GED.

Emergency needs prompt still other adults to learn to read. This urgency may be to read a letter from a loved one, or to write a letter to a son or daughter away from home. Whether or not this motivation is strong enough to hold the learner until reading can be mastered depends on the individual.

Strength of Motivation

Motivation is one of the most important factors in successful learning. This is the drive that forces a person toward a goal. Most adults are self-motivated. They are in class because they *want to be* there, not because they *have to be* there (Warren 1964). However, in the case of the undereducated adult, this self-motivation may be weak because of a life history of failure. He has failed in achieving the American values of success—that is, efficiency, work, practicality, equality, and freedom. Because of these failures, he is easily discouraged and frequently demonstrates an attitude of almost complete resignation to his fate (National Association of Public Continuing Adult Educators. *Adult Basic Education* 1969).

Two types of motivation concern the teacher. The first is the motivation to enroll in the reading class. The second is dependent on the first, but is not as clear-cut. It is that of developing motivation to continue in the class and to learn, even when there are difficulties.

Since the adult usually has a ready-made motive or purpose when he enrolls in school, learning is of great consequence and is therefore worthwhile. Thus, it is possible to create and maintain an intense desire to learn. However, for these people, education is only a part-time interest. In most cases many things compete for time and interest. Learning experiences are supplementary or complementary to some major occupation other than education.

The original drive to enroll in the classes may not be strong enough to maintain that interest and to sustain attendance in the face of difficulties. Participation in a reading class to meet the obvious needs—to learn to read and write—is seldom an adequate motivation. Obviously, some people could get along without these skills. They have been doing so for years! Their status quo may not always require such abilities, and there is *much* difficulty to overcome in attending classes regularly.

Commonly, the individual may not be willing to reveal to the teacher his true reasons for wanting to learn to read. Sometimes this happens because he fears that his reasons might appear to be unworthy in the eyes of the teacher. But regardless of how unworthy the reasons appear, the teacher must respect them. If they are weak, the teacher must utilize these motivating forces as an impetus toward developing other, more powerful motivations that will sustain the learner through many weeks of instruction. This doubtlessly will prove to be difficult or discouraging at some points.

Greenwood's study of 3,813 adult students in four schools yielded interesting conclusions regarding the strength of the participants' motivations to learn to read (Kirchner 1966). The study indicated that black students appeared to have a higher persistence to the task at hand than did whites. It also appeared that the influence of transportation to class was a strong factor. Those who used public conveyance and took a long time to get to school had an equally high rate of persistence as did those who lived nearby. However, the middle-time group and those using cars had the lowest rate of persistence. This may indicate that the amount of effort exerted in order to get to class is a pertinent factor in the establishment of persistence. Another conclusion of this study was that if the influence for the choice of which type of course to take came from within the school rather than from any other source, the persistence rate was higher.

Although motivation cannot create an ability to learn, and will not overcome all of the instructional discouragements in the adult basic education process, the stronger the motivation, the faster the learning process.

Learning to read requires a concentrated effort and an indeterminate amount of time.
(Courtesy of Kishwaukee College, Malta, Illinois Adult Basic Education Program.
Photo by Jan Wiseman.)

The weaker the motivating force, the slower the learning. Thus at times, absence or weakness of motivation has resulted in the neglect of potential ability (Kirchner 1966).

It would follow then that successful teaching is concerned with this highly individualistic factor. It becomes necessary for the teacher both to determine what-the basic motivation for participation in the reading program really is, and to assess its strength. One way in which this is sometimes accomplished is by asking questions, such as, "What would you like most to be doing ten years from now?" Certainly, if the honest answer to this query indicates a thought-out plan for continued learning achievement, then one could be confident that motivation to achieve is probably sufficient to insure persistence to success. However, if the answer reveals a lack of any plan for future development, vagueness, or a strong discrepancy between reality possibilities and wishes, then the teacher would probably be wise to use every tool at his command to build stronger drives for achievement (Seaman 1971; Warren n.d.). Relevance and immediate success under these conditions are mandatory. Each success must be used as a stimulus to proceed one step further toward reading proficiency.

Hostility Toward the School World

At least 95 percent of the illiterate population lack literacy skills because of some school-oriented problem, whether or not they ever spent time in any school (Barnes 1966, p. 18).

Of the many reasons for the existence of illiteracy, unhappy school experiences are probably the greatest factor. Therefore, if the illiterate adult is to be taught to read, it is imperative that some of these factors be considered.

Educational Reasons for Illiteracy

For some people, schools simply were not available to them. Others were forced to leave school at an early age by external social forces for family survival. Many undereducated adults in this present generation are simply casualties of the Great Depression of the 1930s and of World War II during the 1940s. For these people, the decision not to finish their schooling may have been an involuntary one.

Through the practice of social promotion, some underachieving pupils have been allowed to remain in school until their proper time of graduation, but the experience has usually been one of frustration and endurance rather than of fulfillment and learning. In the case of the pupil with a behavioral or learning disability, failure to learn may have been because the school's curriculum rigidity could not minister to individual needs, or because the school was unable to furnish the needed expertise in learning disorders. However, for some of this group the fault may not have been with the school, but rather within the individuals themselves. Mental retardation, or the severity of the learning disorder, possibly precluded success. Although some such pupils did graduate, many more of the unsuccessful youth could not endure the painful frustration and simply dropped out of school as the only escape from an intolerably punishing experience.

Demand for Courage

Whatever the reason for his present illiterate condition, to most such adults the school represents a world that has either been denied to him, or has been a severely penalizing previous experience—one which, understandably, he is hesitant to risk repeating. Therefore, he may view education and educators with deep-seated fear, suspicion, and contempt.

Moreover, this adult, who has failed to achieve our cultural minimum standard of a high school education, often possesses an extremely low self-concept and hides pangs of intense guilt. He comes to think of himself as unacceptable as a learner, and therefore undesirable as a person. Because of this distress and his reluctance to admit his illiteracy to friends and neighbors, even though some of them may be in the same situation, he carefully avoids any discussion of education or of his past inept experiences (Allen 1972).

To return to school at this stage of his life would be to risk again the possible mortification of public exposure and the intolerable possibility of failure. He knows that in the previous schooling experience he *did not learn,* and now is haunted by the unvoiced fear that he *cannot learn.* If he has been away from school for some period of time, this fear and insecurity may be magnified by the fear of scholastic competition with younger people. Embarrassment and insecurity may be further exaggerated by the prospect that the paragon of knowledge—the teacher—may even be younger than he is.

A tremendous amount of courage is required for the illiterate adult to return to the classroom. By participating in an adult basic education program, what he is really saying is,

> Look, world, look at me! I can't read or write! I'm stupid and a failure! I need to be taught like a six-year-old child! (Barnes 1966, p. 18)

Adults can attend their local elementary schools during after-school hours in many school districts. Their motivation to learn is the key factor. (Courtesy of Albuquerque Technical-Vocational Institute, Albuquerque, N. M.)

A Profile of the Undereducated Adult

Placing his foot on that first step of the schoolhouse i:
for the adult illiterate. To go into the room and sit at a de
much courage for the illiterate as is required of a soldier
battle. The successful teacher quickly recognizes this cc
the empathy he displays he awards medals of honor for bi
soldiers. He dispenses encouragement and assurance of su
ing experiences, rather than more failures, which would tend to confirm
their worst fears about themselves—that they *could not learn.*

Summary

"It's just bugging me," said one illiterate, *"that my little kid already knows more than me (Wallace 1965, p. 6)."*

This chapter has profiled the undereducated adult as an individual who may be found in all walks of life. He has a variety of needs, all very important to him.

The many motivational factors that impel him to try once again to learn to read are important for the teacher to know. Most learners offer short-term motivational goals as their reason for participating in a reading program. These are seldom strong enough to maintain the learner in the program long enough to build adequate reading skills. Therefore, the skillful teacher uses daily successes and encouragement to build higher motivation that will be capable of sustaining the individual until his goals are reached.

The undereducated adult who returns to school is pictured as a courageous person worthy of esteem. Since for many the school has been a punitive environment and a prime factor in their reading difficulties, such courage in risking the reopening of old wounds deserves the highest commendation. It behooves the teacher to expend every effort to make certain that it does not go unrewarded.

Physical Factors Related to Adult Learning

Psychological methods in teaching the adult must be directed toward overcoming the inertia of age, but at the same time protecting the innate pride of a grown-up person (Weiskopf 1951, p. 410).

For the older person, it is particularly important to recognize how the dynamics of learning may involve adjustment to aging (Verner and Davison 1971, *Physiological Factors in Adult Learning and Instruction*). There are many changes in health and vigor during adulthood that affect the learning process, either directly through the lessening of some physical capacity or indirectly through ego threats involved in the loss of youth.

Organic health factors that may have been operative during childhood as inhibitors of success in learning to read may in adulthood still be involved in the learning process. Oettinger (1963) lists eight genetic deficiencies that may unfavorably influence the development of reading behavior. These are as follows:

1. Hypomentia.
2. Inherited dysrhythmias.
3. Inherited metabolic diseases.
4. Inherited visual defects.
5. Inherited speech and hearing defects.
6. Inherited dominance defects.
7. Slow maturation.
8. Epilepsy.

Beyond these genetic deficiencies that may have unfavorably influenced the development of reading behavior to varying degrees, various other acquired conditions may have further complicated the problem. Oettinger (1963) refers also to five of these that may be of importance in adult learning. These are as follows:

1. Mental retardation.
2. Traumatic brain injuries.
3. Visual defects.
4. Auditory defects.
5. Epilepsy.

The teacher of reading in adult basic education will be concerned about the existence of these conditions as plans for proper instruction are made.

22

Information regarding these health factors can often be secured through welfare caseworkers, neighborhood clinics, or through tactful interviewing of the adult himself.

Neurological Factors Involved in the Reading Process

The main goal in planning for adult classes is the development and growth of each student. Accent the positive! Be cheerful, optimistic and relaxed! (Curriculum Guide to Adult Basic Education: Beginning Level 1966, pp. 91, 93)

There has been much research into the genetic and acquired organic conditions that can possibly interfere with the development of potential reading behaviors in children. Reading has rightfully been defined as being at least partially a physical and a neurological process. Since all data upon which any organism (person) must act has to be introduced to the brain by being fed through one or more of the five senses, or modalities, development of reading proficiency depends in part on the adequacy of these senses to perform their task. Thus, either inherited or acquired physical deficiencies of the senses cannot help but interfere with the learning process. Low vitality, poor nourishment, and other factors that lessen the efficiency of these modalities will inevitably impede learning, regardless of the individual's level of intelligence.

Once the data from the external world has been introduced to the organism through one or more of the sensory modalities, it must then be interpreted to the brain through the individual's neurological or central nervous system. This entire process could be roughly compared to the process of telegraphy, with the telegraph wires representing the central nervous system. If there is a disturbance somewhere along the wires, the signal, even though it had originally been correctly sent, will be distorted when it is received. However, the functioning of the central nervous system in relation to learning is far more complex in nature than the functioning of telegraph wires. This functioning is not only regulated by genetic strengths and weaknesses, by acquired assaults or damage, by idiosyncracies in development and in function, but also by learned perceptual practices.

For most motor functions of the brain, it has been possible for neurologists to establish cerebral areas that control these functions. For example, the area of the brain that controls the motor functions of the arms and legs can usually be pinpointed. The area of the brain that is the receiver of auditory and visual signals is generally designated. Therefore, when a dysfunction that cannot be ascribed to the physical organ itself appears, the competent neurologist can generally investigate causes within the cerebral control centers themselves.

Unfortunately, the cerebral centers governing the various learning processes—reading, writing, etc.—cannot be so easily mapped out. That such centers do in all probability exist is attested to by the observation of various types of asphasia in adults following accidents or illness. Frequently, it is noted that only the ability to read is lost, while all other mental functions appear to remain intact. Current literature concerning the neurological factors of learning seems to express the opinion of neurologists that the development and location of such learning centers may be uniquely individualistic within each person.

The genetic characteristics of the central nervous system are also related to reading development. There have been some studies to indicate that genetically males in particular families appear to be endowed with central nervous systems that are not receptive to the interpretation of graphic symbol systems. In these families there also appears to be a weakness in the system for the establishment of patterns of laterality, with more incidences of either left or mixed laterality, than of right laterality.

Assaults to the neurological system or developmental idiosyncracies and the difficulties are also pertinent to reading. With children who are failing to learn to read, the diagnostician explores the child's neurological history with particular interest in prenatal, perinatal, and early childhood circumstances of oxygen deprivation, persistent high fevers, or other conditions that could conceivably cause some minimal neurological dysfunction. The diagnostician is also interested in the child's milestones, that is, his rate of neurological development. For many reasons, it is also generally noted that males tend to develop neurologically somewhat slower than do females. Hence, at six years of age, some boys may not be neurologically ready to learn. By the time such maturity is reached, in many cases, beginning reading instruction is passed and the child is left behind.

Although the functioning of the brain and the neurological system in the encoding and decoding process of graphic symbols and in the higher cognitive processes of comprehension is not perfectly understood, it is generally agreed that within the boundaries of the factors thus far discussed, this neurological interpretive process (perception) is a *learned* behavior. The interpretation of graphic symbols may have been distorted at the time of the initial attempt to learn to read, but because of one or more of the factors discussed here, it is possible in many instances to *teach* the neurological system the accepted interpretation. Thus, reading problems that, in all probability, were originally neurological may have been lessened through proper teaching or may have become amenable to instruction in adulthood.

However, there is also the possibility that the neurological inaptitude that may have originally been a factor in the lack of success in learning to read may in adulthood still prevent adequate learning in this area. At the present time, not enough objective evidence is available for making it diagnostically possible to determine which reading disabilities with probable neurological etiologies will yield to competent instruction and which will not. Therefore, it is expedient that competent, optimistic instruction be offered for all cases. Yet, the teacher needs to be extremely alert to the student's feelings of frustration, and sometimes, futility in the effort. In some *very few* cases, wisdom would indicate that efforts toward further improvement should either cease, or at least be redirected.

Auditory Factors Involved in the Reading Process

One listens, sees, and perceives selectively. Many sensory experiences are ignored until they are required to give meaning or content to some need of the individual (Kidd 1959, p. 52). The perceptual experience of reading has been ignored for a lifetime.

In discussion of the auditory factors involved in the reading process, we are concerned with both auditory acuity and auditory perception. Acuity involves the ability of the hearing mechanism to properly receive audio information from the acoustical environment. Auditory perception is concerned with the interpretation process of that acoustical information.

Auditory Acuity

Changes in auditory acuity may affect learning, both directly and indirectly. Auditory acuity reaches maximum at about fourteen years of age, after which it normally declines at a slow rate. For the majority of adults, the decline is so gradual that considerable loss of acuity may have been suffered without awareness, creating psychological problems of varying degrees. Sometimes such an adult becomes somewhat paranoid, believing that the indistinct conversations around him are actually whispers about him. He may feel left out of peer and family activities. A marked hearing loss may also be accompanied by feelings of insecurity and fear, thus depressing learning ability. In addition, there are many older people who suffer little actual acuity loss, yet find it considerably difficult to follow rapid speech (Cass 1956).

Generally, the perceptive teacher can recognize the symptoms of such auditory loss. He will notice certain tense facial expressions of straining to hear, the tilting of the head in order to catch all of the sound, and the inability to respond verbally to questions when the listener does not see the speaker's lips.

Since learning to read is seldom accomplished with proficiency without the ability to hear sounds, this is a health problem that deserves the teacher's immediate tactful attention. A suggestion to the learner that he secure an audiogram from the nearest audiologist is in order. If the financial cost of such attention is a problem, it might be advisable to work through the welfare agency or another community service. Certainly the teacher must do all that is possible within the classroom itself to accommodate the learner. Seating the individual in a position where he has the best opportunity to hear all that is said around him will increase his learning. It is important that he be able to see the teacher's lips at all times. Some people with poor auditory acuity subconsciously develop such dependence. It is not helpful to raise one's voice to speak to the person with a hearing problem, but wise teachers consciously endeavor to slow their rate of speech for the entire class, thus unobtrusively auditorily accommodating handicapped people. Special effort must be made to assure these people of their worth to you as the teacher and to the group, as well as to enhance their feelings of acceptance and belonging.

Auditory Perception

Auditory perception is a neurological interpretive process of the auditory signal. As such, it is both circumscribed within the boundaries of genetic and developmental factors, as well as learned factors (Wepman 1968). Studies with disadvantaged children have frequently noted significant deficits in auditory discrimination. It is presumed that for these children, life in surroundings plagued with confusion, over-crowding, and too much noise has forced them to *learn* to shut out such noise. They learn *not* to hear sounds and speech. Thus, they must be taught to listen to speech and the differences in the sounds of English phonemes (Havighurst 1970). Since such discriminative ability is a necessary facet of the reading process, remediation of observed deficits in this area must be provided for within the instructional framework of the curriculum.

Visual Factors Involved in the Reading Process

Reading is only incidentally a visual process. It is the brain which imposes order and meaning on what is presented to the eye (Smith 1970, p. 83).

In considering the visual factors involved in the reading process, we are concerned with the ability to acquire information through visual sources. As with the auditory modality, the visual modality also has several aspects that concern educators. Visual acuity is concerned with the ability of the eye to receive visual stimuli with sharpness and clarity. Visual performance is concerned with the eyes' ability to move properly and to perform together. Visual perception involves the processing and interpretation of visual information.

Visual Acuity

Changes in visual acuity also cause learning difficulties for adults. Maximum acuity is attained at about eighteen years of age, and then generally declines slowly, but continuously thereafter. After the age of thirty-five, people generally show a preference for a bright light when reading. This tendency is especially marked in persons between the ages of thirty-five and fifty, probably because their eyes begin to lose the ability to refract light during this period. Changes in visual acuity can be so rapid during these years that corrective lenses may need to be changed often (Cass 1956).

Presbyopia, the loss of accommodation, also may become an acute problem of the middle-aged adult. This inability of the muscles of the eyes to shift rapidly from near-to-far-point vision tasks causes strain in the classroom. When endeavoring to shift between the near-point tasks (books) and the far-point tasks (the chalkboard), the weakening muscles of the eyes and the resistance of the lens to make necessary changes cause blurring and fatigue. This accommodation problem appears to cause the most strain with near-point tasks.

Bifocal lenses may be the solution to the problem in most instances. However, it is not uncommon for undereducated adults to have neglected visual examinations for years. Therefore, encouragement to have such checkups needs to be given. For many, the cost of glasses may be prohibitive. Here again, welfare services, and other community agencies such as the Lions Clubs can often help defray the expense.

Visual Performance

Visual acuity is not the only factor involved in the vision problems related to learning to read. The ability of both eyes to move across the lines of print in a controlled fashion; the ability of both eyes to work together as a pair; the development of eye-hand coordination, depth perception, shape, size, and form perception are all physical visual performance tasks not related to acuity—that is, the sharpness of the visual image.

Nevertheless, these factors may be interfering with the ability to learn. It is quite conceivable that such an unrecognized difficulty may have interfered with learning to read during childhood. While such inadequacies may have been compensated for in the tasks of everyday life, for the adult returning to the classroom, the problem as related to reading ability may yet be unsolved. One of the most poignant accounts of an adult coping with such problems is found in Jess Oppenheimer's autobiography *All About Me* (1972).

Vision specialists, as a rule, do not check these visual performance factors unless specifically requested to do so. However, through the use of a telebinocular screening device the teacher can determine the possible presence of such a difficulty before referral is made to a vision specialist.

Visual Perception

Visual perception is the neurological process of interpreting the visual signals received from the outside world. As with auditory perception, this process is both genetic and learned (Wepman 1968). With children, dysfunction in this area has been noted as a factor in reading difficulties, because of distortion in figure-ground relationships, placement and rotation in space, directionality, constancy of form, etc. (Frostig 1968). Although by adulthood most difficulties in these areas have either been compensated for or remedied as far as possible, there is the possibility that this could have been the inhibiting factor in past attempts at learning to read. In a minority of cases, visual perception difficulties might continue to be an inhibition to learning in adult education.

Motor Factors Related to Adult Learning

> For very few activities that adults may wish to learn, is the factor
> of decline of physique of such magnitude that they need to be discouraged from any attempt (Kidd 1959, p. 73). But the illiterate, fearful
> adult does not know this!

Peak motor abilities are generally reached between the ages of twenty and twenty-five, and thereafter begin to slow down. This decrease in physical ability many times prevents the adult from taking part in some leisure-time activities.

However, verbal abilities do not decline (Fox 1947). Therefore the age at which eminent people generally do their best work does not coincide with their physiological prime. This indicates that the human organism, consciously or unconsciously, adjusts to physiological change. Perhaps one of the more subtle adaptations to physiological change is the slowdown in work tempo, which may have many implications for teachers (Berdrow 1965).

Provisions for Physical Needs in Adult Learning

Be a clock watcher. Plan the work for the period in terms of time. Your class sessions will have more "zip" if you do this (Curriculum Guide to Adult Basic Education: Beginning Level 1966, p. 93).

In order to achieve the maximum learning efficiency, these changes in health and vigor as adults mature must be respected and provided for. The adult requires more constant and ideal environmental conditions in order to work efficiently. He has restricted powers of adjustment to external temperature changes and to distractions (Reissman 1962). Improper room ventilation, odors, noises, poor lighting, as well as improper or uncomfortable seating can be distractions from learning, which are more damaging for adults than they are for children.

The location of the reading classes is also important in providing for the learner's physical needs. It is intolerable to schedule an adult basic education class either on the second floor to which an elevator is not available, or back in some unattractive basement or storeroom. Such environmental conditions add to the adult's existent feelings of self-worthlessness and depression.

The pattern of the class schedule is also important. In participating in learning activities, most adults will have to overcome the fatigue resulting from a strenuous full day's work prior to class. Research has shown that fatigue is a potent factor in the lowering of motivational forces necessary for achievement (Koehler 1968). Allowing smoking, when it can be done without infringing on the rights of others, and providing frequent coffee breaks can help to counteract this fatigue.

Coffee breaks are important not only to combat fatigue, but also to give time for a closer interaction with the learners in a somewhat social situation. This helps to facilitate the communication and the solidarity of the group (Cass 1956).

Psychologists generally agree that the first hour is the best for learning. Therefore, taking this into account when planning the curriculum, as well as allowing adequate changes of pace and activity, contribute to the holding power of the program by providing for the physical needs of the adult learners involved.

Summary

*A habit cannot be tossed out the window; it must be coaxed down
the stairs a step at a time (Mark Twain).*

This chapter has been concerned with some of the most important physical factors that will influence learning in adult basic education. The important concept of this chapter is that everything regarding the learner's physical being has some influence on both his past failures in learning to read and on the success of his present endeavor.

A wise adult education teacher is aware of health and nutritional problems, neurological inadequacies, auditory and visual problems, and motor limitations. These needs are provided for within the setting of the adult education program.

4.
Sociological
and Environmental
Factors

*The deprived person is often super-
stitious and may believe that everything
is a matter of luck. On the other hand,
he believes that the reason his luck
is so often bad is that the dice are loaded
against him. He sees himself as a
gambler in a crooked game in which the
rest of society is cheating him. In a
sense he is right. . . . He stands in awe
of the pillars of this society—including
policemen, politicians, and teachers—
because to him they are big and
powerful. But he dislikes and mistrusts
them at the same time because they
represent a corrupt society which is
continually against him (Ulmer 1969,
p. 20).*

The illiterate lives in an entirely different world than that of the middle-
class American. At one time, he may have had the same hopes and aspirations as the mainstream of society, but because of illiteracy, he now
has little prospect of ever bettering himself or achieving his aspirations.

It is hardly accurate to consider the illiterate as just another segment
of society, but rather an extreme necessity to protect what is left of self-
respect and ego weld these people together into a distinctly separate
society with its own system of values, its own hierarchy, and its own power
structure (Barnes 1966). The rules of the game of this culture, the patterns of communication, and the ways of dealing with the larger system
are usually unknown to the teachers who have their roots in the mainstream culture (Greenlee Associates 1965).

The Different Value Structure: A Pragmatic One

*These are the people behind the American looking glass. . . . .
Being poor is not a choice for them, but is a rigid way of life. . . . For
the rebel who seeks a way out of this closed circle, there is little
help (Chilman and Sussman 1961, p. 161).*

The pervasive needs of survival mold the value system of people in this
illiterate society. Brazziel (1965) points out that although the needs to
provide next week's rent, or even the next day's family food may seem
commonplace and mundane to the middle-class teacher, these most powerful of psychological needs will govern and influence behavior in many
ways. Brazziel further characterizes these people as "scramblers" or
"strugglers" who have never known relief from these rigors and have
been led to expect none during their lifetime—that is, until the opportunity
for adult basic education presented a glimmer of hope. Furthermore, when

things are bad, such as witnessed in large cities during prolonged spells of bad weather, often the rise in theft and robbery can be attributed to the "forager." If such stress becomes too great, society is forced to deal with the "pathology of poverty."

Reissman (1962) describes these people as "overly pragmatic" with highly developed concerns for individuals within their own group. He further comments that their motivation for long-range planning and self-evaluation appears to be stunted. Instead, the undereducated adult appears to be prone to overprojection of the causes of his difficulties. Brazziel's study (1965) of the value system of low-income groups paralleled Reissman's conclusions, which indicated:

> high pragmatism and low needs for achievement, such as writing novels, holding high office, low aesthetic, political and economic values, and low needs for either dominance or autonomy. There were, on the other hand, manifestations of high social and religious values and high needs for nurturance and affiliation (Brazziel 1965, pp. 44, 45).

Other Poverty-related Factors in Adult Learning

> *The poor are also taught to be docile and not to endanger public safety or the public treasury. In other words, a major object in educating the poor is to control them, while the purpose of education of affluent adults is their self-realization. But social control from outside interferes with enabling poor adults to assume self-responsible adult roles and thus reduces their motivation to become educated at all (Haggstrom 1965, p. 148).*

The effects of poverty on adult basic education programs is immeasurable. It alienates. It oppresses. It becomes a way of life. Illiteracy causes poverty and poverty causes illiteracy. No adult reading program will ever "get off the ground" unless those responsible for its development pay attention to these factors.

Minority Group Status

Minority group status also affects adult learning. Brazziel (1965) calls attention to the conclusions reached by most investigators, indicating that lowered self-concept, suppressed and displaced aggressive urges, in-group aggression, degrees of alienation from mainstream values and participation, and exorbitant uses of opiates and defense mechanisms (i.e., hedonism, substitutive behavior and overprojection) occur in varying degrees to members of minority groups in societies where their groups are placed at a serious disadvantage. So, in addition to the general psychological portrait of the disadvantaged worker, teachers must also add the extra psychological burdens of minority group status. Either, alone, can be a powerful deterrent to learning. Together, they represent formidable stress and interference with the modification of attitudes.

Orientation and Interests Delimited by Illiteracy

The illiterate's interests are different from those of the mainstream of society. He becomes more physically than mentally oriented. Because he lacks the facility to understand and function in a verbal world, he is far more likely to communicate by actions and violence than by words.

Since he cannot read, he is cut off from information and happenings in society transmitted through printed media, such as newspapers and magazines. Therefore, he prefers watching the ball games and fights on television, and is limited in his understanding of the world around him by the narrow and sometimes biased commentaries and reports as presented by this video media (Warren 1964). Being denied the vicarious experiences of the printed page, the nonreader becomes imprisoned by his own meager environment. Fader (1965) has commented that the poorest man in all the world is the man who cannot read; who cannot see through the prism of time, but is shackled by his own experiences in the prison of time. Thus, he cannot comprehend the world outside the paradigm of his own experiences.

Without knowledge of the many functions of the institutions of society, the illiterate is unable to understand or interpret the motives, regulations, and the many factors that determine the behavior of an institution toward him. The seemingly oppressive institution may be the school, the welfare agency, the police, or any other agency of society (Greenlee Associates 1965). Since he cannot read a ballot, he does not vote, and the world of politics and government lack reality to him. Never does he expect to have a voice in his government, or any kind of control over his fate, but moves about either as a hapless robot or in anger strikes out against the society in which he is unable to find peace and fulfillment.

Probably the only institution that reaches his life to any significant degree is the church. Nothing really ties him to the mainstream of society. His job, at the lowest end of the occupational hierarchy because of its menial nature, may in itself breed frustration, which can only be taken out on those who are even weaker than he is—his wife and children. The illiterate is extremely vulnerable at the hands of community institutions. That is, if a member of his family gets involved with the police, there are fewer resources available to him to assist or to intercede with the legal processes. He has fewer means of protecting himself and his family against exploitation and attack; thus confirming his position of powerlessness and alienation from the larger mainstream group (Greenlee Associates 1965).

Necessity for Acceptance

The oppressiveness of such an existence creates a society with values and mores far removed from those familiar to middle-class morality, strivings, and behaviors. However, it is imperative that he be able to understand and to accept a completely different, and sometimes extremely dissident and almost unfathomable hierarchy of values among those whom he would teach. Such acceptance must be offered without undue reproach or denunciation of the individual, else he will not be able to cope with the pressures, defenses, and problems that become an unescapable part of the educational milieu. It almost becomes necessary for the teacher to be able to stand outside his own personal cultural frame of reference and view the behaviors of his students without making any value judgment, accepting the implication that for these people, their nonmiddle-class system of values and mores may be useful, relevant, and valid in a way of life forced on them by the hard fact of illiteracy.

It is profitable for the teacher of undereducated adults to imaginatively place himself in the shoes of his students. What would it be like never to hear Standard English spoken in your home or community? Never to have had a newspaper, book, or magazine in your home? Never to have seen anyone in your home write anything? Never to have had anyone tell you a story or read to you when you were a child? Never to have had anyone speak to you except in terms of command or abuse? Never to have traveled more than a few blocks from your home? (National Association of Public Continuing Adult Educators. *Adult Basic Education* 1969)

Without such consideration, it will be impossible for the middle-class teacher of illiterates to demonstrate that all-important true empathy for his pupils and acceptance of them as human beings, worthy of more than frustration and defeat, and generally capable of being taught. Only when the illiterate trusts and accepts the teacher as a person capable of such empathy will he be willing to be taught and will an adult education program become totally effective.

Family Maintenance Problems Related to Adult Learning

The poor get sick more and longer than anybody else in society.
This is because they live in slums, jammed together in unhygienic
conditions; they have inadequate diets, and cannot get decent medical

care. When they become sick, they are sick longer than any
other group in society. Because they are sick more often and longer
than anyone else, they lose wages and work and find it difficult
to hold a steady job. . . . This is caused by slums, unhygienic conditions,
and poor diet. And because of this, they cannot pay for good
housing, for a nutritious diet, or for doctors. At any point in the circle,
particularly where there is a major illness, their prospect is to move
to an even lower level and begin the cycle, round and round, toward
even more suffering (Harrington 1963, p. 22).

Continued participation in an adult education program will not be solely
dependent on what happens within that program. The external factors of
what is happening within the family cluster may be an equally potent force.

Economic Factors Related to Adult Learning

Usually participation in any adult education program means some economic adjustment for the undereducated adult and his family. Generally,
some curtailment of income is to be expected. Most programs find it
necessary, and desirable, to charge some fees, because seldom is value
attached to what is received gratis through charity. However, fees must
be modest, and when needed, provision must be made for payment by
means other than money. Occasionally, one finds employers in sympathy
with the problem to the extent that they will pay the fees for their employees participating in a program. Beyond this cost of the program itself, there are the costs of transportation to class, supplies, books, baby-
sitters and sometimes the cost of appropriate clothing.

In some cases, adults attempting to learn to read have found it necessary to curtail the number of hours they work. For most, working hours
are long and sometimes irregular, making a consistent attempt to learn
to read sometimes difficult. The adult, usually ashamed of illiteracy, may
not seek the employer's support in adjusting the work load and schedule
so that he is able to handle both work and school efficiently.

Aware of these difficulties, the interested teacher will do all he can to
relieve the strain by judicious consideration of homework assignments
and by giving much encouragement along the way. The adult student
must be assured that the sacrifices being made in order to learn to read
are really worthwhile.

Familial Factors Related to Adult Learning

Beyond the money problems sometimes imposed on a family when an
adult enters a basic education program, there are other possible sources
of difficulty that can influence learning.

It is not easy for adults to come to school after a hard day's work. (Courtesy of Chicago Urban Skills Institute and City Colleges of Chicago. Photo by V. Bacon.)

For most of these people, there is little reading material within the home. Crowded conditions, with the accompanying distractions, prevent any regular study. Many will not have the sympathetic support of the other members of the family. There may even be feelings of jealousy on the part of the spouse and the children toward the time that the adult student needs for study and classes. It is even possible that lacking the ability to organize time efficiently enough to accomplish everything that is desired, there might be neglect of household responsibilities or the care of children or resident invalid members of the family, resulting in further resentment toward the learning situation itself.

In many cases, after caring for the family or after working all day, the parent is too tired to go to school in the evening. Just getting there requires a supreme effort—in addition to learning while he is there!

Since attending must be achieved over personal and family obstacles, the adult learner has little tolerance for busywork or other forms of time-wasting. Being usually just a part-time student, he is free to walk out if he feels that he is not getting what he wants. The adult student has many other demands on his time, other interests and responsibilities, that interfere with education. Therefore, it is imperative that his reading instruction be carefully planned.

Summary

Except during times of national crisis, literacy education for native-born adults has been dominated more by sentimentality than by sense. . . . Sporadic campaigns by individuals and church-related groups were the only ones concerned. . . . National economics forced the federal government to admit that poverty and illiteracy are no longer just an individual's bad luck, but a social problem and a social responsibility (E. Smith 1970, pp. 3-6).

This chapter has overviewed the important social and environmental factors that are pertinent to adult education. The intent has been to give the adult reading teacher, who is most likely a product of the middle-class American value system, a general picture of the background of the undereducated adult who wants to learn to read. When the effects of an environment of poverty and the difficulties in maintaining a family are understood, it is more likely that one can teach with true empathy.

5.
Psychological Considerations in Teaching Undereducated Adults

The illiterates today are aware of being unused and unusable material; rejected, ignored, and involuntary allies of those anonymous forces which expel them from civilized society, but try to become even more inert. . . . These are the people who seldom dare to ask for help, but who need it most of all (Burnet 1965, p. 30).

In public school education, teachers have long known the importance of building a positive self-concept if learning is to take place. In adult education this emphasis is even more important because the learner's self-concept has been battered for years by illiteracy and poverty.

Psychological Consequences of Illiteracy

As educators have thought for many years in terms of the "whole child," so perhaps, must we begin to think in terms of the "whole adult" (Brazziel 1965, p. 40).

The consequences of illiteracy are far-reaching. The effects extend from personal humiliation, to vocational frustration and loss to society (Isenburg 1964). Struggling to survive, the undereducated adult is fearful and devises many charades to cover his inadequacies.

The Experience of Personal Humiliation

Imagine the countless, almost-subconscious daily activities requiring literacy skills that are considered to be within the capacities of every individual. For the nonreader, the all-important name signature becomes only a humiliating and faceless X. Imagine the frustration of shopping for groceries by pictures on the labels, rather than by the product names, and the humiliation of never being certain that you were being given the right amount of change from a purchase.

Imagine the indignity imposed on the illiterate of having to just accept what is given to him as a week's wage, without knowing whether the amount is correct, and suspecting that he may have been cheated, yet being helpless to challenge the paymaster.

Think of the embarrassment of having to ask simple directions to a nearby building, or not being able to use public transportation because you could not read the bus and street signs?

Few middle-class literate teachers ever really understand the heartbreak of the illiterate mother who cannot read the letters from beloved children away from home, but is too ashamed to ask a neighbor to read the letters to her.

It is readily seen that it is hardly possible for the illiterate adult to separate himself from the consequences of his illiteracy for even an instant. Hostility and paranoid feelings are almost an expected reaction to such severe limitations.

Vocational Frustrations of Illiteracy

The problem is summarized by Coates (1966) as he quotes a St. Louis woman.

> You can hardly get a job without some learning. I had a job at a box factory, but I couldn't advance. I had to read the directions and set the machine and I couldn't do it. If you look for a job, other people have to fill in your forms, and then you are told, "We don't want you if you can't fill in your own forms (p. 30)."

The consequences of illiteracy may become tragic, as well as frustrating. Such tragedy is emphasized by the incident of the newly employed automobile worker in Detroit who threw away a list of safety directions because he could not read them. Moments later his hand was seriously injured when caught in a machine (Cass 1956).

In today's economy of inflation and recession, industry finds that it is too expensive maintaining employment for illiterates. Because of their problems, incidences of absenteeism soar higher than that of the middle-class population. Because they cannot read, they learn their jobs by either observation or trial-and-error. This is slow and costly to an employer. Therefore, when there is a need for industry to cut back employees, the undereducated are the first to lose their jobs (American Bar Assoc. 1974; Kent et al. 1971; Northcutt 1975; Schrank and Stein 1970; Sticht 1972, 1974; Sticht and McFann 1975).

"Face-Saving" Psychological Defenses in Adult Learning

> Those who think illiteracy disappeared from the American scene with the buggy whip and the bustle couldn't be more wrong. In fact, to be illiterate today is infinitely more frustrating than it was fifty years ago, when illiteracy was felt to be America's greatest adult education problem (Coates 1966, p. 30).

In affluent America, illiteracy is viewed as a badge of dishonor, causing extreme feelings of inadequacy and hostility toward society. The self-concept of many illiterates has been so bruised that no extreme in attitude or behavior appears to be unwarranted if it assists in disguising the fact that they do not possess the literacy skills.

The illiterate tends to hide his lack of education behind many meticulously developed habits and a fanatic system of defenses. Usually he carefully avoids educated people and organized meetings or places of education. In some instances, the illiterate develops an apparent superfluency in the use of oral language, whether standard or nonstandard, as a distraction away from the inadequate or nonexistent reading skills.

In other cases, this deficiency is camouflaged by a blatant display of a multicolored array of ballpoint pens carried in a shirt pocket. When cornered into the precarious position of being unmasked by the demand to use one of the pens, the ego-threatened illiterate may plead a hand injury or an arthritic finger—thus, once again escaping admission to the world that he cannot write. Commonly, a nonreader may carry a newspaper under his arm, or pretend to read a paperback while riding the subway to work. When this facade is in danger of being penetrated, the undereducated adult pleads a nagging headache, which blurs vision, or eyestrain, or just suddenly notices that his glasses have been misplaced.

A successful teacher of undereducated adults is quick to recognize these pretenses for just what they are—simple defense mechanisms to help preserve pride or whatever ego still survives. As long as such an individual feels the need for these defenses, they should be respected and left intact (*Curriculum Guide to Adult Basic Education:* Beginning Level 1966).

The Challenge of Empathy—Not Sympathy

You know the old saying, "I am as good as you are." Try to change
it around to "You are as good as I am." This has quite different conno-
tations that are most important when one is dealing with
illiterates (Wallace 1965, p. 13).

It is difficult for the middle-class educator to realistically understand the psychological dynamics involved in illiteracy, because he has no equivalent experiences with which to make comparisons. Therefore, it is often profitable for the teacher of adult illiterates to participate in role-playing activities in which the educated teacher assumes the role of the frustrated illiterate.

The teacher of undereducated adults has a better chance at success if he can demonstrate true empathy; the teacher needs to know what it feels like to "walk in their shoes." They do not want anyone to feel sorry for them. Pity and sympathy are demeaning and the adult learner is quick to "turn off" to these artificial offerings. To be able to feel and to express genuine empathy toward his learners as he skillfully teaches them language skills becomes the preeminent challenge of teaching adults to read. Nothing less is really acceptable in successful adult education.

The Dynamics of Fear and Anxiety in Adult Learning

If I'd had people who understand me like these people do and had a teacher like the one I have now when I was a child, I don't think they'd ever got me out of school (Barnes 1966, p. 20).

Fear and anxiety as independent entities are not capable of being judged either as good or bad, productive or unproductive, as far as their relationship to learning is concerned. Being inherent factors of personality structure, their *degree* of functioning within each individual is one of the most potent determiners of mental health, and thus, of psychological readiness to learn.

Too little fear and anxiety may be just as symptomatic of emotional distress as is an excessive fear-anxiety level. Occasionally encountered is the genuinely self-centered, "id-level" functioning psychopathic personality; he represents a real danger to society because he apparently lacks any fear-anxiety development. At our present stage of knowledge, prognosis is very poor for these rare individuals, since some fear-anxiety level appears to be necessary for successful therapy. More often, one encounters the antithesis of this personality; that is, the individual whose fear-anxiety structure is so weak that he may be in danger of producing physical harm to either himself or others, simply because he is not afraid to try anything.

One would be wary to undergo surgery at the hands of a doctor with such a low fear-anxiety level that he was not deeply concerned about the success or failure of the outcome. Neither would a person feel secure in the hands of a doctor whose fear-anxiety level was so excessive that he could not make adequate professional judgments or control his surgical skills. Either situation could be equally disastrous!

It appears that people must maintain an adequate level of anxiety in order to be productive. Individuals seldom learn when there is no anxiety at all attached to the learning situation. Projects that engender little anxiety are seldom completed. A person with no anxiety over his inability to read will probably not learn to read regardless of the quality of the instruction. The healthy personality functions best with a fear-anxiety level that generates reasonable caution and maximum productivity.

However, an excessive fear-anxiety level is equally symptomatic and is a deterrent to learning. The mind protects itself against an overburdening of these pressures. When such does become excessive, it is sufficiently painful mentally to the individual that the need to alleviate the pressing discomfort takes precedence over all other mental and physical activity. Consequently, learning to read may be interfered with or completely halted until the fear-anxiety factor is lowered to tolerable limits.

Factors Producing High Fear-Anxiety Levels in Undereducated Adults

The causes of excessive fears and anxiety are myriad. These causes as they are related to productivity in adult learning may be classified as (1) threats to the self-concept, (2) resistance to change, and (3) generalized anxiety related to maturity and aging.

Threats to Self-Concept

By the time an individual has matured, he has usually come to regard himself as a certain kind of person. A well-adjusted adult recognizes his weaknesses and accepts himself as a worthwhile person as he tries to improve his inadequacies. But in the case of the undereducated adult, this self-acceptance seldom exists. Generally, these people, being fearful and anxious, dare not recognize inadequacies and thus remain in a constant state of frustration. This lack of reality acceptance, coupled with the conditioning of past failures, causes the undereducated adults to underestimate their ability to learn. The anxiety thus induced can cause almost complete stagnation in learning, because as self-concept is eroded, thinking and memory are inhibited.

Resistance to Change

The possibility of change is a possible source of anxiety for most adults. However, the educated adult has within his grasp many resources with which to make constructive adaptations to the "ever-whirling wheels of change" that are not readily available to the illiterate.

To avoid detection, the illiterate has usually become socially conservative, very fearful of change and afraid of the unknown. Thus, tradition and mores may be more important to him than reason in governing his actions. He seldom evaluates any traditional expectation by rationality. Past frustration and failure have usually taught him in no uncertain terms that survival depends on his conformity with the traditions and demands of his society. Having thus defined his role as an adult in that society, he participates largely to the extent of conforming to that role as he sees it, often to the extent of saying what he feels others expect of him, and suppressing his real feelings (Fay 1966). If he feels that he is expected to understand what the teacher is endeavoring to teach, the threat of possible embarrassment and frustration will cause him to allow the teacher to believe that he really has understood when actually he has not. Thus he avoids the prospect of a possible repetition of the previous classroom frustrations of being expected to read when he cannot; of being expected to learn when he cannot understand; of being tested; and of being taught information that may be incompatible with what has been taught to him at home or within his own limited culture (National Assoc. of Public Continuing Adult Educators. *Adult Basic Education* 1969). Although rationally he may recognize the need for attempting additional education, his motivation to learn is generally somewhat weak and he fears that any change in the status quo might endanger his precarious existence and his very survival.

Generalized Anxiety of Maturity and Aging

Learning may be further inhibited by the effects of the increased anxiety observed as a person becomes older. Many factors contribute to this heightened anxiety state. Some persons become anxious and fearful because of change, instability, and confusion in the home or on the job. Of course, this can be further complicated by the fear of being replaced on the job by a younger person.

The changes in health and in vigor caused by increased age present another source of anxiety, frequently resulting in the breakdown of needed social contacts. Also the changes in physical appearance and attractiveness, which accompany advancing age, may be destructive to the ego, causing one to feel unworthy and undesirable (Berdow 1965).

Adults experience other anxiety-producing changes in their world. The possibility of death ceases to be a remote abstraction, but an imminent concern, as they witness the death of parents and contemporary friends. Their children grow up, leave home, and are no longer dependent on them. Fear of being alone, unneeded, and unwanted can be traumatizing, often resulting in the rigidity of attitudes and intolerance observed in some older people (Berdrow 1965; Birren 1964; Bischof 1969; Cleugh 1970; Eisdorfer 1973).

Adjustments to Anxiety

Well-adjusted adults recognize their anxieties for what they are, and then employ constructive problem-solving approaches to alleviate these anxieties. But for the not-so-well adjusted, particularly the undereducated, many forms of maladaptive behaviors are employed to cope with anxiety. Since they cannot read, they cannot make use of bibliotherapy, as do educated people for identification, release of emotion, and as a source of knowledge and strength. They are far more likely to be physically rather than mentally oriented. Thus they are apt to be governed more by emotions than by reason. The undereducated adult will not react to threat, criticism, and failure in the same manner a child does. Rather, he will tend either to explode or to withdraw completely from any ego threatening experience.

Withdrawal Adjustments to Anxiety

Such withdrawal may take the neurotic form of psychosomatic illnesses that inhibit learning. Some manifestations of this may be asthma, headache, nausea, or high blood pressure. In effect, what these symptoms accomplish as anxiety alleviators for the adult is to give him legitimate excuses for not participating and for not succeeding in an educational effort or some other life experience. It is less punishing to the individual to be too sick to try, than to try and consequently risk another failure. There is no pretense of illness here—no dishonesty. The symptoms are real enough, but they may be subconsciously induced by fear and anxiety, rather than have a strictly organic genesis.

The extreme psychosomatic reaction might take the form of a hysterically produced impairment in vision, hearing, or other sensory or motor capacity. Some authorities attribute many severe reading disabilities to this type of hysterical reaction (Oettinger 1963). This could possibly have been a factor in the adult's original failure to learn to read, and is still functioning as a part of his behavioral repertoire. In effect, this is to say that at some time in the individual's life the behavior of not being able to read was in some way reinforced as a defense against an intolerable fear or anxiety. The hysterically produced incapacity legitimized the lack of skill development and provided a way to avoid the painful reality. Although the original stimulus for such a reaction may have long since become inactive or unimportant, the response, not having been recognized and dealt with constructively, remains an inhibiting factor in the adult's present efforts toward literacy.

Unable to cope with anxieties, some undereducated adults will not employ psychosomatic illness or hysterical reactions as defenses, but instead will use rationalization as a withdrawal technique. This is manifested by the too frequent excuse from participation in activities, continued absences on weak excuses, unwillingness to complete assignments, inability to get started or to continue to work alone, as well as procrastination or "forgetting" (National Assoc. of Public Continuing Adult Educators. *Adult Basic Education: A Guide for Teachers and Teacher Trainers* 1969). These forms of withdrawal from threat can sometimes stretch the patience of even the most understanding of teachers!

Another form of psychological withdrawal observed in undereducated, anxious adults is the retreat into fantasy and the too frequent or too prolonged daydream. Besides being constructively unproductive as an anxiety alleviator, this kind of retreat from reality may present serious psychological problems. If such behavior is or becomes habitual, it becomes increasingly difficult for the person to distinguish the real world from his fantasy world, thus grossly complicating the educative process.

Antisocial Adjustments to Anxiety

An often observed maladaptive compensation for anxiety is hostility and sociopathic-type behavior, characterized by low self-control and a tendency to get angry when values are threatened. There is also the tendency to react to threat and anxiety by the swing of a fist or a tirade of profanity rather than by rationality.

Such defense mechanisms, a result of the feeling of helplessness, may become obvious in the classroom. Sometimes they are manifested by overt hostility exhibited toward the teacher, the class participants, or the subject matter itself, which may be accompanied by a tirade against the society in which verbal communication skills are a necessity. The teacher may encounter this hostility as a persistent bewilderment or blocking when skills are taught, in spite of repeated explanations. Being afraid of the unknown and of possible failure, the adult learner psychologically refuses to understand. Nevertheless, it is the task of the teacher to give these people the ability to communicate adequately with words rather than by violent action.

Countering Anxiety in the Classroom

An undereducated adult's past inept attempt to learn to read may be either the symptomatic consequence of fears and anxieties, or may be the generating cause of these emotional reactions. The extent of involvement in the reading act of such emotional factors cannot usually be accurately determined in advance of attempting some form of reading instruction. However, since it is generally true that reading difficulties usually encountered in the adult illiterate are associated with personal disorganization and social aberration, which may have no necessary physiological involvement, and the teacher of adults must recognize these as important elements that function almost universally in the adult educative process (Otto and Ford 1967).

Therefore, at this level, instruction that is exclusively concerned with building communication skills while ignoring the concommitant emotional factors generally fails to achieve its goals. Conversely, attention given solely to negating the effects of emotional maladjustments on the personality, when there is also considerable lack of skill development, similarly fails to achieve maximum gains. The reading act itself appears to be a behavior of the *whole* personality. Therefore, a maximally productive instructional strategy would not minister exclusively to one end or the other of the problem, but would encompass the entire problem, working simultaneously with all aspects.

Need for Encouragement

Conditioned by a past history of failure experiences, the illiterate becomes extremely sensitive to nonverbal clues presented by the teacher. Thus he tends to judge people more by the actions he observes than by the words he hears. To counter the effects of this conditioned anxiety on learning, it is extremely necessary for the adult student to be supported by continual encouragement that is believable in terms of the nonverbal clues presented by the teacher's behavior, as well as by the verbal statements he makes (National Assoc. of Public Continuing Adult Educators. *Adult Basic Education* 1969).

Adult learners need verbal encouragement as well as nonverbal reinforcement. They appreciate the teacher's friendly interest in them; his concern for their physical and emotional welfare, as well as with their mental and educational growth. To achieve this, the atmosphere needs to be a friendly and relaxed one, where opinions can be freely expressed without fear of either verbal or nonverbal censure. Each person needs to be made to feel that his opinion is important and honestly respected. (Patterson 1968). These people do not respond to the falseness of condescension, but appreciate being treated honestly as adults and accepted as individuals, not just as "cases" or "students." Only then can these learners identify themselves as active participants of the group rather than just as onlookers. Only then are they able to accept the teacher as a person from whom they can learn, rather than as a judgmental outsider.

Need for Immediate Success

The illiterate's need for praise and encouragement can only be matched by his need for immediate success experiences in order to alleviate the

Adult learners require continual encouragement and immediate success. (Courtesy of William Rainey Harper College, Palatine, Illinois.)

inhibitory anxieties that block learning. Certainly he must learn to cope with failure and the fear of not succeeding. But this cannot be accomplished until his self-concept becomes strengthened such that he perceives himself as a person capable of success. For most, this will be a new feeling. Success generates further success, but failure becomes a breeding ground for additional failure and greater anxiety. There has already been enough failure within the life of an undereducated adult, in more ways than the teacher will probably ever know. Even *one more* is more than can be tolerated! (Wallace 1965)

Need for Understanding

For any adult student, his frame of reference is not the school. It is his family, job, or neighborhood. Unlike young children taught in public schools, an adult learner's total energy cannot be concentrated toward a goal in learning. Most of these people have families dependent upon them for survival. Thus, their energies may be dispersed in many directions. For them, learning to read is only one goal—and they may *not* consider it as high a priority need as does their teacher.

The adult learner does not leave personal problems, concerns, feelings, and desires outside the classroom. Thus, he can be—and usually is—

easily distracted from learning by personal problems. It is not possible for the teacher to blindly ignore the interference to learning thus presented. Neither is it possible for the teacher to escape some responsibility for concern by the naive comment that everyone has problems and that learning simply must go on in spite of them! It may well be that the teacher himself has achieved such mental self-discipline that he is able for the moment to suppress personal problems and proceed with the learning task at hand. But it can be safely assumed that the undereducated does not have this type of emotional steadfastness. To assume otherwise is unrealistic and can defeat a program. The adult learner's personal anxieties and problems, though they may be transient in nature, can cause mental anguish to the point that the need for alleviation of this overpowering fear-anxiety level assumes preeminence over any need to learn to read.

Recognizing these priorities, the empathic teacher of adults does not offer impersonal sympathy, which is generally unacceptable to them. But instead, he allows opportunity, either in a group or on an individual basis, for the troubled student to talk about the things that concern him without arousing guilt feelings for wasting the teacher's or the class's time, and without fear of belittlement, censure, or judgment. Thus the teacher becomes an understanding listener, advising in such a way as to direct the individual toward a more objective understanding and acceptance of the problem and toward finding his own solutions. There may be very little that anyone other than the individual himself can do toward actually solving a particular problem. But the opportunity of sharing the concern with either the teacher or the group functions toward the goal for learning or of lessening the fear-anxiety level so that mental energies can once again be channeled toward mastering the skills of reading.

The adult learner's emotional development has other, even more direct, effects on the teaching of reading. The meanings that individuals attach to particular events (or words) are influenced by their emotions. If the concept of "home" represents to the individual a place of insecurity, fear, or tension, then the word "home" will usually present reading difficulties. Psychologically, the individual may reject learning as a disagreeable or painful experience. The same dynamics operate in relation to longer conceptual units, such as sentences or paragraphs.

Emotional meanings of words provide overtones for adults that are outside the experience of youth, and as such, may present an obstacle to learning. Because of this, it has been observed that adults may have an easier time learning completely new responses than they will have in reorganizing old ones (Koehler 1968).

The Counseling Expertise of the Teacher

It is not intended to imply within this discussion that the successful teacher of undereducated adults must be a bona fide psychotherapist or psychologist. Neither is it the intention for the teacher to impinge on the domain of the adult basic education project's counselor, social worker, or psychologist—if, indeed, the project employs such specialists. Certainly all of these valuable resources need to be cooperatively utilized in dealing with the total illiteracy problem.

The important concept here is the realization that the interference with learning caused by a personal or emotional problem occurs in a teaching situation. Like a road barricade, the problem exists and usually learning cannot proceed until it is dealt with. In terms of time economy, the immediacy of the need, and the student's confident rapport with the teacher, responsibility is focused squarely on the teacher, who may then mobilize the counseling and social services available, if the adult student is willing to accept such "outside" assistance.

Both group and individual counseling sessions, generally occurring on an impromptu basis, but also as planned activities, become a vital part of any successful program in teaching undereducated adults to read. Therefore, it behooves the prospective teacher of such classes to become as knowledgeable as possible in the areas of both individual counseling techniques and group dynamics (National Assoc. of Public Continuing Adult Educators. *Counseling and Interviewing Adult Students* 1969; Weber 1971).

For the illiterate adult, a prime requisite to learning will be the fulfillment of his need for adaptive, constructive problem-solving techniques, as well as his needs for fulfillment as a person in gaining community and economic status, in vocational achievement, in success as a parent, and in thinking of himself as a person worthy of respect (Fay 1966). His anxieties and fears may well prevent such fulfillment unless he can depend upon an understanding teacher who never for one instant doubts that he is a person who can be taught, and who can learn to be more than he now is (Warren 1964).

Psychological Supports to Increase Staying Power in Adult Basic Education Programs

A major goal in adult basic education is the deepening of insights necessary to cause the student to become more ambitious, orderly, and productive. Basically, for many of the undereducated, these aspects of personal growth will entail a major change in general attitude. While such a change is sometimes difficult to obtain, it is not at all impossible.

Social psychologists follow a general set of rules or principles in their attempts to change attitudes:

1. The experiences of association, transfer, and need satisfaction are the basis for learning new attitudes.
2. Impersonal lectures and mass media are not as effective in causing new attitudes to be transferred, as are face-to-face contacts and group discussions.
3. The process will be enhanced if a person realizes that the change of attitude is to his advantage.
4. Structured experiences to engender new ways of thinking and acting through associations are of great benefit (Lambert and Lambert 1964).

The entire range of experiences in an adult basic education program can be structured to lend this impact. Here is the opportunity for the adult to meet new people, contemplate new ideas, and see new alternatives.

Such new possibilities come through the development of increased competencies in reading, language arts, number skills, human relations, consumer economics, and occupational information.

Reissman (1962) also identifies many psychological strengths of this individual. These have helped him in the past in making his way in a hostile world and should be valuable as supportive and sustaining factors in his attempt to better his lot. These strengths are the lack of strain that accompanies competitiveness, their equalitarianism, informality, humor, freedom from self-blame, and the ability to relax and have fun.

Drop-out rates in adult basic education classes are usually high. Like adolescent dropouts, they can be attributed to a myriad of reasons. Unlike adolescents, however, adults' life experiences fit them unusually well for learning. The use of those as adult basic education materials can do much toward increasing the staying power of the program.

Lack of staying power for the long haul, and the stress of poverty are the big challenges in holding power in the classes. Classes can be linked to jobs and life. They can be ungraded to keep the learners challenged. Many adults have an unusually long attention span and can make startling increases in competence over a short period of time when they have motivation to work at learning.

Because of the seriousness of real poverty, there needs to be, to the greatest extent possible, material support of the participants in a program. Such material support in the form of stipends on a part-time or on a full-time basis must be incorporated into the program planning from the beginning, and competently administered by the personnel services staff. This kind of immediate reinforcement can act as a powerful motive toward holding participants in a program until some basic learning can be achieved.

A broad program of professional assistance is necessary for adults with personal problems. A full-time social worker is needed to meet this need. If such is not available, then the teacher must function to the best of his ability and opportunity in this additional capacity. A multitude of problems beset people in this strata of society. Things just seem to happen to them.

Utilizing the strengths of undereducated adults, while providing these supports to them, will do much toward increasing the holding power of the adult education program.

Summary

What everybody in this world loves most is somebody who will discover an unsuspected diamond in him . . . so you must learn to love people, not for what they are now, but for what you know you can help them become (Laubach 1960, p. 36).

Since the development of adequate reading skills depends not only upon effective and appropriate teaching, but also upon the physical, psychological, and cultural milieu of the learner, these factors have been considered within this chapter. Primary emphasis has been placed on those factors that necessitate the implementation of teaching strategies that do not parallel those used with child learners.

Considerations of adults as learners with problems, needs, experiences, and abilities that differ from those of children generally becomes the most significant factor in structuring successful learning experiences in adult reading classes. Therefore, an understanding of these dynamics of adult learning is a prerequisite for the successful teacher of reading in adult basic education.

6.
The Learning Ability of Adults

Contrary to popular opinion, you can teach an old dog new tricks and he will learn them like a puppy! (E. Smith 1968, p. 3)

One of the greatest deterrents to adult basic education is the notion that undereducated adults do not have the ability to learn to read. Friends taunt the adult student by saying, "You're too old to learn! School is for kids!" Thus, the unspoken fear that these observers may be right becomes an inhibition to the full utilization of the learning powers that the individual does possess. In reality, in most cases, the truth concerning the learning ability of adults is quite the contrary. Because of their handicap of not being able to read or write, for years these people have been forced to "live by their wits" in a reasonably well-educated society (National Assoc. of Public Continuing Adult Educators. *Adult Basic Education* 1969).

Adult Intelligence

Robert Bridges finished his greatest poem at age eighty-five; Tennyson's last volume came out when he was eighty; Verdi was still composing sacred music at eighty-five; Wundt completed his memoirs at eighty-seven (Kidd 1959, p. 75); Golda Meir worked twenty-hour days in her midseventies; Justice William O. Douglas is as keen and alert as ever at seventy-five—the list is unending.

It is difficult to define intelligence beyond a generality. Psychologists have endeavored for decades to develop definitive ways of measuring intellectual capability. But the very diversity of the composition of human thinking and learning capabilities defies exact measurement or even exact definition. It would appear that the best that can be done at this time is to describe intelligence in terms of the factors that are known to be involved.

Intelligence is more than the innate genetic capability to think and to reason. This genetic capability was once considered to be a predestined constant quantity, unchangeable throughout a lifetime. It is now known that the genetic capability to think merely forms a base upon which real intelligence is built. Perceptual-motor development, experiences, cultural environment, training in concept formation, verbal development, vocabulary, and practice are but a few of the building blocks of intelligence. Deprive the genetic intellectual base of any of these building blocks and the resultant structure becomes warped and mis-shapen, developing only a fraction of its original potential.

Therefore, adult intelligence is different from that of a child. In some ways, learning is easier for adults because their brains are better developed than those of children. Their life experiences give them considerable advantage over children. A dull adult with an IQ of 85 (below average) may learn considerably faster than a child of six or seven with average ability. The effects of experience and practice may account for this superiority in functioning of the adult over the child (Botwinick 1971; Smith 1968).

Limitations in Measuring Adult Intelligence

The persistent myth that intellectual functioning slides downhill from adulthood through old age may have very little basis in fact, yet continues as an accepted axiom in the lives of many adults (Hurlock 1975). There are several reasons why this occurs. As we have already seen, adult intelligence is a difficult concept to describe, much less to define. This vagueness leads to inadequacies in measurement and evaluative techniques. Moreover, investigating the intellectual functioning of adults is an overwhelmingly difficult task. Research designs have understandably been faulty and inadequate.

Cross-sectional Versus Longitudinal Research

Cross-sectional studies involve the comparison of one section of the population with another section; that is, at any particular point in time, comparing the performance of a group of adolescent learners with that of a group of middle-aged people. The research design assumes that with the exception of the factors being compared, the populations are equal. Thus, conclusions are drawn such as the faulty one that eighteeen-year-olds have a greater intellectual functioning than fifty-year-olds. Such research does not account for the differing backgrounds of the two groups, nor the fact that for the younger group school learning has been a more potent factor in their lives than for many of the older group. Neither does such research account for the effects of the slowdown in motor skills concomitant with age, or any visual or auditory handicaps and other physical deficits that may have developed with age and inhibit functioning on some of the tests of intelligence, but not in thinking itself.

Longitudinal research, on the other hand, looks down through the years at the functioning of a particular group of people. It compares their per-

formance on a task for example, at age twenty to that at age forty and
again at age sixty. No other group is involved. This research design would
appear to be more suited for judging the maintenance of a human ability
over a period of years. Yet the number of years that would be required
before conclusions could be drawn, much less the researcher's problem
of holding onto a sample population long enough to study, is almost an
overwhelming problem (Butcher 1973).

Shaie and Strother (1973) suggest that the conclusions drawn from
cross-sectional and longitudinal research will continue to produce discrepancies, even if compensations are made for the factors mentioned.
These investigators suggest that a full understanding of development requires an experimental design combining both kinds of approaches.

Research Sample Problems

In researching problems related to children's learning abilities, there is
little problem in drawing a research sample population. Children are in
school and are otherwise available to researchers. However, with adults
the problem is not as simple. Adults are involved in vocations, supporting
families and other things. They are mobile. The general adult population
is seldom willing to be "guinea pigs" to be studied by psychologists. Therefore, for the most part, research sample populations used to investigate
factors related to adult learning ability have traditionally been "captive
audiences"—those in prisons, retirement homes, and other types of institutions. It is probably risky to generalize these findings to the general
adult population in the United States (Kidd 1959).

Problems with Measurement Techniques

Intellectual ability is measured by an individual's achievement on various
tasks of an intelligence, or IQ, test. Most of the problems arise from the
nature of the test and the assumption upon which the test is built. The
most faulty assumption that interferes with measurement is that intellectual functioning is constant or that it is the same thing for adults that
it appears to be for children. Most of the intelligence tests are not based
on tasks dealing with real life situations that are of interest to an adult.
Neither are they separated from the physical factors inhibiting adult performance, such as speed of performance. Most instruments are heavily
weighted toward school learning, and are merely revisions of children's
tests.

However, it is with these instruments that investigators have formulated conclusions regarding the intellectual functioning of the adult in

the real, everyday world. Perhaps a recognition of all of these difficulties in making judgments about adult intelligence will cause adult educators to be more wary of long promulgated myths and poorly founded generalizations.

Changes in Adult Intellectual Functioning

Life is not the same at forty-five as at twenty-five; nor are we the same kind of people (Hurlock 1975, p. 260).

The fact that intellectual functioning does change in some ways as one ages is not disputed. But the kind and degree of this change is still an open question (Kidd 1959).

Early Concepts of Adult Intellectual Functioning

In the past it has been assumed that mental deterioration inevitably accompanied physical decline. The work of Jones and Conrad (1959) in the 1920s was designed as a cross-sectional study to plot the trend of intelligence through most of adult life. This study seemed to show rapid intellectual growth to about eighteen or twenty years, then a gradual steady

It is never too late for an adult to enter the magic world of reading. (Courtesy of Venice-Lincoln Technical Center, Venice, Illinois.)

decline. Scores on information and vocabulary did not show any decline; therefore, he erroneously concluded that these areas were the least valid indications of intelligence and that speed of performance was the most important factor with which to be concerned.

Thorndike's famous studies of adult intelligence were similarly based on speed of performance (Lorge 1940; Thorndike 1928). He made three general observations about adult learning.

1. The most capable man and the most ordinary man show the same curve of ability to learn. The influence of intellect on this curve is negligible.
2. People appear to learn best between twenty and twenty-five years of age.
3. Ability to learn declines about 1 percent per year from age twenty-five to about age forty-two.

Wechsler (1955—*The Measurement of Adult Intelligence*) also published data stating that human intellectual functioning reached its peak at about age twenty-five and thereafter steadily declined. However, his findings were later revised to indicate that the total score on the *Wechsler Adult Intelligence Scale* (1955) climbs steadily from adolescence to about thirty-five years of age, and then declines, but not to the degree that Wechsler thought.

Reasons for Apparent Decline

Other than the research and measurement problems previously discussed, this apparent decline in intellectual functioning may be explained in other ways.

An apparent measured decrease in intelligence quotient may be the result of disuse of knowledge, lack of motivation, remoteness from school, or other physiological, educational, or psychological reasons (Baltes and Shaie 1974; Hurlock 1975; Kidd 1959). This phenomenon can occur at any age and is frequently observed even in children who are underachievers in school, or who are emotionally disturbed. Such occurrence would appear to confirm one of Thorndike's Laws of Learning (1928), which says that a skill not practiced or a knowledge not used will largely be lost or forgotten.

The decline in *rate* or speed of learning and performing accounts for much of this finding. But it must not be assumed that because speed has been slowed, that power or capacity to learn has in any way been affected. This is a separate factor. Lorge (1959) concluded that this decline in rate of learning was due to losses in visual acuity, auditory acuity, and reaction time. Fear of failure and different attitudes of adults also caused the slowdown. Lorge (1956) further concluded that intellectual power in and of itself does not change from twenty to sixty years of age. Probably the decline in rate from age forty-five is not significantly different, so a person of sixty-five could expect to learn at least half as much per hour as could be learned at the age of twenty-five, but more than could be learned at the age of eight or ten.

Some studies have pointed out that this decrease in the rate of learning as the individual advances in years was far less for gifted people than it was for those who were functioning on lower levels (Owens 1973; Terman and Oden 1959). Other studies pointed out that there is a difference in the way younger and older people view "correctness." Therefore, the finding that the older person was slower in responding may simply be the result of deliberate slowness in the interest of greater accuracy, or because the adult can see more alternatives than the younger person can (Kidd 1959; Welford 1951).

Follow-up Studies of Adult Intellectual Functioning

A recent study by Kangas and Bradway (1971) indicates that contrary to previous findings, intellectual functioning tends to increase slightly during middle age, especially among the more talented people. This finding would appear to substantiate an earlier finding by Terman and Oden (1959) that there was no decline in midlife among those with better than average intellectual abilities. There appears not to be any specific age at which mental decline takes place, nor is there a pattern of decline that is characteristic of all older people. Each is individualistic, and it appears that if there is any decline, such loss is not a part of the normal aging process (Bayley 1965; Wilkie and Eisdorfer 1971).

In an impressive study, Baltes, Shaie et al. (Baltes and Labouvie 1973; Baltes and Shaie 1974; Labouvie-Vief et al. 1974; Shaie 1970, 1972, 1973) reported that in abilities heavily dependent on knowledge gained from the culture and from school, such as reasoning, verbal meanings, or numbers, there is no significant longitudinal loss. This study extended over many years during which a single group of people from age twenty-one to seventy were evaluated at various times during adulthood. Four fairly independent general dimensions of intelligence seemed to emerge from the thirteen areas of cognitive functioning that were studied.

1. *Crystallized intelligence,* the area that IQ tests attempt to measure, includes the kinds of skills gained through experiences with education and acculturation.

2. *Cognitive flexibility* indicates one's ability to shift from one way of thinking to another within familiar contexts, as when one must provide either a synonym or an antonym to a word, depending on whether or not it appears in either uppercase or lowercase print.

3. *Visuo-motor flexibility* is concerned with a similar, yet independent skill—that is, the ability to shift from a familiar to an unfamiliar pattern in tasks requiring coordination of visual and motor abilities, such as when one must copy words, but interchange uppercase with lowercase letters.

4. *Visualization* is the ability to organize and process visual information. It involves such tasks as finding a simple figure hidden in a complex one, or identifying a picture that is incomplete.

When this data was analyzed longitudinally rather than cross-sectionally, a definite decline was noted in *only one* of these four dimensions. That was visuo-motor flexibility. Indeed, there was a systematic *increase* in the most important dimension of intelligence, crystallized intelligence, as well as an increase in visualization.

It would appear from this study that differences in intellectual functioning between young people and older people may be caused by differences in generations rather than in chronological ages. In this study, people who were fifty years old in the 1950s did not score as high as those who were fifty years old in the 1960s. This suggests that the measured intelligence of the population is increasing. The reasons for this can only be speculations. Perhaps different educational methods, such as reliance on reasoning, rather than on memory, as well as the increased mobility of the population and the extensive vicarious experiences through television, could partially account for this observation.

Baltes and Shaie (1974) also reported Riegel's observation (1972) that during five or less years before death there appeared to be a sudden deterioration of intellectual abilities. One could only speculate as to the reason for this, but it was judged most likely to be the result of both neurophysiological deterioration and psychological variables that contribute both to the drop and to biological death.

Shaie (1972) concluded that in older adults it is difficult to distinguish between a person's competence and his actual performance. Handicaps, such as fatigue and visual and hearing problems, which have nothing to do with intelligence, often interfere with test performance.

Dwindling reinforcements may also affect the performance of the older adult. In our culture of youth worship, some young people have a negative view of old age and tend to withdraw reinforcement from the elderly. Moreover, the environment of the elderly population may be socially and intellectually impoverished. As adults put aside intellectual activities in acceptance of the stereotype of decline with age, the condition becomes a self-fulfilling prophecy.

Memory and Retention in Adult Learning

A retentive memory may be a good thing, but the ability to forget is the true token of greatness (Elbert Hubbard).

Someone has tersely commented, "Studying is a vicious circle; the more I learn, the more I forget." However, memory and forgetting cannot be explained away in such a precursory manner.

Forgetting is not just a fading away process, but follows certain highly individualistic dynamics. The rate of forgetting is increased by fear and anxiety, as well as affected by the individual's general ability pattern of learning, and his intent to remember.

Contrary to popular opinion, the passage of time since the original learning took place does not appear to be as important a factor of retention as what has occurred during that time. Memory is conditioned by previous learning, the emotional undertones of the learning, and the cultural attitudes and biases toward the learning. When there is a disagreement between new and old materials, or when there is no established relationship between the new and the old learning, the material appears to have been forgotten. However, this apparent loss of data from storage seems to be more of a psychological retroactive inhibition to remembering, rather than merely a loss caused by the passage of time (Farquhar, Krimboltz, Wren 1960; Wayne State Univ. 1967).

Adults appear to surpass children in their capacity to memorize material immediately. Nonetheless, within a few weeks after the original learning, memory of it generally declines. Trying to learn too much material too quickly may also inhibit retention. Therefore, distributed learning over a number of periods of time instead of attempting mastery of an entire task at one longer, but equivalent period appears to be more efficient (Verner and Davison 1971).

Some researchers have commented that immediately after a lecture, students were able to retain only 62 percent of the ideas given. Then after eight weeks, only 23 percent was retained (Farquhar, Krimboltz, Wren 1960). Thus, the rate of forgetting appears to be very rapid during the time immediately following the learning, with the loss of retention curve flattening out after that period of time. Purpose and relevancy of the learning are important factors in retention. The retention rate of nonessential ideas appears to be only one-fourth that of essential facts (H. K. Smith 1970).

The efficient utilization of study skills also appears to be an important dynamic of retention. Research emphasizes the fact that the proper organization of study skills may be as important a factor in academic achievement as is mental ability (Haffner 1965). On any university campus may be found countless students of average or somewhat-below-average ability plodding along and making passable grades because they have mastered effective study techniques, while there are far too many students of superior mental ability just barely getting by or completely falling by the wayside because they lack such organizational skills.

With the preceding evidence, it can be seen that it is probable that for adults the years of experience, anxiety, and other physical and psychological occurrences have in some ways affected the ability to remember, with apparently greater difficulty in remembering isolated facts than information acquired through relational learning. It has also been observed that things are remembered best when presented with the greatest intensity.

Therefore, these dynamics of memory are different for the adult learner than for the child in the classroom. Moreover, for these adults to whom failure to learn is already a familiar and expected experience, it is essential that the teacher make clear the specific purposes for studying. He must point out the structure and organization of that material, showing the learner how to study it, and give him much supervised practice in efficient study skills. Along with fostering motivation by dynamic, varied, and interesting presentations, these become important teaching techniques in increasing retention in adult basic education.

The Relation of Verbal Ability to Intelligence

Age has no veto power over learning, for any period of the natural life span (Miles 1952, p. 86).

It has already been shown that verbal ability does not decrease with increasing years. Since the usage of language is one of the major modes of demonstrating one's reasoning and learning ability, such usage deserves consideration.

Language Facility

In the case of the undereducated adult, atypical nonstandard linguistic practices frequently cause mismeasurement of learning ability. Such aberrant language development may have little to do with intellectual functioning. Frequently, the customs and activities of the group to which the learner belongs dictates his linguistic habits. These may involve production of language—how and when it is used, as well as other practices that inhibit intellectual growth or performance. Discrepancies between dialect and Standard English, as well as logistic differences altering the language content itself become additional barriers to communication. Moreover, individual idiosyncratic language patterns, as well as those caused by the interference of a second language, may also be inhibiting factors. Since the teacher is likely to be middle-class oriented, such language differences may pose a communication problem in the classroom, as well as interfere with an accurate assessment of potential learning ability.

Vocabulary

Vocabulary, another important facet of measured intelligence, increases with age if the new words learned are put into active use (Fox 1947). Since his experiences are much broader, the adult nonreader generally has more words in his oral vocabulary that can be converted to the reading vocabulary than does the child nonreader. This is one of the reasons that the reading skills may be taught more quickly to adults than to children. The verbal deficiency that may be noted in adult learners may be the result of anxiety, rather than a lack of word knowledge or a lack of ability. It is generally alleviated as the fear-anxiety level of the adult learner is lowered and the self-concept is enhanced.

Correlates of Adult Learning Ability

It is really not that "a little education is a dangerous thing."
A little education is one step better than no education. More education
is better. But the role of education is to give people tools for doing
things and tools for further exploration and further thinking
(Rauch 1972, p. 22).

Whether the genetic intellectual capacity becomes useful to the individual to its broadest limits is determined by many factors. In the case of the undereducated adult, one may assume that maximum development of this ability has usually not taken place, else the present learning problem would not exist. Many of the deficiencies that cause the adult basic education student to *appear* less than average in learning ability may be modified within the course of his educational program if these are recognized and purposefully dealt with. The most important avenues through which these deficiencies can be remedied are experience background, motivation, attitudes, and emotional inhibitions and interests.

Experience Repertoire and Relational Learning

For all learners, regardless of age, a repertoire of experiences is basic to the development of the intellectual capacities. Adult experiences differ from those of children both in quantity and in kind, as well as in organization (American Bar Assoc. 1974). Because adults have lived longer than children, they have had more varied lives. Much of their experience is related to firsthand activities. These older learners bring to the learning situation a background of life experience that is not available to younger pupils. Most of them have raised families and held jobs. Many have been in the service, and all have faced the challenges and frustrations of survival in the uncompromising struggle of daily living.

Adult experiences, unlike those of children, are not restricted to activities primarily with their own age level. The adult learner lives a less-prescribed existence than does youth. Despite all tendencies toward conformity in adulthood, this wider range of activities available to him produces more diverse experiences (Whipple 1957). He has infinitely more knowledge of the world around him than does the most advantaged child. This experience repertoire provides life examples for generalizing. Thus, the adult learner demonstrates insights and the ability to see relationships that are not discerned by children. Moreover, this wide range of experience makes it unnecessary for him to learn what words mean before learning to read them. First, he needs to learn how to read the many words that have already become the verbal abstractions of experiences for him. In the same way, the adult's experience with mathematical concepts facilitates his learning of mathematical skills.

In spite of the fact that he has been denied a formal education, the illiterate adult has been educated by living. He is a graduate of the "school of hard knocks." Generally, he is able to deal with problems and has a sense of what is and what is not likely to work—a sort of accumulated wisdom. The handicap of educational deprivation may actually have sharpened his senses so that he cultivated shrewdness, the ability to think, and a high level of common sense (Ulmer 1969).

Professional literature abounds with educators' statements abhorring the fact that these people have not had experiences. It would seem that this generalization is erroneous and misleading. These people have lived their lives within some sort of society. So they must have had some sort of experiences. Living is in itself the essence of experience. So without doubt, the undereducated must also possess experience and intelligence—although neither has served them very well in schools.

The problem is two-fold. First, the facets of intelligence developed by the undereducated adult in order to survive within his own cultural boundaries may not be those we commonly measure on intelligence tests geared to the prediction of academic success; or they may not be those facets needed in order to achieve success in the verbal academic world of reading. However, the various abilities that they have demonstrated in the process of survival must be thought of in terms of intellectual functioning.

The second aspect of the problem appears to be the quality and kind of experiences common to the undereducated adult. Partially because the adult basic education teacher is usually middle-class oriented, it may be difficult for him to understand the experiences of his students, but he must make use of them as structures for learning. However, the tenet that it is necessary to use a child's experience background as the basis of building reading skills is equally important for adults. His experience repertoire—atypical, foreign, or abhorrent to the teacher—must be used as a basis to build reading skills. There is no other way, because words are no more than the verbal symbols for these experiences. Conceptual ability is no more than the trained ability to organize these experiences in some meaningful, logical, and productive way.

Therefore, the successful teacher of adult basic reading skills must become a sensitive, nonjudgmental listener to, and communicator with, his adult learners. He must also become familiar enough with their cultural experiential background, and this can be used as the foundation upon which to build reading skills.

Relevancy and Motivation in Adult Learning Ability

Within the past decade, the term "relevance" has acquired an importance—or at least a new notoriety—in education. Warren (1970) comments:

> This concept was familiar to teachers of adults long before it achieved its "now generation" popularity with teachers on other levels. The adult student is more likely to learn a piece of information or to master a particular skill if he knows "what's in it for him," if he can see a fairly immediate use of his new learning. This is just another way of saying that the teacher should help the student see the "relevance" (p. 1).

Although adults may be slower than children to learn isolated facts and piecemeal information, it has been emphasized before that they are far superior in learning relationally. *Relevance* is the key factor here. Generally, it is true that adults can learn anything that they *need* to know at the time that such learning is needed—whether they are sixteen or sixty! By relating learning activities *directly* to the everyday affairs of life, the experiences of adults can and should become the raw data for much of the basic curriculum. Teaching can utilize as learning vehicles the work, child care, homelife, and local politics of the student's immediate life and experiences. Instruction that begins with these very concrete, pragmatic problems will serve as a motivating force for these very pragmatic people. Later in the course of instruction, learning can become more abstract (Brazziel 1965).

If the student's ultimate goal is to be able to write a letter to a grown son away from home, then it becomes the teacher's responsibility to show him how to express himself within the format of a letter. If his goal is to be able to secure a better paying job, then the skills involved in filling out application blanks or partaking in successful interviews become the relevant tasks for the teacher to use for instructional purposes. Showing the student that misspellings on a job application will lessen his chances of getting the job establishes the relevance of word recognition and spelling knowledge, particularly when the wise teacher has chosen spelling words that would likely be needed in such situations.

The learner tends to be impatient. He wants to learn fast and be able to put his learning to immediate, practical use. Generally, he quickly becomes annoyed at anything that he considers "busywork." Thus, setting purposes that establish relevance for every learning activity is a teaching necessity; it allows the adult learner to become actively involved in the worthwhile utilization of the short time available to him for learning purposes. Only then can he know that his struggle to get to class has been worth the effort.

Attitudinal and Mental Rigidity

Platitudes such as "experience is the best teacher" tend toward the belief that all older people really have learned adequately from their experiences. Older people are supposed to have superior judgment and more stability than younger ones. As such, they are often characterized as filled with the "wisdom of age." Realistically, however, the situation may be somewhat different. Instead, many appear to be slower and more conservative, with a tendency to prejudge from experience instead of experimenting flexibly with new concepts and ideas (Otto and Ford 1967).

Objectivity may also become a problem, in that there is a tendency to allow one's ego and opinions to become so intimately involved with an event that not much is learned from it. This causes experiences to be interpreted differently according to the aspect of reality selected by the individual for emphasis. This perception of reality is sometimes distorted by neuroses in the direction of some overwhelming personal need or anxiety.

Fear of change often converts the somewhat natural conservatism of the adult into a mental rigidity that can pose a problem in the process of adult education. In a manner of speaking, the older adult may tend to become passive toward events—in a rut—just allowing them to happen rather than becoming active agents in their happening. The undereducated adult may be tempted to just coast along, making no effort to investigate new activities, new points of view, or new goals. This is probably the result of many previous negative experiences that have tended to cause an overly cautious, suspicious attitude (Berdrow 1965).

This general attitude of being overly cautious and somewhat suspicious can be a deterrent to learning in the classroom. The adult learner may be suspicious of the teacher's motives in urging the acquisition of learnings and behaviors. This sensitive area requires an indirect approach. In some ways, presentation of new ideas or methods of performance challenge the worth and validity of already established ones. Thus, the worth of the individual himself may be challenged. Therefore, the teacher of adults will approach such areas gradually and cautiously.

The effects of practice and the strength of long-standing habits is also a factor in this mental rigidity. It is frequently observed that older people tend to make the same errors more often than younger learners do. Doing things in a particular way over a long period of time without challenge establishes a firm habit that sometimes requires a long time to modify. Especially is this true with language habits and patterns. Because of this tendency toward rigidity, it is necessary for the teacher to provide the student with much reinforced practice. Teachers can soften this experience for the adult learner by explaining that this is a common problem and not especially peculiar to the individual (Warren 1964).

Relation of Adult Interests to Learning Ability

Although attitudinal and mental rigidity are often barriers to adult learning, as demonstrated by their lack of willingness to adopt new ways or even to try new methods of doing things, if the relevance of their learning has been established and their priority needs are being met, their interest in the pursuit of their learning goals tends to be steadier than that of younger learners. Because of this mature interest, they are also usually cooperative and persistent, and this enhances learning.

Adult interests differ from those of children. The child's interest world is more or less circumscribed by the boundaries of the immediate environment. This is not true for the adult whose interests range far and wide. Interests do not tend to change in adulthood, but their value or depth may vary (Cass 1956).

An adult learner will sometimes be more knowledgeable than the instructor about a particular subject being studied. He enjoys having his talents and information made use of in a teaching situation, and often this can be the greatest teaching resource available. Utilizing these interests can add such excitement and depth to the learning transaction as simply cannot be found in a class for children (SWAP Newsletters). In addition, it boosts a person's self-concept and gives greater confidence in the ability to learn when the teacher occasionally looks to him for expertise and advice concerning his special knowledge of an area of his own interest (Wallace 1965). Adults appreciate this special concern with their experiences and interests which the perceptive teacher demonstrates.

Summary

*The mind of an illiterate person is like an unplanted seed. Inside
the shell, there is a germ of life waiting to be awakened and quickened.
If it does not germinate, it will not grow. Natural, full growth must
come from within; and so your job is to create the conditions
for it (Wallace 1965, p. 6).*

The uniqueness of adult intelligence and learning ability has been the topic of this chapter. Although earlier studies appeared to indicate that aging deteriorates the quality of the adult's intellectual functioning, later studies have shown that this is not generally the case. During adulthood the rate of learning slows down somewhat. Memory may become selective and the adult may encounter difficulty in learning isolated facts. In some adults, anxiety has caused a decrease of verbal fluency. Some have yielded to passive attitudes toward life, thus some mental rigidity may have been created. For many adult learners, atypical linguistic habits and cultural differences may be creating conditions that make it appear that the adult does not have adequate learning ability.

However, the adult also has many advantages in learning that are not available to children. His concepts are probably better developed. He has wider interests, broader experiences, a larger vocabulary, and may be learning relationally.

In considering both the positive and the negative aspects of adult intellectual functioning, it can be said that generally adults can learn anything that they *need* to know at the time such learning is needed—whether they are sixteen or sixty!

Part 2

Developing
Reading Skills
for the
Adult Learner

7.
Teaching Reading in Adult Basic Education: An Overview

The title of "teacher" will continue to be used in schools. In teaching adults, especially, remember that it not only describes one who shows, directs, and guides, but that it also describes one who listens, sympathizes, encourages, support, challenges, and applauds (Curriculum Guide to Adult Basic Education: Beginning Level 1966, p. 95).

This chapter contains some pertinent facets of the reading process and some productive strategies for teaching basic reading skills to undereducated adults. In teaching people to read, the end objective, which is the production of self-motivated, efficient readers, remains the same for the adult learner as for the child. However, the route the teacher must take to get the adult learner to this goal is far different from the route that can

be taken with the child learner. It is the purpose of this chapter to emphasize these necessary modifications in instruction, as the reading process and successful teaching strategies are discussed.

The Nature of the Reading Process

A teacher is the only person who can say to you, "Get lost!" Of course, he means, "Get lost in your book." Then nothing can bother you and you can read and study with good results. If your family sees you reading and studying, they may decide it is a good idea and they will read and study also. Just think how much quieter your house will be then! (Curriculum Guide to Adult Basic Education: Beginning Level 1966, p. 90).

The fields of medicine, neurology, psychology, linguistics, and education all are combining research efforts designed to unravel the mysteries of reading; but to date, there is still much concerning the process that is only inferred, and not thoroughly understood. Thus, attempts to define the process often become descriptions of a particular facet of the process rather than a comprehensive definition. Yet, it is mandatory that adult basic education teachers attempt to define, or to at least describe adequately, the process they intend to teach so they understand how it operates. Such a description or definition becomes the teacher's rationale for strategies and objectives.

The Physiological Facets of the Reading Process

The individual must be endowed with an adequate physiological structure in order to accommodate the reading process. The function of the *sensory modalities*[1] of vision and hearing is obvious. No reading can be accomplished unless the individual is able to focus his eyes properly on the page and to move them systematically across the lines of print, and make the proper return sweep. He must also be able to *hear* the sounds of oral language and of word parts if the reading process is to develop smoothly.

Beyond the accommodation of these obvious sensory modalities, the maturation and development of the *neurological channels*[2] is also essential to learning to read. This central nervous system functions as the brain's conveyor and interpreter of stimuli received through the sensory modalities. Abstract visual symbols and images, auditory impressions, and tactile and kinesthetic stimuli are thus processed by the central nervous system to the brain for discrimination, interpretation, comprehension, utilization, and/or storage. The individual learns to utilize perceptual clues, such as size, shape, combinations of letters and sounds, figure-ground relationships, relationships of the parts to the whole, sequencing, and ordering (Ruddell 1970). Thus, the development of these perceptual processes—visual, auditory, and tactile—along with verbal expression and syntactical maturity are important neurological components of the reading process.

There is also an increasing amount of evidence that learning in general, and reading in particular, may also be related to the individual's general condition of health, vitality, and nutrition, and particularly to the individual biochemical and endocrine functioning (Smith and Carrigan 1959). Biological studies into the relationship of *DNA* and *RNA*[3] to learning also seem to promise a better understanding in the future of many of the heretofore perplexing disabilities in reading and learning that plague children as well as adults.

The Psychological Facets of the Reading Process

Basically, reading is a thinking process requiring intellectual and emotional reaction from the reader. As an intellectual process, it involves ver-

---

1. The sensory modalities are the body's receptors that take in information. The generally accepted list of sensory modalities includes vision, hearing, smell, taste, temperature, pain, pressure, and touch.

2. Neurological channels refer to the central nervous system. The nerve structures in the brain, spinal cord, and the peripheral systems of the body convey and process information received from the sensory modalities.

3. The human gene consists of protein material containing an acid—deoxyribonucleic (DNA)—that forms a template on which other nucleic acid molecules of precise structure are synthesized. There are two kinds of nucleic acid: deoxyribonucleic acid (DNA) and ribonucleic acid (RNA). They are chemically similar, but functionally different. The DNA is the carrier of genetic information. Learning appears to involve a change in the way the brain biochemically synthesizes this protein and the giant molecule, RNA (Goldberg and Schiffman 1973).

bal reasoning, perceiving relationships, classifying data, making critical judgments and evaluations, generalizing, solving problems, imagining, memorizing, and being able to comprehend abstract symbols and ideas.

Hence, Gray's (1960) definition of the act of reading as a four-step process: perception of the word, comprehension of its meaning, reaction to the meaning in terms of what one knows, and integration of the idea into one's background of experience emphasizes the psychological thought processes as most pertinent to the reading act.

Ephrom (1953) delineates the psychological aspects of the reading process in a broader sense by stating that essentially reading may be considered a "complex, but unitary psychological function involving ideational, emotional, and motor aspects, as well as the adaptations of the reader to the reading experience." Such a concept has led some behaviorists to view the reading process as *only one* behavior of the individual's total personality, and as such, subject to the same dynamics as any other behavior, depending on the individual personality structure. Thus, how the individual feels about himself and others in his world, and his emotional security and characteristic patterns of dealing with frustration and anxiety—all are determinants of how well the person will succeed in learning to read. *Defense mechanisms,*[4] rationalization, repression and inhibition, projection, and aggression are but a few of the responses to anxiety revolving around the reading behavior that will be primary factors in determining success or failure in learning to read.

The Cultural-Experiential Facets of the Reading Process

Words are meaningful only in that they function as the abstract symbols for either a real or a vicarious experience or concept. Thus, experience becomes the foundation stone of the reading process. Horn comments that

> The author does not really convey ideas to the reader; he merely stimulates him to construct them out of his own experience (Zintz 1975, p. 15).

Therefore, since to a large extent one's culture controls the quality and the quantity of experience available to the individual, the concept of reading as a cultural-experience process remains a valid one.

Reading is also augmented by self-reliance, social acceptance, and cooperation in a group. Attitudes, such as loyalties, prejudices, and conflicts affect reading. Negative factors, such as broken homes, second language problems, and cultural values in conflict between the home and

4. A defense mechanism is any psychological behavior that the individual engages in, either consciously or unconsciously, to protect his self-concept against unpleasantness, shame, anxiety, or loss of self-esteem.

the educational experience also influence reading (Ulmer 1969). Thus, the social aspects of the reading act become relevant to the adult basic education reading teacher.

The Linguistic Facets of the Reading Process

The linguistic facets of the reading process include the syntactic (or grammatic) and semantic (or meaning) elements in the process of decoding and encoding print into meaningful concepts. Effective reading requires the mastery of phoneme-grapheme relationships, as well as the mastery of the suprasegmental phonemes of the langue; that is the stress, pitch, and juncture (pauses) we use in speech in order to convey meaning. It also requires an understanding of the structural aspects of the language and facility in the use of context to determine meaning. The importance of language varieties, of cultural influence on language, and of the appropriate usage of nonstandard language are linguistic qualities that differentiate success for learners in mastering reading.

An Operational Model of the Reading Process

> *Mere literacy—unaccompanied in the process of its acquisition by training to learn to be understanding and critical of what is being read—is no way to the salvation of the problems of the underdeveloped countries of the world. . . . Literacy without skill and competence is useless; without character and moral principles, it can be dangerous (Orata 1966, p. 66).*

An operational model is an attempt to graphically describe the sequential functioning of a process. Because reading is such a multifaceted process, such graphic presentations can become exceedingly complex, but are very helpful to the adult basic education teacher who is attempting to determine areas of the process that are functioning inadequately or not at all, and to teach reading skills in a sequential, meaningful way. Figure 7.1 illustrates such a model.

The Major Aspects of the Reading Process

Robinson (1966), in a revision and explanation of Gray's model, identified four closely related basic steps in the act of reading that can be expected to develop sequentially, particularly for the immature reader; but may occur almost concurrently in the case of the mature, efficient reader. These four basic steps—word perception, comprehension, reaction, and assimi-

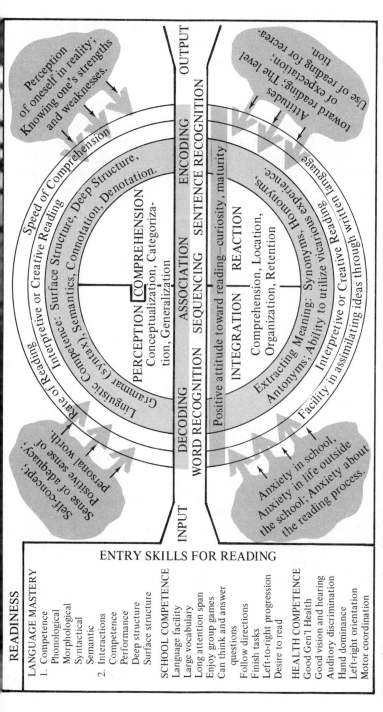

Figure 7.1. Operational model of the reading process. The four parts of the circle show reading as a **four-step thinking process**; perception, comprehension, reaction, and integration. The cognitive process also includes interpretive or creative reading in a word recognition-sequencing process. The linguistic process includes the syntactic, semantic, and meaning (deep structure) in decoding-encoding print into meaningful concepts. The affective processes are interactions of self-concept, attitudes, and anxieties. All of these affect a reader's facility in assimilating ideas through written language—that is, his speed of comprehension in reading. (From *Corrective Reading*, 2d ed., p. 14, by Miles V. Zintz. Dubuque, Ia.: Wm. C. Brown Co., Publishers, 1972; 3d ed. in press. Reprinted by permission.)

73

lation—are circumscribed by a fifth aspect, rates, that depends on the development of the other aspects as shown in the interior quadrants of the circle and its outer ring in figure 7.1.

Word Perception

Word perception involves the identification of the printed symbol, and the identification of the meaning the author had in mind when he wrote the word. For example, one identifies the combination of letters, b - a - n - d as *band* and not *bank* or some other word like it. It is not *bind, bend,* or *bang.* The printed word, then, acts as a trigger to release a meaning the reader already possesses.

To accomplish the task, commonly referred to as the decoding process, certain skills are required, such as the ability to:

1. Use an adequate sight vocabulary and configuration memory.
2. Use contextual clues to determine pronunciation and meaning.
3. Determine pronunciation and meaning through an analysis of the structure of the word according to its parts—that is, roots and affixes, and inflected and derived forms, referred to as structural analysis.
4. Relate the sound of the spoken word to its visual, or graphemic symbol, referred to as phonic analysis.
5. Use a dictionary to determine pronunciation and meaning of words that are resistant to analysis through the use of other skills.

Comprehension

Comprehension of ideas requires the fusion of meanings of separate words into a chain of related ideas, which are usually those that the author had in mind when he wrote the passage. It occurs at two levels: the literal level and the implied level. The individual initially reads the passage for an understanding of what the passage *says*—that is, understanding main ideas, relevant details and facts; recognizing sequence of time, place, events, or steps; and following stated directions or identifying *stated* conclusions. Only when this level of comprehension has been achieved can the reader address himself toward comprehension on the implied level— that is, understanding the *total* meaning of the passage. This involves drawing inferences; determining characterization and setting; sensing relationships; anticipating outcomes; making comparisons and contrasts; drawing conclusions; making generalizations; and recognizing the author's purpose, tone, and feelings; and thus clearly understanding the ideas the author wanted to express.

Reaction

Reaction to these ideas includes the ability to judge their accuracy, quality, or worth in the light of what one knows, and on this basis, accept or reject them. Such intellectual judgments are the result of critical reading and of being able to reason logically as the reader ascertains the validity of the material. Reaction also occurs on the emotional level, which requires value judgments, experience background, and the ability to recreate sensory images. Reaction occurs only as comprehension is fully realized. How much one already knows about the subject and the amount of previous experience one has had with it determines one's ability to react to what is written.

Assimilation

Assimilation of the ideas gained is determined by how the reader reacts. As ideas are accepted or rejected, they become a part of his total life experience. Ideas are then assimilated with what is already known, thus broadening the reader's total background and becoming the building stones for the creation of new insights and concepts. Thus, one may gain insights, understandings, interests, and attitudes; he may develop improved patterns of behavior or become more stable emotionally.

Rates

Rates refer not only to the speed with which the reader decodes the visual symbols, but also to the speed of comprehension, reaction, and assimilation. Thus, rates become dependent on the development and proficiency of the other aspects of the reading process for its functioning. Since these will probably show much variation, rates become plural, used to encompass the range from very slow in some aspects of the process to very rapid in others. Rates of reading need to be flexible, being appropriately adjusted in accordance with the reader's purpose and to the difficulty of the material being read.

Other Aspects of the Reading Process

In figure 7.1, Robinson's five major aspects of the reading process are overlaid by other factors that other investigators have considered to be essential. The necessary entry skills for success in learning to read; the cognitive factors in word recognition, sequencing, and sentence meaning described by Geyer (1970); the linguistic factors in decoding, associating, and encoding the significant meaning in the language used (Ruddell 1970); and the affective factors exhibited in the self-concept; and one's perception of himself, and attitudes toward reading (Athey 1970) have been incorporated into the diagram (Zintz 1970).

In light of the most current research in the fields of psycholinguistics (Geyer 1970; Goodman 1969; Hillburn 1973; Ruddell 1970) and of cognitive psychology (Gibson and Levin 1975; Lindsay and Norman 1972; Robeck and Wilson 1974; Smith 1970, 1975; Sticht 1974), the foregoing discussion of the reading process is undoubtedly superficial, incomplete, and overly simplistic. However, for fear of clouding the issues in adult basic education, the temptation toward further explication of the complexity of the act of reading is resisted. For such excursions, the reader is directed to sources cited.

Summary

Meaningful reading is like meaningful listening. As you listen to a speaker you do not respond to each word he says. Instead, you respond to groups of words—to ideas (Paul Witty).

This chapter has attempted to orient the reader to complexities of the reading process and to present a simplified model of the process upon which the adult education teacher can build teaching strategies. Along with the presentation of the model, implications for teaching have been made.

8.
Teaching Reading as a Developmental Process

Teaching adult illiterates has many skids! Educators who look upon the illiterate as a hopeless case share one thing in common with him—they believe that little or nothing can be done for him (Wallace 1965, p. 11).

Reading develops in an orderly, sequential pattern regardless of the learner's age. Teachers who fail to recognize this fact often cause confusion to the learner. A mathematics teacher would not expect a learner to be able to do multiplication and division before he had learned addition and subtraction. Neither can a reading teacher expect a learner to develop competent skill in comprehending the words on the printed page before he has mastered those words on an oral level.

Readiness for Reading

Proceed from easy to more difficult lessons step by step. Don't be afraid of the one-room-schoolhouse idea where beginning students get to hear the more advanced students recite. Beginners can learn much in this way (Curriculum Guide to Adult Basic Education: Beginning Level 1966, p. 91).

Readiness for reading and reading success is probably most related to vocabulary development. An adult will probably learn to read more quickly than a child of comparable ability. The readiness for reading factors that the kindergarten and first-grade teachers endeavor to develop in a child are generally already matured in the adult. He probably has developed better visual and auditory perception. Through the years he has most likely had some type of experience working with shapes, colors, sizes of objects; and in noticing directionality. He is also probably better motivated, better organized, and better able to concentrate than a child in the first grade. Also, he has most likely had extensive practice with oral language and recognizes most of the letters of the alphabet. He is very well aware of what words are—he has been using them for years! Therefore, in adult education, there is seldom a need for an extensive reading readiness program to prepare learners to learn to read.

Nevertheless, the culturally different adult may experience difficulty in dealing with abstractions. Limited vocabulary, bilingualism, and dialectical differences may also be inhibitions. Most certainly, there will be interferences with learning to read caused by the psychological and sociological factors discussed in other chapters.

The Sequence of Language Development

> A *tribute to adult basic education:* "The Teacher IS good He
> Taught me What I know and I tank him for What he done for me.
> When I came to School I could not Rite So tank to all Who Were
> the cause of This" (Witty 1966, p. 61).

The basic premise that reading is *only one* step in the sequential process
of the development of language, as illustrated in figure 8.1, is just as important for adult learners as it is for children.

As pictured in figure 8.1, language functions on two levels: (1) the
auditory-motor level, which involves only that language that can be heard;
and (2) the visual-motor level, which involves only that language expressed through symbols that can be seen. On each level, language is

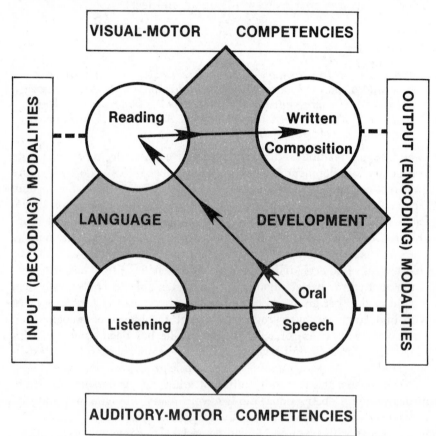

Figure 8.1. Sequential development of language.

received and decoded, or comprehended, by the individual through an input modality. The input modality on the auditory-motor level is listening ability, and is reading ability on the visual-motor level. When there is a need for the individual to be a transmitter or generator of language, the output, or encoding modalities, on each of the levels, is available for use. These are speech and writing, or composition ability. A certain degree of competency in the use of the input modalities must be attained before effective use of the output modalities can be made. The individual cannot use words to generate thought until he first recognizes and has assigned a meaning to the words involved. Also, research has shown that usually visual-motor level competencies are not developed substantially without a substructure of effective functioning on the auditory-motor level. Thus, a sequence for the teaching of language skills is implied.

The sequence proceeds in this manner. Initially, effective listening abilities and adequate auditory discrimination must be cultivated. The use of oral language, developed with practice through the imitation of the language structure that is heard, is an outgrowth of listening abilities.

Concept formation and categorization, as well as the thinking abilities of abstraction, discrimination of significant differences, and problem solving generally must become proficient on the oral language level *before* the language development has the capability of proceeding on to the next level, which is reading.

At the reading level, the first step is the conversion of the individual's stock of already acquired oral language concepts into the printed symbols that can be utilized and manipulated as a thinking process, much in the same way as oral language was used. The second step of language development at the reading level is the addition of concepts presented in printed symbols that may *not* already be a part of the individual's stock of oral language concepts.

The final level of language development, writing and composition, is the utilization of the written symbols of language to creatively express feelings, ideas, and concepts. Just as speech is patterned from the structure of the oral language that has been heard in the individual's environment, written expression also needs a foundation of reading ability from which to initially model and then subsequently to develop an individualistic style.

The importance of this sequence of language development cannot be overly stressed. The difficulty in applying it to the teaching of adults to read is that because of their years of experience, they have already progressed through the developmental sequence, even though many of the learnings at this earlier time may have been inadequate or fixated at a particular level. The adult basic education teacher's problem is in identifying the inadequacies on the various levels and then systematically remediating these weaknesses while continuing sequentially from the point of fixation toward the development of adequate language skills.

The teaching of these skills becomes an everwidening spiral process. One skill is developed to a minimum competency, whereupon the next one is attended to. As a new skill is added, the established skill is purposefully reinforced and expanded. Then this expanded skill is used as a foundation for the development of further skills and concepts. Instruction in this forward and backward spiraling pattern proceeds until there is sufficient competency developed in all four of the language areas.

The Sequential Development of Auditory-Motor Level Competencies (Oral Language)

The development of oral language as the basis of reading instruction begins with the first class period and continues throughout the last one. Experience with both input and output modalities—listening and speech —need to be provided through a variety of experiences.

Listening Skills

Several writers (Chapman 1965; *Curriculum Guide to Adult Basic Education: Beginning Level* 1966; Havighurst 1970; Jones 1962), have commented on the lack of listening skills and auditory discrimination abilities observed in culturally deprived areas. This has been attributed to overcrowding and the excess of confusion and noise. In the culture of poverty, it has been assumed that the individual defensively shuts out sound, particularly speech, purely as a means of surviving the environment. Whether or not this is the real reason that this behavior occurs, it is nevertheless true that with undereducated adults the teacher must first develop conscious listening as opposed to hearing or mere awareness of sound.

Auditory discrimination needs also to be developed through affording practice in listening to initial consonants; long and short vowels; sound-alike words, such as *pen* and *pin;* and rhyming words. Later on, this listening skill must be related to the printed symbol for the sound. For both those adults who are learning English after speaking a nonstandard dialect, or those who are learning English as a second language, it will be imperative that they have intensive oral language patterning and sound discrimination instruction using the techniques for teaching English to speakers of other languages, which are discussed in a later chapter. This

Learning to hear and to speak the language must precede learning to read. (Courtesy of Kishwaukee College, Malta, Illinois Adult Basic Education Program. Photo by Jan Wiseman.)

includes ample opportunity to hear the patterns of English and to compare these with the patterns of the native tongue or dialect.

Learners must also be *taught* to actively think while they listen, becoming conscious of the main idea, supporting details, sequences of events, and context clues. They must have opportunity to manipulate ideas orally by listening, for the purpose of making inferences, predicting outcomes, distinguishing fact from opinion, or drawing conclusions. Adult learners need conscious training in oral memory and conscious practice in following directions. The art of summarizing ideas while listening, as well as learning to evaluate, and to use ideas presented to them via radio, television, film or speeches is essential. Later on, these thinking skills will be transferred to the printed page as comprehension or reading-study skills.

Extending Oral Language

The development of this output modality depends on opportunity afforded the learners to talk. In a really successful class, it has been found that most of the oral communication taking place is from student-to-student and from student-to-teacher, rather than predominantly from

teacher-to-student. Initially, development of this competency can com-
mence by providing an atmosphere conducive to group interaction, with
opportunities for the sharing of experiences, problems, and ideas. Such
interaction leads naturally to participation in both large and small group
discussions. Having enhanced the self-concept with these fairly nonthreatening activities, more facility with oral language can be fostered
by involving students in role-playing activities, such as interview situations utilizing class-prepared questions. As content area activities develop,
oral reports presented by groups, committees, and individuals can contribute to this competency. In this manner oral vocabulary is developed,
supplying the individual with the tools to express himself spontaneously
and exactly. He learns to orally generate and evaluate ideas, defend positions, clarify issues, explain concepts and think creatively.

The Sequential Development of Visual-Motor Level Competencies (Written Language)

The language skills mastered at the auditory-motor level must now be
transferred to the level of the printed symbol. For some undereducated
adults, development of language on this level must be initiated with train-

As competency develops in oral communication, the adult learner is able to express
ideas and explain concepts to other class members. (Courtesy of Chicago Urban Skills
Institute and City Colleges of Chicago. Photo by V. Bacon.)

ing in visual-motor coordination, including experiences designed to develop awareness of left to right progression of the printed page, as well as the ability to make the return sweep with accuracy.

Reading: Decoding Tools

In order to become efficient readers, learners need to be able to determine which of the decoding skills are appropriate in a particular situation, and then be able to use these skills with ease. Specific instructional emphasis needs to be given to each of the five word recognition skills: (1) sight-configuration skills, (2) context skills, (3) structural analysis skills, (4) phonic analysis skills, and (5) the use of the dictionary. Consider what is involved in each of these.

Sight-configuration skills. Visual discrimination must be developed. The neophyte reader must be taught to recognize all the letters of the alphabet in both lowercase and uppercase, and to accurately discriminate significant differences in letters and in letter configurations. He must also learn to identify at sight a stock of basic service words.

Context clues. Throughout the process of learning to identify words, the reader needs to understand that there are many words, for example homographs, that defy pronunciation and comprehension through the use of any other clues except the redundancy of the language supplied by the context. For some words, placement in the sentence or paragraph can supply clues for identification. Effective use of these syntactic and semantic clues of reading must be fostered *without* developing an over-dependence on this one tool to the exclusion of the usage of the others.

Structural analysis. As word identification abilities develop, the learner also needs to use word structure as a tool for decoding. Initially, the function of such inflectional endings as *s, es, ed,* and *ing* is mastered. This is gradually expanded until he achieves competence in the usage of root words, affixes, compounds, contractions, and combined forms, and is then able to combine this tool with phonic analysis in the mastery of syllabication.

Phonic analysis. The sounds of the language mastered on the oral level must now be attached to their appropriate visual symbol. Just being able to *hear* rhyming words, initial and final consonants, vowel sounds, diphthongs, digraphs, blends, and words that sound alike, is not enough. He must also be able to recognize the visual representation for these sounds—

the grapheme, which may be a letter cluster or only a single letter. He also must learn the orthographic, or spelling, function of graphemes that have no sound at all. Through much exposure and practice with these clues, the learner is helped to gradually form generalizations regarding the regularities of the written language, and is then enabled to utilize these in decoding new or unfamiliar words. Of course, words that were originally identified through such phonic analysis, or indeed any other mediated process, must be practiced until they become a part of the sight-recognition vocabulary.

Dictionary usage. Preferentially, as a method of word identification, this tool ranks last. Realistically, however, the English language has many words that defy identification in any way other than referral to a dictionary. Thus, the development of techniques of dictionary usage can not be ignored in an adult reading program. Nevertheless, the goal of teaching efficient word identification skills is to enable the reader to be as free as possible from the need to refer to the dictionary.

Reading: Comprehension Skills

As pictured in figure 8.2, the roots of comprehension in reading are the mastery of the word-identification skills. If the visual symbols are not recognized, it is certain that the reader will be unable to attach meaning to the printed page.

Comprehension develops in stages progressing from the simple understanding of concrete concepts to the mastery and manipulation of abstract and creative ideas. Given proper instruction, and barring neurological, physiological, or emotional problems that become stumbling blocks to learning, nearly all adult basic education learners will be able to master the word identification skills. However, the *degree* of mastery of comprehension skills depends on the learning potential and psychological adjustment of the individual, as well as his experiential and cultural background. Therefore, the teacher must provide successful learning experiences on several levels of comprehension, helping each person to master the reading skills within that level before progressing to the next level (Miller, Beasley, and Swick 1974). Although Bloom (1956) and Sanders (1966) suggest five to seven levels of comprehension, the three suggested by Herber (1970) are adequate for our needs in adult basic education.

Literal comprehension. This basic level of comprehension involves concrete or factual understanding. The reader is only concerned with what

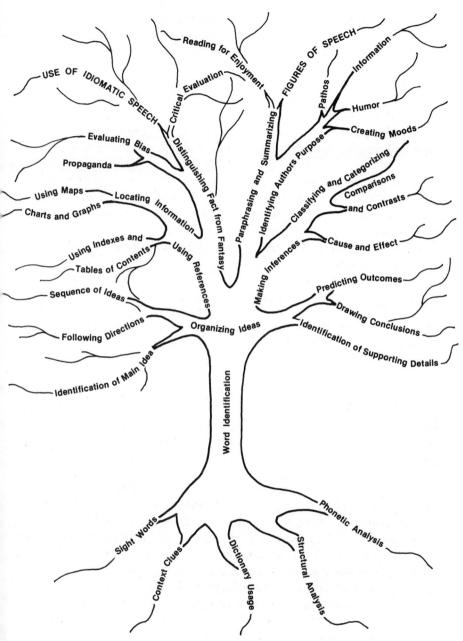

Figure 8.2. Hierarchy of comprehension skills.

the writer's words actually say. He is concerned with the recognition of facts, such as the main ideas and supporting details; the sequence of events; following specific directions; and the use of context clues to supply meaning.

Interpretive comprehension. On this level, the reader asks the question, "What did the writer *mean* by what he said?" The reader is concerned with making inferences, predicting outcomes, judging the author's mood, tone and purpose, and engaging in such evaluative thinking as is possible.

Applied comprehension. At this highest level of comprehension, critical reading—the comparison of what the author says with some external criterion drawn from the reader's experience—permits creative applications of what has been read. The reader is concerned with comparing and contrasting ideas, distinguishing fact from opinion, drawing conclusions and forming new concepts.

Writing and Composition Skills

The ability to use this output modality to express oneself in some written form sequentially follows the development of reading abilities. On the oral level, speech is patterned from listening experiences. Similarly on the visual level, creative composition is patterned to a degree from what is heard, but more importantly, it is patterned on what is read in print.

The development of writing and composition skills is the culminating application of all language development. Skills in this area will be developed in ways that are *directly* applicable to the adult's present world, such as writing a letter.

Handwriting skills. Some adults will need to be given instruction in holding a pencil and in the motor coordination necessary for handwriting. Although there is disagreement among authorities, it is probably best in most cases to develop manuscript writing before cursive skills are taught. The similarity of the manuscript letters to the ink marks on the printed page reduces the amount of visual discrimination required in this early stage of reading. However, it is also probable that the learner will want to learn to write his name in cursive style as quickly as possible. There is no substitute for the ego boost involved in the ability to sign one's own name! This can probably be accomplished very early in the program by teaching him to recognize the cursive configuration of the whole name and to copy that, rather than at first painstakingly teaching him to identify and reproduce the individual letters.

Composition skills. The development of composition skills begins initially with such simple activities as dictating sentences and brief stories to the teacher; then, in turn, copying the dictation after it has been read. Eventually, the learner will be able to write simple sentences dictated by the teacher. The third step is the independent writing of simple thoughts that have *not* been dictated. These skills are expanded until they can be applied first to simple paragraphs, then to more complex ones. As rapidly as possible, composition skills are applied to practical problems, such as writing letters, addressing envelopes, taking notes, making reports, filling out forms, etc.

For some learners, the development of such skills is only a beginning. They go on to develop latent creative writing talents. But for most, writing and composition are pursued only to the extent of meeting definite, pragmatic needs of the individuals involved.

Summary

It is important to note that excellent teaching is like an iceberg. There is much more to it than appears on the surface (Hunter 1972, p. 25).

This chapter has been concerned with the sequential development of reading skills, beginning with basic readiness for reading and progressing on through composition skills. The underlying concept throughout this chapter is that language skills develop in an orderly and sequential manner. Effective teaching of adults provides for this sequence.

9.
Learning Theory Applied to Adult Reading Instruction

Whether a person is six or sixty, he must learn the basic things—the "simple" things first. . . . Practicing scales seems terribly unimportant, when one's object is to play the "Moonlight Sonata" (Wallace 1965, p. 10).

Teachers of reading to undereducated adults will need to develop their programs over a period of time to meet the needs of many widely different individuals who perform at different levels of ability. Because of this wide variation in the needs and characteristics of the learners involved in adult basic education, it is not possible for this text to offer a "cookbook" step-by-step, detailed plan of instruction, complete with a money-back guarantee for success in adult reading. The authors recognize that each of the principles suggested is basically theoretical, requiring tailoring and modification to meet the specific needs of the particular situation.

The worn-out cliché, "Take the learner where he is," is as significant to adult education as it is to the education of children and will often be even more difficult to implement. The teacher will undoubtedly have considerable difficulty in identifying the exact point of beginning; but once this is done, instruction should proceed in a well-ordered sequential manner.

Basic Principles of Learning

There is no way that a teacher can ever be replaced, because there is no machinery or system that can think as rapidly, make assumptions about the cause of a problem, or figure out a possible solution and try it on a short-range basis and discard it if necessary (Puckett 1972, p. 8).

Regardless of the age of the learner, there are certain principles that appear to be basic to successful instruction. McCreary (1967, pp. 138-42) offers ten principles that apply equally well at all ages.

1. Students enjoy learning when they learn about things that are relevant to their past or present circumstances, problems, or difficulties; when learning is meaningful, significant, and timely in terms of their own concerns.

2. Because individuals differ so much in so many ways, learning experiences should provide a maximum diversification of materials and activities and ways of evaluating what has been learned. Interests, abilities, needs, and concerns are cues to individual learning.
3. Students with disadvantages, like most learners, prefer to be active learners rather than passive receivers. They often respond to opportunities to dramatize, role-play, or pantomime.
4. Students are more likely to enjoy learning if they are able to help others or associate with others in learning experiences.
5. Students find learning experiences more satisfying when they participate in defining what they are trying to learn and in judging their success at learning it.
6. Pupils enjoy learning experiences most when they are provided frequent opportunities to express themselves in a variety of ways—physically, intellectually, and emotionally—in speech, drama, art forms, and creative compositions.
7. Pupils are likely to enjoy learning if they are permitted the widest possible freedom of choice of curricular emphases, learning materials, and learning activities. Much that most interests and concerns many adolescents, whether or not they are "disadvantaged," lies in the areas considered controversial or dangerous for public schools to consider—civil rights, war, juvenile delinquency, sex, law enforcement, school practices, etc.
8. Pupils experience special satisfactions when their work gains the recognition of others, especially their peers. Such recognition does not have to be achieved in purely competitive activities.
9. Learning experiences are peculiarly satisfying and mastery and retention are promoted when students are encouraged to discover for themselves important relationships and principles.
10. Pupils experience satisfactions when they realize that they are needed, when they can perform in roles of real significance, and when they can help others in meaningful ways.

McCreary concludes his article by saying:

... Any serious application of learning principles to schools would involve a reduction in competition, a much greater freedom in curricula, a very much greater attention to individual pupils, and a massive shift in the involvement of all pupils in school affairs and decision-making (p. 142).

Beyond these well-stated basic principles, which are applicable to learners of all ages, there are other considerations with which we must be concerned.

Involvement

Students do not learn as a result of what *teachers do,* but as a result of what teachers *get students to do* (Mager 1965). Relying solely on the lecture method of instruction is most likely to produce frustration and disappointment, rather than real learning. Learning is an *active* process, focusing primarily on the student rather than on the teacher, and is capable of producing a behavioral change in the learner. Such changes do not actually become a part of a person until the changes have been reinforced through personal use. For example, a learner can memorize the directions for making a cake, or he can memorize all the words on his vocabulary list. But until he actually has the experience of making the cake or using the new vocabulary words in the various contexts of his own environment, it is doubtful that any real learning has taken place.

Therefore, it becomes essential that learning activities be structured to be relevant to the learner's needs, interests, and environment. In accomplishing this, the teacher must check on the learner's understanding of useful concepts. Those utilized in a beginning program for adults should be those most useful in the community in which the adult lives. In the beginning reading lessons, the episodes should be drawn from home, neighborhood, and community. Different concepts will be reflected

Adults enjoy helping in the selection of their instructional materials. (Courtesy of Venice-Lincoln Technical Center, Venice, Illinois.)

if the learner's life is rural rather than urban. After this, concepts regarding technology, vocations, and the job world can be introduced.

Allow the learners to do most of the talking in the classroom because they contribute much from their own fund of information and knowledge. Incorporating their ideas into lesson plans will assure the utilization of relevant material from which to teach the reading skills. Thus, the learning experience becomes pupil-centered and life-centered, rather than curriculum-centered. Moreover, the learner becomes actively involved in the learning process—and that is the secret of effective education on any level.

Interaction

Learning should not be primarily a lonely process. Opportunities for learning in both small and large group activities, as well as through self-instructional strategies and in one-to-one tutorial sessions will counteract this danger.

Intragroup classroom organization functions best when the structure is kept fluid and flexible. On some occasions, groups will almost spontaneously organize around a particular need or interest. At other times,

Small groups are usually more successful in teaching English as a second language. (Courtesy of Kishwaukee College, Malta, Illinois Adult Basic Education Program. Photo by Jan Wiseman.)

groups will need to be organized for a specific learning activity according to differences in learning ability. Such grouping insures that those having the greatest problems will not feel outstripped by those to whom the learning comes easier, and also prevents the more able learners from feeling impeded by those who progress at slower rates. Still other groupings occurring on a sort of random-selection basis will be appropriate for some needs.

Learning in groups is enhanced through the utilization of such tools as dramatization, round table or panel discussions, and "club" activities, even with frequent rotation of officers. Training in the democratic process and development of self-concept occurs as everyone learns to participate and to contribute to the group without either monopolizing the teacher or the group, or withdrawing from it as a spectator. Thus, the traditional atmosphere of a classroom, which many adult learners remember with distaste, may be transformed into a warm, personal experience, making reading a delightful adventure.

The Function of Effect

Behaviorists point out that people tend to accept and to repeat those responses that are pleasant and satisfying, and tend to avoid annoying experiences. If the adult enrolls in a course expecting to learn to read, and quickly finds out that he *is learning* to read and *is enjoying* the process, he will tend to continue to come to class.

As Chapman (1965) stresses, it is satisfying to the undereducated adult to feel appreciated for what he is *as a person* and not condemned for what he does not know *as a learner;* that he is understood and liked as a friend, in spite of his faults. Nothing succeeds like success!

The Importance of Primacy

First impressions are the most lasting. Therefore, the interest and sense of need cultivated during the first classes is all-important. It is also of concern that skills and concepts be learned correctly the first time presented, since, for adults particularly, relearning that which has been originally mislearned appears to be most difficult (Thorndike 1928).

The Effect of Practice

The more often an act is repeated, the more quickly a habit is established. Practice makes perfect *if* the practice is the right kind, but practice can be disastrous if it is the wrong kind. In teaching adults to read, instructional provision must be made for many repetitions, much practice, and frequent reviews. Designing such instructional reinforcement, which can provide the learner with the security of working with that which is familar while striving for new skills, without the monotony of doing over exactly what was done before, is one of the most creative challenges of teaching (Thorndike 1928).

Dangers of Disuse

A skill not practiced or a knowledge not used will largely be lost or forgotten. Therefore, the function of *immediate* reinforcement of newly acquired skills is most important. The period of time immediately following the learning experience appears to be the most critical in terms of retention. Therefore, it is urgent that important knowledge and skills be reviewed soon after the initial instruction occurs, and then frequently thereafter (Speer 1972, *Part IV: Final Report*).

Teaching for Transfer

Ellis (1965) has cautioned that if learning is to be truly utilized by the individual, we must teach for transfer. He cautions that in order to be truly useful, a skill must be taught within as close a proximity as possible to the area in which it is to be utilized. Skills learned as isolated entities as an end unto themselves may be virtually useless to the learner.

Reading is a *skill*, and as such has no content or subject matter of its own. Therefore, for a learner to be taught to read effectively, it is necessary to fuse the teaching of the reading skills with the content area learning. Except for instances in the very beginning stages of learning to read, reading instruction should never be divorced from the teaching of the remainder of the adult basic education curriculum of social studies, science, arithmetic, health, consumer education, and vocational education. Because the reading teacher is primarily concerned with the teaching of certain specified skills rather than particular content-oriented concepts, he is at liberty to select from the various areas those materials that can best be adapted to teaching that specific skill. Thus, as a side benefit, as the skill is being acquired, content learning also takes place. Additionally, as the skill is being learned, it is being learned in the context of a particular subject matter, and thus, transfer of the skill can be expected to take place.

The Use of Behavioral Objectives

I think you have to be a good learner in order to be a good teacher.
You've got to always remember how it is to have to learn what you're
asking them to learn (Puckett 1972, p. 48).

Endless wanderings through learning can be avoided by defining instructional goals behaviorally, that is, in terms of measurable, observable attributes that state what a successful learner will be able to do at the end of the learning activity. This is accomplished in three steps:

1. Identify the terminal behavior by name. We can specify the kind of behavior that will be accepted as evidence that the learner has achieved the objective.
2. Try to further define the desired behavior by describing the important conditions under which the behavior will be expected to occur.
3. Specify the criteria of acceptable performance by describing how well the learner must perform to be considered acceptable (Mager 1965).

An example of a reading objective stated behaviorally might be as follows:

Given opportunity for practice in small group instruction, the learner will be able to identify at sight ten of the common signs of the road with ninety percent accuracy in reading.

When the teacher and learners together specify instructional goals behaviorally, each learner experiences the security of knowing just what is expected of him at the present time and in the future. Such "mapping out" procedures in adult education can be important in alleviating anxiety and promoting motivation to learn.

Summary

Once we've gotten a learner to feel successful at a task, no matter
how simple, we've usually overcome one of the major stumbling blocks
to learning (Newman 1971, p. 43).

This chapter has been concerned with the principles of learning with which adult education teachers should be familiar. Considerations discussed include the need of learners to be involved, the need for interaction, the application of the laws of effect, primacy, practice and disuse, and teaching for transfer. The chapter was concluded with a brief definition of behavioral objectives and a statement about their importance to the teacher as a map for learning.

10.
Orienting
Beginning Reading
Experiences
to Adult Learners

The teacher's theme song: "My time is your time." I am here to help you. Ask questions. If I seem to be busy, don't hestitate to interrupt me (Curriculum Guide to Adult Basic Education: Beginning Level 1966, p. 93).

Today, the successful teacher thinks of the teaching of reading from a selective viewpoint. This statement does not infer that the successful teacher may not be using one particular approach that has generally proven adequate for his instructional needs. However, as the field of reading develops, as new materials become available, and as the teacher himself develops professional expertise, he is constantly evaluating his instructional procedures. He does not become slavishly bound to any one system, but chooses his approach and material according to the particular needs of those he is teaching. On those occasions when his usual methods are not working, the successful teacher has alternative approaches available to him. He does not feel threatened, disloyal, or inadequate if his learner's needs dictate a change of approach or material.

In order to develop such a repertoire of approaches, the reading teacher requires the opportunity to critically examine new materials as they are published. These should be reviewed in light of the needs of particular learners, the skills that need to be developed, and what the teacher knows about the reading process itself. An annotated listing of current materials for adult basic reading instruction is found in appendix A.

Adults, like children, must first learn auditory and visual discrimination. This is followed by the development of a basic sight word vocabulary. Phonic and structural analysis skills for unlocking new words must be learned. The ability to use contextual clues in word identification as well as in dealing with meaning is also important. Such skills are a prerequisite to the development of comprehension strategies. Moreover, effective oral language and writing skills must become supportive of the reading skills. Beyond the mastery of some basic skills, becoming mature readers is a long-term process that may require many years.

The difference between teaching reading to adults and to children is not in the skills taught, but in the *approach* taken to the learning of these skills. The adult learner is seldom content to learn only one of the language skills without almost simultaneous accomplishment in the others. That is, he wants to be involved in oral language improvement as well as in reading and writing. Moreover, he is not often satisfied to concentrate only on isolated word identification skills, but insists on dealing with meaning and comprehension almost from the beginning. Therefore, the teacher's problem is to formulate an instructional approach that is comprehensive and flexible enough to meet *all* of these needs. At the same time, interest and motivation must be sustained to keep the learner actively involved and persevering until learning goals are reached. Thus, the teacher must be perceptive to individual needs, continually diagnosing problems and tailoring programs to meet *specific* learning requirements.

Problems in the Selection of an Approach to Beginning Reading

> *If we have more than 20 million adults who are functional illiterates and if you have a quarter of the school population who need tutor assistance in reading; if, in effect, we have, say, 35 million Americans who need help, then, in fact, we could use 10 million people who could give a couple of hours a week to help that kind of problem (Emery 1972, p. 6).*

Professional literature abounds with reports of the successes and failures in the use of many different approaches to adult beginning reading (Aukerman 1971; Boone and Quinn 1967; Dell 'Apa 1973; Ferndale Adult Basic

The teacher must accept the responsibility for finding the proper materials and using methodology to maintain a high level of learner interest. (Courtesy of Kishwaukee College, Malta, Illinois Adult Basic Education Program. Photo by Jan Wiseman.)

Education Curriculum, 1971; Hiemstra 1973; Jonas 1968; Klevins 1972; Langerman 1974). To help understand their differences and usefulness in adult basic education, some of the types of programs currently marketed are considered from the viewpoint of the undereducated adult.

The Phonic Approaches

Typically, adults are learners in a hurry, lacking the time resources usually available to children. Hence, they are impatient with many of the leisurely approaches used successfully with younger learners, even though attempts have been made to make these materials more sophisticated. Few will tolerate a laborious *synthesis approach* to decoding.[1] Too much time is involved in dissecting words rather than in reading sentences and paragraphs. Olsen (1965) wisely cautions:

> In the teaching of reading, a sentence rather than a word approach should be used, because even adults without sufficient word-attack skills have already internalized the word order of our language. Beginning with a letter or a word approach makes adults feel like children and therefore, antagonizes them. After some sentences have been learned, word-attack skills can then be taught in terms of the words already known. These skills can then be further developed and extended with other kinds of varied exercises. All new learning should be quickly rewarded (p. 458).

Thus, an initial emphasis on phonics *without* attention to the greater language needs of the adult learner can be self-defeating.

These approaches that emphasize the sounds of language are based on three assumptions. First, they assume that English is an encoded *sound* language. Second, the approach assumes that if you can decode the symbols into sounds, you can pronounce the words by synthesizing that decoding into a word. Finally, it is assumed that if the learner can produce words that are probably words he knows, then he will be able to read. However in evaluating such approaches, it must be remembered that teaching reading is not merely a process of helping learners combine symbols with sounds. People learn differently; some have an auditory memory, some have a visual memory, and some appear not to remember any kind of correspondence with any reliability. Therefore, this kind of approach may not be appropriate for every learner (Wepman 1968).

---

1. The synthesis approach to decoding involves learning individual sounds of letters first, and then attempting to blend these together into words. It is really an artificial separation, since the sounds of letters are not independent of each other and cannot be taken apart and reassembled in this way.

The Phonemic Approaches

Teaching reading with so-called specifically phonemic, or linguistic, approaches of the 1960s presents problems similar to those encountered with the phonic systems. These differ from the phonic systems in that they are built on the assumption that reading approaches that utilize phonics in isolation are very difficult and that the purpose of learning phonics is to read. Generally, such systems offer immediate practice in reading, although for the most part the reader spends more time "playing around" with words than with reading. The phonemic approaches also call attention to the observation that the reading approaches in the phonic or basal readers is generally too irregular. Several sounds of a vowel might be presented within the same segment of instruction (Aukerman 1972).

Phonemic approaches are presented to teachers as linguistically systematic and logical. However, these systems still fail to put meaning at the center of the reading process. In few cases will this approach be a fruitful activity if used alone. There are serious limitations in such approaches, since they tend to deemphasize comprehension and provide the reader with nonsensical stories. Although initially amused by such passages as "Can Dan fan Nan?" and "The fat cat sat on a mat," adults will soon tire of this kind of material, even though the construction is logical and regular.

The Basal Approaches

Adult learners are also usually dissatisfied with the stilted language of a basal reader (see fig. 10.1). Some are written in typical preprimer style, with a large picture and one sentence on a page. Later primers have more printed material on the page, but are viewed similarly. Adequately supplemented, these very structured, controlled vocabulary books may provide a good beginning. However, it is the *format* of instructional approaches such as this that becomes a stumbling block. Even though the material has been specifically *written* for adults, it *looks* like children's stories, and unhappily reminds adult learners of unsuccessful childhood experiences.

The Programmed Instructional Approaches

Programmed instruction, whether labeled phonic or phonemic in nature, is sometimes useful for reinforcement practice, but as a basic approach to beginning reading, it becomes very lonely learning. All too often the learner is given a program, then allowed to proceed on his own. He may

Figure 10.1. (From *Reading Newsreport* 6 (February 1972):42. Used by permission.)

soon be unintentionally ignored or forgotten by the teacher. Also, it has been noted in many large adult education projects, such as the Job Corps Centers (1972), that there is a tendency for the user to be unable to transfer skills apparently mastered in programmed materials to other books. This phenomenon may occur in part because the adult learning to read needs opportunity to make mistakes so that he can note signifi- cant differences and form categories. Programmed learning, theoretically errorless learning, denies the learner the benefit of making mistakes (F. Smith 1970).

Other Approaches

Other approaches, such as configuration systems (Boning 1970; Carrillo 1970), and special alphabets (Gattengo 1962; Pitman 1960; Woodcock 1968), may possibly be useful for some adults with special problems, but are not usually found to be entirely adequate for a general basic reading approach in adult basic education. Their value lies chiefly in their unique- ness, which may meet some motivational needs.

Using the Approaches

Recognizing the inadequacies and problems of the above described ap- proaches to beginning reading for adults is *not* intended to imply that all such materials are useless in an adult reading program. Nothing could be farther from the truth. Certainly, each of these approaches offers help for an instructional need that must be met under the skillful guidance of a teacher. It is only recommended that the teacher be aware of the possible limitations and that he pick and choose from the many approaches commercially available *only* those portions that appear to be appropriate to the *specific needs* of the individual learner. Such a selective approach seems to offer the greatest chance of success with these previously "turned- off" learners.

Probably the most relevant learning materials of all will be the ones that the teacher and learner will create together. Figures 10.2, 10.3, 10.4, 10.5, and 10.6 are examples of reading materials created by various adult education projects for their own participants. "Homemade" stories and books are an essential part of the curriculum for adult basic reading classes.

Tutorial Considerations

The task of teaching adult nonreaders usually becomes one demanding more one-to-one tutorial instruction than in most other instructional settings. Beyond various group activities, most programs utilize the services of lay tutors to meet the individual instructional needs (Brown 1972; Dell 'Apa 1973; Geeslin 1971). Indeed, some programs are committed to the proposition that reading for adults can *only* be accomplished on a one-to one tutorial basis. Regardless of the situation, lay tutors add an invaluable dimension to any literacy program. Usually they are teaching without re- numeration because they are concerned about the adult who is held back in obtaining life goals for lack of literacy skills. This commitment toward the needs of people is an enrichment to any program, creating an atmos- phere conducive to a maximal learning experience.

Nonetheless, the use of lay tutors in an adult basic education program creates certain needs. Not being a reading professional, the tutor may not know effective techniques for teaching reading skills. Therefore, the approach selected for the lay tutor's use must be highly structured as compensation for the absence of professional pedagogical skills. In this situation, the expertise of teaching reading is built into the system and

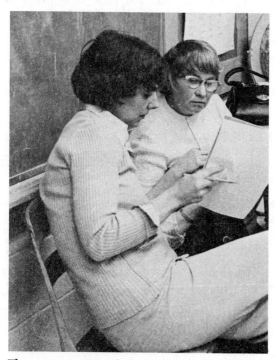

The one-to-one tutorial situation maximizes efficiency in learning and immediate feedback. (Courtesy of Kishwaukee College, Malta, Illinois Adult Basic Edu- cation Program. Photo by Jan Wiseman.)

NO NEED A-PECKING ON THE BLIND

A few years back I was living in Hazelhurst,
Georgia and cutting timber for a living. Every
morning I drove my truck to the Standard Station
on the corner to get diesel oil. Well one morning
I got to thinking and said to myself, "Hell, I'm
going to find me a woman." So I jumped in the
truck and drove through town. There on the walk
was a woman- a fine woman. Well, maybe she wasn't
that fine but she was a woman.

I said, "Hi Babe, what you up to."

She said, "Nothing Mister. How's about a ride."

I said, "Hop in. Do you know some place we
can go to get to know each other better."

She said, "Yea, go down to Church Street and
turn down to the third house on the left."

I shot the juice to that old truck and there
I went. I pulled into that third yard and she
hopped out and I hopped out.

"Just follow me," she said.

We went into the house and there lay a little
baby just kicking and crying.

She said, "Soon as I get this bottle everything will be ready, Mister."

I said, "O.K., Babe."

I reached down and tickled the little fellow
under his chin, kissed its brow and told him to hush
because Mama was coming back with his bottle. She
came back in about three minutes and stuck the bottle

Figure 10.2. Locally created books—Georgia. (Kincaid, J. P., and Thomas Georgelle.
Use of the "peer-prepared" method to produce dialect readers for Blacks. ERIC, 1973,
ED 062 982. Used by permission.)

in the baby's mouth.

"Where do you want to go now," she asked, "In the bedroom or out in the country."

I said, "Let's go into the bedroom. It's raining on the outside."

She went into the bedroom and I followed her. She got ready and I got ready and man did we have a good time. When we got through, I fell against the foot of the bed and looked up. The sun was shining.

"Damn, let me out of here," I said.

She said, "Hey darling, what's the matter."

I said, "Look over yonder, the sun's shining. I got to get back to that mill or I'll be fired."

I said, "Don't worry Baby, I'll be back."

I got into my truck and went back to that mill and sawed to black dark. I got to thinking about that gal and I thought that I'd go back and get me a little more of that stuff. Right then I was at home and had to say something to my uncle about going out. I thought I'd say something about needing diesel oil.

I said, "Unc, I'm going to get my diesel oil tonight so I won't waste no time in the morning."

He said, "O.K., hurry back. Supper will be ready in a little while."

I said, "Damn supper. I don't want no damn supper. I'm going to get my diesel oil." Of course, I wasn't studying that diesel oil. I wanted to go see that gal.

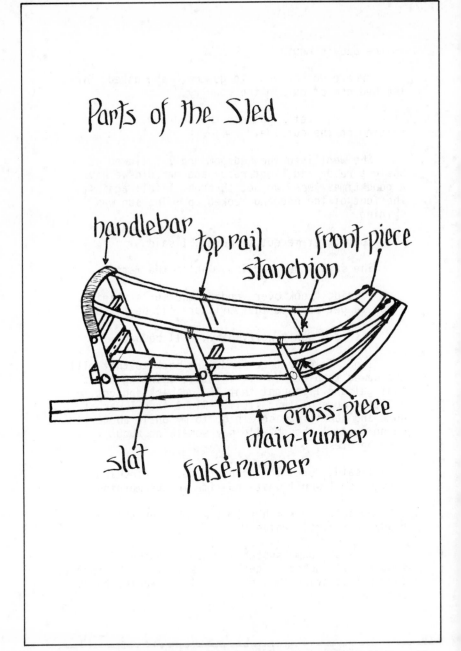

Parts of the Sled

handlebar   top rail   front-piece
                stanchion

slat   false-runner   cross-piece   main-runner

Figure 10.3. Locally created book for a specific culture. (Marsha Million, *Building a Dogsled,* pp. 52-53. 505 W. Northern Lights, Anchorage, Alaska: Adult Literacy Laboratory, Division of Community Services, Anchorage Community College, 1974.)

Introduction

Dogsleds come in all shapes and sizes. There are freight sleds, racing sleds, children's sleds and all-purpose sleds. The sled in this book is a 7 foot sled suitable for general use.

Every village and even every sled builder has his own particular style and his own way of making it. The sled described here was built by Charlie Wulf from Anvik. He builds his sleds the way he learned from his father many years ago.

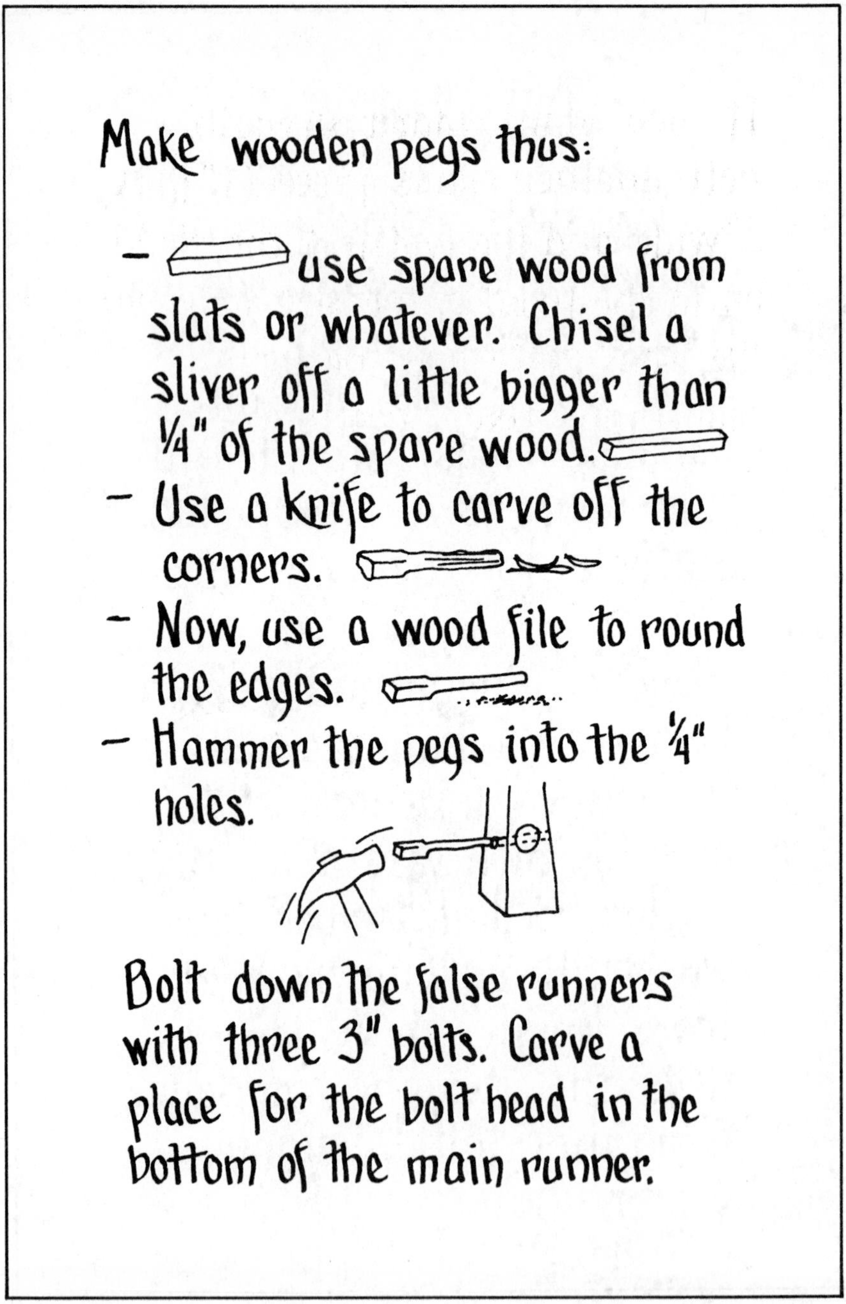

Make wooden pegs thus:

— ⬭ use spare wood from slats or whatever. Chisel a sliver off a little bigger than ¼" of the spare wood. ⬭
— Use a knife to carve off the corners. ⬭
— Now, use a wood file to round the edges. ⬭
— Hammer the pegs into the ¼" holes.

Bolt down the false runners with three 3" bolts. Carve a place for the bolt head in the bottom of the main runner.

Figure 10.4. Locally created book for a specific interest. (Marsha Million, *Building a Dogsled,* pp. 52-53. 505 W. Northern Lights, Anchorage, Alaska: Adult Literacy Laboratory, Division of Community Services, Anchorage Community College, 1974.)

If you want added strength,
bolt another cross-piece (1" thick,
2" wide and the width of the sled)
on to the front of the sled between
the front-piece and the front
stanchion. Use 2" bolts.

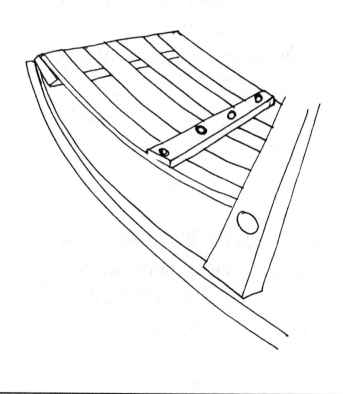

The leader of a meeting is
called the CHAIRMAN. He keeps
order. He makes sure that the
people have a chance to speak.
He makes sure that the people
don't waste time. He sees
that the rules are followed.

Who needs to know the rules?
The chairman must know the
rules so he can run the meeting. The people should know
the rules too. Even if you do
not want to speak, you want
to know what is going on.
It is good if everyone at the
meeting knows the "rules of
order."

Figure 10.5. Locally created book for a specific need. (Marie A. Schouler and Kathleen Lynch. *Holding a Meeting.* 505 W. Northern Lights, Anchorage, Alaska: Adult Literacy Laboratory, Division of Community Services, Anchorage Community College, 1974.)

HOW TO DO BUSINESS IN A MEETING

MAKING MOTIONS

People hold meetings to decide what to do about problems or things they want done. The people have to decide together what is best to do.

First, someone has to say what he thinks should be done. His idea or plan has to be made into a motion so everyone can talk about it.

Outside your house is a
circuit "breaker" or "breakers."

When you push the circuit
breaker button, which is marked
ON and OFF, to OFF then the
circuit is broken.

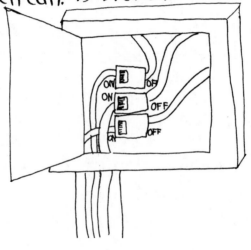

Figure 10.6.   Locally created book for a specific purpose. (From *How to Treat Elec-tricity*, Field Testing edition. 505 W. Northern Lights, Anchorage, Alaska: Adult Lit-eracy Laboratory Division of Community Services, Anchorage Community College, 1973.)

If too many electrical appliances
are being used the circuit
breaker will turn itself OFF.

This is called "overloading the
circuits."

materials utilized, rather than in the individual doing the teaching. Such emphasis is laudable, but limited—even with the help of tutorial handbooks (Criscuolo 1972; Fry 1964; Rauch 1969; Sleisenger 1965)—since *no* approach or system can possibly predict all the idiosyncracies and needs of the human learner. Thus, the conscientious lay tutor utilizing a very fine tutorial system may find himself at a loss, when for some unknown reason, the system does not produce the desired learning results. The lay tutor seldom has alternative approaches available to him in this circumstance. At this point, the lay tutor who does not seek other resources and begins to build his own knowledge of reading beyond the scope of a single instructional system will, in all probability, lose the learner.

The Laubach System to Beginning Reading

The illiterate who has moved into town has the need for reading brought home to him forcefully. . . . A city is in itself a book . . . signs, posters, and billboards everywhere, price tags in shops, labels and instructions for use on tins and packages. . . . We cannot afford to do this job halfway (Burnet 1965, pp. 27, 37).

Although not without difficulties and seldom appropriate for beginning reading in public schools, the Laubach system (1960, 1969) of beginning reading has been used to teach illiterates in more than 300 languages during the past forty years.

With this system it has been noted that an adult can usually learn the sounds of the whole alphabet within a few hours. After that, theoretically, he can decode anything written in the language. The system uses letters and word configuration clues as well as phonic analysis. It capitalizes on adults' superior ability for associative learning by using key words and line-drawing pictures of familiar objects as visual memory clues for learning both the name and the sound of the letters. Sounds are never presented in isolation, but always within whole words and sentences. A sample of the typical beginning Laubach lesson is presented in figure 10.7.

This highly structured code-breaking system may tend to become a "locked-in" approach. Such a structure was necessary to Laubach's original intent that it should be used by the lay person and even by the semiliterate volunteer tutor in order to teach another person to read. "Each one teach one" has become the byword of Laubach literacy campaigns around the world.

The system has been criticized because although meaning is stressed from the beginning lessons, some students of the Laubach system have

Some people learn better by themselves than in groups.
(Courtesy of Albuquerque Technical-Vocational Institute, Albuquerque, N. M.)

tended to become expert word callers and code breakers without adequate comprehension and critical reading skills (Orata 1966).

Nevertheless, thousands of people around the world have been made
at least partially literate through the use of this system. This attests to
the fact that the system does indeed work, although success is probably
higher in languages other than English that have a more regular grapheme-
phoneme equivalence. In other words, with languages that can be phonetically *sounded,* it is easier for an adult who speaks it to learn to read it.

Like any system, however, the Laubach approach cannot meet all
needs and will not do the total job of teaching any illiterate adult to read.
Be that as it may, except with learners who do not appear to be able to
hear language sounds, Laubach's *New Streamlined English Series* (1968)
is one very good starting point for reading instruction. Learners move rapidly through the lessons. When a minimum number of sight words have
been mastered through this approach, it can easily be combined with
language experience that will utilize the learner's own language for building reading skills.

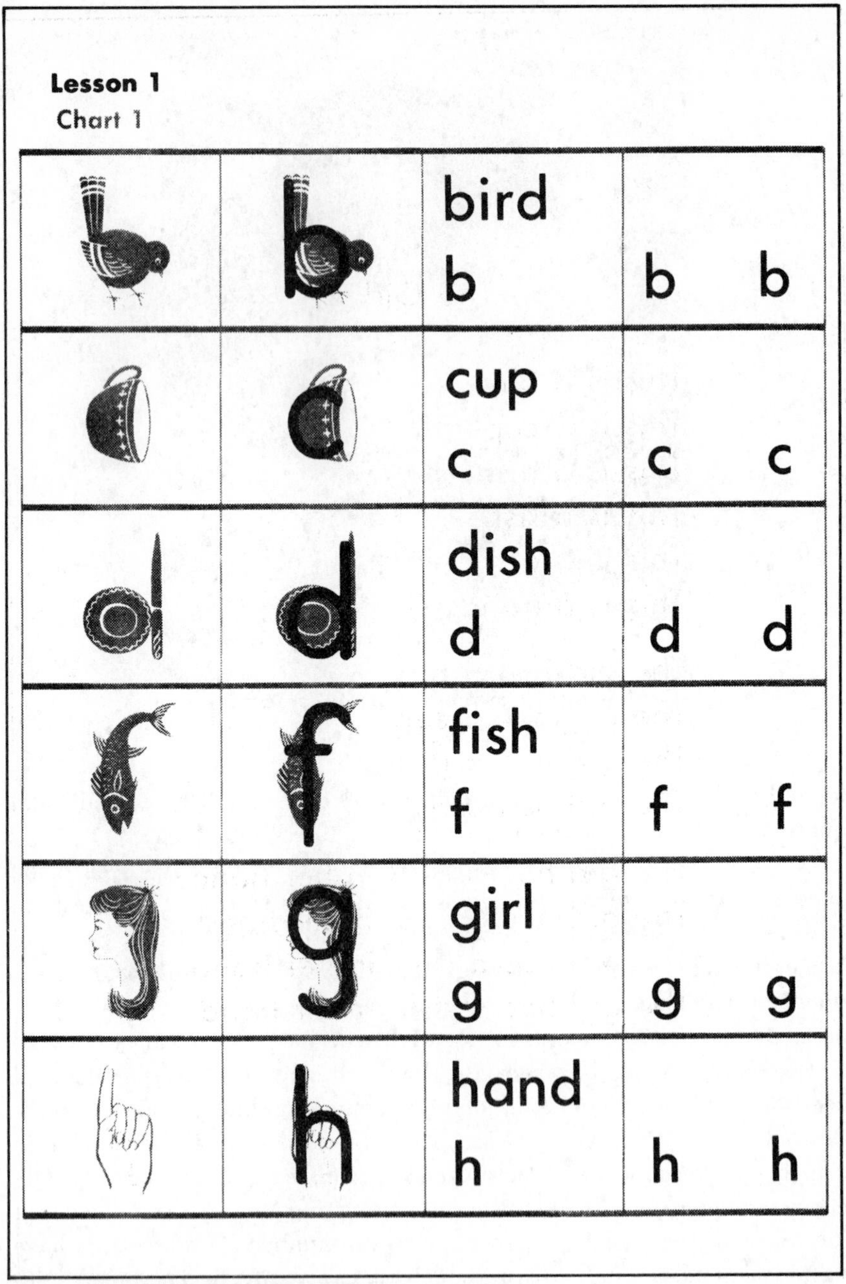

Lesson 1
Chart 1

		bird b	b	b
		cup c	c	c
		dish d	d	d
		fish f	f	f
		girl g	g	g
		hand h	h	h

Figure 10.7. (Frank C. Laubach, Elizabeth Mooney Kirk, and Robert S. Laubach. *The New Streamlined English Series: Skill Book 1—Sounds and Names of Letters,* pp. 2-3. Syracuse, New York: New Readers Press, Division of Laubach Literary International, 1969.)

The Girl

This is a bird.
This is a cup.
This is a dish.
This is a fish.
This is a girl.
This is a hand.

The girl has a bird.
The girl has a cup.
The girl has a dish.
The girl has a fish.

The girl has a bird in her hand.
The girl has a cup in her hand.
The girl has a dish in her hand.
The girl has a fish in her hand.

The Use of a Language-Experience Approach

Special caution: Don't lecture! You may enjoy it, but your students will not! (Curriculum Guide to Adult Basic Education: Beginning Level 1966, p. 95).

In all probability the adult illiterate comes to his first reading experience already able to understand and attach meaning to many words. This fund of experience is a gold mine of raw material for beginning literacy teaching. Helping adults to read in print the words that are already useful on an oral level can achieve initial success quicker than by other isolated methods.

An Unstructured Approach

Unlike the Laubach system, the language experience approach to beginning reading is unstructured and without manuals of precise directions. Hence, it is fraught with perils for the inexperienced teacher. A large share of the materials must of necessity be student- and teacher-made to match the particular need and interest of the individual. Therefore, it is important that the teacher have a good understanding of the word identification skills that must be taught, so that the language experience stories can be utilized to teach or to reinforce these skills. Teaching through this approach becomes a continuing diagnostic process that involves identifying needed skills and keeping individual records of those that have been learned. Although this is a more complex procedure for the teacher than other approaches, with practice and experience, a teacher will become comfortable either using this approach as the basic method or as a supplement to other methods of code-breaking instruction. It can also function as a reinforcement of word identification skills and as an aid to conceptual development through the learner's own oral language.

In making use of this approach with adult learners, Stauffer (1970) comments,

> When the adult learner is given the opportunity to produce his own learning material, to use his own interests, choose his own vocabulary and to articulate his own experiences, he is quick to notice the degree to which his wealth has been recognized and honored. By tapping his experience—language wealth, his thinking is fostered, and this, in turn, becomes stimulating to him . . . he is asked to talk about what he is doing and, in turn, to internalize his knowledge and experience. The ideas that he voices and the nomenclature that he uses become comprehensible in print and excite further attempts at use (pp. 255-56).

Becker (Hill 1972), Stauffer and Cramer (1967), and other investigators also report that the use of the language-experience approach in adult basic education projects fosters far greater motivation than only the use of either an adult-oriented "look-say" basal approach or the other approaches discussed previously.

The specific techniques for teaching reading through a language-experience approach are detailed by Lee and Allen (1970), by Stauffer (1970), and Van Allen (1976). Modified for adults, the approach becomes more sophisticated. Instead of recording the stories on chart paper, the chalkboard or an individual notebook is used. Instead of child-oriented story content, the adult language-experience story might be something like the following very simple, straightforward story:

> My name is Mr. Brown.
> I am a factory worker.
> I work at Firestone.
> I live in Normal, Illinois.

As instruction progresses, the stories become more complex, yet remain within the idiom of the student, for example:

> Last night my old lady and I went to look at a set of wheels.
> We don't want a new set, just a secondhand job.
> Al's, down on Main Street, showed us this old heap.
> You never seen such a piece of junk!

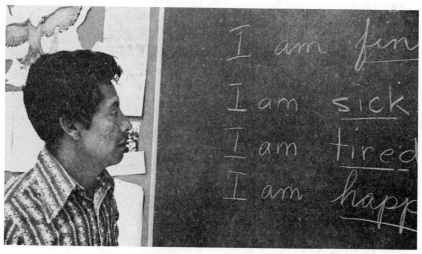

Even in the earliest lessons, the language must be relevant to the learner. (Courtesy of Albuquerque Technical-Vocational Institute, Albuquerque, N. M.).

And the bread he was asking! It was a rip-off!
Then we walked over to Honest Abe's lot.
He had this red job that was decent.
But the bread he wanted was out-of-sight.
I tried to talk him down, but it wasn't my day.
Guess we'll have to look some more.

Although the last sample story is far from what is commonly referred to as Standard English, the ideas talked about, the syntax, and the colorful words used to express those ideas become comprehensible in print because they are already useful to the adult on an oral level. Even these words can be located in print in various places, such as newspapers, signs, advertisements, or booklets. At a later time, after the adult student has achieved some success and independence in reading, the teacher can show him more socially acceptable ways of expressing himself, both in terms of vocabulary and syntax.

Building Sight Vocabulary Systematically

*Literacy has a changing meaning. Once it meant simply the ability
to read simple words and write your name. Today it is necessary to
complete high school in order to qualify for 97 percent of the
jobs. Even shoeshine parlors, groceries, etc., ask for high school graduates. Newpaper advertisements for janitors, office clerks, cashiers,
and truck drivers often say, "Apply only if you have had some college
or business school background" (Chapman 1965, p. 13).*

Service words, or sight vocabulary, as far as possible need to be taught in context rather than as isolated words. Such skills, begun with the Laubach or some other approach, can be successfully reinforced and expanded through language-experience stories.

In most cases, service words do not become easily recognized sight words until they have been used approximately twenty times in various contexts. Thus, it can be profitable to utilize reading charts or other sentences such as these:

Today is Monday.
This is a lovely day.
Mr. Sanchez went to Chicago today.
Today is Mr. Brown's birthday.
It is snowing today.
Mr. Kelley went to the store today to buy a suit.

In the above sentences, there is opportunity for practice with the service words *to,* and *day,* and with *today,* which is a compound of the first two words. Students can be guided to notice the word *today*, as it is used in various positions in the sentences. Further practice could be gained by asking students to notice the parts of this word, *to* and *day*, as they are used in other words, such as in *birthday*, or separately as *to* and *day*. Other service words from the above sentences that might be practiced are *is*, *it*, *the*, and *a*. These will be learned only after they have been read many times. Since such words are to be used over and over, it is absolutely necessary that the student learn to recognize them at *sight*.

Additional practice in developing sight-word competence can be obtained from published materials. Many of these approaches provide excellent practice exercises. However, care must be taken that practice does not become isolated from other reading, monotonous, or just another worksheet that must be done. The adult student who is expected to spend much time with isolated lists or who practices repeating words or copying them is very apt to lose interest. Rather, it is better to work on this for brief periods of time, preferably as learning-recreational activities using word games, such as those created by Alcock (1953), Burie and Heltshe (1975), Dolch (1952), Herr (1969), Platts (1972), Russell (1963), Thompson (1973), and Wagner and Hosier (1961).

Sight words can be chosen from many standard lists, such as the *Mitzell Adult Basic Word List* (1966), or the *Stone List* (1950). Also the 220 words of the *Dolch Basic Sight Word List* (1952) is an important source. Although the Dolch and Stone lists are oriented toward children's basal readers, Johns (1971, 1972, 1974) and the work of Kucera (1967) indicate that these words are also basic to most adult reading choices in magazines, newspapers, and signs. Therefore, the lists are important for our purposes.

Learning the Alphabet

Being the first-grade teacher so many of them never had . . . while remembering that these are adults learning a child's lessons . . . never take for granted that "Anybody would know that!" (Patterson and Larsen 1967, p. 51).

With children, the teacher might be concerned that the alphabet be at least partially taught before beginning to learn to read words. However, with adults it is not likely that the letters will be complete strangers. Moreover, adults are extremely anxious to get on with the business of learning words and sentences.

Rather than expect learners to first *learn the alphabet*, the teacher will do well to present information about the alphabet at appropriate times when beginning to teach a few words that include common letters. As sight words are taught, the names of the letters that appear in these words can also be taught. The learner can then work on the spelling of these common service words.

Basic facts about the alphabet that should be taught are the following:

1. Altogether, there are twenty-six letters that have a definite alphabetical order.
2. Some letters are vowels and some are consonants.
3. Some letters are used much more than others in the first words to be learned.
4. The letters x, q, and z will appear very seldom in easy reading, while e, m, and t will appear quite often.

The use of the Laubach charts (1968) or some other system of letter identification along with letter sounds within the context of words will suffice for this need. Moreover, this learning can be integrated with experience stories in the following manner:

Mr. Sanchez, look at this sentence on the chalkboard:

Mr. Sanchez went *to* Chicago *to*day.

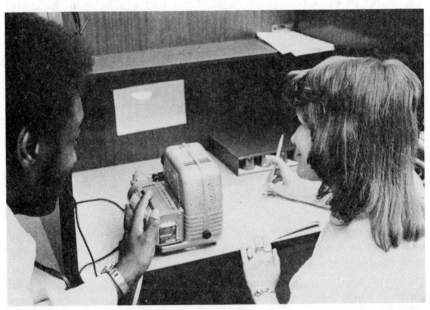

This young woman is reading an Educational Development Laboratories filmstrip. (Courtesy of Albuquerque Technical-Vocational Institute, Albuquerque, N. M.).

The word *today* begins with the letter *t*. Can you underline another *t* in that sentence? Fine. Yes, there are two *t*s in that sentence. Now, listen to the sound of that *t* as I say these words: *Today . . . went . . .* Listen to the sound of the *t* at the beginning of the word . . . *today . . .* and at the end of the word . . . *went . . .* Now, you say the words as I point to them.

In this manner, within the context of meaningful words and sentences, the learner becomes conscious of both the identity and the sound of the letters that they are using (Bureau of Vocational, Technical and Adult Education 1965). The teacher should not feel compelled to "test" the hearing of every sound. The concept is presented, reinforced a few times, and then the learner moves on to the next activity.

Developing Word Identification Readiness

Keep it simple . . . keep it relevant . . . keep it moving!
(Chapman 1965, p. 44).

Successful word identification is dependent on three subordinate skills: discrimination, memory, and blending (Wallen 1972). Development of each of these begins with the earliest stages of reading instruction and continues to be refined until the learner has become a mature reader.

Visual and Auditory Discrimination

It is necessary for the reader to be able to hear the difference between similar sound patterns in oral language, and be able to see the difference between similar visual patterns of written language.

In teaching discrimination on both the auditory and visual levels, the teacher begins with patterns containing gross differences, then progresses to those with moderate differences, and finally attacks those with very minimal differences. Practice is first given in identifying initial letters and sounds, then endings, and finally those sounds in the more difficult medial position. The groups of words presented to the students are varied in order to clarify the distinctive look or sound of specific language patterns. Then the student's attention is guided through verbal and nonverbal clues to the distinguishing features of the patterns involved (Olsen 1965).

For the completely illiterate, the teacher may have to begin by associating the letters and sounds met in the Laubach (1968) lessons or in the beginning experience stories (Ferndale Adult Basic Education Curriculum 1971; Stauffer 1967) with the people and the objects in the classroom. For example, the teacher might say something like this:

Mr. Brown, look at your name on the chalkboard. (The teacher points
to the name that has been used in the context of a very simple sentence or experience story.)
Is there anyone else in our group whose name begins with this same
sound?
That's right. Mr. Burns, Mrs. Baker, Betty.
What objects do you see in the room that are identified by names be-
ginning with *B?*
You are right on target! (Always reinforce a correct response by a
smile and a compliment.) The book, the basket, the bell on the
wall.
Are you wearing anything that begins with the letter *B?* Yes, a belt, a
billfold, a bracelet. No, not a bikini! It's too cold today for that!
(Never be afraid to use humor in teaching.)
Now, what are some businesses downtown that begin with the letter *B?*
Very good. A bar, bank, billiard parlor, beauty shop.

Such practice can go on indefinitely, until the letter and the sound used
in all positions are thoroughly associated with the student's environment.

The next step might be to use one of the words referred to previously
in a word-grouping practice that requires the student first to make a
gross discrimination, then a discrimination of moderate differences, and
finally a minimal difference. The teacher might proceed in the following
manner:

Listen to these words.
    belt, come, tell
Say the one that begins with the sound of this letter. (The teacher writes
a letter *B* on the chalkboard.)
Fine. Now, look at these words on the chalkboard.
    melt, belt, welt, salt
    Listen to me as I pronounce them. Which one begins with *B?* (The
    teacher writes the words on the chalkboard as he pronounces them.)
You are doing great. (The teacher then erases the chalkboard.) Now,
    look at these words and tell me which one begins with the *B* sound?
    felt, dealt, belt, velvet

Next, follow the same procedure on the visual level by eliminating the
auditory clue, requesting the learner to circle the proper word.

With sounds for which discrimination appears to be particularly difficult, the learner should watch the teacher's mouth and tongue movement as the sound is formed, then imitate this movement himself as he
uses a mirror to watch his own mouth and tongue. When memory of the
visual form appears to be troublesome, learning can be reinforced through
the use of Fernald techniques (1943), a summary of which appears in
appendix 1.

Memory and Blending

The two subordinate skills of memory and blending develop almost concurrently. According to Wallen (1972), the most complex of the three subordinate skills for word identification is blending. If a learner is successful in the blending stage of word identification, the teacher can assume that he already possesses the less complex skills of discrimination and memory, since blending utilizes both of these subordinate skills. Given purposive attention to these subskills, they will develop as the broader skills of phonic and structural analysis are explored.

Memory Principles

A student has sufficient knowledge of a phonic or structural language pattern when he can remember what the letter or pattern sounds *and* looks like, and when he is aware of the element as encountered and applied in new contexts (Wallen 1972). Much of this is achieved when adequate discrimination skills are developed.

Blending Principles

Beyond being *aware* of a particular letter or pattern as it is seen in new contexts, the student must be able to *apply* this knowledge by blending that letter or pattern into the new one. In other words, the student perceives the *b* of the word *belt*, not as buh-ĕl-tuh, but is able to blend that sound into the entire word as *belt*. He applies the phonic and structural principles that he remembers. It is seldom productive for the teacher to pronounce unfamiliar words for the student every time they are encountered in reading. Instead, the student should be guided to use the learned phonic and structural principles to unlock the new word for himself. An approach such as this may be used.

TEACHER: What is the sound of the first letter of this word? (Pointing to the *b* in the word *belt*, written on the chalkboard.)
STUDENT: Buh, like in *boy*.
TEACHER: Right. Now, you said that this word was *melt*. (Writes the word *melt* on the chalkboard.) Does it begin with the "buh" sound? Listen carefully. (Pronounce the word *melt*.)
STUDENT: No.
TEACHER: You are right. Now try this word again, and remember the beginning sound. (Teacher points to the word *belt* on the chalkboard.)
STUDENT: Belt?
TEACHER: Great. Now go back and read your sentence.

Or the teacher may later work with a structural skill in the same manner:

TEACHER: (Student is having difficulty with the *tion* in the word *election.*)
I think we can figure this word out. Look at this word that you already
know. (Teacher writes the word *action* on the chalkboard.) Now, say
it. (Teacher gives clue by saying, "Ak - - -.")
STUDENT: Ăk-shun.
TEACHER: Right on. Now say this one that you already know. (Teacher
writes the word *attention* on the chalkboard. He again clues the stu-
dent if he feels it is necessary.) "A-ten - - - -."
STUDENT: A-tĕn-shun.
TEACHER: Very good. Now look back at that troublemaker in your sen-
tence. Can you say it now?
STUDENT: Ē-lĕk-shun.
TEACHER: Fine. (Reinforce the learning by stating the generalization *after*
the student has arrived at it by his own reasoning and directed practice.)
Remember, "tion" on the ends of words is usually pronounced "shun"
(Wallen 1972).

In this way the word identification generalization has been used within a
meaningful context. The practice can be repeated in different ways as
often and as long as necessary.

Developing Structural and Phonic Analysis Competency

*The attitude of praise for your students relieves tensions and makes
for better relationships among students and teacher. Most adults
sacrifice a good deal to attend class. Not all are willing to make the
sacrifice. Appreciate it (Curriculum Guide to Adult Basic Education:
Beginning Level 1966, p. 93).*

In actual practice, instruction in structural and phonic analysis cannot be
separated (Parker 1961). However, for the purposes of explanation, an
artificial separation will be made.

Structural Analysis Skills

Structural analysis is based on two assumptions about language:

1. A root retains one of its basic meanings in inflected or in derived forms
as well as in compounds.

2. Affixes and inflectional endings in themselves are meaningful parts of
   words.

Thus, the root *appear* retains its meaning in such inflectional forms as
appears, appeared, appearing, and is used with affixes such as *disappear,*
disappearance, and reappear. These inflectional endings and affixes also
contribute meaning to the word. In addition to this principle, whole words,
such as *side* and *walk,* each retain one of their basic meanings when joined
together in the compound word *sidewalk.*

Developing adequate structural analysis skills is one of the most rapid
methods of increasing a learner's pronunciation vocabulary. From one
familiar configuration, the learner quickly learns to master many new

Much time may need to be spent in developing word-identification skills. (Courtesy
of Chicago Urban Skills Institute and City Colleges of Chicago. Photo by M. Jones.)

words. Instruction in the use of this tool is accomplished in three stages. First, the learner needs to be able to recognize simple forms such as inflections, compounds, and easily derived forms. Second, he progresses to the more difficult affixes and roots. In the third stage, the structural knowledge thus acquired is related to spelling generalizations, and inflections and affixes are classified according to meaning and function (Burmeister 1971; Carlton 1970; Gray 1960).

Inflected Forms

The understanding of inflectional forms is the simplest place to begin instruction in structural analysis. The inflected endings *s, es, ed, ing, er,* and *est* are commonly used with nouns, verbs, adjectives, and adverbs to indicate number, person, tense, and comparison (Carlton 1970). The learner must not only be aware that *s* and *es* signify a plural, but also discriminate inflectional endings from the occasion when the letters do not function in this manner, such as in the words *gas* and *does*. Development of competence will depend on many opportunities to examine both root words and their possible inflections, such as those listed under "Common Prefixes and Suffixes" in appendix 5. Guided experience with these forms will lead to the formation of generalizations governing their use (Carlton 1970).

Derived Forms and Affixes

As with inflected forms, it is necessary that the learner recognize when a letter combination is actually an affix and when it is not by calling attention to such pairs of words as these:

*re*gion—*re*quest	*table*—not*able*
*pre*gnant—*pre*view	*list*—reception*ist*
*dis*cipline—*dis*miss	*trial*—termin*al*

Appendix 5 presents a list of common roots and affixes.

Although one must learn to recognize structural forms, it is never wise to teach a learner to look for the little words in big ones. Too often such configurations are neither roots, compounds nor affixes; and this leads to faulty generalizations. For example, the *aunt* in *dauntless* has nothing to do with a parent's sister. In learning compounds and affixes, pronunciation is the key to recognizing familiar words that have been joined together. Generally, a configuration of a small word within the boundaries of a larger one should not be identified unless it retains its original sound.

Application of Structural Analysis

At this third stage of development, structural analysis becomes increasingly meaningful and helpful in the promotion of good comprehension in reading. Conceptualization is aided by classifying affixes according to meaning and function.

CLASSIFICATION ACCORDING TO MEANING

Negative prefixes: dis, non, un, in, a, anti
Locational prefixes: under, over, circum, pre, post, sub, trans
Numerical prefixes: uni, mono, bi, tri, quad
Degree prefixes: hyper, hypo, arch, ultra, super

CLASSIFICATION ACCORDING TO FUNCTION

Noun suffixes: ation, hood, ist, th, ant, ent
A person who: ist, ent, ant, ee, eer, ster
Adjective suffixes: -tive, -ic, -ous, -ish

Structural analysis is also applied to spelling patterns. Such spelling functions as doubling of letters, dropping the final *e*, and changing *y* to *i* are important for language mastery. It may also be helpful to call the students' attention to the derivation of roots and affixes as borrowed from other languages. This information may be of particular benefit to those for whom English is a second language.

Phonic Analysis Skills

Sounding out words, or applying the phonic principles of language to decoding, is at least partially useful for about eight percent of the English words. The most important generalization with which the teacher should be concerned are listed in appendix 6. Success in the use of phonic analysis is predicated upon the understanding that words are made up of sounds, and upon the ability of the individual to recognize auditory and visual likenesses and differences in words.

Vowels and Consonants

In developing competency with phonic skills, consonants should be taught before vowel sounds.

Whether or not the teacher teaches long vowels before short ones, or vice versa, is somewhat a matter of preference. On one hand, long vowels are somewhat easier to learn because the sound says the name of the letter. However, more of the first words that beginning readers use have a short vowel sound. Whatever choice is made, it is important to be consistent. The learner should not be confused with a second sound of a vowel before he has had practice with the first. He should not be required to make the fine discriminations between the close sounds of some of the vowels until he has mastered the grosser differences.

Neither should a learner be encouraged to analyze a new word by sounding it out from left to right, *letter by letter*. Instead, he should not think of sounds in isolation, but as part of the whole (Rauch 1969). Such habits will build smooth blending and fluency in reading. Because vowels are extremely irregular, teaching them is somewhat more complex than teaching consonants.

Syllabication

Syllabication is taught throughout the instructional experience, as the opportunities are presented. The learner needs to understand that syllabication visualizes speech, not vice versa. The syllabication principles in appendix 7 can be utilized as a guide for the teacher.

Suprasegmental Phonemes

The suprasegmental phonemes of English—stress (accent), pitch, and juncture (pauses)—are important sound components of the language that must be mastered if communication is to be meaningful.

Stress. Since stress, or accent, also visualizes speech, it needs to be taught auditorially before being taught visually. Certain principles concerning accent that will be helpful to the teacher are listed in appendix 8.

Pitch. Although English is not strictly considered a tonal language, the voice pitch—low, middle or high—that the speaker employs in the delivery of an oral communication determines a portion of its meaning. Declarative statements generally end with a falling pitch, while interrogations end with a rising pitch. Moreover, the entire meaning of an utterance may be altered by changing its tonal pattern. Of course, in written discourse, pitch cannot be heard, but must be inferred through context, the use of punctuation marks, and occasionally through the use of underscoring or italics to indicate emphasis. Practice with the pitch patterns of language is mandatory for students who are speakers of other languages, and also sometimes needed by native speakers.

Juncture. It is necessary to teach most students that sentences are group-ings of separate words rather than just a conglomerate sound. This is accomplished auditorily through listening activities, then is helped visu-ally in many ways. One method is to place words on cards for matching or rearranging in flannelgraph pockets. Students must learn that such an expression as "Wherdjago?" really consists of four words, "Where did you go?" The auditory language must then be matched to the visual forms that will be encountered in books.

Summary

Teachers frequently ask, "What do you do when the student cannot read the book? The answer is, "Who is the teacher, you or the book?" (E. Smith 1968, p. 6).

This chapter has been concerned with the development of a productive approach to teaching undereducated adults to read and with methods of promoting competency in various basic word identification skills.

It has been stated that a selective approach to beginning reading is the most useful in adult basic education. We believe that most successful teachers will basically do two things: First, he will follow some system-atic approach to the teaching of reading, which has been chosen to meet the specific needs of the learner. Second, he will help adult learners to expand oral language and comprehension by discussion of topics and recording these ideas as a language-experience approach similar to that used with young children.

Many published materials and teacher-made materials will be useful for adult reading instruction. Of utmost importance in the development of basic reading skills is the continual emphasis on relevance and appro-priateness of the reading materials to adult experience (*Reading Curric-ulum Guide for Adult Basic Education* 1972). Only as this prerequisite to reading instruction is adhered to can the development of comprehension be assured as word identification is developed.

11.
Achieving Independence in Word Identification

Treat your student like a king! If you heard a king mispronounce a word you would never say, "Your Majesty, you didn't pronounce that word right." When it is necessary to correct him, do it in an indirect way. For example, if he should mispronounce "Hat," calling it "hate," you could point to a hat and say, "Yes, what a pretty hat you have!" Give him a compliment instead of a correction (Laubach 1960, p. 36).

Since without decoding skills the act of reading cannot occur, it is imperative that the teacher determine which skills need to be taught and weave this need into the whole fabric of instruction. In developing such skills, the greatest success will be experienced if several skills are taught concurrently. All language skills are closely related and will reinforce each other. Opportunity must be provided to hear the words, say the words, use them in conversation, write them on the chalkboard, read them, use them in word games, spell them aloud, and write them in sentences and in paragraphs (Carrillo 1970; *Guide for Trainers of Teachers of Undereducated Adults* 1967).

The overall sequence of developing these skills will vary to some degree according to the needs of the individual student. Barbe (1970) and Guszak (1972), among others, have already developed comprehensive sequential lists of these skills that need to be learned. Although developed for children, these lists are appropriate for adults as a sequential guide. However, the grade-level assignments of the skills are meaningless in relation to adult basic education.

Lessons dealing with word skills should usually be short, since the undereducated adult lacks study habits and usually has a short attention span for this kind of activity. Introduce a few words at a time, using, as far as possible, words that the learners have already become familiar with, or words that represent their real life experience. Words may also be introduced by labeling objects, writing simple sentences, directions, or news stories of current interest on the chalkboard. Demonstrate the importance of "little words" by having learners circle these in a newspaper or a magazine article. Some of the words that prove to be troublesome can then be placed on flashcards or on tachistoscopic devices. Learners can then work in pairs to study them. They may also keep a notebook of new words found in their reading, underline unfamiliar words in their books, or make lists of words from common roots, guess the meaning, and then check the definition in a dictionary.

More interest in word identification can be promoted by supplying additional information about the words, such as a picture, a filmstrip, an audiotape or simply an interesting account of the word's history.

Twenty General Principles of Teaching Word Identification

The decade of the 70s will see the 200th anniversary of our nation.
A most appropriate celebration of that event—a celebration that would
honor the true spirit of the democratic concept, and recognize
the fundamental importance ascribed to education from the beginning
of our nation, would be to secure for all of our citizens that right
to read, which so long ago made possible the feasibility of a demo-
cratic society and continues to undergird its strength (James E.
Allen, former U.S. Commissioner of Education—now deceased; quoted
in Rauch 1972, p. 22).

Regardless of the general approach or the detailed sequence of skills that the teacher chooses to follow, certain general principles of teaching word identification skills are pertinent.

1. *Proceed from the simple to the complex,* from the known to the un-known. Present minimal pairs before multidiscriminations are required. Give plenty of practice where clues to the skill are provided before the learner is required to utilize the skill without clues.
2. *The oral modality should be the vehicle for the initial presentation of a skill.* Learners should have much practice in auditory discrimination and in pronunciation before being presented with the visual forms of words.
3. *Approach the task from various modalities* when learning a particular skill is proving somewhat difficult for an individual learner. Let him hear it, say it, feel it, read it, and then write it. Fernald (1943) techniques may be appropriate when difficulty is encountered. A summary of these is found in appendix 1.
4. *Teach a skill at the time it is needed.* Never teach a skill in isolation from a meaningful context, but always at the time when the reading situation demands it. Avoid drill on isolated words.
5. *A vocabulary of fifty to seventy-five sight words is needed before in-struction on structural and phonic analysis advances very far.*
6. *Identification of sight words should be achieved through the use of general configuration and visual clues.* The learner should be taught to distinguish the gross differences in visual forms (Chapman 1965).
7. *Establish the habit of using the context* for the identification of words before applying other word identification tools (Chapman 1965; Smith 1970).

8. *Use word games and interesting activities* in seeking to make the identification of sight words automatic. Repetition is the key to such mastery, but the teacher must be inventive to maintain the interest. A few such games are:
   a. *Dolch Word Games and Phrase Cards* (1952).
   b. *Grab* (Alcock 1953).
   c. Word Wheels (Durrell 1960).
   A few sources of games are:
   a. *Reading Games: Strengthening Reading Skills,* by Guy Wagner and Max Hosier (1961).
   b. *Reading Aids Through the Grades,* by David H. Russell and Etta E. Karp (1963).
   c. *Learning Activities for Reading,* by Selma Herr (1969).
   d. *Reading With A Smile: 90 Reading Games That Work,* by Audrey Ann Burie and Mary Ann Heltshe (1975).
   e. *Energizers for Reading Instruction,* by Richard A. Thompson (1966).
   f. *Rescue* (Platts 1972).
   g. *Spice* (Platts 1972).
9. *From the beginning, establish the left-to-right direction in attack on new words.* Help the learner to see differences and similarities in the configuration of words. Help him to see similar beginnings and endings, and to notice the details of words. Help him to detect significant differences. When difficulty is encountered in establishing left-to-right directionality, these techniques may be useful:
   a. Use the finger under the word from left to right.
   b. Cover the word with a card, moving it slowly from left to right.
   c. Draw arrows under the words, left to right.
   d. Have learners type the words.
   e. Practice choral reading.
   f. Require the student's name to be written on the left side of the paper and words to be written down the left margin.
   g. Capitalize on the learner's knowledge of traffic light colors by making experience charts that teach left-to-right. Write the first word of every line in green (for go) and the last word in red (for stop). Tell the learner that every time they get to a red word they stop and make their eyes find the next "go" word (Kaulfers 1954).
   h. Use a classroom calendar as a left-to-right teaching tool. Point out that the days are recorded left-to-right (Kaulfers 1954).
   i. Make "mirror-image" flashcards—for example, a card showing a boy facing right. Distribute one set and display their opposites

(facing left) at the front of the room. Learners find the mates to their cards (Kaulfers 1954).

j. Whenever you erase words or sentences from the chalkboard, begin at the left and work toward the right (Kaulfers 1954).

k. Use alphabetizing exercises.

l. Emphasize word beginnings rather than endings.

m. Use the Fernald (1943) tracing-sounding-writing method.

n. Hold up left hand. Notice that thumb and forefinger form the letter *l*.

10. *Teach identification skills so that they function in an integrated manner*, rather than as separate techniques for word mastery.

11. *Teach structural analysis and phonic skills together*, rather than separately. Do not expect complete mastery and use of a skill at any one level. Rather, the teacher will endeavor as quickly as possible to convert words learned through either structural or phonic analysis to words identified instantaneously by sight. This is accomplished only after much exposure to the words in various contexts.

12. *Fit the word-identification program to the needs and abilities of the individuals*, allowing each to progress toward independence at a rate commensurate with his own abilities (Otto and Ford 1967).

13. *In pronouncing multisyllabic words, structural analysis precedes phonic analysis.* Word parts must be recognized before phonic elements can be identified. Continued practice in structural analysis will help the learner divide new words into parts that represent meaning and pronunciation units; then use this skill in identifying new words.

14. *Phonic analysis should be taught gradually and only as a functional tool for unlocking new words.* Isolated drill on phonics can be deadly!

15. *Except for words that are easily phonetically regular, help the learner to analyze a word visually before trying to analyze it phonetically.*

16. *The goal of developing word identification skills should be to make learners as independent as possible of the dictionary* in pronouncing and attaching meaning to new words. Continued practice and help in utilizing the word identification principles that unlock the small words to longer, more complex structures will accomplish this goal.

17. *Never introduce a "gimmick" or a "rule" that has to be unlearned later.* Gray (1960) gives an example of this problem:

"ap" may say "ăp" in words like *map, cap*, or *lap*. But because of syllabic division and accent in long words (*apron, maple, approach*), this rule cannot be applied to many words of more than one syllable (p. 34).

18. *Guide learners in formulating generalizations and spelling rules.* Then provide much practice in the application of generalizations. *Do not*

teach rules. Because of the irregularity of the English language, such phonetic generalizations are at best of limited value, since exceptions function a large percentage of the time (M. H. Bailey 1971; Burmeister 1971; Clymer 1971; Emans 1971).

19. *Use of the dictionary as an aid to pronunciation and meaning should be taught systematically* along with instruction in structural and phonic analysis. For adult basic education a simplified dictionary is probably the most appropriate (*Curriculum Guide to Adult Basic Education: Intermediate Level* 1966).

20. *Repeat—and repeat—and repeat!* One adult educator has commented:

It's not easy to remember things that are completely new and strange to you—as you know if you've ever studied a foreign language. Words must be read over and over again. Many opportunities for word drill must be given—in the guise of games, contests, or any method that the creative teacher can think of to make repetition interesting. (Warren 1970, p. 2)

Using several types of materials at the same level of difficulty (Otto and McMeaney 1966), such as Durrell's *Word Analysis Cards* (1960), the SRA *Reading Comprehension Laboratory* (Parker 1961), *Reading for Concepts,* Levels A–H (Liddle 1970), or the *Be Informed Series* (1970), permits the learner to work on the same skills from one activity to another—or from one day to another. Reinforcement occurs when vocabulary is repeated from one activity to the next. "That word on that card we did yesterday was in my spelling lesson today."

Expanding Language Experiences

A tribute to adult basic education: "Since I came to school I have learned many things. I learned to spell more words. I learned to write better letters and best of all, I have learned to read the Newspaper. . . . I appreciate what you done for me. I take a shoar every day and shave every day. I am not a messup any more" (Witty 1966, p. 61).

Gradually expand the one-sentence exercises on the chalkboard into short conversations with perhaps two sentences for each of two people. First, practice *saying without reading.* Then ask two members of the class to read the sentences as conversation. Here is an example:

JUAN: Good morning, Pedro.
PEDRO: Good morning, Juan. How are you today?
JUAN: I'm fine, thanks. And you?
PEDRO: I'm fine, thank you.

Adult students need much practice in the development of oral language. This student is learning to speak, read, and write English. (Courtesy of Chicago Urban Skills Institute and City Colleges of Chicago. Photo by V. Bacon.)

Or perhaps, a conversation like this:

JUAN: Please tell me what time it is.
PEDRO: It's five minutes past nine o'clock.
JUAN: Thank you, Pedro.
PEDRO: You're welcome, Juan.

After such practice, gradually expand the one sentence reading on the chalkboard into a short experience story told by the group, recorded in manuscript on the chalkboard by the teacher, and then read first by the group and finally by individuals. Such stories might be like these:

1. John works on a beet farm in the valley.
   John works five miles from here.
   John works for about six months each year.
2. Mr. Tanaka is a beet farmer.
   He farms in the river valley.
   He lives in Malheur County.
   He lives a few miles south of Ontario.

As this type of practice is pursued, identification of sight words and individual letters and sounds is expanded. Such practice should continue until everyone has learned a stock of sight words from a selected sight vocabulary list. After the group has learned a short list of words, the teacher can select books or stories that will contain enough of the same words to enable some of the group to read them.

With this beginning, the class can read some of the easier titles in adult education materials, such as the *Reader's Digest Adult Series Mystery of the Mountains* (fig. 11.1); *In the Valley,* and *City Living,* by Frank C. Laubach and Elizabeth Mooney Kirk (figs. 11.2 and 11.3); possibly *Stories for Adult Readers* (fig. 11.4); or "homemade" stories and books, which were discussed in the last chapter. Much of the published beginning reading instructional materials may also be adapted to supplement and expand on the language experience thus begun by rewriting some of the stories employing parallel constructions and substitution drills. For example, peruse the story of Bill Jones provided in *Book 2, English 900, Unit 1* (1965). This story could be rewritten as follows:

NEW WORDS TO BE LEARNED AS SIGHT VOCABULARY	BILL JONES
my, name, is	My name is Bill Jones.
his	His name is Bill Jones.
her	Her name is Bill Jones.
your	Your name is Bill Jones.
am, I, a	I am a student.
student, he	He is a student.
she	She is a student.
are, you	Are you a student?
and	My name is Bill Jones and I am a student.
first	My first name is William.
	His first name is William.
	Her first name is Mary.
short, for	*Bill* is short for William.
was, born, in	I was born in a little town.
	He was born in a little town.
	She was born in a little town.
	José was born in a little town.
	Francisco was born in a little town.

country, not, from, here   I was born in a little country town
not far from here.
Maria was born in a little country
town not far from here.[1]

Here is another rewrite of a paragraph in *Book 4, English 900, Unit 4* (1965), with examples of a planned oral sentence pattern practice, to be followed by group rather than individual reading:

BUYING CLOTHES

Bob and Don go to the same school.
They needed some new clothes for school.
They decided to go shopping together.
They went to a new department store.

The two boys went to Men's Wear.
They found the department where there were suits.
They found suits for high school boys.
The salesman helped them find the right size.
Don tried on a light gray suit.
It was a good fit.
He liked it right away.
He bought the light gray suit.

Bob found several suits that he liked.
He could not make up his mind about just one.
The boys talked about the suits.
Bob did like the navy blue one.
Don told him he should take it.
Finally, he tried it on and it fit very well.
He decided to buy it.

Next, they went to the shoe department.
The clerk measured their feet.
He asked what style they wanted.
He brought several pairs for them to try on.
They each soon selected a pair.
It is easy for boys to buy shoes.

Then, they went to the shirt department in the store.
Don needed a white shirt.
Bob decided to look for a sweater.
While Don picked out a shirt, the right size for him,
Bob went to look at the sweaters.

1. The story of "Bill Jones," from *Book 2, English 900,* Unit 1. Copyright © 1964 Macmillan Publishing Co., Inc. Rewritten by permission of the publisher.

The Balloon That

Grassy and I were high in the air. We were in the basket of Balloon 161. The Army used this big balloon as a lookout during World War I.

Grassy and I did not know much about balloons. But we were not

Figure 11.1. (From *Mystery of the Mountains,* pp. 12-13. Pleasantville, New York: Readers Digest Services, 1964. Used by permission.)

Got Away

afraid. A big rope held Balloon **161** to the ground.

After a while it was time to come down. I called to the men to pull us in.

Then a strong wind hit us. Wham! The big rope broke. Our balloon was flying away!

Then we WERE afraid! Higher and higher we went. What could we do?

Mr. Hill Visits Sam's Shop

This is Sam's shop.

The shop is in the valley.

Sam sells fish and apples in his shop.

Sam sells eggs and olives in his shop.

Sam sells zippers in his shop.

Sam sells cups and pans in his shop.

Figure 11.2. (From *In the Valley*, p. 13, by Frank C. Laubach and Elizabeth Mooney Kirk. Syracuse, New York: New Readers Press, Division of Laubach Literary International, 1969. Reprinted by permission.)

lift, into

Jimmy Linn works with a big lift truck.
Jimmy brings the glass to big boxes.
Jimmy brings the glass with his lift truck.
Jimmy does not let the glass drop.

Jack and Jimmy put the glass into the boxes.
The glass fills the boxes.
The boxes fit the glass.

Figure 11.3. From *City Living,* p. 15, by Frank C. Laubach and Elizabeth Mooney Kirk. Syracuse, N. Y.: New Readers Press, 1969. Reprinted by permission.)

A Penny Spent Is Five Dollars Earned

By

Jean Bryant

Miss Hill ran up the back steps of Mrs. Cook's house.

"Oh, Flo," she cried, "I'm a criminal, I'm going to be arrested!"

Mrs. Cook opened the back door and Miss Hill went in. "Be quiet, Emma. You're carrying on so I don't understand a word you are saying. Sit down at this table. I'll fix some iced tea."

Miss Hill sat down. " A policeman just called. He said he had a warrant for my arrest. I have to go down to the police station. Oh, Flo, what can I do!"

"Now, now Emma, everything will be all right. Why are they going to arrest you?"

Emma sniffed and wiped her nose. "Flo, do you remember when I went to town two weeks ago to pay my light bill? Well, I only parked a minute to run in to pay my bill. I was only gone a little minute. That policeman gave me a

Figure 11.4. (From *Stories for Adult Readers*, p. 1. Tallahassee, Florida: Florida Department of Education, 1972. Used by permission.)

Bob tried on all the sweaters in his size.
After Don had picked out a new white shirt,
he went over to the sweater counter to talk to Bob.
He helped Bob decide to buy a blue wool sweater.[2]

Here is another example of a progressively more difficult sentence practice. These are simple sentences, using repetition and parallel sentence construction to provide an interesting story about a topic in which the class was interested.

Most of the land in the Snake River Valley was dry.
The land was a dry desert.
The land did not grow any crops.
There was no rain on the land.
Only a few people lived here in those days.
The land was fertile.
The land could grow crops if it had water.
The land could grow crops if it would rain.
If rain would fall, the land would grow different crops.
But there was no rain.
There was no water for the crops.
The Snake River Valley was a desert.

People knew that the land was fertile.
People knew that crops could grow if there was water.
People knew that they must get water for crops.
People knew that there was water in the Snake River.
People knew that there was water in the Weiser River.
People knew that there was water in the Malheur River.
People knew that there was water in the Owyhee River.
People knew that if that water were on the land, they could grow crops.

With water, they could grow potatoes.
With water, they could grow sugar beets.
With water, they could grow onions.
With water, they could grow hops.
With water, they could grow alfalfa.
With water, they could grow corn.

About twenty-five years ago, Mexican migrants came to the Snake River
    Valley to help with the crops.
Mexican migrant farmers came to plant the large fields of potatoes.
Mexican migrant farmers came to weed the large fields of potatoes.
Mexican migrant farmers came to harvest the large fields of potatoes.
Mexican migrant farmers came to work for potato farmers.
Then they went back to Texas.

2. The story about "Buying Clothes," from *Book 4, English 900*, Unit 4. Copyright © 1965 Macmillan Publishing Co., Inc. Rewritten by permission of the publisher.

Mexican migrant farmers came to plant the sugar beets.
Mexican migrant farmers came to thin the sugar beets.
Mexican migrant farmers came to harvest the sugar beets.
Mexican migrant farmers came to work for the sugar beet farmers.
The sugar beet farmers needed the migrant workers very much.
Then the migrant farm workers went back to Texas.
Mexican migrant farm workers came to plant onions and work in the
    hops.
Mexican migrant farm workers came to work in the fruit.
Mexican migrant farm workers came to do stoop labor.
The farmers in the Snake River Valley needed the help very much.
They were glad that the migrant farm workers came to help.

Then, new machines were invented.
Then, fewer and fewer men could tend to the crops.
There is a machine that drops the potatoes.
There is a machine that digs the potatoes.
There is a machine that sorts the potatoes.
There is a machine that does almost every part of growing potatoes.
Mexican migrant farm workers have less to do.
Getting work done with machines is called *automation.*
Automation has taken away many of the jobs.
The jobs that were stoop labor were very hard work.
It is better if a machine can do the hard work.
It is better if stoop labor is done by a machine.
It is better if machines can do hard work for us.

Then, there must be other work for the migrant farm worker.
Then, the migrant farm worker must learn other skills.
First, the migrant farm worker must learn to speak English.
Then, he can talk directly to the people who might hire him.
Then, he can talk directly to all the people in the town.
He can speak to the man in the drug store.
He can speak to the man in the grocery store.
He can speak to the man in the clothing store.
He can speak to the man in the hardware store.
He can speak to the man in the gasoline station.
He can speak to the man in the restaurant.
He can speak to all the people on the street.
He can understand the lessons that his child has in school.
He can learn to say everything in English that he knows in Spanish.
Then, he can be just like all the other people in any town in the Snake
    River Valley.

Care must be taken that new words are not introduced too rapidly for
beginning readers. After the student can produce successive prepositional

phrases early in oral language, the teacher needs to provide practice in reading common prepositional phrases used in adult materials, such as:

of her house
for her family
with her family
to the store
to the grocery store
of the groceries

Return to the story of Bob and Don's shopping trip. Notice how this story can be rewritten to provide this kind of practice.

Bob and Don went to the store	to buy a new suit to wear to the school dance on Friday night.
Bob bought a new suit	to wear to the school dance on Friday night.
Don asked Bob to go	with him to the store to buy a new suit to wear to the school dance in the gymnasim on Friday night.
Bob needed a new shirt	because he tore the old one when he went through the fence on his uncle's farm hunting rabbits.

Many stories can be adapted in such a manner. The "List of Important Prepositional Phrases" in appendix 9 will be helpful in devising practice exercises as the student works with this skill until phrases are read and comprehended with ease.

Summary

*Some people assume that an illiterate does not think. He does think,
but his method of thinking is not the same as an educated person's. . . . .
Educational deficiency is not a sign of mental retardation . . .
most ABE students complete what is equivalent to one grade for each
month that they spend in school (Wallace 1965, p. 7).*

This chapter has been concerned with the utilization of word-identification skills in the expansion of language experiences.

Twenty general principles of teaching word-identification skills were given. Such skills cannot be taught as isolated entities, but are utilized in the process of unlocking words that are appropriate to the needs of a particular student at a specific time. Only through the development of competent word identification skills can the goal of independence in reading ever be reached.

As the ability to identify new and unfamiliar words is being developed, word identification skills are immediately applied to sentences and paragraphs. Much practice is necessary in the usage of language-sentence expansions, conversations, and language patterns. To accommodate this need, teachers will rewrite stories employing parallel constructions and substitution drills. The mastery of these enables the beginning reader to then achieve success in reading the stories, newspapers, advertisements, and other things that have been outside his reach for so long.

12.
Comprehension
Skills
in Reading

*Everyone who understands the proc-
esses of education would agree that
some subjects are more important
than others and that reading is the
most important of all. Reading is the
skill which supports all other methods
of learning, enlarges the horizons
of the mind, permits us to move freely
across space and time to establish
contact with those with whom we have
a community of interest, and corrects
the distorted or narrow views which
we often get from first-hand observation and from other methods of
learning (Houle 1964, p. 83).*

Making sure that the content read is meaningful should be the major concern of every reading teacher. Synthesizing meanings, grouping words
into concepts, and anticipating meaning in lines of print become objectives in reading. In this text, primary concern has been with all the affective and cognitive needs of the underachieving adult, rather than with
developing a person who already reads into a mature, critical reader. For
this reason, this chapter will introduce the teacher to many types of exercises in reading comprehension that will enable the adult who is learning to read to progress beyond the elementary stages and perhaps go
directly to work in commercially prepared materials to meet requirements of the General Educational Development Tests. The techniques
for arriving at adequate meanings constitute the comprehension skills of
reading (Grindstaff 1971).

This chapter will contain examples of some of the literal comprehension
skills and the interpretive comprehension skills. Organization skills, evaluation skills, and creative reading skills required of the mature reader may
also be utilized in these elementary reading exercises.

Reading with comprehension enables the individual to use the reading process as a problem-solving tool. Problem-solving through reading
matter is a four-step process. First, one must be able to state the problem
that he seeks to solve; second, he must be able to locate the information
he needs in order to solve it; third, he must read sources of information
until he understands the solution to the problem; and finally, he must
be able to synthesize what he has read and summarize the information so
that he can state or write the solution to his problem concisely and clearly.

The skills illustrated in this chapter include:

I. Finding information.
  A. Identifying specific information in brief passages (answering who,
     what, where, when, why, and how).

    B. Skimming.

    C. Finding topic sentences.

    D. Getting meaning from pictures, cartoons, the TV guide, maps, and figures.

II. Comprehension exercises.

    A. Reading to find details.

    B. Reading to grasp the general significance.

    C. Reading to organize ideas read.

    D. Recognizing antecedents in the use of pronouns.

    E. Determining if the sentence tells how, when, or where.

    F. Answering riddles.

    G. Classifying; putting things into categories.

    H. Understanding function words or word markers in sentences.

III. Learning to anticipate meaning in context.

    A. Completing the sentence meaningfully.

    B. Practicing the cloze procedure.

IV. Extending vocabulary.

    A. Multiple meanings.

    B. Antonyms, homonyms, synonyms.

    C. Analyzing word structures (affixes and compound words).

    D. Dictionary exercises.

    E. Sample vocabulary lists in GED subject matter.

  V. Readability.

 VI. Remembering what one reads.

Finding Information

The desire to read soon dwindles if success that the reader can see and feel is not readily attainable. The reader 'psychs out' and no amount of drill or tutoring is effective until his attitude is changed (McGarry 1971, p. 33).

Finding information is an important skill in any learning situation. But for the adult learner who is not in the habit of looking for main ideas, supporting details, and specific information instruction must be detailed. The teacher cannot take for granted that the learner already possesses these skills.

Identifying Specific Information

It is important that adults be shown how to find specific information, such as telling who, which, what, when, where, and how. To help learners de-

Teachers ask questions about the content of the reading selection to help develop the reading-thinking abilities. (Courtesy of William Rainey Harper College, Palatine, Illinois.)

velop confidence at the most elementary level with this ability, exercises like these might be provided.

1. Tom chased the chickens in the yard.
   Who chased the chickens?
   What did Tom do?
   Where did Tom chase the chickens?

2. Ben rode his Honda to work yesterday. He showed it to all of the workers. He rode it home after work.

   Who rode his Honda to work?
   What did Ben ride to work?
   When did Ben ride his Honda to work?
   Where did Ben ride his Honda?

3. Pigeons like to come to the park where people feed them crumbs of bread. Pigeons like people and are not afraid of them.

   Who comes to the park?
   Why do pigeons come to the park?
   What do the people do?
   How do pigeons feel about people?
   What do pigeons like to eat?
   Which birds like people?

4. Polar bears are large white animals. They live in the far north where it is cold. Polar bears have heavy fur coats. Polar bears like to swim and play in the water.

   What are polar bears?
   What color are polar bears?
   Where do polar bears live?
   How do polar bears keep warm?
   Why do we know polar bears like the water?
   What is the Far North like?

Skimming

Skimming is one of the skills involved in locating information. It is moving the eye quickly over a passage to locate specific items. Smith (1963) distinguishes between skimming and scanning in a way that may be helpful to some teachers.

> The term *scanning* is generally used to designate the process of quickly locating a particular word, phrase, sentence, fact, or figure within a selection, while *skimming* is used for the process of quickly passing over an entire selection or passage to get a general impression of it. A person *scans* when he sweeps his eyes over the list of items in a television schedule to find the time of a particular show. He *skims* when he glances through a short article on "How to Increase Your Energy" to catch a few phrases now and then that will give him a general idea of what suggestions the article holds (p. 364).

Skimming enables a reader to quickly find a statement in a passage, to instruct someone else, to win an argument, or to prove a point. Skimming also enables the reader to look quickly for a given fact that will make it possible for him to find related information, and other related topics to add breadth to the material he has immediately at hand. When factual material is written in brief, condensed style, one can often pick up many details by looking only for the specific detail that will be the needed answer to a question. For example, if the paragraph tells when the astronauts first orbited the moon and there is only one date in the paragraph, one need only scan quickly for that date.

Finding Topic Sentences

A well-written paragraph deals with only one topic. It should contain a topic sentence. All the details of a good paragraph develop the topic sentence. The topic sentence may be the first sentence in the paragraph. If it is, it helps the beginning reader to know what the paragraph is going to be about. However, it may be a summarizing sentence and appear at the end of the paragraph. Students may practice reading paragraphs, identifying the main idea in the topic sentence, and developing the beginning of outline form by finding the details in the other sentences that further explain the topic. Read the paragraph below.

Before there were trade schools for boys to attend, there was another way for a young man to become a craftsman. *First* he had to decide what kind of craftsman he wanted to be. *Then* he had to find a craftsman with those skills and become an apprentice. *After* he had been an apprentice for a long period of time and the craftsman was satisfied with his work, he became a journeyman. He could work for more pay *then* with another craftsman. He had to do a piece of work that was judged by the master craftsman to be satisfactory before he could become a master craftsman. *Now* he no longer had to work with another master craftsman and he could teach other apprentices.

The first sentence in this paragraph is a topic sentence. Notice the words *first, then, after, then,* and *now,* and think about how they help to relate these sentences in a sequence that tells how the young man goes through all the steps in becoming a master craftsman.

The student may then read paragraphs like the following and decide that the first sentence here is also the topic sentence.

A puncture wound is a very dangerous type of wound that needs careful treatment. You may get a puncture wound from such accidents as stepping on a nail or being struck by a sharp-pointed object. Sometimes puncture wounds do not bleed enough to clean the wound of dirt and germs. Then there is danger of infection and lockjaw. You should try to clean the wound as well as you can and then put iodine or some

Newspapers are useful in the development of the ability to find topic sentences of paragraphs. (Courtesy of Venice-Lincoln Technical Center, Venice, Illinois.)

other antiseptic on it. You should have a doctor see it as soon as possible if it is a deep puncture or if you are not sure that you have treated it thoroughly yourself.

What is the topic sentence? ───────────────────────

───

Getting Meaning From Pictures

Pictures, signs, and other graphic symbols are read in the same way that words are read. A good example is found in figure 12.1, showing the many road signs on Mexican highways to help those drivers who cannot read Spanish. The symbols can be read in any language.

In cartoons, it is often possible to grasp a complete concept with no words or one short sentence. This, too, is reading. Ford Button expresses current concepts in interesting cartoons (see fig. 12.2).

The TV guide, with scheduled hours for local channels should be read critically, and parents should guide the selected viewing for both themselves and their children. A *few* programs should not be missed. The TV Log for Albuquerque, dated 17 April 1975 (fig. 12.3), lists both *Sesame*

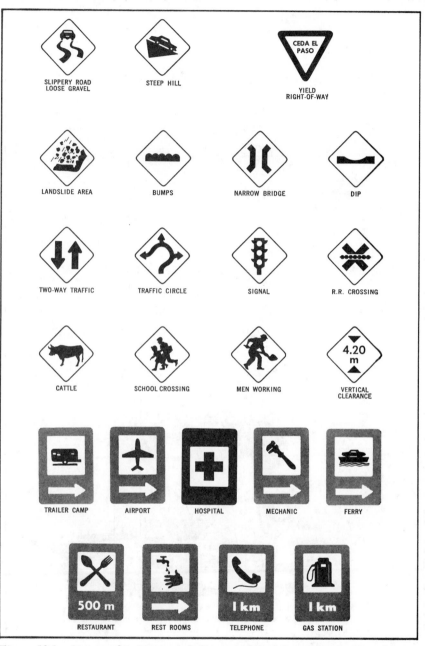

Figure 12.1. Signs used in Mexico to help automobile drivers from the United States who cannot read Spanish. (From Mexico and Central America, 1969-1970, p. 375. American Automobile Association, 1712 G. St. N. W., Washington, D. C. 20006. Used by permission.)

Figure 12.2. Cartoons carry important messages without extensive reading. (Cartoons by Ford Button from *Instructor,* copyright © 1974, © 1975 by The Instructor Publications, Inc. Used by permission.)

Daily **TV LOG**   Thursday, April 17, 1975

LISTINGS IN THE FOLLOWING PROGRAMS ARE FURNISHED BY THE TELEVISION STATIONS AND THE JOURNAL IS NOT RESPONSIBLE FOR CHANGES IN PROGRAMS THAT OCCUR AFTER COPY DEADLINE.

Thurs. April 17	4 KOB-NBC	5 KNME-PBS	7 KOAT-ABC	13 KGGM-CBS
6 :00 :15 :30 :45	Today Show			CBS Morning News: Rudd
7 :00 :15 :30 :45			AM America	Captain Kangaroo
8 :00 :15 :30 :45	Celebrity Sweepstakes Wheel of Fortune	Prelude Lilias, Yoga & You		Joker's Wild Gambit
9 :00 :15 :30 :45	High Rollers Hollywood Squares	An Ounce of Prevention Color Bars Time Out A Performance	Dick Van Dyke Brady Bunch	Now You See It Love of Life
10 :00 :15 :30 :45	Jackpot Blank Check Floyd Kalber w/the News	Sesame Street	Password Split Second	Young & Restless Search for Tomorrow
11 :00 :15 :30 :45	Somerset How to Survive a Marriage	Kaleidoscope On the Trail Villa Alegre	All My Children Let's Make a Deal	Guiding Light As the World Turns
12 :00 :15 :30 :45	Days of Our Lives The Doctors	Misterogers Neighborhood Consumer Survival Kit	$10,000 Pyramid Showdown	TV-13 Report: Andrews, Black, Smith Forum 13
1 :00 :15 :30 :45	Another World	The Electric Company Kaleidoscope Science Potpourri	General Hospital One Life to Live	New Price Is Right Match Game
2 :00 :15 :30 :45	Merv Griffin	Sound Go Round History of the Motion Picture	Money Maze Dialing for Dollars: "Les Miserables"	Tattletales Edge of Night
3 :00 :15 :30 :45	Here's Lucy	Prism University Journal	Michael Rennie	That Girl Beverly Hillbillies
4 :00 :15 :30 :45	Andy Griffith Partridge Family	Sesame Street	Mickey Mouse Club	Bonanza
5 :00 :15 :30 :45	NBC Nightly News Bewitched	Misterogers Neighborhood Villa Alegre	Action News: Beimer, Murray, Nelson ABC News	Hogan's Heroes TV-13 Report: Milligan, Thorne, Smith
6 :00 :15 :30 :45	Eyewitness News: Wilk- erson, Roberts, Edwards Wild Wild World of Animals	The Electric Company Hablemos Espanol	Action News: Knipfing, Boggio, Morgan Family Affair	CBS News: Cronkite The Price Is Right
7 :00 :15 :30 :45	Sunshine The Bob Crane Show	Feedforward Projections in Education	Barney Miller Karen	The Waltons
8 :00 :15 :30 :45	"The Law" Part III	Bill Moyer's Journal: Intl. Report	Streets of San Francisco	CBS Thursday Night Movie: "Hot Rock"
9 :00 :15 :30 :45	Lucas Tanner	The Quarterly Report	Harry O	
10 :00 :15 :30 :45	Eyewitness News: Wilk- erson, Roberts, Edwards Tonight Show		Action News: Knipfing, Boggio, Morgan W/W Special: "Geraldo Rivero"	TV-13 Report: Milligan, Thorne, Smith Nightwatch Movie: "What a Way to Go"
11 :00 :15 :30 :45	12:00 Tomorrow 1:00 Eyewitness News Briefs		Goodnight America"	12:30 CBS Late Movie: "Fade In" Burt Reynolds

Figure 12.3. The TV Log for 17 April 1975. (From "The Daily TV Log" *Albuquerque Journal.* Albuquerque, New Mexico 17 April 1975.)

Street and *Villa Alegre* for young children, and world and local news for adults. An elementary Spanish lesson, *Hablemos Español,* is also available for interested viewers.

Figure 12.4 presents an illustrated glossary of twenty-four terms needed for reading geography. Beginning readers of textbooks need instruction in understanding the terminology of each subject.

Figure 12.5 shows the four time zones of the forty-eight states. One needs to be aware that Alaska and Hawaii are not included in these time zones. Part of Alaska is in the same time zone as Hawaii.

Comprehension Exercises

Reading is not a matter of going from words to meaning, but rather from meaning to words. To read words effectively, you need to have a good idea in advance of what it is that you are reading (F. Smith 1970, p. 35).

The act of reading does not take place unless there is comprehension of meaning on the printed page. However, this does not take place accidently. It is a purposive skill that can be taught.

Reading to Find Details

One of the necessary skills of comprehension is the literal task of finding the details contained in a paragraph. Such an exercise is illustrated below.

Directions: Read the following paragraph and find six things a farmer must do to grow a crop of corn.

The farmer needs to do six things to grow and sell his crop of corn. He must *prepare the soil* by plowing, disking, and raking it to get a fine soil on top. If it is needed, fertilizer must be added to the soil. The farmer needs seed that produces good quality corn. He *plants the seed* in rows so the corn can be cultivated to kill the weeds and keep the soil in good condition. He may *cultivate the field* three or four times. Now there must be enough rain to finish growing the crop. The ears of corn must be large and well formed before frost kills the plant. After the frost comes in the fall, the farmer *harvests the crop.* He will *keep all he needs* as feed for his livestock. Then he can sell or store the rest. He must *decide whether to sell* at harvest time. If he sells then, the price may not be as high as it will be in the late winter or early spring. For this reason, he may store the corn in large bins to sell at a better price.

altitude – height above sea level.

bay – a part of an ocean or a lake which extends into the land.

canal – a man-made waterway dug across land for transportation or irrigation.

canyon – a deep, narrow valley with steep sides, often with a stream at the bottom.

cape – a point of land extending into a sea or lake.

desert – a very dry region, with little water and few plants.

divide – a high ridge of land that separates river basins.

equator – an imaginary line around Earth, halfway between the North Pole and the South Pole.

foothills – low hills at or near the base of mountains.

highland – land that is high above sea level, often mountainous or a high plateau.

inlet – a narrow strip of water that extends into the land from a larger body of water.

isthmus – a narrow strip of land, with water on both sides, connecting two larger bodies of land.

lowland – low and, usually, level land.

marsh – swamp; low, wet land, covered at times by water.

mountain range – a row of mountains.

plain – a region that has mostly level land.

plateau – a region of high land that is usually rather flat.

prairie – a large stretch of level or rolling land with grass but few or no trees.

rain forest – a woodland region where the rainfall is very heavy.

reef – a ridge of rocks at or near the surface of an ocean or lake.

river basin – land that is drained by a river and its tributaries.

strait – a narrow channel of water that connects two larger bodies of water.

tributary – a stream that flows into a river or larger body of water.

valley – low land between hills or mountains.

Figure 12.4. An illustrated glossary of terminology for geography. (Reprinted by permission from *Map Skills Project Book III* by Loretta Hunt. Copyright © 1967 by Scholastic Magazines, Inc.)

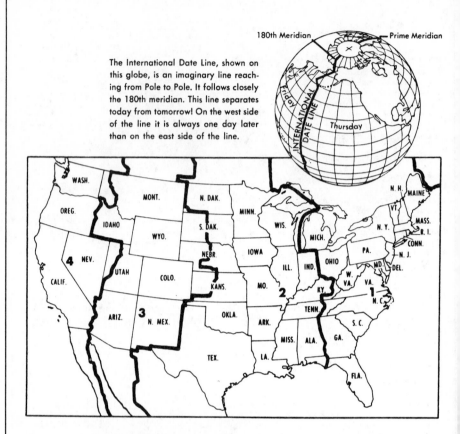

The International Date Line, shown on this globe, is an imaginary line reaching from Pole to Pole. It follows closely the 180th meridian. This line separates today from tomorrow! On the west side of the line it is always one day later than on the east side of the line.

The world is divided into 24 time zones. Each time zone is based upon longitude and is about 15° wide.

As Earth rotates, the position of the sun seems to change. Every hour the spinning Earth moves 15° and the noonday sun is directly overhead in another time zone.

This map shows the four time zones of the U.S. except Alaska and Hawaii. As you move from east to west, each time zone is one hour earlier. When it's 4 P.M. in Vermont, it's 3 P.M. in Iowa, 2 P.M. in Wyoming, 1 P.M. in Oregon.

Figure 12.5. Time zones on a map of forty-eight states of the United States. (Reprinted by permission from *Map Skills Project Book III,* by Loretta Hunt. Copyright © 1967 by Scholastic Magazines, Inc.)

The six things that the farmer does to grow a crop of corn are:

1. _____

2. _____

3. _____

4. _____

5. _____

6. _____

Many students need help to complete such exercises. Key words may be italicized, as above, or the group may select together, with teacher guidance, the key ideas.

Reading to Grasp the General Significance

After reading a paragraph, the alert reader should be able to interpret the author's meaning so that he can identify the significant concept presented. The two paragraphs below illustrate this.

Directions: Read the paragraph below and then select the best answers to the questions.

Ben had decided he really didn't want an operation. At the plant where he worked, he did heavy lifting. Now the doctor said he needed to have an operation for a hernia. Ben knew that this was true but he couldn't face it. He had asked the doctor to put it off. He had asked his wife to talk to the doctor. He even talked about the possibility that he might not live if he had the operation. Nothing the doctor said made Ben feel any better about having an operation.

Which word best describes how Ben felt?
confident　　　　angry　　　　*afraid*　　　　strong

In 1972, I was traveling in South America and I visited a large city in Columbia. When I arrived at my hotel, I learned that there was an international festival of orchid growers in the city at that time. I was amazed to learn that there was an international organization of orchid growers. I had been delighted with the great numbers of different kinds and colors of orchids I had seen in Columbia, but I could hardly believe it when I met people from the United States, Africa, Australia, and Europe—all in this city for an orchid festival. The beauty of the

Sometimes "machines" are good motivators in initial learning, and are useful in learning to read to grasp general significance. (Courtesy of Albuquerque Technical-Vocational Institute, Albuquerque, N. M.)

orchids on display was *out of this world.* There were several thousand varieties in the total exhibit. Can you imagine that?

What word best describes how the writer felt about this visit?
great surprise   disappointment   curiosity   interest

Take time to pronounce these words together before reading.

trav · el · ing	in · ter · na · tion · al	fes · ti · val
or · chid*	or · gan · i · za · tion	de · light · ed
dif · fer · ent	dis · play	sev · er · al
thou · sand	ex · hi · bit	va · ri · e · ties

*Point out that *ch* has the *k* sound.

Such specific help as is suggested above with pronunciation will be needed by some adult readers, and not by others.

Reading to Organize Ideas Read

Utilizing the two previous skills, the reader is ready for initial outlining skills in the organization of ideas. The essays below have been designed to make possible such a lesson on organization.

Directions: Read the essay "Through the Year."

THROUGH THE YEAR

In the United States, there are four seasons of the year. The change from one to the next makes an interesting year. The names of the seasons are fall, winter, spring, and summer. Fall and spring are warm but not hot. Winter is cold but summer is hot.

September, October, and November are the months of fall. Football is very popular in the fall. People harvest gardens and farm crops in the fall.

December, January, and February are the winter months. December is the last month of the year and January is the first. Some people like skiing and skating in the cold weather. Some people wish the weather would always be warm.

March, April, and May are the spring months. Everyone is glad to see the winter end and to have warm weather every day. Baseball is popular in the spring. People plant their gardens in April and May.

June, July, and August are the summer months. Some places are very hot and humid. Then we like very much to have air conditioning.

After reading the exercise, the student should be able to recognize two or three ways to organize the passage to remember the key ideas.

1. There are four seasons of the year.

   Fall
   Winter
   Spring
   Summer

2. The four seasons.

   The fall months are Sept., Oct., Nov.
   The winter months are Dec., Jan., Feb.
   The spring months are Mar., Apr., May
   The summer months are Jun., Jul., Aug.

3. Or, through the year.

   A. The four seasons are

   _____

   _____

   _____

   _____

B. In the fall, people

_____

_____

C. In winter, people

_____

_____

D. In spring, people

_____

_____

E. In summer, people

_____

_____

Directions: Try to discover the author's details. Always try to connect these details to the major points that they explain or develop. In the paragraph below, discover the main idea, the three major types of programs, and the details related to them. Then, complete the outline.

There are three major kinds of programs offered in the junior college or the community college. *One kind* is the terminal program. Among the purposes of this program is to prepare students for a career or a job, to train students in particular skills, or to provide organized general education beyond high school. *Then* there is the college transfer program. This program provides the courses required for the first two years of college. It also helps to relieve the congestion and need for added facilities for the freshman and sophomore years at the four-year college. The *third kind* of program is the community service program. Two major purposes of this program are to provide community special-interest courses for adults and to train students in particular skills needed by local business or industry (Joffe 1972).

Main idea _____

_____

_____

I. _____

    A. _____

    B. _____

    C. _____

II. _____

    A. _____

    B. _____

III. _____

    A. _____

    B. _____

Directions: Working together, or with teacher guidance, students should be able to outline the following passage about the grasshopper and his life story.

THE GRASSHOPPER

Late in the fall the female grasshopper looks for a place to lay her eggs. She is most apt to choose a place where the ground is dry and hard, sometimes in paths or fence rows. This kind of place is not very likely to be too wet for the eggs that lie in the ground all winter. Many of the eggs are eaten by the young potato beetles but the beetles do not work so well in hard ground. Then the old grasshoppers live until cold weather, but since they have no home and do not store food for winter as the ants do, they freeze and die when the weather is cold.

Early in the spring, as soon as we have a few warm days, the young grasshoppers hatch from the eggs in the ground and crawl out of the hole where they have been all winter. The little grasshoppers are called nymphs. They look just like the old grasshopper except they do not have wings. They are very, very hungry and eat all the time. Their hind legs are very stout and they can jump very great distances. That is one way they can get away from their enemies. Since the nymphs eat so much, they grow very rapidly. They do not have bones as we do in our bodies, but their skin is a tough covering over their body. This is the only protection they have. This skin does not grow as the nymph inside does, so he soon eats himself out of it. The skin splits and he comes out of it altogether. He doesn't have any protection until he grows a new skin so he has to hide carefully from his enemies. Losing his skin is called a molt. Before he is full-grown, he molts five or six times.

The full-grown grasshopper is called an adult. Adults live until cold weather kills them. They have six legs all fastened to the middle part of their body, which is called the thorax. The other parts of the body are the head and the abdomen. The adult has four wings—two on each side, and he makes a noise by rubbing the one over the other. The thick skin over his body is called an exoskeleton. He has two large compound eyes and three single eyes giving him a very keen sense of sight. He breathes on the side of his body through spiracles. There are two antennae on his head that are his organs of smell.

The grasshopper has big jaws that help him devour more food. These insects come in swarms and often eat whole fields of grain. Many farmers in Iowa have lost much of their corn crops in different years because of the grasshoppers.

Recognition of Antecedents

One of the basic needs in understanding many English sentences is recognizing antecedents, or pronoun referents, in the sentence. Some examples are given below in which the reader is asked to write the noun on the space following the pronoun which is its referent:

1. The first day Jack worked at the plant, he wasn't sure about the right bus to ride home. He said to his foreman, "Can *you* tell *me* which bus will take me to the corner of Washington and Central?

   you refers to ——————; *me* refers to ——————.

2. All of the women in the reading class asked the teacher for *his* permission to have *their* bake sale during one of the class meetings.

   his refers to——————; *their* refers to——————.

3. The students *who* were in the protest march told *their* teachers that *they* had permission to be absent from class.

   who refers to ——————; *their* refers to ——————;

   they refers to ——————.

4. Mr. and Mrs. Morgan lived next door to the Smiths. When *they* moved to Alaska, they gave *them their* old, second car. *It* was a Ford that had already run over 100,000 miles.

   they refers to the ——————; *them* refers to the ——————;

   their refers to the ——————; *it* refers to the ——————.

Determining if the Sentence Tells How, Why, When, or Where

This is a useful exercise to insure that beginning readers are thinking of the meaning in the context as they read.

Directions: Decide whether the sentence explains *when, where, why, how,* or *who.* Then write the correct word in the blank space at the left.

1. I will go with you *after I get off work.* _____
2. After people get married, they should live *happily* ever after. _____
3. There was a terrible tornado *in Missouri.* _____
4. He will be at work from *four until midnight.* _____
5. He came home because *the library was closed.* _____
6. He found the newspaper *out in the street.* _____
7. They couldn't play ball *because it rained.* _____
8. He brought his lesson *to the teacher.* _____

Answering Riddles

This should be an enjoyable activity for a small part of the reading activity. Students may share these in small groups if they are sufficiently facile with reading; the teacher may use these as motivating exercises to encourage some students to practice reading more so that they may enjoy such riddles by themselves.

A few of the easy riddles that might be used are:

1. I am small and gray.
   I can gnaw ropes in two.
   My teeth are sharp.
   I like to eat cheese.
   I have a long tail.
   What am I?
   A mouse

2. I am blue during the day.
   I am black at night.
   I rhyme with fly.
   What am I?
   The sky

3. Many people march in me.
   They play music and carry signs.
   I rhyme with afraid.

   What am I?
   A parade

4. I am big.
   I travel through the air.
   I carry many passengers.
   I have jet engines.
   I can go very fast.
   What am I?
   An airplane

5. I am a part of your house.
   I have a knob to turn.
   I open and shut.
   You can lock me at night.
   I may have a small window.
   What am I?
   A door

There are some elementary books of jokes that may appeal to some of the students and they may be motivated to read them if introduced to them in such a way that they feel confident that they *can* read them.

Bruce, Dana, ed. *Tell Me a Riddle.* New York: Platt and Munk, Publishers, 1966.

Bruce, Dana, ed. *Tell Me a Joke.* New York: Platt and Munk, Publishers, 1966.

Cerf, Bennett. *Bennett Cerf's Book of Laughs.* New York: Beginner Books, A Division of Random House, 1959.

Gardner, Martin. *The Arrow Book of Brain Teasers.* New York: Scholastic Book Services, 1959.

McGovern, Ann, ed. *Summer Daze.* New York: Scholastic Book Services, 1961.

Rockowitz, Murray. *Arrow Book of Word Games.* New York: Scholastic Book Services, 1964.

Putting Things in Categories: Classifying

Classifying things in groups will serve beginning adult readers as a thinking exercise as well as a word recognition exercise.

Directions: Following are four categories. On the right side of the page is a list of nouns that fit into one or the other of these categories. Put the things in the proper categories.

1. Things that are round.
   a. _____
   b. _____
   c. _____
   d. _____
2. Parts of the face.
   a. _____
   b. _____
   c. _____

apple	floor	orange
ball	flower	roof
cheek	leaf	root
chin	marble	stem
door	mouth	wall
eyes	nose	window

     d. _____

     e. _____

3. Parts of a house.

     a. _____

     b. _____

     c. _____

     d. _____

     e. _____

4. Parts of a plant.

     a. _____

     b. _____

     c. _____

     d. _____

There are many categories that may be used, for example:

> Things sold in a grocery store.
> Things sold in a hardware store.
> Things to ride in on the water.
> Vegetables that grow underground.
> Furniture in our houses.
> Articles of clothing.

Understanding Function Words

In a monograph published by the International Reading Association, Jenkinson (1966) suggests that the understanding of *function* words be developed systematically because in context they may carry the burden of precise interpretation. She lists function words that suggest:

1. cause and effect—because, since, or so that
2. condition—if, unless, although
3. contrast—whereas, while
4. relationships—as, before, when, after, during, while
5. parallel ideas—however, therefore, nevertheless, hence, accordingly

Learning to Anticipate Meaning

The search for meaning, the process of making sense of the world, is central to development of language (F. Smith 1975, p. 176).

Reading is more than just decoding words. It is extracting meaning from the printed symbols on the page. Learning to use context and the redundancy of the language in extracting this meaning is an important skill.

Completing the Sentence Meaningfully

When the reader is thinking about the meaning of the sentence, he will be able to complete it if one or two words are omitted. In such sentence structures, when all the other words are in place, there is only one answer (or a very limited number of answers) that could be used in the blank spaces. Consider this exercise.

Directions: Read the following sentences and supply the missing word or words:

1. The glass was so fragile that it broke into a thousand _____ when she _____ it.
2. There was an accident at the sharp curve in the_____.
3. The tornado destroyed all the_____in the village.
4. The flashlight suddenly lighted the dark_____.
5. He was careful with his arithmetic because he wanted all his answers to be _____.
6. Mother sent Bob to the _____ to get a loaf of _____.
7. Bill wanted to play_____ that afternoon so he took his baseball glove to school with _____.
8. An illiterate person cannot _____ _____ _____.
9. She exclaimed, "Those pearls are not imitation, they are _____.
10. When people crowded around the accident, the police made the crowd _____.

Teachers should, of course, encourage students to think of multiple responses. For example, the response to number 4 will likely be *room* but it could also be *cave, tunnel,* or possibly *attic.*

The Cloze Procedure

Cloze is a procedure in which the reader attempts to anticipate meaning from the context so that he can accurately supply the deleted words from a message. In this procedure, every *nth* word is omitted after the topic sentence has given the idea of the passage. Redundancy in writing provides the reader many clues as to what is coming next. General language facility, breadth of vocabulary, native language aptitude, and motivation are factors in determining one's ability to grasp the total idea, even though every *nth* word has been left out. Research suggests that if the reader can supply 40 percent of the missing words in a passage that contains fifty deletions, this represents probable instructional level of reading. This technique as an evaluative device will be discussed in later chapters.

In a study of the use of the cloze procedure in adult basic education, Sherman and Klare (1970) found that cloze is generally useful and that learners enjoyed the procedure. As an instructional technique, the authors suggested a deletion rate of one word in nine or ten (every ninth or tenth word).

In professional literature is found many discussions and recommendations regarding the use of cloze procedures for instructional purposes (Bormuth 1969; Froese 1975; Ohnmacht 1974; Peterson and Carroll 1974; Ramanauskas 1972). Some researchers suggest the deletions of various parts of speech and some recommend various rates of deletions. But however done, it has proved to be a useful device to help people learn to use context clues and the redundancy of language in the improvement of comprehension. For example, in the passage below, every seventh word has been deleted.

IN A NUT SHELL

The hummingbird is a tiny bird. It is so light, it can——————— on a flower. No other bird———————so small. A hummingbird's nest would ———————into one side of a nut———————. It holds two eggs. The eggs ——————— as tiny as bees. Four baby ——————— ———————would fill a teaspoon. A hummingbird——————— beautiful, bright feathers. Its wings move———————fast, it can seem still in———————air. Like a helicopter, it can——————— straight up. It can fly straight———————. It can fly to the back, ———————the front, or to the side. ———————wings make humming sounds because they ———————so fast. That is how the ——————— got its name.[1]

Extending Vocabulary

It is one of the maxims of the civil law that definitions are hazardous (S. Johnson 1751, p. 193).

Comprehension skills develop in tandem with the extension of the reader's vocabulary. As with comprehension skills, vocabulary seldom grows with-

1. Copyright 1960, McGraw-Hill Book Company, Clarence R. Stone and Ardis Edwards Barton, *New Practice Readers, Book A*, page 32. Used with permission of Webster-McGraw-Hill.

out purposive attention. Adult learners need help in broadening word skills.

Multiple Meanings

The English language is saturated with words that are used in many different frames of reference. So many words in the English language have multiple meanings, or are sometimes called polysemantic, that adults learning to read must become adept at shifting from one meaning to another with each context. The connotation from one sentence to another may be a completely different frame of reference.

RUN

The dog can *run* much faster than his master.
Trains *run* between the cities every hour.
Vines *run* along the whole side of the house.
Does the water *run* all the year round in the creek?
Will the colors in the blouse *run* when it is washed?
The shelves will *run* around three sides of the room.
The wells *run* dry every summer when there is no rain.
You can almost see the thoughts *run* through his mind.
How do the stitches *run?*
Will the senator *run* for president?
She has a new *run* in her stocking.
We had a *run* of good luck with our garden this year.

In addition we talk about *in the long run, to run out of, to run through,* or *to get run over.*
Learners should be able to give numerous examples such as these.

CALL

Please *call* Jack back to the group.
Did you answer the telephone *call?*
What do you *call* your dog?

DOWN

Jack fell *down.*
I went *down*town.
Elevators go up and *down.*

Exercises such as the one below can be used as a study exercise for a small group or as a homework assignment to give emphasis to this facet of multiple meanings. In the exercise, the learner should match *a*, *b*, *c*, or *d* with the sentence numbered *1*, *2*, *3*, or *4*, in which the italicized words have the same meanings.

BLOCK

b 1. We had a *block* party last   a. The streets were *blocked* with
      night.   traffic.
c 2. They put the *blocks* away.   b. They live in the same *block*.
d 3. She walks twelve *blocks*   c. The big boys ruined the *blocks*.
      to school.
a 4. The roads were *blocked*   d. The grocery store is five *blocks*
      with snow.   away.

BOARD

b 1. Saw the *board* in half.   a. He serves on the *board* of health.
c 2. *Board* the ship at two   b. The *board* is four feet long.
      o'clock.   c. They were on *board* the train.
d 3. Mrs. Jones gives good
      board.   d. I must pay for my room and
a 4. The *board* of education   *board*.
      will discuss it.

BREAK

d 1. Mary will *break* my doll.   a. The doctor will *break* the news to
c 2. He never *breaks* his   the boy's parents.
      promise.   b. Did someone *break* into the store?
b 3. Did the thief *break* into   c. People who *break* the law are
      the house?   punished.
a 4. How will we *break* the   d. Plates *break* into many pieces if
      news to his mother?   you drop them.

Antonyms, Synonyms, Homonyms

Antonyms can be practiced by merely having oral exercises in which the student gives the opposite of the stimulus word.

before–after	halt–advance	deny–confess
bold–timid	capture–free	common–rare (uncommon)
remain–leave	smooth–rough	sunny–cloudy

Or the word opposites can be practiced in sentences in which the word omitted is the opposite of the *italicized* word:

1. *Many* of the boys left, but a <u>few</u> remained.
2. An elephant is *enormous,* but a mouse is <u>tiny</u>.
3. If you *begin* your work on time, you should <u>finish</u> on time.
4. When mother said, "Be sure to *remember*," Jack said, "I won't <u>forget</u>."
5. Each student listed both his *strengths* and his <u>weaknesses</u>.

Synonyms can also be practiced and students need to be required to make these responses. Sometimes, however, a synonym is appropriate only in its given context, so it is better to use words in sentences and then ask for words that can substitute for the stimulus (*italicized*) word.

1. It was *rich* food.   full of fat, or sugar
2. He has a *rich,* deep voice.   full, brilliant, very pleasing
3. He is *rich.*   wealthy, a land owner, has everything
4. She speaks with a sharp *tongue.* severe, critical manner
5. I like to eat *tongue.*   meat, the tongue of an animal, for food
6. He spoke in a strange *tongue.* language unknown to his listeners

Think of some synonyms for the italicized word in each sentence.

1. He has a *breezy,* enthusiastic   brisk, lively, jolly
   manner.
2. The experience was *foreign* to   strange, unusual, entirely new
   her.
3. My father walks at a fast *pace.* rate, gait, speed
4. Did you *seal* the letter?   close tightly, fasten, shut
5. It was a *tragic* accident.   sad, unfortunate, dreadful

Homonyms can be used in the same types of exercises. Oral lessons can quickly demonstrate whether the students can use both words in the pair of homonyms correctly. The words must be used in sentences in order to test the correct meaning.

steel—steal   main—mane   stairs—stares
through—threw   waist—waste   strait—straight
herd—heard   throne—thrown   seller—cellar

After learners demonstrate some facility in recognizing these words in pairs, they may enjoy reading exercises like this one, in which they must supply the missing word.

1. I *knew* that you would wear your <u>new</u> necktie.
2. John went to the doctor because his *heel* would not <u>heal</u>.
3. We cannot *see* the <u>sea</u> from our house.
4. I have *heard* that he has a large <u>herd</u> of cattle.
5. We praised *him* for singing the <u>hymn</u> so beautifully.
6. Tell us the *tale* about the monkey that lost his <u>tail</u>.
7. The boy said he *would* come to chop the <u>wood</u>.
8. Mary was *weak* in arithmetic so she studied it all <u>week</u>.
9. The building *site* was in plain <u>sight</u> from the top of the hill.
10. He had been in a *daze* for several <u>days</u>.

Analyzing Word Structures: Affixes

There are only a few most commonly used prefixes in the newspaper and magazine reading commonly done. Therefore, it will be helpful if adults who want to read independently know those common prefixes and suffixes that they will meet. In the case of prefixes, a word may begin with the prefix spelling but in that specific word it may not be serving as a prefix. So, it is necessary to understand the meaning of the word or check with a dictionary. In the word *disapprovingly*, there is a prefix, a root, and two suffixes.

By discussing the following examples, the group can decide that the prefix *dis,* according to the following root word, means *not, separation, negation, privation,* or *difference.* All of these words are almost sure to be in both the listening and speaking vocabularies of the adult learner.

disability	lack of fitness, e.g., physical
disable	to deprive of power or to incapacitate
disagree	to differ in opinion
disagreeable	unsatisfactory or not pleasing
disappear	to remove from sight
disbelieve	to think of as untrue
discontent	not satisfied
discourage	to lessen the courage of
dishonest	not honest
disrespect	to show lack of respect

Similarly, the group can conclude that the use of *less* as a suffix in the words *countless, needless, penniless, motionless, powerless, restless, effortless,* or *childless* means *without* or *unable to.*

Common Prefixes

PREFIX	MEANING	EXAMPLE
ab	from; not	abnormal
ad	to; near	adhere
com, col, con	together; with	collaborate; compact; congregate
de	down; from	depress; depart
in	in; not	invade; incomplete
pre	before	premature
re	back; again	retain; renovate
un	not	uncooked

Common Suffixes

SUFFIX	MEANING	EXAMPLE
ness	full of	goodness
less	without; unable	countless
full	full of or characterized by	bucketful; helpful
ly	in what way or manner	rapidly
hood	state of being	manhood
ment	result, process, or state of being	achievement, government, astonishment

A quick perusal of the front page of a morning newspaper showed that all of the following compound words appeared: *classrooms, hand-delivered, chairman, newspaper, firearm, high-speed, ditchbank, somebody, today, downtown, spokesman, something, Sunday, weekend, single-engine, aircraft, himself, afternoon, automobile.* Immediate word recognition is a primary need in fluent reading.

Dictionary Exercises

The dictionary tells you three things about a word:

1. How to divide it into syllables.
2. Which syllable to stress or accent.
3. Pronunciation by respelling.

Look up these words. Copy them in syllables and put in the accent. Copy the respelling to show the pronunciation.

WORDS	SYLLABLES AND ACCENT	RESPELLING WITH MARKS
1. separate	_____	_____
2. exclamation	_____	_____
3. refinement	_____	_____
4. understanding	_____	_____
5. appreciate	_____	_____

Selecting the best definition. Word study through the use of the dictionary: a sample lessson. Using your dictionary, write the meaning of the word *play* in each of the following sentences.

1. Children like to *play* during recess.
   Definition of play: Fun, sport, action to amuse oneself.
2. She will *play* the piano at noon today.
   Definition of play: Have fun; do something in sport; perform.
3. He will *play* a leading part in the game.
   Definition of play: To take part in.
4. The children gave a *play* at the end of the unit.
   Definition of play: A story acted on a stage.
5. John's dog will *play* tricks.
   Definition of play: Act.
6. We watched the sunlight *play* on the leaves.
   Definition of play: A light, quick movement.
7. Let's *play* that the big paper box is a boat.
   Definition of play: Make believe; pretend in fun.
8. Tom made the winning *play* in the checker game.
   Definition of play: A turn, act, or move in a game.
9. Don't *play* with your pencils.
   Definition of play: Act carelessly; do foolish things.
10. Our team will *play* the other class.
    Definition of play: Compete against.

Sample Vocabulary Lists from GED Textbooks

The adult basic education teacher must be ready to help any student who is motivated to think about challenging the GED examinations for an equivalency high school graduation certificate. Listed below in alphabetical order are selected words from four of the areas tested in the GED examinations. The teacher could plan a variety of kinds of discussion or

writing exercises based on these words. Pronunciation and use in sentences is the first necessary step; determining how many syllables in each
word; explaining or demonstrating the meaning of the concept each word
represents; or, perhaps writing short sentences from dictation in which
these words are used. Of course, teachers should not make use of such
lists as these until students have sufficient word recognition skills to decode them readily. Most adults will know their meaning if they have pronounced them correctly.

MATHEMATICS	SCIENCE	SOCIAL STUDIES	LITERATURE
addition	adult	agriculture	adventure
angles	appendix	archipelago	analyze
area	atmosphere	atlas	autobiography
astronomy	atom	barrier	biography
capacity	bacteria	campaign	caricature
circumference	biology	capital	character
compare	botany	capitol	classic
cubic	chemistry	cartoon	comedy
decimals	chrysalis	colony	comprehend
diameter	conductor	commonwealth	contemporary
dimension	cycle	culture	contradict
distance	dinosaur	delegate	criticize
division	ecology	democracy	description
equals	environment	discrimination	dialogue
equation	evaporation	domestic	drama
equivalent	examination	ecology	emotion
fractions	experiment	economic	enunciation
geometry	force	equator	essay
gram	fossil	federal	evaluate
hundredths	geology	frontier	fiction
isoceles	glacier	geography	hero
liter	gravity	immigrant	humor
mathematics	hypothesis	industrial	interpret
maximum	immature	industry	italics
measure	laboratory	international	linguistics
measurement	larva	latitude	literal
meter	magnetic	legislate	mood
minimum	mammal	longitude	motive
multiply	mineral	majority	mystery
obtuse	molecule	meridian	myth

MATHEMATICS	SCIENCE	SOCIAL STUDIES	LITERATURE
percent	orbit	municipal	novel
percentage	organic	national	paragraph
perimeter	physics	oppose	poetry
proportion	planet	patriot	preface
radius	pollute	poverty	prose
ratio	pollution	propaganda	publish
right	pressure	ratify	review
sphere	pupa	regional	rhyme
square	reproduction	secession	scan
subtotal	reptile	senate	scene
subtraction	revolution	sociology	stanza
surface	rotation	tariff	summary
tenths	satellite	United Nations	theme
total	telescope	urban	topic
triangle	thermometer	veto	verse
weight	vertebrate	welfare	vocabulary
	virus		wit

Readability

*What do adults read? The most common type of reading is the
reading of notices or signs in which about one out of every five persons
engage for an average of five minutes. Letters, memos or notes
are also popular at work as they are read by 16 percent for an average
of sixteen minutes. Among other frequently read items at work
are manuals or any written instructions that are read for an average
of seventeen minutes; forms (21 minutes); order forms, invoices,
or account statements (20 minutes); schedules or lists (7 minutes);
telephone or address books (13 minutes); reports, pamphlets, or articles
in publications (19 minutes); labels or writings on packages (6 minutes);
catalog, brochure, or printed advertising (9 minutes); specific
work-related materials (30 minutes); and legal documents (29 minutes)
(Smith and Fay 1973, p. 3).*

The concept of readability refers to the ease or difficulty with which the
reader can successfully utilize the written material. The readability of a
book refers to those elements within printed material to which the reader
must respond easily in order to interpret the expressed ideas of the writer.
Measuring readability informally is done by elementary teachers when
they explain to children this technique to use in the selection of a library
book.

If you read a full page of print, keep track of the number of words on the page you do not know. Use the fingers of one hand and count the little finger for the first difficult word, the next finger for the next, the third finger for the third, and the index finger for the fourth. If you get to your thumb before you get to the bottom of the page, the book is too hard. Put it back on the shelf and select an easier one.

Or, the teacher asks the person to read a short sample from the book aloud at sight (without preparation) and keeps a record to see that he does not miss more than five words in 100 running words. If he misses five or more words, or indicates that he has not understood the content, the book is too difficult and the person selects a different one.

Measuring readability formally is done by different methods, but generally includes some of these features: vocabulary, number of polysyllabic words, length of sentences, or sentence difficulty (Dale and Chall 1948).

The purpose of the readability formula, graph, or scale is to have the best predictor possible for matching suitability of the material with the functioning level of reading of the individual learner. The Fry Read-

The learner cannot be successful unless instructional materials are readable. (Courtesy of Albuquerque Technical-Vocational Institute, Albuquerque, N. M.)

ability Graph (1968) is an instrument that has the advantage of ease and facility of application with only a little mathematical calculation necessary. For that reason it is presented here as a means by which a teacher can quickly determine an approximate grade level of difficulty for any book he may wish to use. Only two tasks are necessary and they are explained in the directions that accompany the graph, which is found in appendix 10.

For most materials, the Fry Readability Graph is extremely reliable. However, sometimes because of the structure of the material being evaluated, the level yielded by the graph does not seem quite believable. Therefore, another method is needed to verify the results. For this purpose, other readability procedures are given. The Flesch Readability Formula (1948, 1951) is included in appendix 11, and Gunning's FOG Formula (1963) is included in appendix 12. Other procedures, such as the Dale-Chall Formula (1948) are useful although more complex.

Cloze procedures can also be used to assess readability. This process is discussed and illustrated as an evaluative technique in later chapters.

Remembering What You Read

One day after reading an assignment the average reader has 40 or 50 percent of what he had originally learned; two weeks later he has forgotten 80 percent of the material! This information helps to explain, but not solve . . . (N. B. Smith 1963, p. 364).

Teachers have a direct responsibility in guiding learners into setting up specific purposes or finding key ideas with which to associate the details in the reading matter as they read. For example, there is some key idea or thread of continuity that holds a chapter or a book together. The teacher needs to explain what this thread of continuity is when learners are ready to begin independent study at this level. Learners may need help to clearly differentiate between main ideas and some of the details in the reading. They need to understand the relationship to the main idea and the degree of importance of such details as dates, names, places, and definitions. If there are pictures, maps, diagrams, or charts, they were included because they relate to the written material. Adult learners must be encouraged to study these carefully before, during, and after reading the text.

All learners must be encouraged to utilize some method, such as the SQ3R (Survey, Question, Read, Recite, Review) as an approach to the reading of the text. Reading the summary at the end of the chapter first may be very helpful in finding out the organizational pattern of what the author has written. The path the reading is taking, the relationships of the parts to the whole, and the relationship of the details to the main ideas need to be within the grasp of the reader.

Mnemonic devices are helpful to many people when there are lists of things to remember, either as subordinate points or in categorizing. In music, many children have remembered the notes for the lines of the staff, *e, g, b, d, f,* by remembering the sentence "Every good *boy does fine.*" And for the spaces, the letters *f, a, c, e* spell the word *face.* In science class, if the learner must remember the names of the planets in order (of distance from the sun), the sentence, "Mary Virginia eats my jam sandwich until Ned protests," may help to associate *Mercury, Venus, Earth, Mars, Jupiter, Saturn, Uranus, Neptune* and *Pluto* in their proper sequence. Mnemonic devices are a valid way of remembering things for anyone who can use them effectively. It is doubtful that the mnemonic device for spelling *arithmetic,* "*A rat in the house might eat the ice cream,*" is any easier to remember than the correct spelling of the word *arithmetic.* However, if it is easier to remember, then it is a useful mnemonic device.

Teachers should be prepared, in making reading assignments, to give their adult learners direct suggestions or possible cues to help in remembering before the learner attempts to study his lesson or to read for enjoyment.

Summary

One study revealed that learners who surveyed an assignment before reading it read the material 24 percent faster than students who read without first surveying it (N. B. Smith, 1963, p. 364).

This chapter has contained a discussion of many of the skills needed in order to comprehend well when one reads. Illustrative exercises were provided to show ways in which specific skills might be practiced. Houle emphasizes the necessity of a well-planned time, place, and strategy in order to develop a regular pattern of learning.

Reading is the skill which supports all other methods of learning, enlarges the horizons of the mind, permits us to move freely across space and time to establish contact with those with whom we have a community of interest, and corrects the distorted or narrow views which we often get from first-hand observation and from other methods of learning (Houle 1964, p. 36).

13.
Integrating
Handwriting
Experience
with Reading
Instruction

*For Americans it is learn to read—
or be dependent on the welfare check!
Cook County, Illinois paid $8,000,000
monthly to functional illiterates
during the late 1960s. (Chapman 1965,
pp. 9, 13). Think what it must cost
today!*

Many adult educators stress the importance of developing reading and handwriting skills simultaneously (Bauer 1966; Buchanan 1967; Chapman 1965). For example, the initial lesson of *Getting Started* (Bauer 1966), as shown in figure 13.1, provides the opportunity for the learner to write his name, as well as to begin to read whole words. Some other programs (Hall 1967; Henney 1965; Wardhaugh 1969) also provide such experiences. The rationale for this is that one of the most satisfying experiences available to the illiterate adult is to learn to write his name. Such positive reinforcement may be the inducement for the insecure learner to attend the next class meeting.

If anyone is expected to learn to read very well, he will also need to learn fundamentals of writing the language he is trying to learn to read. In teaching children, teachers will teach a sizable basic sight vocabulary before they expect young learners to write and spell words. Certainly, spelling words in sentence writing can never get ahead of word identification abilities. At least, writing practice can never serve a useful purpose if one is trying to write words he cannot pronounce.

For the typical adult learner in basic education who must learn the habit of writing, learning how to hold a pencil or a pen, learning how to form the letters either in cursive or manuscript writing, as illustrated in figure 13.2, and spacing of letters into legible words is a difficult mechanical process, since he is most likely putting to work fine muscle coordination for the first time. His problems of writing the words he is learning are difficult for him, but the need to read a large number of words before he has a use for them in writing is *not* the same as it is for the child. He is ready to learn to write *service* words as soon as he recognizes them in print. And he can learn to use the basic sight vocabulary in writing as soon as he recognizes individual words while reading in print.

Writing skills in undereducated adults can be developed through two types of exercises—both of which will seem completely utilitarian to the student: (1) filling in forms, and (2) writing dictation exercises.

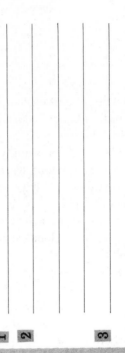

A B C D E F G H I J K L M N O P Q R S T U V W X Y Z

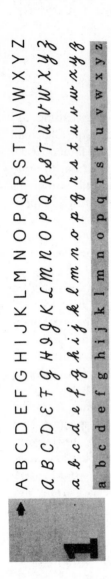

On the top of the page you see four ways of writing the letters of the alphabet. These are the letters that you will be learning to read and write. There are only twenty-six letters, and it will not take you long to learn them. Start by reading the large printing letters—the ones after the arrow. Say each letter right after I say it, and point at each letter as you do.

Look at your name where I have written it on the first line. Look at each letter of your name; then try to find each letter in the large and small writing alphabets. (**Note:** Explain which alphabets are meant.)

1 Trace your name by writing it on the tissue right over what I have written.

2 Now copy your name three times on the next three lines.

3 The first letter of each of your names begins with a large, or capital, letter. These capital letters are your initials. (**Note:** Explain what initials are.) On the next line, write your initials.

Figure 13.1. The initial lesson. (From *Communications I—Getting Started*, rev. ed. by Josephine Bauer. Copyright © 1965, © 1966 by Follett Publishing Company, a division of Follett Corporation. Used by permission.)

Handwriting experiences need to be built into the reading lessons. (Courtesy of Venice-Lincoln Technical Center, Venice, Illinois.)

Filling in Forms

Eighty-six million Americans cannot compute their car's gasoline mileage. An estimated 52 million can't determine if they qualify for a job listed in the classified ads, 48 million can't figure out how much change they should get back from a store purchase, and 39 million can't find their Social Security deduction on their paycheck stub. Those projections, based on results of a sample survey conducted for the U.S. Office of Education, may lead to a new and broader definition of functional illiteracy in the United States (Associated Press 1975, p. 2).

The most crucial need for writing by any adult is the giving of his signature and personal information when it is called for. Any teacher can use a very simple procedure for getting the class roll taken at the beginning of the class that will, at the same time, require each participant to write his name and some other bit of information he is learning to write. At first, perhaps each person will write only his name on a three-by-five-inch index card. Preferably the card should be prepared so that the word *Name* is situated under the line he is to fill in. This is the way it will appear on forms to be completed later. As soon as the adult is able to write his full name—first name, initial, and last name—the teacher should substitute other words as found in common forms under the line, so he will be

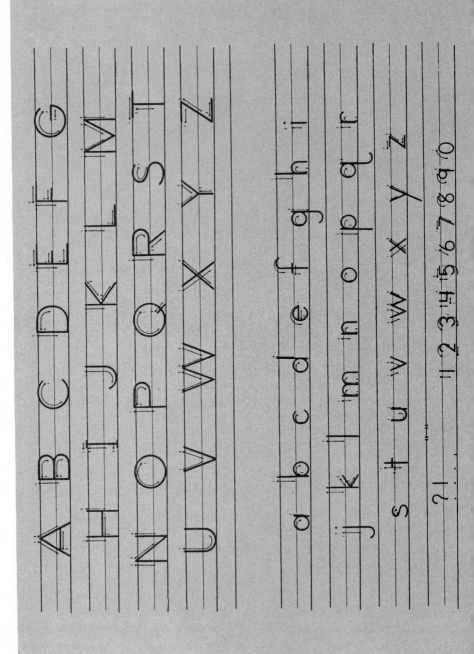

ABCDEFG
HIJKLM
NOPQRST
UVWXYZ

abcdefghi
jklmnopqr
stuvwxyz
1234567890
?.,:;!

184

Figure 13.2. Cursive and manuscript writing. (Copyright © 1975, Zaner-Bloser Inc., Columbus, Ohio. Used by permission.)

185

able to recognize any one of the several ways in which business forms request one to write his name. The progression would be similar to this.

Name

Name in full

Give your full legal name

Name   Last   First   Middle

Name (your usual signature)

As soon as adult learners have mastered the signing of their full names, and the recognition of various ways this information is requested, the teacher should add one additional requirement to the "signing-in" process as each old one is mastered. The second bit of information needed is the date. Then, the signing-in process is like this:

Date

Name in full

or like this:

The date today

Name: Last   First   Middle

When the date can be written legibly, the learner should be taught to write his address. If he writes it every day for six weeks, he will begin to habituate it. If, in a three-month class, each person learned to write legibly his full name, his street address, and the date for all the months of the year, he would have accomplished a great deal.

Beyond this, of course, he needs to be able to write additional information, such as the names of family members, telephone numbers, social security number, zip code, etc. It is important to remember that not all adults will move at the same rate of learning to perform these writing functions. Therefore, the teacher should set up a very flexible routine so that each one progresses as rapidly as he is able to the next step in the lists of skills to be mastered.

There are many kinds of forms in everyday life that each citizen must know how to read and to fill out. Working with various forms can be a good experience in both reading and writing. Most businesses are willing to furnish the adult basic education teacher with sample copies of job application forms. Banks will provide sample checks and other banking forms, such as loan applications that can be used in class instruction. The Social Security office likewise will furnish forms for instructional purposes. However, the most efficient way of providing learners with experience in using forms is through the utilization of some of the newer instructional material on the market, such as Scholastic's *Scope Visuals 13: Getting Applications Right* (1973). This material is furnished in the form of overhead transparencies and ditto masters. Another good workbook that can be a resource to the teacher is Learning Trends Company's *Forms in Your Future* (Goltry 1973). Still other material of this nature can be found in New Reader's Press *Be Informed Series* (1970), or their *Everyday Reading and Writing* (Laubach 1970). The two latter materials both go beyond just filling out forms to offer the adult experience with other things, such as writing letters, reading signs, using newspapers and magazines, using the telephone, etc. Examples of some of the kinds of forms that are most important to an adult's everyday needs are shown in figure 13.3, "A Social Security Form"; figure 13.4, "A Job Application Form"; figure 13.5, "A Mail Order Form"; figure 13.6, "An Application for a Driver's License"; and figure 13.7, "A Credit Application."

It must be emphasized that the instructional goal in using forms as a part of the adult basic education curriculum is not only for the development of writing skills, but also for the development of reading, following directions, critical thinking, and evaluation.

Learning to fill in forms correctly also presents opportunities for the extension of the learner's vocabulary. The vocabulary word may be introduced by writing it on the chalkboard. Then, the teacher may ask for volunteers to write some of the words on the board, or he may call on the more confident learners to do this. Vocabulary commonly associated with the filling out of application blanks and other forms will probably include:

family name	age	quantity
middle name	sex	signature
maiden name	occupation	description
print or type	signature	department
married	telephone number	deposit
single	health	bank references
widowed	height	credit references
divorced	weight	line of credit

2—SOCIAL SECURITY APPLICATION

SCOPE VISUALS—GETTING APPLICATIONS RIGHT

APPLICATION FOR A SOCIAL SECURITY NUMBER
(Or Replacement of Lost Card)
Information Furnished On This Form Is CONFIDENTIAL

See Instructions on Back.   Print in Black or Dark Blue Ink or Use Typewriter.

———— DO NOT WRITE IN THE ABOVE SPACE ————

1 Print FULL NAME YOU WILL USE IN WORK OR BUSINESS   (First Name)   (Middle Name or Initial – if none, draw line ___)   (Last Name)

2 Print FULL NAME GIVEN YOU AT BIRTH

6 YOUR DATE OF BIRTH   (Month) (Day) (Year)

3 PLACE OF BIRTH   (City)   (County if known)   (State)

7 YOUR PRESENT AGE (Age on last birthday)

4 MOTHER'S FULL NAME AT HER BIRTH (Her maiden name)

8 YOUR SEX   MALE   FEMALE

5 FATHER'S FULL NAME (Regardless of whether living or dead)

9 YOUR COLOR OR RACE   WHITE   NEGRO   OTHER

10 HAVE YOU EVER BEFORE APPLIED FOR OR HAD A SOCIAL SECURITY, RAILROAD, OR TAX ACCOUNT NUMBER?   NO   DON'T KNOW   YES   (If "YES" Print STATE in which you applied and DATE you applied and SOCIAL SECURITY NUMBER if known)

11 YOUR MAILING ADDRESS   (Number and Street, Apt. No., P.O. Box, or Rural Route)   (City)   (State)   (Zip Code)

12 TODAY'S DATE   **13** TELEPHONE NUMBER   **14** Sign YOUR NAME HERE (Do Not Print)

TREASURY DEPARTMENT Internal Revenue Service   Return completed application to nearest SOCIAL SECURITY ADMINISTRATION OFFICE
FORM SS-5 (7-69)   **HAVE YOU COMPLETED ALL 14 ITEMS?**

INSTRUCTIONS

One Number Is All You Ever Need For Social Security And Tax Purposes
Special Attention Should Be Given To Items Listed Below

Fill in this form completely and correctly. If any information is not known and is unavailable, write "unknown." Use typewriter or print legibly in dark ink.

1 Your social security card will be typed with the name you show in item 1. However, if you want to use the name shown in item 2, attach a signed request to this form.

3 If not born in the USA, enter the name of the country in which you were born.

5 If a stepfather, adopting father, or foster father is shown, include the relationship after name; for example, "John H. Jones, stepfather."

10 If you have ever before filled out an application like this for a social security, railroad, or tax number, check "yes" even if you never received your card. If you check "yes," give the name of the State and the approximate date on which you applied. Also enter your social security number if you did receive the card and remember the number. You may find your number on an old tax return, payroll slip, or wage statement.

11 If you get your mail in the country, without a street address, show your R.D. Route, and Box number; if at the post office, show your P.O. Box No.; if there is no such way of showing your mail address, show the town or post office name. If mail under your name is not normally received at the address which you show, use an "in care of" address.

14 Sign your name as usually written. Do not print unless this is your usual signature. (If unable to write, make a mark witnessed by two persons who can write. The witnesses preferably should be persons who work with the applicant and both must sign this application. A parent, guardian, or custodian who completes this form on behalf of another person should sign his own name followed by his title or relationship to the applicant; for example, "John Smith, father.")

✷ GPO : 1969 OF—356-795

FOR DISTRICT OFFICE USE

FOR BUREAU OF DATA PROCESSING AND ACCOUNTS USE

Figure 13.3. A Social Security Form. (From *Scope Visuals 13: Getting Applications Right* by Jeri Schapiro. Copyright © 1973 by Scholastic Magazines, Inc. Used by permission.)

JOB APPLICATION

POSITION APPLIED FOR				DATE	

NAME IN FULL — MR. MRS. MISS	LAST	FIRST	MIDDLE	MAIDEN NAME	SOC. SEC. NO.

NUMBER AND STREET	CITY	STATE	ZIP	TELEPHONE NO.

MARITAL STATUS ☐ SINGLE ☐ MARRIED ☐ SEPARATED ☐ WIDOWED ☐ DIVORCED	DATE OF BIRTH — MO. DAY YR.	PLACE OF BIRTH

IN CASE OF EMERGENCY NOTIFY	NAME	RELATIONSHIP
	ADDRESS	TELEPHONE NO.

HEIGHT	WEIGHT	WEAR GLASSES ☐ YES ☐ NO	HANDED ☐ LEFT ☐ RIGHT	ANY PHYSICAL DEFECTS ☐ YES ☐ NO	EXPLAIN

EDUCATION

TYPE OF SCHOOL	NAME AND ADDRESS	YRS. ATTENDED	YEAR LEFT	GRADUATED	COURSE OR MAJOR
GRAMMAR OR GRADE					
HIGH SCHOOL					
COLLEGE					
BUSINESS OR TRADE					

MILITARY EXPERIENCE

BRANCH OF SERVICE	DISCHARGE DATE AND RANK	DRAFT CLASSIFICATION	TYPE OF DISCHARGE

SKILLS

WHAT KIND OF WORK CAN YOU DO	TYPING SPEED
WHAT MACHINES CAN YOU OPERATE	SHORTHAND SPEED

PRIOR WORK HISTORY

LIST IN ORDER, LAST OR PRESENT EMPLOYER FIRST — MAY WE CALL YOUR PRESENT EMPLOYER ☐ YES ☐ NO

DATES FROM TO	EMPLOYER	RATE OF PAY START FINISH	JOB TITLE AND SUPERVISOR'S NAME	REASON FOR LEAVING
	NAME			
	ADDRESS			
	NAME			
	ADDRESS			

REFERENCES (Other than Relatives or Former Employers)

	NAME	ADDRESS	OCCUPATION
1.			
2.			

IT IS AGREED AND UNDERSTOOD THAT ANY FALSE STATEMENTS ON THIS APPLICATION MAY BE CONSIDERED SUFFICIENT CAUSE FOR DISMISSAL, WHEN DISCOVERED.   SIGNATURE_____

Figure 13.4. A job application form. (From *Scope Visuals 13: Getting Applications Right* by Jeri Schapiro. Copyright © 1973 by Scholastic Magazines, Inc. Used by permission.)

This is the order form.

SEARS, ROEBUCK AND CO.

| ADJ | 155 | A/8 | SPEC. | 2/N | C/A |

Sears

Date_____196__

PLEASE BE SURE TO INCLUDE
ZIP CODE IN YOUR ADDRESS

————————SATISFACTION GUARANTEED OR YOUR MONEY BACK————————

PLEASE DO NOT WRITE IN SPACE BELOW

FIGS
C? 0

Order No. — Date — Batch No. — Type of Sale — No. of Tickets

NAME;
ADDRESS;
CITY ZONE;   Total for Goods   Route Code
STATE—

R FIGS
K K1   Tax Code

FIGS
ACCOUNT NUMBER   G;   Cash Received   R   K

PLEASE PRINT PLAINLY ONE LETTER IN EACH BLOCK
All members of the same household should order under one name

NAME

Mailing Address

Additional Address

Post Office   State

ZIP CODE   Area Code   Tel. No.

PLEASE GIVE COMPLETE DELIVERY INFORMATION
Be sure to give complete mailing address at the right, filling in the correct information on the lines provided. ON FREIGHT ORDERS, IF YOU DO NOT HAVE A STREET ADDRESS, additional information is needed for delivery by truck. The name and/or number of the road or highway, landmarks such as a church, gas station, fire house or bridge are important guides.

PLEASE DO NOT WRITE IN SPACE BELOW

IF YOU WISH THIS ORDER SHIPPED TO ANOTHER ADDRESS THAN YOUR OWN please give complete directions on the lines below:
NAME

Mailing Address

Additional Address

Post Office   State   ZIP CODE

IF YOUR ADDRESS HAS CHANGED since last order, give old address here:
Mailing Address

Post Office   State   ZIP CODE

ALWAYS STATE COLOR OR PATTERN CHOICE BY NUMBER WHERE REQUIRED

CATALOG NUMBER	HOW MANY	COLOR NO. Pattern, Finish, Etc.	SIZE Measure to be sure	NAME OF ITEM	PRICE Ex. Yd. Pr., Etc.	TOTAL PRICE Dollars	Cents	SHPG. WT. Lbs.	Oz.
								R K	
								R K	
								R K	
								R K	
								R K	
								R K	
								R K	
								R K	
								R K	
								R K	

HOW SHALL WE SHIP?
(mark X in proper square)

☐ PARCEL POST (Mailable Items Only)
☐ PACKAGE DELIVERY SERVICE

In Metropolitan areas, merchandise can be delivered by fast package delivery service at higher cost.

☐ FREIGHT (Truck or Rail Where Available)
☐ RAILWAY EXPRESS

IF THIS IS AN EASY PAYMENT or MODERNIZING CREDIT ORDER, CHECK HERE ☐

IF A REVOLVING CHARGE ACCOUNT, CHECK HERE ☐

MY ACCOUNT NUMBER IS_____
RECHECK Have you given all information such as size, color, pattern, finish, etc.

ADD TAX for orders delivered to:
CONNECTICUT......................3½%
(No tax on meals or clothing for children under 16 years)
DISTRICT OF COLUMBIA................3%
MARYLAND..........................3%
NEW JERSEY (Good tax on exempt clothing).....3%
NEW YORK STATE*....................2%
*If your city or county in New York has a tax, include the additional tax required.
OHIO..............................4%
PENNSYLVANIA......................6%
(Don't tax on food, clothing, except swim wear, formal wear, furs and clothing designed primarily for sport activities)
VIRGINIA..........................3%
WEST VIRGINIA.....................3%
Tax rates based on information available at printing and subject to change

At which Sears Store?_____

and fill-in and sign the top form on other side.
Do not send identification card or plate.

TOTAL FOR GOODS

← AMOUNT FOR TAX

If credit order, we will figure and bill this is for you   POSTAGE

Amount I owe Sears on previous order

TOTAL CASH PRICE

AMOUNT ENCLOSED
Sears Checks
Money Order or Check

	Total Pounds	Total Ounces
Total Weight in Pounds	
Enter Parcel Post Zone No.	

P

(Pa.) (Conn.)

Sears 561

Figure 13.5. A mail order form. (Used by permission of Sears, Roebuck & Company.)

1 Puff sleeve knit Top. Pretty pullover with banded sleeve edge. Two solid colors and one print to choose from. Round collar and casual three button placket front. Polyester and cotton. Machine wash, warm.

Girls' sizes S(7–8) M(10–12); L(14). State size letter S, M or L, *not number size.* See Chart 1, page 373.
77 A 7318F—Multicolor flowers. Shpg. wt. 6 oz. . .$5.99
77 A 7317F—Red   77 A 7316F—Gold
Shipping weight 6 ounces 5.49

(2 and 3) Denim Overalls. Large bib pocket and two front patch pockets. High back. Step-in style with adjustable straps and side buttons. Reinforced triple needle seams and flare legs. Railroad stripe and navy fabric is blended of polyester and cotton. Machine wash at warm temperature.

Girls' sizes 7, 8, 10, 12, 14. Avoid disappointment, *state correct size.* See Chart 2 on page 373.
(2)   77A4518F—Navy solid
(3)   77A4517F—Navy, white stripe
Shipping weight 1 pound 2 ounces $8.99

4 Embroidered trim Overall. Old-time auto decorates pocket on bib front. Adjustable buttons on straps. Zip and button closing in back. Navy woven fabric of polyester and cotton. Machine wash at warm.

Girls' sizes 7, 8, 10, 12, 14. Avoid disappointment, *order correct size.* See Chart 2 on page 373.
77 A 4532F—Shpg. wt. 14 oz. $9.99

5 Short sleeve knit Top. Choose from three solid colors. Styled with pointed collar. Sporty detail includes three button placket front.
Polyester and cotton. Machine washable at warm temperature.

Girls' sizes S(7–8); M(10–12); L(14). State size letter S, M or L, *not number size.* See Chart 1 on page 373.
77 A 7460F—White
77 A 7461F—Navy
77 A 7462F—Red
Shipping weight 6 ounces $3.99

6 Patchwork print Overall. Red, white and blue woven fabric of polyester and cotton. Front bib. Adjustable shoulder straps with white button closures.
Zipper at back waist. Machine washable at warm temperature.

Girls' sizes 7, 8, 10, 12, 14. Avoid disappointment, *order your correct size.* Measure to be sure. See Chart 2 on page 373.
77 A 4577F—Shipping wt. 15 oz. $8.99

Just call Sears and say "Charge it". . see page 532

4–DRIVER'S LICENSE APPLICATION

Department of Motor Vehicles REQUEST FOR ORIGINAL DRIVER LICENSE	Write Below This Line	Pending Number

1. Check Type Desired
☐ Jr. Oper.
☐ Oper.

Chauffeur
☐ Class 1 ☐ Class 3
☐ Class 2 ☐ Unclass.

Restriction
☐ Birth Certificate   Check   M.O.
☐ Baptismal Cert.
☐ Passport
☐ Other Proof.............................

Learner's Permit N

2. PRINT Full Name	First	Middle	Last

3. Mailing Address	Street & No.	City or P.O.	County	State

4. Legal Address	Street & No.	City or P.O.	County	State

5. Date of Birth   6. Sex   7. Weight   8. Height   9. Color of Eyes

Mo.   Day   Year   ☐ Male ☐ Female   Lbs.   Ft.   In.

Examined by .... date ....

	Yes	No
10. If you answer "Yes" to any part of Question 10, fill out and attach form MV-22. (a) Have you ever had a convulsive disorder, epilepsy, fainting or dizzy spells, or any condition which caused unconsciousness?		
(b) Have you ever had a heart ailment?		
(c) Do you have any physical disability? Have you suffered the loss of, or the loss of the use of, a leg, hand, foot or eye?		
(d) Have you had any mental illness for which you have been confined to any hospital or institution?		
11. Is it necessary for you to wear glasses or contact lenses while driving a motor vehicle?		
12. Have you ever been found guilty of ANY crime, offense or traffic infraction (except parking violations), or forfeited bail in any court either in this state or elsewhere?		

If yes, list all convictions and forfeitures of bail below (If additional space required, fill out and attach form MV-22):

Date	Crime, Infraction, Offense	Court and Location

13. Do you have a valid current Driver License? If yes, give state and license number. _____		
14. Have you ever had a learner's permit or a license to operate a motor vehicle refused, suspended or revoked, cancelled or an application for a Driver license denied, in this state or elsewhere? If you have answered "Yes" give reasons. If accident was involved, give date and place:		

Where do you desire your road test examination? _____

Signature of Applicant _____

Figure 13.6. An application for a driver's license. (From *Scope Visuals 13: Getting Applications Right* by Jeri Schapiro. Copyright © 1973 by Scholastic Magazines, Inc. Used by permission.)

CREDIT APPLICATION

MISS ☐ MRS. ☐ MR. ☐	FIRST NAME	INITIAL	LAST NAME	Husband's or Wife's Name	Widow ☐ Divorced ☐ Separated ☐
	PRESENT ADDRESS				HOW LONG
	CITY		STATE	ZIP CODE	PHONE NUMBER
FORMER ADDRESS					AGE

NUMBER OF DEPENDENTS INCLUDE SELF AS ONE	RESIDENCE (CHECK ONE) OWN ☐ RENT ☐ ROOM☐ LIVE WITH PARENTS ☐

E M P L O Y M E N T	HUSBAND OR SINGLE PERSON	EMPLOYED BY	POSITION & BADGE NO.	SALARY
		ADDRESS	BUSINESS PHONE	HOW LONG
	WIFE	EMPLOYED BY	POSITION & BADGE NO.	SALARY
		ADDRESS	BUSINESS PHONE	HOW LONG
	FORMER EMPLOYER SELF ☐ SPOUSE ☐		POSITION	HOW LONG

BANK	BRANCH OR ADDRESS	Savings ☐ Reg. Check ☐ Spec. Check ☐

PLEASE LIST FIRMS THAT HAVE GIVEN YOU CREDIT

FIRM NAME	ADDRESS	Account Number
1		
2		

PERSONAL REFERENCE	ADDRESS	PHONE NUMBER

AUTHORIZED BUYER	RELATIONSHIP	YOUR SOCIAL SECURITY NUMBER

RETAIL INSTALLMENT CREDIT AGREEMENT

I may, within 25 days of the closing date appearing on the periodic statement of my account, pay in full the "new balance" appearing on said statement and thereby avoid a FINANCE CHARGE; or, if I so choose, I may pay my account in monthly installments in accordance with the schedule below. If I avail myself of the latter option, I will incur and pay a FINANCE CHARGE computed at a periodic rate of 1½% per month (an ANNUAL PERCENTAGE RATE of 18%) on that portion of the previous balance which does not exceed $500.00 (subject to a minimum charge of 50¢) and 1% per month (an ANNUAL PERCENTAGE RATE of 12%) on that portion of said balance which exceeds $500.00. For convenience, however, there will be no FINANCE CHARGE on balances of $5.00 or less. The FINANCE CHARGE will be computed on the previous balance without deducting any payments or other credits and without adding current purchases.

Notice to the buyer: 1. Do not sign this credit agreement before you read it or if it contains any blank space. 2. You are entitled to a completely filled in copy of this credit agreement at the time you sign it. 3. You may at any time pay your total indebtedness hereunder. 4. Keep this agreement to protect your legal rights.

PAYMENT SCHEDULE	If Indebtedness is	$ .01 to 10.00	$10.01 to 60.00	$60.01 to 90.00	$ 90.01 to 120.00	$120.01 to 180.00	$180.01 to 240.00	Over $240.00
	Monthly Payment is	Full Balance	$10.00	$15.00	$20.00	$30.00	$40.00	1/5 of Balance

APPROVED BY:_____ BUYER'S SIGNATURE:_____

Figure 13.7. A credit application. (From *Scope Visuals 13: Getting Applications Right* by Jeri Schapiro. Copyright © 1973 by Scholastic Magazines, Inc. Used by permission.)

separated	salary	dependents
list employers	special skills	loans
work experience	application	debts
educational history	application blank	mortgage holder
supply information	position	installment
previous employment	fill out	real estate
describe briefly	names of schools	lien holder
describe fully	circle grade completed	checking account
reason for leaving	elementary school	savings account
location of company	junior high school	M. O. (money order)
out-of-town	vocational school	proof of age
night shift	length of time	apartment number
job and duties	regular line of work	spouse
dates: from___to___	employment references	C.O.D.
mailing address	personal references	military experience
permanent address	character references	agreement
temporary address	defects or disabilities	security
marital status	Social Security Number	Pay to the order of

Thus, from the beginning, writing practice and vocabulary expansion can be directed toward the vocational needs of the adult learner.

Writing Dictation Exercises

The woman looks warily around the Post Office for a face she can trust, an individual who will not demean her. She needs to find someone to write an address on her package for her. The young man slumps against the booth in the diner, intently studying the bill of fare. But he orders a hamburger, as usual, because he can't decode the words on the menu. These people are illiterates, two of an increasing minority of American adults who cannot read (Weber 1971, p. 27).

Adults in basic education classes need to master a controlled vocabulary of sight words. Teachers can rely heavily on the 220 service words in the Dolch *Basic Sight Word List* (1952) and the 95 commonest nouns identified by Dolch. Any words used in daily lessons in working with an adult should of course be given priority in preparing writing lessons. The words utilized should have high utilitarian value. A writing lesson might be structured as follows:

My name is_____.
His name is John.

Her name is Mary.
His first name is John.
His last name is Jones.
Her first name is Mary.
Her last name is Jones.

If the new words in the lesson are *can* and *work*, perhaps the adult learner can write:

He can come to my house.
I work at my house.
He can work at my house.
He can come to my house to work.

The best lessons will grow out of discussions with the learners. If it is the season to dig potatoes, then the men might both read and learn to write a sentence such as the following:

We worked in the potatoes today.
We dug potatoes all day.
We worked very hard.

Workbooks offer much material from which the teacher can develop dictation practice and reinforcement experiences and vocabulary skills. (Courtesy of William Rainey Harper College, Palatine, Illinois.)

The following sentences were composed using only the words in the first 500 of the *Gates Primary Word List* (1947). Most of the words on the *Dolch List* are included on this list with the addition of many nouns. These sentences will serve only to illustrate that good sentences can be formulated and dictated for learners who know only a few sight words. The more "local" vocabulary that can be injected into the sentences, the greater the interest that may be generated among some of the learners.

1. I can do the work for you.
2. He can do the work for us.
3. I will do it if you will help me.
4. Is it time for me to go home now?
5. He and I are going to go at six o'clock.
6. All work and no play is no fun.
7. They are very happy at their work.
8. Monday is the first school day of the week.
9. Write a letter to your mother on Sunday.
10. Be sure to call me if you cannot come.
11. I want to go fishing with my father.
12. His car is on the left side of the road.
13. He did not tell me who did it.
14. My father will help you build your house.
15. The bird in the tree in the yard was singing.
16. She will wash the dish and put it away.
17. I will do my best to help him with his work.
18. You may begin with the little one on your right.
19. My car is the little one on the left.
20. His car is the big one on the right side of the road.
21. He left the door wide open.
22. You are one of my very best friends.
23. The family went to the park to eat their lunch.
24. He carried his lunch in a brown paper sack.
25. I am going to eat apple pie for dinner.

After a sufficient vocabulary of words has been mastered, one can scramble the words of a sentence and let the learners sort out the meaning. *Linguistic Blocks Series, The First Rolling Reader* (1963), may provide the adult educator with ideas of how to develop such basic experiences for adult learners. This kind of assistance is particularly helpful for learners for whom English is a second language. Here is an example of a sentence scrambled in such a manner:

Scrambled: big, went, yesterday, to, sister, baseball, the, game, my
Unscrambled: My big sister went to the baseball game yesterday.

Further development of oral language is encouraged by asking a series of related questions and then requesting learners to respond in an oral paragraph. Only those with a sophisticated knowledge of reading and spelling can compose the writing paragraph. An example of such an exercise is the following:

TEACHER: Where and when were you born? How many brothers and sisters did you have? When did you start to school? When did you come to the United States? What have you been doing since you came here? What are you going to do after you learn English?

LEARNER: I was born in Guatemala in 1940. I have three brothers and two sisters. I started school in 1947. I came to the United States last year. I have been working at the cannery since I came here. After I learn English I am going to work in a factory.

Another opportunity for writing that can be followed naturally after any of the oral activities of the class are describing an object in the room, writing conversations for pictures or comic strips with empty balloons, finishing incomplete stories or dialogues, or experience stories. Care must be taken to make certain that any teacher-written stories furnish an adequate model of *good* cursive or manuscript for the learner to emulate.

Some adults are motivated to attend adult basic education classes in order to learn to write letters to family members in distant places. Therefore, as writing skills are developed by exercises such as those above, they should as quickly as possible be applied to practical situations, such as letterwriting.

Summary

Banks (1965) reported the variety of abilities in reading in adult basic education classes as varying all the way from the learner who had tried to study "on his own" and could perform at high school level, to many who possessed primary-grade reading ability to the one who entered the classroom and proudly said, "Ma'am, I can't read, but I can call off all the letters on this page."

Adult learners must develop writing skills as the reading skills are being taught. They can begin writing exercises utilizing reading vocabulary as rapidly as sight words are mastered. Personal data—spelling one's name, address, and names of one's immediate family, learning one's social security number, telephone number, and zip code number—should seem most immediate to the learner's needs.

Stress should be laid in learning how to correctly fill in forms. Vocabulary can be expanded utilizing the words commonly found in all kinds of forms that are pertinent to the adult's everyday personal life as well as to his vocational needs. Then, writing easy sentences containing the service words from dictation should review, reinforce, and habituate the commonest words in beginning reading materials.

14.
Teaching Reading to Adults from Non-English-Speaking or Nonstandard Dialect Origins

Few teachers realize that all of us speak dialects. Many teachers assume that dialect is bad, that the word dialect *refers only to the speech of someone who is in a minority position and is in a class considered low. Teachers should realize that all of us speak a particular dialect; that some dialects are prestige dialects and some are not (Seymour 1972, p. 49).*

There are many problems encountered when the adult learner who is beginning reading arrives with a nonstandard dialect of the teacher's Standard English, when he arrives with a very limited knowledge of English because it is not his native language, or when he comes to the school with a set of cultural values that are not the same as, or even similar to, those of the teacher who wishes to help him learn to read. Some of these problems are mentioned in the chapters discussing the areas of socio-psychological values, life-styles, and beliefs of the individuals, and the economic differences that exist between the teacher and many of the students who may enroll in his classes. Some of the specific understandings necessary in cultural awareness in the "normal" usage of nonstandard English as a means of communication, and in the techniques of teaching English either as a second language or as a second dialect will be discussed.

Cultural Awareness

Teachers should . . . realize that by teaching people the standard dialect they're teaching them something they need to know, but not something that is intrinsically better than what they already know (Seymour 1972, p. 48).

The teacher who extends his services in adult basic education must ask himself frankly and honestly how "open," how "accepting," and how "culturally pluralistic" he can be in his perspectives. Basically, teachers, like all other people, are ethnocentric. We carry within us a high degree of feeling that our own culture is the best and the most significant and that our ways of behaving are the "right" ones. Habits and values learned in early childhood last a lifetime. Seymour Fersh (1968) expressed it this way.

From the moment of birth, the infant in all cultures is encouraged to be ethnocentric—to believe that his homeland, his people, his language, his everything is not only different but is superior to those of other people. The elders (by demonstration and remonstration) teach that the ways in which *we* do things are the "natural ways," "the proper ways," and "the moral ways." In other places, they—"barbarians," "infidels," "foreigners,"—follow a "strange" and "immoral" way of life. "Ours is *the* culture; theirs is *a* culture (p. 132)."

In the Chinese language, the words for the name of their country means "middle kingdom," not some vague faraway place we call the *far east.* The Navajo people call themselves *Dineh, the* people—not insignificant Indians on an isolated reservation, but "*the* people."

Fersh (1968) asks teachers to think critically about values learners will learn if they encounter experiences like these.

> Why . . . should a photograph in an American textbook which shows an Indian woman and her children have a caption which reads, "even though they live in mud huts, Indian parents love their children"? What is a teacher implying when, in her introductory remark to students, she says, "although the people of Asia and Africa are backward, there is no reason for us to feel superior (p. 128)"?

It is neither necessary nor possible for a person to stop being to some degree ethnocentric. One cannot be expected to deny his strongest loyalty to those people and experiences through which he was inducted into his culture. However, one's awareness of his own ethnocentricity should enable him to understand the differences and make contrasts and comparisons in a logical frame of reference. Fersh (1968) wrote:

> Ignorance about others perpetuates ignorance about one's self because it is only by comparison that one can discover personal differences and similarities. The "glass" through which other cultures are viewed serves not only as a window; it serves also as a mirror in which each can see a reflection of his own way of life (p. 134).

Adult learners need to be made aware that anthropologically one culture is *not* "better than" or "superior to" another, nor has it any greater claim to ultimate truths. Teachers need to guard against the use of such words as *underprivileged, backward,* or *inferior* when used in patronizing or demeaning ways.

> As Pogo once said, "We have met the enemy—and he is us." We Americans do so much that is fine and good both here and abroad that we tend to think we have no flaws, when in truth our Achilles heel in international relations is our tendency to be basically proud, provincial and unprepared for cultural shock. We do not really appreciate fully our own subcultures, let alone understand the rest of the world and its awesome problems. To a degree we are still insular, as if that were necessary to our mental health (p. 126).

A Chinese graduate student in this country, writing in *Quinto Lingo,* records anecdotes that illustrate clearly how severe a barrier the language differences can be:

We students have problems when we begin to learn English. The results, more often than not, are ludicrous. Perhaps the following letter will give some idea of how we Chinese students, in our peculiar way, do violence to, and are done violence by, the English language. It was written by a Chinese boy as a birthday tribute to his English teacher, an attractive American lady:

"Dear teacher: To express my gratitude for the excellent English you have taught me, I wish to take this opportunity to celebrate your honorable birthday. I send you these roses.

The roses are beautiful, but you are more beautiful. The beauty of the roses will soon pass away, but your beauty is perpetual.

The roses are fragrant, but you are more fragrant. The smell of the roses will soon be gone, but you will smell forever (Rodale 1969, p. 2)."

Kaulfers (1954) illustrates clearly how language is an integral part of a people's culture. Language is the means by which thoughts and feelings are expressed; language guides our thinking about social problems and processes. Kaulfers says:

How translation can defeat its own ends if words are merely transverbalized without regard for their pleasant or unpleasant associations is illustrated by the difficulties missionaries have sometimes in trying to convert remote populations to Christianity. Most Eskimos, for example, eat no bread. Few like it because it has no taste or smell. Consequently, early missionaries found it difficult to explain the phrase, "Give us this day our daily bread." To win the natives, they had to substitute walrus, polar bear, and deer. This illustration is but one of many that could be cited to show how an expert command of a second language always requires a thorough understanding of the attitudes, likes, dislikes, customs, and standards of values of the people (p. 82).

Young (1972) explains from his depth of understanding of how the Navajo uses language, some of the conflict teachers will face in their "usual" use of English.

The concept of coercion, in the sense of imposing one's will on another person or animate being without physical contact or force, is part of the Anglo-American cultural heritage, and the English language is replete with terms expressing various aspects of the concept—cause, force, oblige, make, compel, order, command, constrain, must, have to, ought to, shall, come quickly to mind. They are part of the heritage of a culture with a long history of kings, emperors, dictators, deities, governments, and family patriarchs whose authority to impose their will on others has been long accepted as part of the worldview of the communities participating in the system. So deeply engrained is this area of habitual acceptance of the compelling, coercive need to do certain things that we are astonished and annoyed by the lack of concern in the same area on the part of people like the Navajo, as reflected by the paucity of terms in the language of the latter corresponding to those listed above.

Navajo culture does not have a heritage of coercive religions, political or patriarchal family figures and in the Navajo scheme of things one does not usually impose his will on another animate being to the same extent, and in the same ways as one does from the English point of view. "I *made* my wife sing" becomes, in Navajo, simply "even though my wife did not want to do so, she sang when I told her to sing. . . ." From the Navajo point of view, one can compel his children to go to school in the sense that he drives them there; or he can *place* them in school, but none of these terms reflect the imposition of one's will independently of physical force—the children do not comply with a mandate. They are animate "objects" with wills of their own.

The Navajo parent is likely to ask a child if it *wants* to go to school, rather than issue a mandate to the effect that it must go. By the same token, coercive laws are distasteful from the Navajo point of view, and the Tribal leadership has long preferred persuasion to force, even in applying "compulsory" education laws on the Reservation (p. 41).

Mace (1959) illustrates the miscalculations that result from assuming that other cultures hold the same values as one's own. He writes about an experience he had in India when discussing Western "romance marriages" which he assumed would be the envy of those who were "doomed" to marriages that were arranged by the parents:

"Wouldn't you like to be free to choose your own marriage partner?" I asked. "Oh, no!" several voices replied in chorus. I was taken aback. "Why not?" I asked.

"Doesn't it put the girl in a very humiliating position?" one girl said. . . . "Doesn't she have to try to look pretty, and call attention to herself, and attract a boy, to be sure she'll get married? . . . And if she doesn't want to do that or if she feels it's undignified, wouldn't that mean she mightn't get a husband? . . . Well, surely that's humiliating, it makes getting married a competition, in which the girls fight each other for the boys. And it encourages a girl to pretend she's better than she really is. She has to make a good impression to get a boy and then she has to go on making a good impression to get him to marry her. . . . In our system we girls don't have to worry at all. We *know* we'll get married. When we are old enough, our parents find a suitable boy, and everything is arranged. . . . How could we judge the character of a boy we met? We are young and inexperienced. Our parents are older and wiser, and they aren't as easily deceived as we would be. I'd far rather have my parents choose for me. It's important that the man I marry is the right one. I could easily make a mistake if I had to select him myself (pp. 50-51)."

A Navajo teacher speaks out, asking for our acceptance and understanding. This is what he says:

Too often, to many prominent and influential educators, equal education means the same education, without regard to cultural, racial, linguistic, or ethnic differences. They assume that everyone speaks English (or must), believes in Christianity, watches television, eats the same foods, and quite possibly believes in White Supremacy. It's no wonder that some people, to which these assumptions don't apply, will have difficulties attempting to obtain an education without first being ruined or brainwashed.

If the shoe were on the other foot, in accordance with today's educational standards, our schools would teach or infer that Whites are inferior, barbarians, villians, that their religions are mere superstitions, that they are filthy and without "sanitation," and that their culture isn't really "best for them."

Our school systems would be based on assumptions that everyone speaks Indian, believes in Indian religions and in Indian supremacy, and eats fried bread. In this way, our education would do for us what White education is now doing for them. It would be relatively simple for White children who attended such schools, to develop inferiority complexes, negative self-concepts and self-identities, become void of self-confidence and self-responsibility, and many would probably drop out of school.

Nonstandard English

The inner-city black child is failing in our schools. . . . His failure to acquire functionally adequate reading skills not only contribute to alienation from the school as a social institution, but it goes on to insure failure in mainstream job success (Yaz 1973, p. 21).

The language model that a person has always used in his communication with others should not be considered a deficit model of school language. It is a different dialect of the language. The dialect is a complete, systematic, functioning language that is correct for the speaker who uses it at certain times, in certain places, and under certain circumstances.

The language that the learner brings to school is a valuable personal possession, and the people about whom he cares cannot be judged as incorrect or inferior because they do not use the school's language.

The root of the problem is not in the nonstandard English itself, but in the attitudes about it that are expressed by teachers and other adults.

Teachers should:

1. Teach Standard English as a second language to those persons who have habituated an oral nonstandard language pattern.
2. Permit the use of nonstandard dialect in written form for beginning reading (Baratz 1970). If we start reading with a language-experience approach, this is no problem.
3. Be sure that the speaker understands clearly that there are two variations of the same language. His pronunciation fits the "written-down" language too if the teacher emphasizes understanding.

Labov (1973) writes:

> There is no reason to believe that any nonstandard vernacular is in itself an obstacle to learning. The chief problem is ignorance of language on the part of all concerned. . . . Teachers are being told to ignore the language of Negro children as unworthy of attention and useless for learning. They are being taught to hear every utterance of the child as evidence of his mental inferiority. As linguists, we are unanimous in condemning this view as bad observation, bad theory, and bad practice (p. 43).

There is abundant evidence that traditional teaching of "language" to speakers of nonstandard dialects of English has been ineffective. Most culturally different students leave school after twelve years still using the nonstandard variety of English they were using when they came to school.

Many teachers still project the attitude that the language used by the nonstandard speaker is inferior; that all nonstandard dialects are substandard.

Sherk (1970) analyzed the language produced by five-year-olds in Kansas City and reported:

> Language is a very personal thing. Pupils whose language is always criticized soon come to feel that it is themselves who are being criticized, and this reflects on their parents, their neighbors, and their whole world. Because teachers refuse to accept their words, pupils feel they are not accepted as persons. In turn, pupils reject their teachers, and thereby in effect they reject school language, textbook language, and the language of the larger society (p. 291).

Reading difficulties appear when students must reconstruct meanings for symbols they have decoded. The nonstandard language user is apt to become an ineffective reader when there are not enough pictures and the meanings are subtle.

Standard English is a language system. So is nonstandard English. Nonstandard English has features that deviate from Standard English in systematic and predictable ways. Nonstandard English provides a functional, efficient, and satisfying means of communication among its members. In order to work effectively with those students who speak a nonstandard dialect of English, teachers must understand the spoken dialect. Teachers must first accept the language of the learners; second, analyze carefully the language they hear the learner use; and third, decide whether some of the features in the learner's language need to be the focus of formal language instruction. The formal language instruction would likely be practice exercises patterned after methodology in teaching English to speakers of other languages.

Standard English is needed by the learner as an alternate dialect. In critical situations, the learner must be able to communicate in Standard English without embarrassment; he must recognize these situations in which only Standard English is appropriate.

Black English

*The complex maze of norms labelled "Standard English" can be
one of the most imposing obstacles facing a young black today. . . .
it is a fact that blacks in significantly high numbers frequently
lack this language skill both when they enter school and when they
leave it (Stewart 1972).*

Houston (1973) explains that the English of some black people in selected areas of our country is not inferior, it is only different. The following paragraph is the way Rabbit began telling Houston the story of the "Three Little Pigs."

This story bout three lil pigs. One day, the lil pigs went out to play. They made lil house. One made a dog house an one made a hog house. One made a pen. Then the fox came. "Let me in!" "No no my shin shin shin!" An then he say, "I'l blow you lil house down!" He blow it. He puff, he rough, an he tough, and he blow the house down. An the lil pig run to the other house (p. 46).

Dillard (1973) records another bit of black dialect as a vivid description that probably could not have been told so flavorfully in Standard English.

I can skate better than Louis and I be only eight. If you be goin real fast, hold it. If its on trios and you be goin and you don't go in the ring, you be goin around it. You be goin too fast, well you don't be in the ring. You be outside if you be goin too fast. That man he a clip you up. I think they call him Sonny. He real tall (p. 1).

There is sufficient evidence to show that blacks are not less verbal, but their nonschool language may vary considerably from that of so-called Standard English.

Kincaid et al. (1972) collected stories told by a group of black adults that related to their own life experience. Black dialect is evident, as are words and phrases used by blacks in urban settings and words and phrases used by blacks in rural settings. The tape-recorded stories were transcribed and evaluated by graduate students studying reading at Georgia Southern College and by trainees in a Public Service Careers Project on the same campus. The investigators concluded that peer-prepared materials have obvious merit in adult basic reading programs for particular cultural or ethnic groups. The stories were judged to be interesting, authentic, and appropriate.

"Big Red" is a story with a readability index of fifth grade but would probably have a very high interest level for black readers. Slick Pete is a hustler who drinks too much in the tavern, brags about his money belt, and leads Big Red to believe there is money in it. When Big Red gets his money belt on the pretext of taking good care of it, he starts driving home and fails to stop at a red light. The story ends like this.

Big Red had put in a hard day. The time to tip was getting closer and Red couldn't wait. Maybe that's why he ran the light. Red and Slick. He soon found out what Slick's hustle had been.

The car was stolen (Grand Theft Auto).

Heroin in the hubcaps (Possession of Narcotics).

Red was high (Driving under the influence).

The big surprise to Red was heroin in the money belt he was wearing (Possession of Narcotics).

For the first time in his life, Red had met a police officer that treated him with dignity.

The officer politely said to Big Red and Pete, "You have the right to remain silent (p. 14)."

GLOSSARY OF TERMS

Tip—Leave; as in "Make off with the money."

Hustle—To act as a hustler; also to engage in other types of illegal or antisocial behavior, generally for personal gain.

Hustler—One who exploits a person or situation.

Some of the differences in Black English can be described in the following way:

Initial consonants are usually standard except *th* which is *d.*

A few initial consonant clusters are altered: *stream* for *scream.*

*R*s are generally omitted: *guard* becomes *god.*

*L*s are frequently omitted: *tall* becomes *toe; help* becomes *hep;* and *fault* becomes *fought.*

M and *n* are nasalized rather than clearly distinguished: *ram* sounds like *ran.*

T, d, s, and *z* are lost in final clusters: *past* becomes *pass; bites* becomes *bite; played* becomes *play;* and *nest* becomes *nes.*

Sometimes *sk* becomes *ks; ask* becomes *aks.*

Final consonants may be weak or missing: *ba* may represent *bat, bad,* or *bag.*

Voiced final *th* may be sounded *v: breathe* becomes *breav.*

Before *m* and *n,* the vowels *e* and *i* may be pronounced the same: *pen = pin; ten = tin.*

Dorothy Seymour (1971) has listed a few of the grammatical forms that teachers will find to be typical of Black English.

GRAMMAR	STANDARD ENGLISH	BLACK ENGLISH
1. *Verb usage*		
Present tense	He runs.	He run.
Present progressive	He is running.	He run.
Past tense, irreg.	He took it.	He taken it.
Past perf., irreg.	He has taken it.	He have took it.
Future	I will do it. I am going to do it.	I am a do it.
Present habitual	He is (always, usually) doing it.	He be doing it.
Past habitual	He (always) used to do it.	He been doing it.
2. *Negation*	I don't have any. He hasn't walked.	I don't got none. He ain't walked.
3. *Question*	How did he fix that?	How he fix that?
Indirect question	I asked if he fixed that.	I asked (aksed) did he fix that.
4. *Treatment of subject*	My brother is here.	My brother, he here.
5. *Noun plural*	those books men	them book mens
6. *Pronouns*	We have to go.	Us got to go.
7. *Possessive*	Jim's hat The hallway of Jim's family's building	Jim hat Jim and them hallway

In summary, teachers who teach students who habitually use nonstandard English must study and accept the language and, in the course of the student's educational experience, teach him to use both nonstandard and Standard English efficiently and appropriately. Some generalizations upon which this statement is based are:

1. There is such a thing as Black English. Black English and Standard English differ phonologically and syntactically. They also differ in vocabulary.
2. Generally, in the past, nonstandard English has been rejected. However, insistence by teachers on the use of only Standard English has not led to satisfactory achievement in curriculum practice.
3. A child brings to school at least six years of life experience when he comes and this represents the cultural, social, economic, and other values acquired during his whole life.
4. Rather than deny any value in the language, teachers must encourage students to use it in positive ways to assure self-confidence and to develop a competent feeling.
5. Teachers must be sensitive when communicating with pupils so they do not reflect a nonaccepting attitude toward the language spoken. The teacher must also be keenly sensitive to nonverbal clues.
6. Students speaking a nonstandard English dialect have a well-structured, sophisticated language and vocabulary that is suited to meeting all of their everyday needs. They must never be looked upon as having *no* language or an inferior language.
7. In itself, speaking nonstandard English is not detrimental to learning how to read. A person with a nonstandard dialect is likely to have the *same capacity to learn* to read as a user of a middle-class standard dialect.
8. Of course, the standard dialect must be taught, and it should be learned. Even though there is nothing inherently *wrong* or *bad* about using a nonstandard dialect, there will be times when it will be detrimental (prevent one from getting the job he wants, for example) to the person who cannot use Standard English.

Many articles have appeared in professional journals during the past five years which can provide the classroom teacher with information about the status of Black English and how to work with it constructively in the classroom (Allen and Campbell 1972; Allen and Forman 1970; Savage 1973; Shen and Crymes 1965; Smith, Goodman and Meredith 1976).

Teaching English as a Second Language

The non-English-speaking learner finds that he cannot compete
successfully with those who during their formative years have lived in
an English-speaking environment. . . . The guiding philosophy
behind a bilingual program is the conviction that one learns best in
in his native language (Levey 1970, p. 49).

Whether the adult basic education class is composed of recent foreign
immigrants, Spanish-speakers who are United States citizens, American
Indians, or culturally different citizens who speak a nonstandard dialect,
principles of teaching English as a second language are basic and primary. Teachers at all levels of education must become aware of the dis-
tinct differences between teaching English as a scond language and teaching Standard English to those who learned some dialect of English in
infancy as the native language.

Preston (1971) points out that adult basic education has addressed itself to the necessary skills and abilities needed by millions of Americans
who are not functioning members of society, and that *"a goodly portion*
of those millions still requires English as a Second Language" (pp. 181-
82). (Italics mine)

During the summers of 1969 and 1970 the USOE has sponsored national teacher-training institutes and workshops in ESL-ABE at the
University of Wisconsin-Milwaukee, and these programs have helped
bring together professionals from both ESL and ABE (Preston 1971,
pp. 181-82).

Patterning English as a Second Language

Teaching English as a second language is not like teaching English to
native English speakers, although teacher preparation in most colleges
of education ignores this very important fact. Most teachers find themselves totally unprepared when they teach in areas where a large percentage of the students enrolled in school are attempting to learn English
as a new language. On the other hand, the fact remains that in order for
the person to adjust in our English-speaking society, he needs to speak
the language of his peers fluently and spontaneously. Some adaptation
of the audio-lingual approach to second language learning is needed to
prepare such students for much more profitable formal school experiences.
For several years, these specific methods of second language teaching
have been yielding efficient results in binational centers all over the world.

Learning a second language is not primarily acquiring a vocabulary

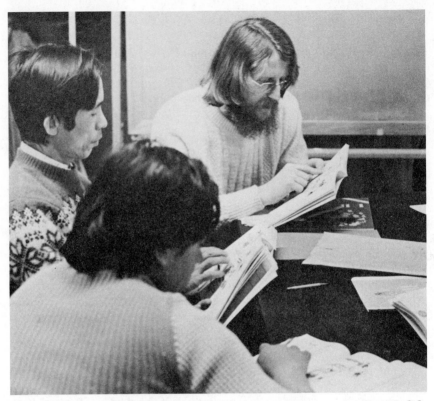

A great deal of oral reading practice will be necessary to learn to read well in English. (Courtesy of Kishwaukee College, Malta, Illinois Adult Basic Education Program.)

in that language. It is much more important for the student to focus his attention on the structure of expression, sentences, or patterns in that language and to engage in practice that will most quickly form habits of articulation, stress, intonation, and word order (Alesi and Pantell 1972; Stevick 1967). The sooner these matters become habit, and not choice, the sooner the student will achieve mastery of the language.

Three Basic Sentence Structures in English

1. Subject-Verb.

   I am going.
   We can drive.
   He studies.

2. Subject-Verb-Object, Predicate noun or adjective.

John shot a deer.
He studied his lesson.
He is class president.
Her dress is blue.

3. Subject-Verb-Prepositional phrase.

It is on the table.
He is in the house.
Mary went to the store.

In the second language acquisition, the learner needs to see the basic "slots" to fill to make words make sense. The basic slots are never fewer than *two:* a subject and a predicate; although they may not be expressed, they are *understood.*

Subject	Predicate
Boys	work
Time	flies
(you)	Jump!

In the sentences below, the subjects, verbs, and objects or predicate nominatives are interchangeable if singular, and plural is adjusted with each combination.

Subject	Verb	Object or Predicate Nominative
Jack	bought	a ball and bat.
		a book.
		a box of candy.
	brought	his homework.
	shot	a rabbit.
	carried	the ball.
	sent	a box of candy.
	played	a game of marbles.
	sang	a song.
He	ate	the apples.
She		

Subject	Verb	Object or Predicate Nominative
They	ate	the apples.
The girls		
The boy and his father		
He	resigned	his position.
Jack	kept	the position.
Mary	left	her position.
John	is	captain of the team.
Mary		my sister.
Miss Smith		my teacher.
He		my friend.
Tom and Dick	are	our friends.
They		our neighbors.
Mr. and Mrs. Smith		cochairmen.
The boys	are	skillful.
The children		helpful.
The work	is	easy.
The cat		black.
Miss Smith		angry.
The manager		shortsighted.

Substitution

Substitution practice is illustrated below, first filling the subject slot with a range of nouns, and second, varying the infinitive phrases:

The	school	is just around the corner.
	store	
	restaurant	
	post office	
	department store	
	house	
	apartment	

The teacher models "The school is just around the corner." The class repeats. Small groups and then individuals repeat. Then the teacher says only the word "store" and the class repeats, "The store is just around the corner." The teacher says "restaurant" and the class repeats "The restaurant is just around the corner," etc.

Please ask Jack to	turn the light off.
	turn the light on.
	leave the light alone.
	turn on the light.
	put the light on the table.

Grant Taylor's book is filled with substitution drills (1962, Drill 153). The one below substitutes different verbs with the third person singular.

He works	every day.
studies	
reads	
rests	
walks	
practices	
listens	
speaks	
watches	
repeats	

This replacement (substitution) drill is taken from a manual prepared for a ABE-ESL lesson (Patterson 1968).

The teacher says:

These	shoes	are	tight.	These shoes are tight.
			cheap.	These shoes are cheap.
	jackets			These jackets are cheap.
	slacks			These slacks are cheap.
			pretty.	These slacks are pretty.
	blouses			These blouses are pretty.
		is		This blouse is pretty.
	shirt			This shirt is pretty.
			tight.	This shirt is tight.
	shoe			This shoe is tight.
		are		These shoes are tight.
This				This shoe is tight.

In the framework below, combinations of any one of the subjects, adverbs, verbs, and prepositional phrases will constitute a good sentence.

Subject	Adverb	Verb	Prepositional Phrase
He	often	comes	on Saturday nights.
My sister	usually	works	after dinner.
Jack	sometimes	stays	after school.
My father	never	studies	during the weekend.

Learners must be taught the structure system in our language. They must *drill* on other words within word classes that can be substituted for each of the words in a pattern.

Did	*he*	go	to the store	this morning?
	she			
	Jack			
	father			

Did	father	*ride*	to the store	this morning?
		walk		
		drive		

			to the *office*	this morning?
			airport	
			station	
			farm	

Did	father	drive	to the farm	this *afternoon?*
				this *evening?*
				this *morning?*
				yesterday?

For those adults who cannot *produce* English fluently and easily and who do not yet easily *understand the sound pattern of the language,* we must teach oral language skills *before* written language skills (Nilsen and Nilsen 1971).

Teachers may find repeating, repeating, and repeating, and the use of endless one-word substitution drills to be monotonous and tiresome, but it is necessary and *the learners do not* find it either tiresome or monotonous if it is motivated and suitably challenging.

Language learning means acquiring the ability to ask and answer questions; to make statements; and to produce the normal expressions used by the native speakers of the language. Answering in complete ideas does not require that one always answer in complete sentences. For example, to the question, "When will it be time to go?"; "at 9:30" is a complete answer.

Vocabulary

Finally, students must acquire the vocabulary of the language after basic sentence structures are learned. However, as already emphasized in the early stages, vocabulary must be subordinated to the sounds and the structures of the language. Vocabulary can be accumulated fairly rapidly as it is needed *after* the sentence sense (structure) is established.

1. The learner acquires the ability to use the language communication skills of English in the order of listening, speaking, reading, and writing. *First*, he hears with understanding; *second*, he reproduces the language he has heard—trying to imitate a "good" model; *third*, he is then ready to learn that part of the language he has heard and spoken; and *fourth*, he can then learn to spell and write the language he needs to use, but only after he has heard, spoken, and read it.
2. The learner learns the "sound system" of the language. The "stream of speech," or the words running together rapidly, is the way the spoken language sounds and *takes precedence over everything* else in learning a new language. Acquiring a vocabulary of many words *is not the important thing* at first. Patterns, intonation, and stress are the elements for the student to focus attention on. Spoken language is the "natural" expression as commonly used by the native speaker and the new language should be learned in that manner. "It's a book" is spoken as "Itza book." Later, when the speaker learns to read and write, he finds that it is written, "It is a book."
3. Language is habit. Language is learned behavior. Native speakers are not conscious of each sound or word they say, nor of the sequence of the sounds of words. They are primarily conscious of the ideas or thoughts they are trying to convey. The stringing of sounds together in a certain position is generally unconscious. It is a habit that is *automatic* by the time children start first grade. The language must be learned through *repetition* in producing it. Guided repetition, correction, and drill are indicated. Drills must be relevant, lively, interesting, and not too long; but they cannot be avoided.
4. Language has *structure*. There are only a few basic sentence patterns in the English language *that are used frequently*. The teacher must *model* the basic structures and make sure that the student learns to repeat them accurately. The teacher tells the student exactly what to say and repeat it until the student can imitate correctly.

English-Spanish structure contrasts. The following English-Spanish contrasts are helpful in explaining problems of Spanish-speakers learning English (Board of Education of the City of New York 1964).

ENGLISH	SPANISH
The use of *not* with verb forms: "Mary is not here."	Usually replaced by *no:* "Mary is no here."
The use of *s* for most plural nouns: "boys, pencils."	A silent *s* is more usual in the Caribbean countries. The tendency is therefore to say: "My two girl are big."
The use of *s* in our simple present: "The boy eats."	Verbs are fully inflected. Learning our comparatively uninflected English, the student tends to drop even the inflections that persist, to say: "The boy eat."
Negatives with *do, does, did*: "He did not go to school."	No auxiliaries exist. The tendency is to say: "He no go/went to school."
English adjectives usually precede the noun: "the red dress."	Adjectives usually follow the noun: "the dress red."
Nonagreement of adjective or gender: "The big rooms."	Agreement of adjective. Tendency is to say: "The rooms bigs."
Adverbs of time appear only at the beginning or end of sentence, usually at the end: "I saw your brother yesterday."	Tendency is to place adverbs of time at the beginning of sentence only: "Yesterday, I saw your brother."
The *ed* past ending for regular verbs: "wanted."	For a comparatively uninflected form, the tendency is to say: "The baby want milk yesterday."
Use of the gerund: "I am ready for reading."	Tend to replace the gerund with the infinitive: "I am ready for to read."
Going to express future time: "I am going to sing."	Tendency is to substitute the simple present: "I go to sing."
The auxiliary *will* in our future: "I will see you later."	Tendency is to carry over the inflection and to say: "I see you later."
The use of *it* to start a sentence: "It is Tuesday."	Tendency to make the ethnic omission of *it* and to say: "Is Tuesday."
Comparison of most adjectives with *er* and *est:* "tall, taller, tallest."	Spanish uses only *more* and *most:* tendency is to say: "more big," "most big."

ENGLISH	SPANISH
Use of *to be* to express age: "I'm twenty years old."	*To have* is used: "I have twenty years."
Use of *to be* to express hunger, thirst, etc.: "I am thirsty."	*To have* is the more common usage; *to be* expressed an extreme: "I am hungry" means "I am famished."
Our negative imperative: "Don't run!"	Replaced by *no:* "No run!"
Questions with *do, does* or *did:* "Does this man work?"	No auxiliaries exist in Spanish. Tendency is to say: "This man works?" or "Works this man?"
Inversion of subject and verb for question: "Is the boy here?"	Tendency is to use rising intonation rather than inversion: "The boy is here?"
Use of continuous present: "I am working now."	Tendency is to use simple present for all forms of the present: "I work now."
Verbs in indirect discourse use the same tense in each clause: "He said that he was sick."	*That* is followed by the present: "He said that he is sick."
The use of pronouns as subjects: "She can go."	Spanish uses verbal inflection to indicate person and number. Tendency is, therefore, to omit the pronoun to say, "Can go."
Verbal contractions: "I'm, we'll."	No contractions exist in Spanish, causing ensuing difficulties in English.
Possessive adjective for parts of body and clothing.	Spanish uses the definite article. Tendency is to say: "The head hurts me."
No definite articles before titles: "I see Dr. Fox."	Definite articles always appear before titles, leading to uses such as "I see the Dr. Fox."

Transformations

In English grammar, transformation is the means by which basic sentences are changed, or modified, into other types of structures. So, the sentence, "There are four chairs in the room," can be transformed into a question by changing the positions of *there* and *are* and asking: "Are there four chairs in the room?"

The nineteen categories below are sentence patterns taught in the *Roberts' English Series* (1962). The categories are:

1. Subject + intransitive verb.
2. Subject + intransitive verb + adverbial of manner.
3. Subject + transitive verb + noun phrase.
4. Subject + transitive verb + noun phrase + adverbial of manner.
5. Subject + "seem" verbs + adjective.
6. Subject + "become" or "remain" verbs + adjective or noun phrase.
7. Subject + "be" + noun phrase.
8. Subject + "be" + adjective.
9. Subject + "be" + adverb of place.
10. Sentences in past tense.
11. Sentences with a model (present or past).
12. Sentences using have + participle.
13. Sentences using be + ing.
14. Negative transformation.
15. Yes/no question transformation.
16. Wh-word question transformation.
17. Combined sentences using such structure words as and, because, if.
18. Passive constructions.
19. Imperatives.

Observe the many *variations* or transformations in the following sentences:

SENTENCE	PATTERN
John ate the apple.	Simple past
John did eat the apple.	Emphasis
John is eating the apple.	Present current action
John didn't eat the apple.	Past negative
John wasn't eating the apple.	Negative
Did John eat the apple?	Question, past
Wasn't John eating the apple?	Question, current action
Was the apple eaten by John?	Question, passive voice
The apple was eaten by John.	Passive voice

Some of Roberts' (1962) basic sentence patterns in transformational grammar are presented below. All English sentences are derived, by various changes and combinations, from a relatively few basic sentence types.

1. "There" transformations.

STATEMENTS	QUESTIONS
A man is at the door. There is a man at the door.	Is there a man at the door?
The day is warm. It is a warm day.	Is it a warm day?

Three boys are in the
    principal's office.
There are three boys in the
    principal's office.
	Are there three boys in the
	    principal's office?

2. Question transformations.

STATEMENT	QUESTION
He is at school.	Is he at school?
He reads fast. (He does read fast.)	Does he read fast?

(These sentences require the intermediate step *to provide the verb* to change positions with the subject.)

He is going now.	Is he going now?

3. Question transformations supplying the question word.

STATEMENT	ASKING THE QUESTION THE STATEMENT ANSWERS
John works here.	*Who* works here?
Robert lives in *Arizona*.	*Where* does Robert live?

The books should have cost
    ten dollars.
	How much should the books have
	    cost?

Bill is in his *office*.	*Where* is Bill?
He studies *geography*.	*What* does he study?
He *works* in an office.	*What* does he do?
He studies *in the afternoon*.	*When* does he study?

4. Passive transformations.

Active Voice	Passive Voice
They built a house.	The house was built by them.
John shot a deer.	A deer was shot by John.
The third grade worked that problem.	That problem was worked by the third grade.
The old man planted the garden.	The garden was planted by the old man.

5. Transformations where the verb is changed to a noun.

John works.	John is a worker.
Julio gardens.	Julio is a gardener.
Mary teaches.	Mary is a teacher.
Ramon farms.	Ramon is a farmer.
Enrique drives a truck.	Enrique is a truck driver.
Mr. Jones practices law.	Mr. Jones is a lawyer.
Marianna cooks.	Marianna is a cook.
Mrs. Chacon makes dresses.	Mrs. Chacon is a dressmaker.

6. Combining kernel sentences into one sentence.

Coordination of Simple Sentences

It is the end of summer.	It is the end of summer and school will begin soon.
School will begin soon.	
Girls work.	Girls work and boys play.
Boys play.	

Coordination—Omitting Repeated Words

The teacher was fair.	The teacher was fair, helpful, and completely honest.
The teacher was helpful.	
The teacher was completely honest.	

Subordination of a Clause

The book was *The Wind in the Willows*.	The book that was lost was *The Wind in the Willows*
The book was lost.	

The man reads in the library most every evening. He knows a great deal about Mexico.	The man who reads in the library most every evening knows a great deal about Mexico.
Some pupils know the story already. They should not tell the ending.	Some pupils who know the story already should not tell the ending.

7. Combining parts of sentences using *because, until,* and *if.*

Because

TEACHER	STUDENT
I came home early. The library was closed.	I came home early because the library was closed.
The farmer didn't plant potatoes. The ground was too wet.	The farmer didn't plant potatoes because the ground was too wet.

Until

TEACHER	STUDENT
I can't go with you. My homework isn't finished.	I can't go with you until my homework is finished.
I have to wait. I get paid on Friday.	I have to wait until I get paid on Friday.

If

TEACHER	STUDENT
I'll stay here. The library stays open.	I'll stay here if the library stays open.
José will work every day. His brother can work too.	José will work every day if his brother can work too.

8. Changing to the past tense.

PRESENT	PAST
I go to work. I need help.	I went to work. I needed help.

I walk to class.   I walked to class.
I bring my books.   I brought my books.
I eat my lunch at school.   I ate my lunch at school.

Regular verbs

PRESENT   PAST

I work.   I worked.
He works.   He worked.
She works.   She worked.
You work.   You worked.
We work.   We worked.
They work.   They worked.

Irregular verbs

QUESTION   ANSWER

Did you tear your shirt?   Yes, I tore it.
Did you pay your bill?   Yes, I paid it.
Did you choose that tie?   Yes, I chose it.
Did you buy that car?   Yes, I bought it.
Did you find your room key?   Yes, I found it.

9. Tag-on questions.

POSITIVE   NEGATIVE

You can go, can't you?   You can't go, can you?
He has the book, hasn't he?   He doesn't have the book, does he?
He is working today, isn't he?   He isn't working today, is he?
He was in your office, wasn't he?   He wasn't in your office, was he?
He will come back soon, won't   He won't come back soon, will he?
  he?

Finocchiaro (1967, 1969) lists five basic steps in language development.

1. The pupils should be helped to *understand* the material.
2. They should *repeat* the material after the teacher models it as often as necessary.
3. They should *practice* the material in as many ways as possible.

4. They should be helped to *choose* the correct structure, word, or expression from several alternatives.
5. They should be encouraged to *use* the new material in many communication situations.

Rivers (1964) also emphasizes the necessity for oral practice of patterns and suggests the same techniques for such practice. She points out that the use of these techniques supports two important ideas, (1) language is speech, not writing; and (2) a language is a set of habits. She feels that audio-lingual techniques aim to provide the learner with automatic control of the framework of the language.

Paulson and Bruder (1976) delineate three levels of language drills: mechanical drills, meaningful drills, and communicative drills.

A mechanical drill is defined as a drill where there is complete control of the response, where there is only one correct way of responding (p. 4).

In a meaningful drill there is still control of the response although it may be correctly expressed in more than one way and is less suitable for choral drilling. . . . Everyone is always aware that these drills are only language exercises and that any answer will do as well as another as long as it is grammatically correct and conforms to the information supplied (p. 7).

The expected terminal behavior in communicative drills is normal speech for communication or, if one prefers, the free transfer of learned language patterns to appropriate situations. . . . The answer to "Do you have a date for Saturday night?" is communicative; here the class gets a piece of information it did not have before (p. 9).

Communicative drill is the level teachers are attempting to achieve as students progress. The emphasis is now on the content of the message; errors that do not cause misunderstanding about the intent can be ignored; and students can both teach and correct each other.

Summary

Children of migrant workers are often among the most educationally underprivileged in the nation. It is comforting to realize that the federal government spends many times as much on assistance to migratory birds as on assistance to the children of migrant workers (Witty 1966, p. 61).

The greatest problem in many adult basic education programs is the inadequate mastery of spoken English. Encompassing several million Spanish speakers, speakers of many Indian dialects, and the newly identified culturally different in our midst, these undereducated adults constitute a large American minority. Teachers at all levels of education must become more concerned with specific techniques for teaching English as a second language or Standard Engish as a second dialect.

The student developing literacy in English must learn communication skills in the order of listening, speaking, reading, and writing: (1) he hears with understanding; (2) he speaks or reproduces the language he has heard; (3) he can then learn to read that part of the language that he has heard and spoken; and (4) he can then learn to spell and write the language *he needs to use,* but only after he has heard and spoken it.

There are only a few basic sentence structures in the English language that are used frequently. Teachers must *model* the basic structures and make sure that the student learns how to repeat them accurately. The teacher needs to be a good model for the students to imitate. The teacher tells the student exactly what to say and motivates the student to imitate correctly.

Teachers need techniques for interesting and varied pattern practice, habituating the signals in the sound system that convey meaning.

A bibliography of commercially prepared texts for sequentially teaching English to non-English speakers will be found in appendix 3.

Part 3

Assessing Reading Needs in Adult Basic Education

15.
Resources
for Assessment
of Reading
Needs

The illiterate, paralyzed with despair,
if you tell him how bright he really is,
tingles from head to foot. I have
seen tears fill many eyes, tears of a new
hope and love (Laubach 1960, p. 36).

In no other area of education is the accurate assessment of reading strengths and weaknesses more important than in adult basic education. In the mainstream of society, the majority of those who enter an adult education program may function on a very low literacy level, but are not completely "ground zero" illiterates. In all probability, some reading abilities already exist and need to be developed, while it is obvious that many other requisites to successful reading are absent. Moreover, most of these people have had past learning difficulties that still may be a present factor in learning to read. The instructor needs to look closely at the learner's strengths and weaknesses, and then build a prescriptive curriculum based on that data.

In no other area of education should formal diagnostic and evaluative testing procedures be used more judiciously than in adult basic education. The very mention of the word *test* to many of these people conjures vivid and painful memories of past frustrations that raise the anxiety level to almost intolerable limits. For some, the intimidation of a test is too much, so these apprehensive individuals join the ranks of adult dropouts. Nevertheless, the data so acquired is important for providing maximum success in the instructional program.

Basic Considerations for Gathering
Pertinent Diagnostic Data

No longer is diagnosis restricted to or reserved for only the
educationally "sick." Rather, such diagnosis has become an intrinsic
part of the teaching art for all learners (Langerman 1974, p. 51).

Diagnosis for the sake of inquiry and probing is wasted time and effort. It is only necessary to look for those factors that have a direct bearing on the learner's effort to learn to read. Nor is it essential that all data be acquired through testing, which when used as either an infallible yardstick or an end unto itself may be a fruitless activity. Much of the data that needs to be known can be secured through other means. Such data is useful only when needed to answer questions that directly relate to designing strategies for effective instruction.

This information can be organized into four categories: (1) analysis of the learner's present reading strengths and weaknesses; (2) estimation of learning potential; (3) investigation of inhibiting factors; and (4) diagnosis of learning style. Some data from each of these categories may be acquired through these four generally used methods: (1) interview and observation; (2) informal diagnostic procedures; (3) standardized testing; and (4) case histories.

Standardized Evaluation of Reading Status

Whether group or individually administered, standardized reading tests attempt to provide a record of observed reading performance. This record can then be compared to some normative standard—that is, how people of similar educational backgrounds and of similar ages have scored on the same test, given under the same circumstances. Standardized test procedures attempt to answer the question, "How am I (or this group) doing as compared with others like me (us)?" Results are reported in the form of standard scores, such as stanines, percentiles, or grade levels. Such scores cannot be averaged, but can be logically compared with each other. To facilitate such a comparison, many test companies prepare a profile of subtest scores that indicate observed strengths and weaknesses.

One of the problems in using standardized tests with adult populations is that most of the tests presently available have been standardized with child populations; they do not really compare an adult's performance with that of other adults. Another problem is that most are also child-oriented as far as the reading content of the test is concerned. Interest and prior knowledge of the subject matter being read is of great importance in eliciting the maximum performance in reading. Thus, it follows that testing an adult with child-oriented materials is not going to adequately measure his real reading ability.

Some standardized tests are constructed to be criterion referenced rather than norm referenced. That is, they are carefully constructed to yield accurate individual scores that are to be interpreted solely in terms of mastery of the content tested according to specific standards for performance that have been determined externally and independently of the measurement process. Scores are reported as percentage of the content mastered, rather than in terms of comparative information internally determined, such as a ranking of students in relation to the performance of peers on the same material (Clymer 1971; Warren n.d.).

Informal Assessment Procedures

Informal reading inventories (IRIs) are usually designed to show the level of the individual's ability to deal with specified skills or areas of knowledge. However, there are no norms or information relative to validity and reliability. Results are evaluated either by some sort of intuitive standard or by the author's hypothesis concerning what should constitute satisfactory performance. Therefore, interpretation of informal reading inventories demands experience and care. However, informal procedures as suggested in this section may often be of more definitive diagnostic value than many of the more structured standardized evaluation procedures. Most teachers will depend on a combination of both standardized and informal evaluation procedures as they attempt to understand the reading strengths and weaknesses of their students.

Using Group and Individual Assessment Techniques

Both group and individual assessment techniques have their place in the evaluation of reading ability. Group procedures are primarily useful for gathering group data; that is, how is this group doing when compared to a specific standard for performance (criterion referenced) or when compared to another group (norm referenced). Care must be taken when one interprets group data in terms of individual performance.

Individual procedures are generally more time-consuming than are group tests. However, usually individual tests do not require the time limitations that are generally characteristic of group measurements. This allows the learner to respond freely, giving answers that seem appropriate to him, and also allows the teacher to probe for the reasons for the answers. This assists the teacher in understanding how a learner thinks, what frustrates him, and how he handles frustration. In a group situation, the student usually responds by selecting an answer from a limited number of alternatives, without such opportunities for expansion or probing.

Another possible difficulty in using group tests is that generally the directions to the test and the test itself must be read. It is difficult for an examiner to determine if those taking the test really understand the directions, or are stumbling over thinking problems simply because they cannot read, rather than because they cannot think.

Most adult basic education programs use a combination of both group and individual tests, the selection being based on the specific diagnostic information needed, or on which instruments will evaluate progress toward specific instructional goals.

Oral and Silent Reading Tests

Although the value of oral reading for instructional purposes is limited and debatable, for evaluation purposes oral reading is indispensable. Oral reading makes demands of the reader that are not made in the silent reading situation. Oral interpretation of meaning, eye-voice span, and pronunciation of words rather than merely recognition of words is demanded. In an oral testing situation, the examiner has the opportunity to *hear* the kinds of errors the student makes, and to view his mental processes as he attempts to unlock unfamiliar words. This type of diagnostic information is simply not available from the silent reading situation. Moreover, there is considerable evidence that errors made in oral reading are also made in silent reading.

Silent reading demands different skills. The reader does not have to know every word in order to answer the comprehension questions. His ability to scan and to pick out essential information aids him in answering the multiple choice literal and inferential comprehension questions. His ability to scan the page and to pick out essential information, as well as to use contextual clues, may be all that he needs. But the examiner is only able to infer the processes that were used in arriving at the response given.

Since each mode of reading involves a different set of skills, it is probably erroneous to expect scores on oral and silent reading tests to be similar. Oral reading, being more complex, will probably score well below silent reading. If it does not, one might wonder if the reader were utilizing context clues at all, or if he were indeed doing any scanning or organizing of the information in terms of main ideas, supporting details, or conclusions. In all probability, this reader would be attempting to pay equal attention to each word in the text.

Observation and Case Study as an Assessment Tool

We are all one-man communication centers: sending and receiving messages every minute of the day. Our messages are often silent and given quite unconsciously—a gesture, posture, facial expression, tone of voice (NAPCAE 1972, p. 43).

The astute teacher uses every contact with a learner to evaluate a learning need. He becomes expert in "listening between the lines" and eliciting autobiographical data that will yield some clue as to why reading development has been inhibited. Generally, he is concerned with four areas: (1) educational experiences and environment, (2) socioeconomic factors, (3) physical and neurological factors, and (4) emotional problems that either predispose to the reading problem or complicate it after the fact.

The astute teacher uses every learning situation to evaluate a learning need. (Courtesy of William Rainey Harper College, Palatine, Illinois.)

Usually the adult learner is really anxious to give an empathic teacher his perception of his reading problem. But he will seldom do so all at one time, or at all, until mutual trust has been built. As facts concerning the learner's past experience become known, the teacher may become aware of repeated patterns of behavior, and may form hypotheses as to the genesis and maintenance of the present reading problem.

Inferences from Oral Language

There is much to be learned from listening to an individual's use of oral language. Cognitive processes are expressed through oral language. Therefore, such factors as vocabulary, syntax, exactness of expression, and the ability to verbalize are but some of the indicators of the learner's ability to use language as a thinking process. From such a judgment, it can be inferred that, barring inhibitions to the process that cannot be bypassed, deficient reading skills can be brought up to function on approximately the same level as the oral language skills. In a very broad sense, oral language can be used as a measurement of potential for learning to read (Durrell and Hayes 1969).

Other hunches about the learner's probable reading needs can be formulated through listening to his oral language. What is his level of vocabulary? Does most of his speech consist of one- or two-syllable words, or is there a richness of expression demonstrated? Does he appear to have enough words available to him to express his thoughts accurately, or is he constantly groping for the words he needs? Does he use descriptive terms, such as adjectives and adverbs, or is his language devoid of color? Or, is his command of descriptive language limited to vulgarity and profanity? In talking about his own experiences, can he do so in "television English," or Standard American English, or is the description of his own experiences limited to a socioeconomic or cultural dialect? Can he listen to television English and readily respond to the ideas comfortably through his dialect? Or, is it evident that he is not able to decode enough of television English to be able to talk about the ideas in his own words?

Listen also to the learner's words in terms of syntax and sentence structure. What is the length of the sentences he uses? Does he converse in simple sentences—subject, verb, object? Or, is he able to use prepositional phrases and dependent clauses? What about his verbs? Is he able to use past and future tenses appropriately? Does he use subjects and verbs in proper agreement? Can he use negatives properly? Can he handle the irregularities in the English language?

Most of these are dialectical problems, but it is important because most of the language that the teacher uses and that the books are written in is television English. If the learner cannot function with this level of language, then it can be assumed that he will have difficulty learning to read. Moreover, there is considerable evidence that the errors noticed in oral language will also be present on the print level. Therefore, such an observation is a good place for the teacher to begin in diagnosing the probable weaknesses in the student's reading.

By using oral speech in this way, as a probable mirror of the individual's reading patterns, the teacher has formulated hunches, or hypotheses, regarding the learner's potential for learning to read as opposed to his present reading achievement. Based on these observations, a level for beginning instruction can be hypothesized and teaching can begin.

Inferences from Public School Cumulative Records

Often the educational records of a learner in adult basic education have been placed in storage files or have been discarded as no longer pertinent and are not available for inspection. But when these records are accessible, a review of this data might present bits and pieces of information that can assist in obtaining a perspective on the learner's past educational experiences.

Many teachers forego a study of a learner's past educational records for fear of prejudging a person's learning needs. However, educators should be able to use these histories with much the same professional objectivity and expertise with which a physician reviews a patient's medical history. Rather than fearing the formation of prejudice, a teacher should review the history looking for data that might have a bearing on the present problem, knowing full well that portions of that record are purely unsubstantiated subjective judgments, and that many of the physical, social, and psychological dynamics that prompted such judgments in the past or caused poor performance in testing and academic achievement may no longer be operative in the milieu of the learner's present environment. Some of the data from past schooling records that might be especially pertinent to the present reading problem might be the following factors:

Attendance Regularity

Reading develops sequentially. Therefore, irregular attendance and/or frequent changes in schools would severely inhibit such skill development. Knowing that these educational opportunities were not previously provided, the adult educator may need only to offer such experiences.

Origin of the Reading Problem

When did the problem seem to begin? Was there a severe perceptual deficiency noted in kindergarten and first grade? Was the student noted as immature? Was he a slow starter? Did he repeat kindergarten or first grade? These kinds of problems may signal a neurological immaturity or dysfunction that interfered with beginning reading. By adolescence, or much earlier, many of these deficiencies are either compensated for or have disappeared. Unfortunately, by this time in a child's life, school instruction no longer centers around learning to read. The late blooming child simply never catches up. Moreover, some neurological dysfunctions may never have been outgrown or compensated for. Thus, these are still pertinent to the present adult reading problem.

Sliding Achievement

Was there ever a time when the individual was working up to school expectations? Did school achievement and testing scores just grow steadily more deviant as he progressed through the grades? Many things cause such a pattern—poor self-concept, lack of motivation, curriculum pressures, inability to function in the learning environment, a too rapid pacing of learning, or getting behind and being unable to catch up. An adult educator who is aware of these previous experiences will be less apt to place a learner in situations where such frustrations could be repeated.

Psychological Evaluation

Note the presence of emotional disturbance that appeared to be related to the reading problem. Were social maladjustment and/or behavioral problems indicated? Was lack of motivation noted? The adult educator will realize that such problems could have been transitory, or that the maturity of adulthood may have dissipated such problems; but nevertheless, such factors probably inhibited the development of reading skills. Frustration in the adult basic education program may again trigger such reactions.

Ability Test Scores

In the learner's cumulative records, you will generally find several different kinds of test scores with very little, if any, notation about their meaning. Most of the test scores reported will be group-administered *verbal* tests that by their very nature should be viewed with some skepticism. For the following reasons, they are seldom as accurate as would appear.

1. The learner was required to read the test.
2. Cultural bias in the test items in favor of the white middle-class society penalizes many learners.
3. Language and dialectical differences interfere with the process of sampling the learner's abilities.
4. The group administration of the test does not allow the administrator control over such factors as motivation, concentration, distraction, and anxiety. These, and other such factors, have a strong bearing on the outcome of the test.

Group *nonverbal* tests, which do not require the learner to read, are somewhat more reliable but still fall prey to the inherent weaknesses of group testing.

Individually administered verbal and nonverbal (sometimes called performance) ability tests are more reliable. The adult educator needs to look carefully at these, paying particular attention to the patterns of scoring rather than to the numerical scores themselves. For instance, scores on the individually administered *Wechsler* test (1955, 1974), in which the verbal score is at least 15 points under the performance score would indicate the probability of a reading problem related to something other than a lack of learning ability. A low score on the coding subtest would indicate difficulty in dealing with a symbolic code, which is what reading is. People who have difficulty remembering a letter or a word from one day to the next often show low scoring in this area. A low score in the picture arrangement subtest may indicate a difficulty in understanding the sequence of events. Difficulty with the Gestalt concepts—that is, the relationship of the parts to a whole figure—is indicated by a weakness in scoring in block design—parts as related to the whole—and in object assembly—the whole as related to its parts—subtests. The vocabulary subtest is an excellent indicator of general intelligence and apparently does not deteriorate with aging.

Of course, it must be remembered that such data gleaned from public school cumulative records may be past history and no longer true for the individual. However, this kind of analysis may be helpful when attempting to identify the many threads of the present reading problem.

Standardized Achievement and Reading Test Scores

Study the scores on achievement test batteries taken periodically during the public school experience. Do the scores drop as the years progress? This is a strong indicator that the learner was just "turning off" to school. Is mathematics reasoning usually scored higher than test areas that required the individual to read words? A curve of scores peaked in this way usually indicates a student with normal learning ability who just cannot read the test. However, a "flat curve" of scores on the lower end of the scale may indicate a slow learner. Such a finding need not frighten the adult educator, since the experience of living and surviving in our society, and maturing into an adult has probably sharpened learning ability considerably since leaving the public school situation.

Reading test scores will frequently indicate the kinds of reading problems that the individual was experiencing in school. The relationships of the subscores to each other are more important than the total, or average score. These relationships will be discussed thoroughly a little later.

Such information gleaned from past records needs to be compared with similar data from the learner's *present* reading performance.

Inferences from Other Records and Sources

The more an educator knows about what motivates the learner, what situations are likely to cause frustrations beyond tolerance, and what his likes and dislikes are, the more probable it will be that productive learning experiences can be designed. However, most of this type of data should come from the individual himself, whether given directly or indirectly. Very seldom will records from agencies and concerns other than the school be available to the teacher. Nor should they be. It is important that in the educator's zeal to diagnose a reading problem and to understand the learner that he not invade individual privacy and actively seek information that is not pertinent to the present problem. Doing this will cause him to be perceived as a "busybody" or a threat. However, there will be occasions in which other agencies or concerns are also interested in helping the individual reach his goals and will appreciate sharing data for the mutual benefit of both efforts. Such assistance may be available from public health and welfare agencies, church organizations, employers, family, and peers.

The Importance of Rapport

Above all, encourage a confident attitude, use their mistakes in a positive way. Each student must feel that he is respected as a person (Wallace 1965, p. 7).

No discussion of assessment can progress very far without attention being given to the importance of establishing rapport between the teacher and the learner in gaining valid data. The following case study will illustrate that fact.

I administered the *T-NAT* [*Test That's Not a Test*] to my client on April 9, 1975. I was already aware that my client was reading on at least a sixth-grade level and that she was *extremely* apprehensive about oral reading. After putting her at ease by telling her the results need not be recorded, we began. On the second-level card she made several mistakes, but, according to instruction, I gave her the third-level card. She did better, but still made more than three mistakes. On my own judgement, I gave her the fourth-level card, and she passed. On the fifth- and sixth-level cards, she not only passed, but read better than she had on the second level. In fact, she made no more than two mistakes on the sixth level and corrected herself on both of these.

Because of the above, I feel that one should be careful in using the *T-NAT* as an initial inventory unless more than a single card is administred beyond the one failed, i.e., the person should be given two or three cards beyond the one he failed. I say this because the adult is bound to be somewhat nervous, no matter what the testing personnel does or says, since this is probably one of the client's first encounters with the person testing him. Even in the case of my client, it took two or three cards for her to completely relax and show her true ability—despite the fact that we have worked together several weeks and she appears quite relaxed around me (Kauffman 1975).

This experience clearly demonstrates the negative effects of anxiety on assessment procedures. It also shows how important the teacher's subjective evaluation of the learner can be in the assessment process. Had not the teacher been aware of the apprehensiveness under which the learner was laboring, she might have stopped testing too soon.

There is no magic formula for establishing rapport with a learner. It requires time. But until it is established, test results are severely affected. One would suspect that teaching is likewise handicapped without sufficient rapport.

Plan for Assessment

We cannot afford to lead people up a blind alley. We must not raise hopes we can't satisfy; we must not seem to promise what we can't deliver. Before we start out, we must have a very clear idea of what rewards we can offer an illiterate, and we must make sure— as far as is humanly possible—that these rewards are really forthcoming (Burnet 1965, p. 37).

Many assessment procedures will be offered in this section. As many contingencies as the authors could predict that might occur in an adult basic education reading program will be discussed. Many avenues of assessment will be traveled. But it is not the intent of this wide discussion to infer that the adult education teacher will need or want to use all of these procedures with each learner.

The important thing is for the teacher to very quickly establish a beginning instructional level for reading, and then design learning experiences and begin teaching. Teach and observe—wait and see if further evaluation is required. *Only test for information that you cannot teach without having and that cannot be secured by a method other than testing.*

As data is accumulated, it should be compiled in the form of a narrative or case study. Gradually, a pattern will emerge, from which future learning behaviors and problems can be predicted. It is important to

For many adults, test-taking presents a threatening situation. (Courtesy of Venice-Lincoln Technical Center, Venice, Illinois.)

record successes and strengths as well as problems and difficulties, and to think positively and optimistically as the case study is being built.

Summary

> As far as [the illiterate] is concerned, he's an outsider who has no place here in the land of the privileged. "Thas the way it is, baby, and thas the way it gonna stay. . . . Society may make you an outsider, but in your dreams, you can belong (Hawkins 1972, p. 70).

This discussion has been concerned with resources available to the adult basic education teacher that can be utilized in the assessment of reading needs. The function of various kinds of evaluation were described, and procedures suggested for gathering that data. Attention was also given to the kinds of data needed in order to understand the adult learner and to plan an appropriate program of instruction for him.

16.
Informally
Determining
Reading Levels

*You must learn to love people, not
for what they are now, but for what
you know you can help them become
(Laubach 1960, p. 36).*

Some adults will know more about reading than they realize, but others
will be far less competent than they think. A teacher will notice which
books the learner picks to look at or read. Often an informal opportunity
will arise for the teacher to evaluate language and reading by listening
to learner-initiated voluntary reading. However, these methods are seldom adequate to give the teacher enough data regarding reading performance.

Probably a more definitive analysis of present reading strengths and
weaknesses will need to be made as early in the instructional program
as possible. Quick assessment is important for purposes of placement, designing beginning instruction, and reporting to funding agencies. In most
programs that are funded by state and/or federal monies, reimbursement
is contingent upon such preassessment and postassessment. The problem
that faces educators is to secure an initial measurement in some logical
terms that can be accurately reported to a funding agency *without* producing the anxiety that usually is generated by an ordinary standardized
reading test. Standardized testing done too early—before sufficient rapport has been established—seldom yields an accurate measurement anyway, since the experience is too closely associated with previous frustration and failure. The learner subconsciously resists such probing. It
cannot be too strongly stated that preassessment data must be gathered
in a nonthreatening manner. Therefore, until rapport is built, informal
techniques are better than formal ones. Beginning hypotheses regarding
the learner's strengths and weaknesses in reading can be drawn from
observations and from informal procedures. On the basis of these, instructional procedures can be designed and learning begun. At a later
time, hypotheses can be further delineated and confirmed by more objective measurements.

Identifying Reading Levels

*His reading dysfunction is just one part of his life fabric of poverty
and failure, and the whole must be treated if he (the illiterate) is to
succeed (Hawkins 1972, p. 11).*

Evaluation of general levels of competency in reading is essential early in the program in order to get learners started on materials that are right for them. Since reading is only one part of the sequence of language arts and does not function independently, evaluation of reading ability should not be done in isolation. Attention should also be paid to language facility and to writing ability.

There are four reading levels with which the educator must be concerned. These are generally designated as (1) independent reading level, (2) instructional reading level, (3) frustration reading level, and (4) hearing-capacity reading level (Betts 1954).

Independent Reading Level

This is the level at which the learner can read without assistance. Words presented to him in isolation by flash techniques are identified with 90 to 100 percent accuracy. Words presented in the context of a sentence are identified with 99 percent accuracy, with a score of at least 90 percent comprehension of that context. His reading at this level is characterized as being free from tension symptoms, such as frowning, body movements, finger pointing, lip movement, and/or subvocalization. His reading is generally rhythmical with a conversational tone and the correct interpretation of punctuation. The rate of silent reading on this level is significantly higher than that of oral reading.

Each person needs the opportunity to read widely within his own interests on this level. There is no better way to build self-confidence in reading than the repeated opportunity to experience success at this level.

Instructional Reading Level

When a learner is presented with materials at this level, he feels secure, but is challenged. He still needs the teacher's help. Most of the material chosen for instructional purposes should be at this level, at which there is 75 to 85 percent identification of isolated words from a flash presentation. Some authorities would expand this identification band from 70 to 90 percent. However, such percentages as these are just general guidelines anyway, so the difference is not that important. Words presented to the learner within some meaningful context are identified with 95 percent accuracy with comprehension scoring at a minimum of 75 percent.

Oral rereading is noted by a rhythmical, conversational tone, correct interpretation of punctuation, and a reasonable eye-voice span. Silent reading is characterized by the ability to use the appropriate word identification techniques for the recognition of new words. As with the independent level, reading is characterized by freedom from signs of tension, such as body movements, subvocalization, finger pointing, and/or lip movement.

Frustration Reading Level

This is the level at which reading skills appear to break down. It should be located *at once*. Then, forever after, the teacher needs to avoid it! Materials presented at this level invite only failure. The frustration level becomes obvious when only 50 percent of the words presented by flash techniques in isolation are identified. Within a meaningful context, word identification may increase to 90 percent; however, comprehension falls to 50 percent or less. Oral rereading performance is not characterized by rhythmical, conversational tone, correct interpretation of punctuation, and a reasonable eye-voice span. Silent reading is characterized by a low rate and the inability to use clues for pronunciation or identification. There is much evidence of anxiety in the form of finger pointing, withdrawal from the reading situation by temper display, attempts at distraction, and/or refusal to read. Reading at this level may cause embarrassment to the adult learner; therefore, it should be quickly established and thereafter avoided.

Hearing-Capacity Reading Level

Performance on this level becomes a rough estimate of learning ability, but may change with instruction. It is the level at which a learner comprehends at least 75 percent of the material read *to* him. At this level the teacher will observe that the learner's own language structure in oral discussion is at least as complex as the written material that was read to him. The learner demonstrates the ability to supply from experience information pertinent to the topic. He pronounces words in discussion accurately, and his use of words is precise and meaningful. However, this should not be confused with verbalism.

Quick Assessment Through Word Lists

An adult's desire to learn demands a businesslike approach, so a good teacher must be well-organized. He cannot waste time or be slipshod (NAPCAE 1969, p. 9).

Word lists as assessment instruments are useful in adult education because they can be administered informally and quickly, and because they

tend to be nonthreatening. There are two kinds of word lists that may
be used for assessment purposes: (1) functional word lists, and (2) grade-
level screening word lists.

Functional Word Lists

Functional word lists are created with little reference to grade levels, but
serve another purpose. They attempt to determine if the learner can identify particular words that are necessary for survival in our society, such
as *danger, caution, men, women,* and *do not enter.* Certainly, these words
are priority candidates for early entry into the learner's stockpile of sight
words.

Rather than establishing a level for placement, such lists indicate to
the teacher which words are already known and which must be taught
as quickly as possible. In appendixes 13 and 14 are found two word lists
of this type: *Wilson's Essential Vocabulary List* (1963) and a list from
the *Curriculum Guide to Adult Basic Education: Beginning Level* (1966).

Grade-Level Screening Word Lists

The grade-level screening lists contain lists of words that the author establishes as typical for that particular school grade level. This is a very
general measurement of only word identification. Usually, there is no
context to the words and learners are not required to give definitions or
to use the words in any manner. Nothing is determined concerning comprehension of the words. Purely on the basis of such sight-word identification, a probable working level for the student can be established.

A valid use of the grade-level screening lists is for the initial assessment that must be made to satisfy funding agencies. Certainly such procedures do not answer many of the questions regarding a learner's
strengths and weaknesses in reading that will eventually need to be answered. But, without undue threat to the learner, it does quickly establish a general grade level at which instruction can be started, and which
can be used as a baseline to measure progress. This is really what such
a requirement for reimbursement of funds from governmental funding
agencies is all about anyway.

There are several grade-level screening lists with which the adult educator should become familiar. These are briefly described among the items
in table 17.2, "Individual Oral Reading Diagnostic Instruments Useful in
Adult Basic Education," page 255. Some of these lists function in slightly
different ways and need a little further discussion than the data given.

The Dolch *Basic Sight Word List* (1952), which is described in table

17.2, is the product of Dolch's survey of children's basal reader series in the 1930s. He found that approximately 80 percent of the vocabulary in these readers could be covered by 220 words, termed as sight words, and an additional 95 nouns. These words were presumably taught during the first three grades of public school. In the last forty years, children's basal readers have changed considerably. Some reading specialists speculated that these word lists are probably outdated, no longer being representative of the words in children's readers. Comparison with recent word lists do not support this, and the reader is reminded that language changes very slowly.

Johns' (1971-1972) research not only disproved this hypothesis, but he found that the words on the Dolch lists comprised nearly 50 percent of the words in most popular adult reading material. Using Kucera and Francis' (1967) listing of 1,014,232 words in order of frequency of usage, he then expanded the Dolch list to include an additional sixty-three words that were common to newspapers, magazines, and popular books. This list is also included in appendix 15.

In using such lists as these for assessment purposes, the following procedures are appropriate. Print each of the words on a card that is approximately 2 x 3½ inches, the size of an ordinary business card. Arrange the cards in groups according to grade level. That is, you will have five groups: grade 1 words, grade 2 words, grade 3 words, Dolch nouns, and Johns' adult words. Some teachers use a different color card for each group. Present only one group at a time. The teacher's instructions to the learner should be something like this:

> So that I might do a good job in teaching you to read, I need to find out which words you already know and which ones you do not know. Please say these words aloud to me. The ones you know we will stack to my right, and the ones you do not know we will stack to the left. Those will be the ones that you will need to learn.

When the stack of unknown words gets as large as the stack of known words, quit testing. It is threatening to the learner to see that stack of unknown words tower above the known ones. Teach the ones that are presently unknown, and then at a later time continue assessment. Under *no* circumstances should all five lists be given in one sitting. Grade level can be established from these particular lists in only the most general terms. However, their utility lies elsewhere—the identification of very important service words that must be known by sight.

The other word lists described in table 17.2 can be used to establish grade level. They are collections of lists that are representative of each grade level, such as the *Slosson Oral Reading Test* (1963) illustrated in appendix 16 and the *Quick Gauge of Reading Ability* (LaPray and Ross 1969), found in appendix 17. None require more than sight recognition and one test can be used to cross-check the results attained on another.

The *Word Recognition Test* and the *Word Opposites Test,* subtests of the *Botel Reading Inventory* (1961) are described in table 17.2 and sampled in appendix 18; they function somewhat differently. The *Word Opposites Test* may be given either on a listening or a reading level and is intended to compliment the *Word Recognition Test. Word Opposites* is a kind of comprehension task. That is, the learner must not only be able to read the word, he must also have some understanding of its meaning in order to be able to identify its opposite. Used at the listening level, the test becomes a rough indicator of learning potential—that is, assessment of ability to comprehend oral language that at present is unreadable to the learner. For those persons who score fourth grade or beyond on the *Word Recognition Test,* the *Word Opposites Test* should always be given to assure valid placement beyond this level.

Fry's *Instant Word Recognition Test* (1972), described in table 17.2 and found in appendix 19 approaches the task somewhat differently. This test requires only sight recognition rather than sight-reading of words, thus simplifying the task. Moreover, the words are presented in the context of a sentence, which further simplifies the task by offering additional clues. The score attained in this manner might not be exactly comparable to one attained through more complex requirements.

None of the word lists were created specifically for adult populations. However, since simple lists of words are fairly neutral in interest, the techniques are useful in adult programs. Few of the word lists offer extensive data concerning normative procedures, or material concerning validity and reliability. But because word lists are used in the context of adult education as informal procedures, merely as a general measurement to indicate a starting point, such lack of data may not be a serious deficiency.

Teacher-made Informal Reading Inventories

> *It is often better to build your own evaluation instruments than use ready-made ones. . . . Everyone concerned with the educative process should be involved in evaluation (Thatcher 1963, p. 180).*

There are many formats for informal reading inventories. Their purpose is to gain as much diagnostic data as possible from reading material that is relevant to the learner. These inventories are generally constructed by the teacher. They differ from standardized reading inventories in that they do not yield normed, standardized types of data in the same way that the traditional oral or silent reading test battery does.

Using Book Passages as Informal Reading Inventories

One method of building an informal reading inventory for adults is to select four books that have a readability range through various stages of reading difficulty. Any series of graded readers from first through eighth grade will do, as long as the subject matter is not childish, and the material is expository rather than narrative. Confirm the readability level of the material using the Fry Readability Formula (1968), the Flesch Readability Formula (1948) or the Gunning (FOG) Formula (1963). These will be found in appendixes 10, 11 and 12, respectively.

Once you have established suitable materials, beginning with the lowest level book, ask the adult learner to read the first sentence on every fifth page or so. Continue doing this in the next book, and so on. Decide in which book the student can read 90 to 95 percent of the words correctly. Then take the book selected during the reading trial and have him read several pages. If he can read and understand most of what he has read, this is his instructional level. If not, try another book on a lower level, or just assume that the next lower level is his instructional level.

The same procedure may be used on any group of passages with at least 100 running words in each passage. In establishing reading levels to work with in instructional settings, the "rule of thumb" is as follows:

Independent level: 1 error per 100 words.
Instructional level: 2-4 errors per 100 words.
Frustration level: 5 or more errors per 100 words: Thumbs Down!

Informal Reading Inventories for Content Skills

Informal Reading Inventories for content skills are especially effective when the teacher wants to know whether or not the learner has the requisite reading skills in order to learn from the printed materials of a particular content area, such as consumer education or social studies. The purpose of this kind of informal reading inventory is to assess the learner's competence in handling particular reading skills on a specified reading material. Such skills that might be investigated in this way are the ability to pick out main ideas, the ability to distinguish supporting details from nonessential material, the ability to follow the author's pattern of organization, the ability to draw conclusions, predict outcomes, and make inferences; the ability to read maps, charts, and graphs; the ability to use an index and a table of contents; and the ability to use parts of the book and source materials. Not all of the skills listed are equally applicable in all content areas. Likewise, there are pertinent skills in some areas that have not been listed. These are merely suggestive of the possibilities that can be pursued. An illustrative example of such an inventory will be found in appendix 20.

The obvious weakness in this type of measurement is that there is no certainty that skills demonstrated on the reading material tested will be generalized or applied to another content area. However, this is an excellent method of determining whether or not learners will be able to profit from the specific material the teacher has in mind.

Commercially Prepared Informal Reading Inventories

> *There is an adage that a good education improves your ability to worry about what is going on around the world. If that be true, I'm for raising all Americans to the level of expert worriers (Thompson 1966, p. 46).*

There are several informal reading inventories either in developmental stages or being marketed commercially that appear to have promise in the attempt to measure the general reading skills of adults. These have been briefly described in table 17.2.

Brown's *Test That's Not A Test* (1974) because of its simplicity and informality appears to be an excellent choice for use as an initial screening instrument for placement and reports to funding agencies. As its title indicates, the instrument does not resemble a test. All test paraphernalia, such as clipboards and stopwatches, are unnecessary. At a later time, an inventory such as Leibert's *Adult Informal Reading Inventory* (1972) or the *Follett Individual Reading Placement Inventory* (1970) can be administered to secure more diagnostic data than is available through either a word list or the *T-NAT*.

For those learners who are already reading at approximately the fifth-grade level, Litchman's *Reading/Everyday Activities in Life* (1972) offers possibilities of assessing the adults' skills in handling the everyday reading tasks. Results of this test can be used to direct the teacher toward relevant instructional materials.

Cloze Exercises Used for Evaluation

> *As one illiterate expressed it: There's no reason to stay in school, so I quit . . . "they acted like I didn exis. I was jus takin up a seat, an it was usually in a corner by myself . . . (Hawkins 1972, p. 19).*

Another method of determining whether or not certain instructional materials are appropriate to particular learners is through the use of cloze exercises. This gives teachers a means of approximating a learner's comprehension of classroom reading materials. Although the cloze procedures do not yield as much diagnostic data as do informal reading inventories and other evaluative techniques, they are simple to prepare and to interpret in relation to the learner's independent, instructional, and frustrational reading levels.

To construct a cloze exercise, select a reading passage from appropriate instructional materials of approximately 275 words. Leave the first sentence intact. Beginning with the second sentence, randomly choose one of the first five words to delete. As you type the selection on a mimeograph stencil or ditto master, leave a blank for the deleted word. Be certain that all the blanks are the same length and will allow enough space for the learner to insert the correct word. If the length of the blank spaces is varied, it would tend to either clue the reader or confuse him. An underlined space of about fifteen typewriter spaces is appropriate. Every fifth word from the first blank space should be deleted for a total of fifty deletions. At this point, copy one more sentence, leaving it intact as you did the opening sentence.

Learners are requested to insert the missing word. Show them that they are using context clues to supply the missing words. In scoring the exercise, only the *exact* word inserted in the blanks may be counted as correct. It has been determined that allowing synonyms to be counted as correct will have little effect on the total score and will have great effect on the teacher's sanity in trying to judge the appropriateness of such responses! The total number of exact reproductions multiplied by two will yield a percentage score that can be evaluated according to the following criteria:

Independent reading level: Above 60 percent.
Instructional reading level: Between 40 and 60 percent.
Frustrational reading level: Below 40 percent.

The important thing to remember about cloze measurements is that a particular score is applicable only to the specific material from which the exercise was taken. This procedure will indicate whether or not a particular instructional material being considered for use with a learner is appropriate, but it will not yield data regarding specific reading weaknesses or the inhibiting factors that appear to be involved, other than the observation that for some reason or other the learner does not seem to be able to utilize context clues and the redundancy of the language to help him read. A sample cloze exercise is found in appendix 22.

Summary

Underprivileged, disadvantaged, undereducated—these are just a few of the words used to describe men and women who are poor and have had little schooling. Teachers would be wise to add a new word to their thinking: underestimated (Warren 1964, p. 6).

This chapter has been concerned with informal procedures that can be utilized for the adult learner's reading levels. These informal procedures are particularly applicable for the establishment of a beginning level of instruction so that learning can proceed. Attention has been given to many types of informal ways of gathering diagnostic data—inventories, paragraph reading, word lists, and cloze procedures. Each has its place in the diagnostic facets of an adult education program.

17.
Standardized
Evaluation
of Reading
Achievement

The scene is your doctor's office. Immediately upon entering, the doctor asks you to orally answer ten standardized questions. If you answer eight correctly he decides you have tonsilitis. If you answer only five correctly, he decides you need major surgery, and sends you off to the clutches of a "remedial specialist" with nary a second thought nor deeper diagnosis. Sound far-fetched? It is—in medical circles. But all too often a parallel situation exists when the diagnosis of reading problems is made on similar flimsy evidence—through improper evaluation of oral reading inventories (Nephew 1971, p. 32).

It is quite possible to misuse standardized reading tests in the manner suggested by the above quote. However, used wisely, and in combination with other types of data, these instruments offer valid help to the teacher in assessing reading needs.

Standardized evaluation differs from informal types of evaluation in two important ways. First, the standardized test has been developed, tested, and validated by professionals in tests and measurements over a period of time. If these experts have done their job well, the test is more likely to consistently measure what it is purported to measure. Data is generally available to the test user regarding its development, the size and kind of population sample used to establish the norms, and the instrument's validity and reliability. Such information should be found in the test manual or in a technical supplement furnished by the publisher. The test user should also consult one of the two sources by Oscar Buros, *Mental Measurements Yearbooks*—seven volumes (1972)—or his *Reading Tests and Reviews* (1968, 1975), which is an extraction from the *Mental Measurements Yearbooks* (1972) of all the data regarding reading tests.

The other important difference between standardized procedures and informal tests is that standardized tests do offer an established set of standards with which to compare data. While most of the norms of these instruments are directed toward the youth in our society rather than toward the adults, the available norms still give the adult educator a point of reference from which to measure progress.

Oral Reading Tests

Oral reading demonstrations . . . point out very clearly the kind of mental and physical frustrations the individual goes through as he reads (Nephew 1971, p. 32).

The diagnostic data gleaned from any oral reading test is far more important than any numerical score. Consider some of the most important implications that can be drawn from oral reading as set forth in table 17.1, "Inventory of Oral Reading Difficulties."

As the learner reads the paragraphs, the teacher records the errors made. These can later be analyzed and summarized on the profile of the oral reading test itself, if such is available, or on a Reading Diagnosis Sheet, such as the example in appendix 23. As stated before, there is considerable evidence that weaknesses noted in oral reading will also be present in silent reading. Such an analysis of errors points the teacher directly to instructional needs of the learner.

Unfortunately, none of the most widely used standardized oral reading tests are built specifically for adult populations, either in terms of content or in terms of norms. Therefore, their usage in adult basic education programs is limited. Of those currently being marketed, a few stand out as being most useful, if the examiner bears in mind the limitations imposed on interpretation by these child orientation factors. Those which the adult educator will probably want to consider are listed and briefly described in table 17.2. "Individual Oral Reading Diagnostic Instruments Useful in Adult Basic Education."

Silent Reading Tests

Many illiterates look upon ability to read as a superior achievement and lack confidence in their own ability to acquire the art (Gray 1966, p. 199).

Silent reading tests are useful to the adult educator for at least three purposes. First, in many adult education programs, time constraints do not permit the teacher to do all of the evaluation through individual procedures. Second, the silent reading test measures somewhat different skills than are tapped in the oral reading inventory. Third, learners need to learn how to take a test, so that the evaluation will be as accurate as possible in sampling their real abilities.

Identifying and Analyzing Abilities Tapped by Silent Reading Tests

Silent reading tests can be classified into two types: (1) product tests, which evaluate the result of learning; and (2) process tests, which evaluate the skills needed to learn. The product instruments, reading achievement tests, usually measure reading in relation to other academic areas, such as mathematics. In many cases, such tests are a part of a much larger battery. Another type of product instrument, generally referred to as a reading survey test, measures reading achievement, but not in relationship to other academic areas. Process tests purport to measure reading skills, such as word identification, comprehension, and study skills. These are usually designed to yield more diagnostic information than the product tests.

The scores attained on silent reading tests are somewhat different than those attained on the oral reading inventories, therefore they need some clarification.

Rate Scores

Usually a rate score, words read per minute, is computed on the basis of a timed reading of from one-to-three minutes. It is erroneous to assume that the rate achieved by the reader on such a short-timed sample is the same rate utilized in reading a book. In the first place, the reader's speed in moving his eyes across the words is not the same thing as his speed in processing the ideas and concepts contained in those words on the page. Neither can it be assumed that the rate achieved in these brief timings is a constant quantity that remains the same for longer periods of time. Since rate is directly related to the reader's prior knowledge of the material, the rate achieved on a particular test may not be the same as that achieved on material written on other topics. Moreover, this measurement is achieved under the pressure of a stopwatch, which further inhibits performance for most adults. The adult educator should view this score with much caution, realizing that without a measurement of comprehension within the same subtest, the score may be invalid, and realizing that performance under time pressure may be the learner's *minimum* performance rather than his maximum effort.

Vocabulary Scores

From this subtest the teacher can learn many things about the reader. Vocabulary scores are important, in that they purport to be a measurement of the words that the learner can recognize in print and can attach meaning to. However, there are some problems of which the teacher should be made aware.

First, the sample itself may not be adequate. An instrument that utilizes approximately 100 words gleaned from dictionary samplings and from word lists, such as Thorndike's (1944), may not be adequate quantitatively or qualitatively to sample the vocabulary of a mature, job-oriented adult.

TABLE 17.1 Inventory of Oral Reading Difficulties

Symptom	Probable Cause	Correction
Reads very slowly—word-by-word.	Poor word identification skills; overdependence on phonics; lack of sight vocabulary; problems with eye-voice span.	Needs easier instructional material; practice in phrase reading; improve word identification skills; build sight vocabulary; use pacers; employ choral reading, and short-timed silent reading on easy material; tape-record oral reading so learner can hear himself.
Reads too rapidly, often at the expense of comprehension.	Nervous; not attending to meaning; inadequate word identification skills.	Build word identification skills; use easier material because he is probably skipping much; show him his inaccuracies; give questions that require details and accuracy; have him underline answers to questions as he reads.
Incorrect phrasing; omits punctuation marks.	Nervous; insufficient word identification skills; unorganized, does not recognize passage structure; not attending to meaning.	Build word identification skills; teach structure; build comprehension by questioning techniques; practice phrase reading.
Poor pronunciation.	Poor word identification skills; Hearing or auditory discrimination defect; weakness in phonic knowledge; carelessness; dialect.	Build word identification skills; check hearing; have learner watch word being pronounced; have him listen through the word; use the word in a sentence; help him analyze the correct pronunciation—disregard dialectical differences.
Often skips words or lines.	Possible visual problem; nervous; difficulty with meaning.	Have vision checked; point out omissions; use marker under lines.
Often hesitates before pronouncing words.	Poor word identification skills; inadequate sight vocabulary; difficulty with eye-voice span; lack of self-confidence.	Build word identification skill and sight vocabulary; practice silent prereading of passage; practice with easy materials; practice phrase reading.

Behavior	Possible Cause	Remediation
(continued)		inforcement of successes; build self-concept.
Often reverses whole words or parts of words.	Poor word identification skills; weak sense of directionality; ambidextrous or left dominant; too-rapid reading; lack of proper instruction.	Build word identification skill; slow down reading; point out differences and critical features of words and letters; use all kinds of exercises to emphasize starting at left of page; use typewriter; choral reading; kinesthetic method.
Often fails to understand what he is reading.	Concentrating on code-breaking at the expense of comprehension; passage is too difficult; does not understand structure of passage, main idea, etc.	Build word identification skills; give questions that require understanding of structure; underline key words; build all comprehension skills; use easier material.
Often adds words to what he is reading.	Lack of comprehension; oral language development may have surpassed reading level; carelessness; if addition makes sense, then it is an effort toward finding meaning.	Build all comprehension skills; point out insertions; ask questions that require exact answer; employ choral reading; read along with tape recording of passage.
Often substitutes words as he reads.	Carelessness; inadequate word recognition skills if substitution is outside the meaning; meaningful substitution may be miscue and considered differently.	Call attention to substitutions; work on beginning syllables and/or sounds that cause difficulty; use words that cause difficulty in multiple-choice sentences; employ choral reading.
Guesses at words.	Lack of systematic word identification skills; not using context clues; not attending to meaning; poor self-concept.	Build word identification skill; present easy practice material leaving blank lines for guessed words; assist with contextual clues; build self-concept.
Fails to recognize consonant sounds.	Probably has not been taught.	Use drills and word games; call attention to difficulties; use key words for initial sounds.

TABLE 17.1 (Continued)

Symptom	Probable Cause	Correction
Fails to recognize vowel sounds.	Weakness in phonic skills.	Build phonic skills through drills, word games, and flash cards.
Often fails to pronounce affixes.	Weakness in structural analysis skills—dialectical characteristic; inability to determine if an affix exists in a particular word.	Make lists of common affixes; use multiple-choice questions calling for proper affix; flash cards; drill; teach syllabication.
Often fails to notice specific parts of words—beginnings, middles, or endings.	Is not picking up sufficient information about the word from its various parts; sometimes a panic situation—reads the beginning and panics at the rest of the word, calling it whatever comes to mind.	Use a card moving from left to right across word, forcing reader to read through the word; teach syllabication skills; flash card drills.
Mispronounces many words on a page.	Reading material is probably at frustration level.	Use easier material; read for pleasure; observe initial parts and endings; give help in enunciation and pronunciation individually; use kinesthetic procedures.
Low sight vocabulary.	In adult, may be visual-memory weakness; lack of instruction.	Use kinesthetic method; copy words on typewriter; word games; experience charts; drill and repetition; practice easy reading.

TABLE 17.2 INDIVIDUAL ORAL READING DIAGNOSTIC INSTRUMENTS USEFUL IN ADULT BASIC EDUCATION

Test Name and Author(s)	Description	Publisher
Adult Informal Reading Inventory (1972) by Robert Leibert.	Provides estimate of adult's functional reading abilities relating to specific instructional needs and his ability to perform at different levels of materials. Constructed in two forms, each consisting of paragraphs ranging from 70 to 150 words on readability levels from grade 1.6 through grade 10. Level of difficulty in the paragraphs progresses in fairly small increments until grade 4. From this point, there is a leap to grades 7-8. Each of the six paragraphs is followed by five literal comprehension questions. Also included are selected word lists from the *Mitzell List* (1966) and the *Bucks County List* (1963). Completely oriented toward adult interest. Yields scores identifying independent, instructional and frustration levels of reading.	Reading Center University of Missouri 52 and Holmes Kansas City, Mo. 64110
Botel Reading Inventory (1961) by Morton Botel.	Although not specifically constructed for adult populations, this instrument is very applicable to adult programs. It provides an easy and accurate estimation of the independent, instructional, frustration, and capacity reading levels, as well as estimates of grade equivalents. There are no paragraphs to read, only word lists. Two forms are offered covering these areas: Phonics mastery (consonants, vowels, syllabication and nonsense words), and word recognition, and word opposites. The last two subtests can be used either as reading or listening tests.	Follett Educational Corp. 1010 W. Washington Blvd. Chicago, Ill. 60607
Boyd Phonics Test (1968) by Robert D. Boyd.	This informal test was constructed for children, but is equally applicable to adult populations. Information is gained about the following abilities related to phonic analysis: ability to hear individual elements; ability to hear blended elements; ability to pronounce individual elements; ability to pronounce blended elements; ability to see and pronounce individual elements; and ability to see and pronounce blended elements. Although no standardized score is available, the diagnostic data gained is very useful in adult programs.	In *Clinical Studies in Reading, III*, edited by Helen M. Robinson and Helen K. Smith, pp. 161-64. Chicago: University of Chicago Press.

TABLE 17.2 (Continued)

Test Name and Author(s)	Description	Publisher
California Phonics Test (1963) by Grace M. Brown and Alice B. Cottrell.	Created specifically for public school grades 9-12, this test is generally referred to as a group test. However, in adult education it may be applicable to individuals. The orientation would not be punitive to adults, although no adult norms are offered. Published in two forms, the test measures the relationships between written and spoken words using five different exercises. These utilize listening and reading to reveal the most common reversals, confusion of blends and of vowels, and other errors that reflect the inability to relate letter combinations to spoken sounds. The five exercises do not measure different kinds of phonics skills, but contribute to the overall pattern of errors a student makes, as visualized on the profile sheet. Detailed analysis can be made by using the diagnostic keys.	CTB/McGraw-Hill Div. Del Monte Research Park Monterey, Calif. 93940
Diagnostic Reading Scales (1962) by George W. Spache.	These eight scales were designed for school-age children with serious reading problems. The child orientation of the paragraphs seriously limits the usefulness for adults. The reading passages and word lists are linked together in a meaningful progression. The word lists are the most useful for adults. The tests evaluate oral and silent reading, and auditory comprehension in a standardized manner. Scores are in the form of grade equivalents for grades 1.6 through 8.5. Scales may be scored separately or together as a battery. Two forms of the test are available.	CTB/McGraw-Hill Div. Del Monte Research Park Monterey, Calif. 93940
Dolch Sight Word Lists (1942) by Edward Dolch.	Originally constructed to test the sight vocabulary of primary children, these lists are quite pertinent to adult reading materials; useful in evaluating adults considered to have almost "ground zero" reading skills. The sight word lists for grades 1-3 and the *List of 95 Nouns* show which service words are already known and which ones need to be taught. Standardized scores are not applicable.	Garrard Publishing Co. 1607 N. Market St. Champaign, Ill. 61820
Follett Individual Reading Placement Inventory (1970) by Edwin H. Smith and	A completely adult-oriented inventory providing grade placement plus a refined analysis of reading difficulties. Consists of five parts: word recognition and analysis (presented first by flash techniques and then for analysis), oral	Follett Educational Corp. 1010 W. Washington Blvd. Chicago, Ill. 60607

summarize and draw conclusions about the data. Scores are in terms of independent, instructional, frustration, and capacity reading levels up to grade 7. Available in two forms.

Fry Instant Word Recognition Test (1971) by Edward Fry.	This criterion-referenced word list is intended to be used in conjunction with *Fry's Oral Reading Paragraphs*, but can be used alone. Appears to be productive with learners who would probably score below 4th grade for an independent level. *Oral Paragraphs* are too child-oriented to be useful in adult education; however, the lists are useful. Words are arranged in forty-eight groups of five words each and are in ascending order of difficulty. Task requires sight recognition rather than the more difficult sight reading skill. Words are also used in the context of a sentence, adding another clue for recognition. Available only in one form.	Drier Educational Systems, Inc. 320 Raritan Ave. Highland Park, N.J. 08904
Fry Phonics Criterion Test (1971) by Edward Fry.	Although created for children, this test is quick and is useful in adult education. Instrument tests ninety-nine phoneme-grapheme correspondences through the use of nonsense words. It is criterion-referenced without norms, but yields good diagnostic information. Only one form is available.	Drier Educational Systems, Inc. 320 Raritan Ave. Highland Park, N.J. 08904
Gates-McKillop Reading Diagnostic Test (1962) by Arthur I. Gates and Ann S. McKillop.	Created for diagnosis of reading problems with children, but of limited usefulness with adults. Oral paragraphs are child-oriented and norms are for children. Subtests cover a wide range of skills: Seven oral reading paragraphs; words—presented by both flash and untimed presentations; phrases—flash presentation; knowledge of word parts—word attack; recognizing visual form of sounds; auditory blending; spelling; oral vocabulary; syllabication; and auditory discrimination. Subtests can be used either individually or as a complete battery. Two forms are available.	Bureau of Publications Teachers College Columbia University 502 W. 121 St. New York, N.Y. 10027

TABLE 17.2 (Continued)

Test Name and Author(s)	Description	Publisher
Gilliland Test of Individual Needs in Reading (1970) by Hap Gilliland.	A screening device for use in assigning appropriate instructional materials and determining the possible problem areas with which the student needs help. Although designed for children, and very much child-oriented in terms of content and norms, some adult programs report successful use of the instrument. Has a profile that graphs subscores on oral reading, comprehension, basic reading level, silent reading speed, use of context, words beginning alike, and word analysis skills (beginning and ending consonants, consonant substitutions, blends, speech consonants, reversals, long and short vowels, vowel blends, blending letter sounds, affixes, compounds and syllabication). Only one form is available.	Montana Reading Publications 517 Rimrock Rd. Billings, Montana 59102
Gilmore Oral Reading Test (1968) by John V. Gilmore and Eunice C. Gilmore.	Standardized test created for public school children, grades 1-8. Consists of ten paragraphs arranged in ascending order of difficulty, each followed by five literal comprehension questions. Early paragraphs are quite child-oriented, but later ones are not. The test yields three standardized grade equivalent scores: accuracy, comprehension and rate. Norms are from grades 1.1–9.8. Stanine scores are available also. No adult norms are offered. Most valuable aspect of the test is the analysis of errors into types: substitutions, mispronunciations, words pronounced by examiner, disregard of punctuation, insertions, hesitations, repetitions and omissions. Four forms are available.	Harcourt Brace Jovanovich, Inc. 757 Third Avenue New York, N.Y. 10017
Gray Oral Reading Test (1963) by Helen M. Robinson and William S. Gray.	Standardized test created for public school children, grades 1-6. Consists of thirteen paragraphs arranged in ascending order of difficulty, each followed by four literal comprehension questions. Early paragraphs are quite child-oriented, but later ones are not. Test yields one grade equivalent score based on the relationship of errors made to time required to read. Comprehension is only for reference. Most valuable aspect of the test is an observation checklist of reading posture and manner, and the analysis of errors according to type—aid, word, omissions, substitutions, inversions, mispronunciations, inser-	The Bobbs-Merrill Co. Inc. 4300 W. 62 St. Indianapolis, Ind. 46206

Test	Description	Source
Idaho State Penitentiary Informal Reading Inventory (1971) by Ernie White and William Kirkland.	Designed to yield data estimating independent, instructional, and frustrational reading levels, as well as to diagnose specific needs. The test utilizes parts of the *Dolch Word Lists* and six paragraphs arranged in ascending order of difficulty. Interest level is geared to adults (perhaps most meaningful to those with a prison background.	Reading Education Center Boise State College Boise, Idaho 83700
Minnesota Percepto-Diagnostic Test (1969) by G. B. Fuller.	This is a visual perception test that is applicable to either children or adults. Norms are given for both. The concepts behind the test are quite complex, but the instrument itself is easy to administer, score, and interpret. The task is to draw six geometric figures as presented by the examiner. The test is scored by the amount of rotation in the drawing. Scores indicate normal perception, personality disturbance perception, or organic perception. Only one form of the test is available.	Clinical Psychology Publishing Co., Inc. 4 Conant Square Brandon, Vermont 05733
New Hampshire Informal Reading Inventory for Adult Basic Education (1972).	The purpose of this inventory is to provide an instrument for measuring reading performance and instructional readability level for teaching purposes. The test has four parts: word recognition and analysis, oral reading, listening ability, and letter and blend recognition. The range is from grades 1–6. Only one form is available.	Office of Adult Basic Education New Hampshire State Department of Education Concord, N. H. 03301
Peabody Individual Achievement Test (PIAT) (1970) by Lloyd M. Dunn and Frederick C. Markwart, Jr.	An individually administered, wide-range achievement battery with items ranging in difficulty from kindergarten through high school. The norms are from ages 6–18.3. This is an untimed power test. Some of the items are child-oriented, but not extremely so. PIAT is a useful tool with young adults to measure achievement in word recognition and comprehension, spelling, general information, and mathematics. Only one form is available. Scoring is in the form of grade equivalents and percentiles.	American Guidance Service, Inc. Publisher's Bldg. Circle Pines, Minn. 53014
PRI Interim Tests (1973).	These criterion-referenced tests are designed for evaluation of performance objectives in reading as built by CTB. The tests will possibly be useful in adult education in determining whether a particular reading skill has been learned or whether further instruction is needed. There are four levels, ranging from grades 1.5–6.5.	CTB/McGraw Hill Div. Del Monte Research Park Monterey, Calif. 93940

TABLE 17.2 (Continued)

Test Name and Author(s)	Description	Publisher
Pope Inventory of Basic Reading Skills (1974) by Lillie Pope.	This informal inventory may be used to evaluate the word attack skills of any problem reader, regardless of age. The primary focus of the inventory is on matching sound with symbol, but also deals with knowledge of left and right and basic sight words. The subtests cover auditory recognition of initial consonants and final consonants, blending, visual recognition of consonants, reading knowledge of vowels, reversals, auditory and visual recognition of consonant blends and digraphs. Only one form is available. No norms are given.	Book-Lab, Inc. 1449 37 St. Brooklyn, N.Y. 11218
R/EAL: Reading/Everyday Activities in Life (1972) by Marilyn Lichtman.	The purpose of this adult-oriented test is to provide a diagnostic and evaluative instrument to assess whether or not the individual is capable of performing reading tasks common to experiences in everyday life. The test is self-paced and can be administered by tape casette, in either Spanish or English. It is not useful for people with less than 5th grade reading ability. Nine reading selections and questions cover these areas: road signs, TV schedule, directions for preparing pizza, narrative selection on drugs, food market ad, apartment lease, road map, want ad, and job application. The test is profiled in criterion-referenced norms. Only one form is available.	CAL Press, Inc. 76 Madison Ave. New York, N.Y. 10016
Roswell-Chall Auditory Blending Test (1963) by Florence C. Roswell and Jeanne S. Chall.	This brief test was developed to evaluate ability to blend sounds to form words when the sounds are presented orally. It gives an estimate of a pupil's ability to blend sounds auditorily into whole words whether or not he has learned to associate the sounds with the corresponding letters and is useful in judging whether or not a person might have difficulty in learning phonics. Norms are presented through grade 5, but this test would be as useful to adults as to children. Only one form is available.	Essay Press P.O. Box 5 Planetarium Station New York, N.Y. 10024
Roswell-Chall Reading Test of Word Analysis Skills (1959) by Florence G. Roswell	The purpose of this test is to provide a means of assessing strengths and weaknesses of selected word recognition skills. Auditory blending tests the person's ability to blend sounds to form words when the sounds are presented orally. Word analysis tests word recognition, mostly phonics. Norms are given for	Essay Press P.O. Box 5 Planetarium Station New York, N.Y. 10024

260

Test	Description	Source
List: Quick Gauge of Reading Ability (1969) by Margaret LaPray and Ramon Ross.	...is a graded word list, taken by drawing words randomly from basal reader glossaries and from the Thorndike list. It was created for children, but may also be useful to adults who have poor decoding skills. It is constructed of eleven ten-word groups. Independent, instructional, and frustrational reading levels can be identified. Opportunity is also offered for analysis of the student's errors.	Appeared in Journal of Reading, January 1969. Also in Teaching Children to Become Independent Readers, by Margaret La Pray. 521 Fifth Avenue, N.Y.C. 10017; The Center for Applied Research in Education, Inc, 1972, pp. 62-64.
Slosson Oral Reading Test (1963) by Richard L. Slosson.	This is an individual placement test of the word list variety. Placement is made on the basis of word identification power only. The test is useful for both children and adults. Twenty lists, ranging in difficulty from preprimer through high school are presented. Scoring is in the form of grade equivalent. Only one form is available.	Slosson Educational Publications 140 Pine St. East Aurora, N. Y. 14052
Sucher-Allred Reading Placement Inventory (1973) by Floyd Sucher and Ruel A. Allred.	Designed for youth, this test is of limited value in adult education, yet reported by some programs as useful. Permits identification of independent, instruction and frustration levels, identifies common word recognition and comprehension errors, and gives a guideline for placement in instructional materials. Range is from primer through grade 9. Only one form is available.	The Economy Co. P.O. Box 25308 1901 N. Walnut Oklahoma City, Okla. 73125
Test That's Not A Test (T-NAT) (1974) by Don A. Brown.	The purpose of this unique instrument is to provide an instrument for initial screening and to indicate instructional levels based on oral reading ability. The test is completely adult-oriented. It consists of six short paragraphs, each on a separate card. The number in the upper right hand corner indicates not only the number of the passage, but the number of errors permitted, and the grade level of the paragraph. Only one form is available.	Basic Education Trade House 1827 26 Ave. Court Greeley, Colo. 80631
Wepman Auditory Discrimination Test (1973) by Joseph M. Wepman.	This test provides a means of determining a person's ability to recognize the fine differences between the phonemes in English speech. Forty single syllable word pairs are presented. The student is requested to indicate whether the pair of words he hears is alike or different. Procedure shows the teacher which phonemes are causing difficulty and must be taught. Two forms are available. This test is just as appropriate for adults as for children.	Language Research Assoc. 175 E. Delaware Place Chicago, Ill. 60611

TABLE 17.2 (Continued)

Test Name and Author(s)	Description	Publisher
Wilson's Essential Word List (1963) by Corlett T. Wilson.	Strictly speaking, this is not a test. But it is a means for the adult education teacher to determine if the student knows words and phrases that are necessary for survival in our society. Such terms as *danger, poison if swallowed, look out,* etc. are presented on a list. Those that the student does not recognize as sight words need to be taught.	Appeared in *The Reading Teacher,* 17 (November 1963): 94-96.
Wide Range Achievement Test (WRAT) (1965) by J. R. Jastak and Sidney Bijou.	Designed for children age five through adults. Norms given for all ages. Test can be given to a group, although it is most often used with individuals. It is a *screening* instrument in reading: letter and word recognition, spelling and mathematics. Scores are reported in grade equivalents, percentiles, and standard scores. Only one form is available.	Guidance Assoc. 1526 Gilpin Ave. Wilmington, Del. 19806
Wold Screening Tests to Be Used by the Classroom Teacher (1970) by Robert M. Wold.	These are visual perceptual tests, created for use with children. However, with the adult who is suspected of having perceptual problems with reading, the careful informal administration of some of these may help to clarify the problem. Tests included are spontaneous alphabet writing, alphabet writing from dictation, sentence writing from dictation, sentence copying, MKM visual letter recognition, haptic letter recognition, MKM auditory letter recognition, recognition vocabulary test, Murroughs phonovisual test, naming test, Piaget right-left awareness test, visuo-motor test, digit-symbol test. Scoring for most of these is in the form of criterion for acceptable performance.	Academic Therapy Publications San Rafael, Calif. 94901
Woodcock Reading Mastery Test (1973) by Richard W. Woodcock.	This battery of tests was constructed for children; however, most of the content is such that it could be used with adults. It is criterion-referenced as well as norm-referenced. Scoring is in the form of grade equivalents and percentiles. The subtests cover letter identification, word identification, word attack, word	American Guidance Service, Inc. Publisher's Bldg. Circle Pines, Minn. 53014

262

Zintz Compound Words (1972) by Miles V. Zintz.	Technically, this is not a test. It is an informal list of words found in representative second grade readers. The list is useful in adult education when the teacher suspects that the individual does not see the configuration of a compound word as two words put together, and is thus having undue difficulty with word recognition. The individual is just required to identify each of the words in the list until the teacher is satisfied as to whether a problem actually exists.	From Miles V. Zintz, *Corrective Reading.* 3d ed., p. 65. Dubuque, Ia.: William C. Brown Co., 1977.
Zintz Lists of Easily Confused Words (1972) by Miles V. Zintz.	Technically, this is not a test. It is two informal lists of words that are easily confused mostly because of reversal possibilities. The lists are useful in adult education when the teacher suspects that the individual is having such a difficulty. The person is just required to identify each of the words until the teacher is satisfied as to whether a problem actually exists.	From Miles V. Zintz, *Corrective Reading.* 3d ed., pp. 66-67. Dubuque, Ia.: William C. Brown Co., 1977.

One must also question why the reader did not answer *all* the vocabulary items. Did he just not know the answers, or did he run out of time? With adults, it has been particularly noted that some will only respond to a small proportion of the available items, but those that are attempted are 100 percent accurate. Usually the teacher is safe in assuming that such a performance is indicative of a reader who fears taking chances and making mistakes. He has set his criterion so high that it interferes with the development of successful reading skills (F. Smith 1970).

Adults do not work well under time pressures. Purely for diagnostic information, it might be productive for the teacher at a later date to offer the learner the opportunity to complete the test without the time limits. If more items were answered correctly, then it could be assumed that, for this individual, time pressures are counterproductive.

The teacher must also consider *why* the reader missed the items he did. Was the item missed because the learner did not know the meaning of the word, or was it because he did not recognize it as a word? Administration of Huelsman's *Word Discrimination Test* (1955), described in table 17.3, "Silent Reading Tests Useful in Adult Basic Education," may help answer this question. If the reader's score on this is significantly below that of the vocabulary subtest, then it may be concluded that his difficulty is not only in connecting meaning with the printed words, but even more importantly, in the very basic skill of recognizing words at all.

The learner may also have missed vocabulary items because he knew quite a different meaning for the word than those that were provided among the multiple-choice items on the test. To check this out, the teacher must read aloud to the student at least a fair share of the items missed. If he responds correctly by providing an acceptable meaning of many of the words originally missed, it may well be concluded that this particular vocabulary test was not an adequate sampling of his knowledge.

The structure of the vocabulary test itself also influences the scoring. Testmakers utilize different avenues to measure word knowledge. Some reading tests incorporate items measuring knowledge of several content areas. The level of the learner's vocabulary may differ in each of the areas, depending on his individual background. Yet, the single vocabulary score makes no such differentiation. Vocabulary words may also be presented in different formats. Some may offer the word in some meaningful context, such as a sentence. Others may simply offer the word in isolation, instructing the learner to pick a synonym from five choices. Some testmakers request the reader to respond with an antonym to the word in question. It may well be that each format is tapping a somewhat different ability. Certainly, there are different conceptual requirements for each of the methods of presenting the task, yet each is reported simply as vocabulary.

Paragraph Comprehension Scores

The test of paragraph reading designed to yield a level of comprehension score usually involves silent reading of paragraphs of increasing length and difficulty. It attempts to measure various comprehension skills through responses to questions that follow the reading. Some merely elicit rote memory, the answering of factual questions covered in the passage. Others require the reader to make an inference or to draw a conclusion based on the information given in the passage. None tap higher level cognitive skills. Thus, the concept of comprehension itself as far as test construction is concerned is somewhat limited.

The examination of the items of a test will reveal whether test items require the reader to ascertain the author's mood, tone, purpose, or intent; to understand the main ideas and supporting details; or to understand literary devices, such as figurative language, the rhetorical sentence, and idiomatic expressions peculiar to our language. Only through a careful study of the actual test items can the teacher get a clear understanding of which skills and abilities the test is measuring, and in which of these the reader appears to show strengths and weaknesses.

Remember also that conclusions regarding the reader's comprehension ability is being based on a relatively small sample of items. Neither has the reader's interest in the subject matter content of the test or his prior knowledge about it been considered in the scoring. Both factors are important enough to have considerable influence on test results.

Comparative Analysis of Subtest Scores

Diagnostic information from a comparative analysis of subtest scores is another productive use of standardized silent reading in adult basic education. Beyond looking at the test items themselves with the question of why the reader responded in the way he did, the teacher should consider *how* the subtest scores relate to each other.

A high rate score with lower scores on vocabulary and paragraph comprehension obviously indicates that the reader's eyes were just covering ink marks on the page with very little attention given to meaning. Such a score is really meaningless, since it is obvious that the reader cannot really process information at such a pace.

On the other hand, a low rate score with higher vocabulary and paragraph comprehension scores would suggest several possibilities. Perhaps the reader is perfectionistic and afraid of skipping any of the words. Perhaps the readability of the material is really too hard for him and he is struggling with the concepts. Perhaps he is attending equally to every word—small and large alike. Or perhaps he is simply having intense word identification difficulties that have slowed him down to a crawl.

A low vocabulary score with a higher paragraph comprehension score suggests that the individual may not recognize all the words, but he is adept at utilizing context clues and the redundancy of the language to perceive meaning. He needs to be given more words to work with. In such a case, vocabulary building activities can be most profitable.

A vocabulary score that is higher than the paragraph comprehension one suggests an individual who is experiencing difficulty with basic comprehension skills, such as finding the main idea, drawing conclusions, predicting outcomes, and making inferences. Or perhaps here is a reader who is reading every word of each paragraph rather than attempting to read for ideas.

Using Tests to Learn Test-taking Techniques

At some point in adult education, adult learners need to learn how to approach the test-taking situation with ease. It is easy for educators to forget that most of these people have been out of school for a long time and may not know how to take a test, much less how to use a machine scoreable answer sheet. Therefore, when they take tests given by employers and employment agencies they may do poorly, partly because of these deficiencies rather than because they lack the abilities being evaluated on the test. Adult learners must be shown how to use the test instrument to demonstrate their maximum competency. Standardized tests should be used often enough in the program so that the student gains this experience.

Do not assume anything in the test-taking situation. Be certain that the individual understands the test directions and that he knows what is expected of him. Show him how to mark an answer sheet and how to make corrections. Sometimes the visual shift from test booklet to answer sheet causes momentary confusion and the loss of precious seconds. A hint to him to use his left forefinger to help mark his place in the booklet while holding his pencil at the last place he marked on the answer sheet to keep his place there can be helpful. Little things, such as just making one heavy mark in the answer space on the machine scoreable answer sheet instead of taking the time to carefully "color in" the space will gain important seconds that can be spent responding to the test items.

Inexperienced test takers have a tendency to spend minutes pondering over an unknown item rather than moving quickly on to the items that are known, and then returning to the problem areas.

In paragraph comprehension tests, experienced test takers quickly read the comprehension questions *before* reading the paragraphs. Then they read for the answers to the questions rather than read every word with equal emphasis. However, the directions in some of the tests will not allow this procedure, and test directions should not be violated.

Such training is favorable for both the learner and the examiner. For the learner, it provides him with confidence and ease in a difficult situation. For the examiner it clears away much of the anxiety and difficulties in mechanical areas that really have nothing to do with the abilities that the test is attempting to evaluate.

Silent Reading Tests Useful in Adult Basic Education

Of the many silent reading tests now on the market, only a few are useful in adult basic education. These have been briefly described in table 17.3, "Silent Reading Tests Useful in Adult Basic Education." It will be noted that some are youth-oriented tests. Others are adult rewrites of youth-oriented tests. A very few are constructed singularly for adults.

Some of the tests described in table 17.3 are product tests useful for the purposes described in this section. Others are process tests that are useful in examining specific aspects of the reading process.

Selecting Assessment Instruments

Many assessment instruments have been listed and described. None are guaranteed to function perfectly. Some instruments yield good data in one situation, but appear not to work in others. Assessment can only be meaningful if the appropriate instruments are selected for use and if the teacher develops expertise in utilizing that instrument.

Therefore, determining the appropriate testing instruments is never a simple task. It should not be done on the basis of publisher's claims for the test, or only on the basis of what has been successful in other programs. The following criteria are helpful in making such decisions.

1. Select instruments that yield information about the specific things you need to know in order to develop an adequate instructional program.
2. Select instruments that assess the skills you feel should be taught in your program—that is, tests that measure your instructional objectives.
3. Do not select an instrument for adult usage that looks childish in any way.

TABLE 17.3 Silent Reading Tests Useful in Adult Basic Education

Test Name and Author(s)	Description	Publisher
Adult Basic Education, Student Survey (1966) by Elvin Rosof and Monroe C. Neff.	A placement battery designed for gross sorting of pupils into groups, as a guide to student growth and a learning experience in test taking. Includes four parts: reading comprehension, word recognition, arithmetic computation, and arithmetic problems. Available in two forms. Scores reported in grade levels, cumulative percent, and T scores. Constructed and normed for adults. Range: grades 1-8.	Educational Opportunities Div. Follett Publishing Co. 1010 W. Washington Blvd. Chicago, Ill. 60607
Adult Basic Learning Examination (ABLE) (1967) by Bjorn Karlsen, Richard Madden, and Eric F. Gardner.	Developed specifically for adults with content for the purpose of measuring achievement as low as first grade level, and to evaluate programs designed to raise their educational level; assists in diagnosing individual strengths and weaknesses. Presented in three levels: level 1 is equivalent to grades 1-4; level 2 is equivalent to grades 5-8; and level 3 is equivalent to grades 9-12. The subtests are reading, vocabulary, spelling, arithmetic computation, and arithmetic problem solving. The vocabulary, spelling and arithmetic problem-solving subtests are administered as listening tests at level 1 to eliminate the contamination of scores by reading ability. Scores are reported in grade equivalents with conversions to stanines and/or percentiles. Two forms of each level are available.	Harcourt Brace Jovanovich, Inc. 757 Third Ave. New York, N. Y. 10017
Adult Basic Reading Inventory (1966) by Richard W. Burnett.	Designed for adults for use in the identification of absolute illiterates, functional illiterates, and individuals who are not illiterate but have reading difficulties originating from other problems. Subtests are vocabulary–picture and word matching; hearing discrimination; vocabulary–synonyms; listening vocabulary; and contextual material. Scoring is criterion-referenced in terms of percentages. Only one form is available.	Scholastic Testing Service, Inc. 480 Meyer Rd. Bensenville, Ill. 60106
American Literacy Test (1962) by John J. McCarty.	Test is based on the proposition that a good literacy test must bear some reasonable relation to ability to use the grammar and mechanics of the English language reasonably. The pupil is required to select one of four options that has the same meaning as the stimulus word. There is no paragraph reading involved. Scoring is in terms of percentiles. Only one form is available.	Psychometric Affiliates P. O. Box 3167 Munster, Ind. 46321

Title / Author	Description	Publisher / Address
Multilevel Achievement Series (1972) by Robert A. Naslund, Lois P. Thorpe, and D. Welty Lefever.	adult education projects. Evaluates achievement in reading: comprehension and vocabulary; (math; spelling; use of sources and science; social studies; and language arts; three levels are available: blue (easiest), green (medium difficulty) and red (most difficult). Test content is only moderately child-oriented. No adult norms given. Scored in terms of percentiles and stanines.	259 E. Erie St. Chicago, Ill. 60611
Basic Reading and Word List (1968)	The purpose of the test is to provide an instrument to determine reading capability for selection in training programs for hard-core or disadvantaged persons. Contains no paragraph reading, but is built to cover a wide reading-vocabulary range. There are eighty true-false items, arranged in an ascending order of difficulty. The range of difficulty is approximately grades 3-8. Scoring is in terms of percentiles. Only one form is available.	Richardson, Bellows, Henry & Co. 1140 Connecticut Ave. N.W. Washington, D. C. 20036
Basic Reading and Rate Scale (1970) by Miles Tinker and Ronald P. Carver.	Measures the rate at which an individual can read very easy material. Appropriate for use in assessing reading rates at all levels of reading ability. The range of difficulty is from grades 3-16. Information about scoring and norms is not available.	Revrac Publications 2200 Forest Glen Rd. Silver Springs, Md. 20910
Basic Studies Inventory (1973) by Raymond J. Hodges, Grace C. Alexander, Arnold R. Rogers, and Casters B. Foster; edited by Barry M. Smith.	Designed for young adults to evaluate four areas: reading, comprehension, writing, listening and mathematics. Scoring is in terms of grade levels and percentiles. This criterion-referenced assessment can be used for level determination and diagnosis. Two forms are available.	P.A.R., Inc. Abbott Park Place Providence, R. I. 02903
Brief Test of Literacy (1968) by Thomas F. Donlon and W. Miles McPeek. (Public Health Service Publication #1000-2-no. 27.)	Developed to assess literacy in reading and writing within the framework of a national health survey. Suitable for use in the general population of adolescents and adults in the U.S. The reading section consists of twelve short paragraphs, each followed by three comprehension questions. The writing section requires the person to write five short sentences from dictation. Entire test takes from 5-8 minutes to administer. Scoring is in terms of a standard score with a cut-off point. Only one form is available.	U.S. Department of Health, Education, & Welfare Public Health Service Washington, D. C. 20402

TABLE 17.3 (Continued)

Test Name and Author(s)	Description	Publisher
California Achievement Tests (1970).	This is an extensive test battery created for use in the public schools at all grade levels. Some adult education projects report acceptable usage of the instrument, although content-wise and norm-wise it is relevant to children rather than adults. Two forms are available with five levels covering grades 1.5-12.0. The subtests evaluate achievement in reading: vocabulary and comprehension, mathematics, and language. The test is also useful in measuring the effectiveness of instruction in these areas. Scores are reported as grade levels, stanines, or percentiles.	CTB/McGraw-Hill Div. Del Monte Research Park Monterey, Calif. 93940
Comprehensive Test of Basic Skills (CTBS) (1968).	An extensive test battery created for use in public schools, grades 2-12, to measure achievement in basic skills. Some adult education projects report acceptable usage of the instrument, even though the content is child-oriented and there are no adult norms. The test covers reading vocabulary and comprehension, as well as language, arithmetic and study skills. Two forms (Q & R) and four levels are available. The scores are comparative in nature and can be used to find strengths and weaknesses. Scores are reported as grade equivalents, stanines, or percentiles.	CTB/McGraw-Hill Div. Del Monte Research Park Monterey, Calif. 93940
Doren Diagnostic Reading Test of Word Recognition Skills (1973) by Margaret Doren.	Designed for individuals whose background of acquired reading skills is unknown. Purports to be appropriate for primary children as well as adults. However, test content is extremely child-oriented and there are no adult norms presented. The test covers these areas: letter recognition, beginning sounds, whole word recognition, words within words, speech consonants, ending sounds, blending, rhyming, vowels, discriminate guessing (use of context clues), spelling, and sight words. Scoring is entirely criterion-referenced on a profile that identifies weaknesses and strengths. Only one form is provided.	American Guidance Testing Services, Inc. Circle Pines, Minn. 55014
Gates-MacGinitie Reading Survey Tests (1965) by Arthur I. Gates and	Designed for the public school at all levels, some of the forms present content that would be acceptable to adults. Purpose is to provide an instrument that reveals specific strengths and weaknesses in reading abilities and indicates the	Bureau of Publications, Teachers College Press, 502 W. 121 St.

...ing from grade ... to for ... read ... are speed accuracy), accuracy), vocabulary, level of comprehension and a total reading score. Test utilizes a cloze procedure for both speed and comprehension tests. Scores are reported in grade level equivalents and in percentiles.

Huelsman Word Discrimination Test (1958) by Charles B. Huelsman, Jr.	An instrument intended to provide a determination of how students use length, internal design, and external configuration in perceiving words. It is helpful in determining whether a low vocabulary score is caused by lack of symbol-to-meaning concept, or lack of recognition of a visual symbol configuration as a word. Consists of a series of ninety-six wordlike forms that progress with increasing difficulty. There is no manual. It is scored by grade equivalents through grade eight. None of the test structure or content is punitive to adults. Two forms are available.	Miami University Alumni Assoc. Miami University Oxford, Ohio 45067
Individualized Criterion-Referenced Testing	Instrument is designed for youth and young adults. Although administered to groups, results are reported for individuals. Covers criterion-referenced items that are correlated with performance in grades 1-8. The test provides a measure of an individual's success with specific objectives in the area of reading, and provides implications for specific prescriptions. Two forms are available.	Educational Progress A Division of Educational Development Corp. 4900 South Lewis Tulsa, Okla. 74105
Iowa Test of Educational Development (1963) by E. F. Lindquist and Leonard S. Feldt.	This is an extensive achievement test battery built for use in public schools, grades 9-12. Some adult education projects report acceptable use of parts of the battery, although the content is oriented toward teenagers and no adult norms are given. The purpose of the battery is to give teachers a comprehensive and objective description of pupil development and for obtaining measures of growth and comparable measures for all pupils. Of the nine tests in the total battery, the following would be appropriate for adult programs, particularly at the GED level: correctness of expression, math, social studies, science, literature. Norms are given in terms of grade equivalents, stanines and percentiles. Two forms, X4 and Y4, are reported to be used in adult programs.	Science Research Assoc. 259 E. Erie St. Chicago, Ill. 60611
Learning Lab Reading Placement Inventory (1968) by Joseph B. Carter.	The purpose of this test is to provide a fast means of initial placement in a learning center. The test is composed of fifty sentences or short paragraphs arranged in ascending order of difficulty. These are to be completed by using	Learning Lab Assoc. Inc. Box 8137 Washington, D. C. 20034

TABLE 17.3 (Continued)

Test Name and Author(s)	Description	Publisher
Reading Placement Inventory (cont.)	the correct word or phrase. Scoring is by a placement chart. Only one form is available.	
McCullough Word Analysis Tests (1963) by Constance M. McCullough.	The purpose of this test is to provide a diagnostic instrument for the measurement of phonetic and structural word-analysis skills that can be used in a group setting. The content of the test is acceptable to both children and adults. Diagnostic information is provided in the following areas: initial blends and digraphs, phonetic discrimination, matching letters to vowel sounds, sounding whole words, structural analysis total, interpreting phonetic symbols, phonetic analysis total, dividing words into syllables, and root words in affixed forms. Only one form is available. No norms are given, but scoring is plotted on an individual profile that visualizes strengths and weaknesses.	Personnel Press, Inc. 20 Nassau St. Princeton, N. J. 08540
Nelson-Denny Reading Test (1965) by M. J. Nelson and E. C. Denny, Revised by James I. Brown.	This reading survey test provides a measurement of reading achievement in vocabulary, paragraph comprehension, and rate. It is applicable for grades 9-12, college, and adults. Separate norms are provided for each level. Two forms are available. Scores are reported in percentiles and grade level equivalents. The content of this test is difficult to handle. It would not be recommended for adult programs working with basic levels, but rather for those preparing for the GED.	Houghton Mifflin Co. 1900 So. Batavia Geneva, Ill. 60134
Prescriptive Reading Inventory (1972) by George R. Burket and William E. Kline.	These tests were designed to evaluate elementary reading skills that are stated in terms of performance objectives. They may be useful to adult projects for diagnostic purposes with young adults, although the content, particularly of the lower levels, is extremely child-oriented. No norms are given. Scoring is entirely in terms of stated objectives. Tests are designed to show which reading skills have been learned and which are yet to be mastered. Most of the skills taught in elementary programs are covered. Four levels of the test are available that generally cover grades 1-6.	CTB/McGraw-Hill Div. Del Monte Research Park Monterey, Calif. 93940

Test	Description	Publisher
(continued from previous page)	to be reliably evaluated by traditional standardized tests. A broad range of ability is covered, from almost "ground zero" to minimal high school expectations. The test is scored to reflect proficiency at five levels: picture-word association, word decoding, phrase comprehension, sentence comprehension, and paragraph comprehension. The highest level passed represents the individual's score.	259 E. Erie St. Chicago, Ill. 60624
Silent Reading Diagnostic Test (1970) by Guy L. Bond, Bruce Balow and Cyril J. Hoyt.	The purpose of this group diagnostic test is to provide an instrument for the assessment of word recognition and analysis skills that are generally mastered in grades 2-6. The areas that are sampled are: words in isolation, words in context, visual-structural analysis, syllabication, word synthesis, beginning sounds, ending sounds, and vowel and consonant sounds. Scoring is in terms of grade equivalents, percentiles, and stanines. However, norms are for children only. Also, much of the material in the test is child-oriented, although the diagnostic profile of scores would also be helpful to an adult learner. Only one form is available.	Lyons and Carnahan 407 E. 25 St. Chicago, Ill. 60616
Stanford Achievement Test (1973) by Eric F. Gardner, Herbert C. Rudman, Bjorn Karlsen, and Jack C. Merwin.	An extensive achievement battery constructed for use in public schools, grades 1-9. Not specifically made for adults, but reported as being used in many adult programs. Much of the content is child-oriented. Norms are entirely for school-aged children. The reading section of the battery covers these areas: reading, vocabulary, comprehension, and word study skills. It is intended to provide a measurement of pupil achievement in these areas yielding information that can be used for grouping as well as curriculum evaluation. The test is furnished in two forms on three levels of difficulty: level I (primary), level II (intermediate), and level III (advanced). Scores can be translated into scaled scores, grade equivalents, percentile ranks, and stanines.	Harcourt Brace Jovano- vich, Inc. 757 Third Ave. New York, N.Y. 10017
Test of Adult Basic Education (1967) by Ernest W. Tiegs and Willis W. Clark.	A battery of tests designed for mature adults to use in the identification of the instructional needs of individuals with severe educational limitations. Level E (easy) is an adaptation of the upper primary level of the *California Achievement Test: 1957 Edition*. Level M (medium) is an adaptation of the elementary level of the *CAT*. Level D (difficult) is an adaptation of the junior high school level of the *CAT*. The battery includes a ten-minute locator test that indicates	CTB/McGraw-Hill Div. Del Monte Research Park Monterey, Calif. 93940

TABLE 17.3 (Concluded)

Test Name and Author(s)	Description	Publisher
Test of Adult Basic Education (cont.)	to the administrator which level of the test is appropriate for an individual. The test measures achievement in vocabulary, reading comprehension, and arithmetc reasoning and fundamentals. Levels M and D include subtests of mechanics of English and spelling. Although some of the test content has been revised to reflect adult interest and tastes, these changes from the original *CAT* have been minimal, with many items still reflective of child experiences. Scoring is in terms of grade equivalents, but no data is given as to whether they were established with adults or just carried over from the youth-oriented *CAT*.	
Triggs Diagnostic Reading Test, Survey Section (1956) by Frances Triggs, George Spache, and Agatha Townsend.	This test battery was created for public schools, grades 4-13. Although oriented toward younger learners, some adult programs report using the instrument. The test measures reading rate, general reading, vocabulary, and paragraph comprehension. The survey section, which appears to be the most useful of the battery, is published in two levels: grades 4-8 and grades 7-13. The lower level has two forms, while the upper level advertises eight. Some of the items on the test are outdated. The test is oriented for the child and younger learner. Scoring is by percentiles. No adult norms are offered.	Committee on Diagnostic Reading Tests, Inc. Mountain Home, N. C. 28758 (Level 7-13 is also distributed by Science Research Assoc.: 259 E. Erie St. Chicago, Ill. 60624

4. Look at the research, both pro and con, concerning a test that you are considering. A good evaluation of nearly all standardized tests can be found in Oscar Buros' seven volumes of *Mental Measurements Yearbooks* (1972), or his *Reading Tests and Reviews* (1968, 1975).
5. Do not select an instrument that requires more expertise than you have to administer, score, and interpret.
6. Write the publisher for a specimen set of the test so that you can thoroughly study it before you use it. Most publishers provide these at nominal cost.

Summary

The old saying "Familiarity Breeds Contempt" only holds true when a friendship is lopsided, with one doing most of the taking while the other does all of the giving. I would rewrite that homily to read, "Informality Breeds Better Learning." Particularly in a tutorial situation, where one isn't concerned with maintaining discipline over thirty or more adolescents (Hawkins 1972, p. 110).

This chapter has been concerned with the use of standardized test instruments in the evaluation of reading. Their uses and limitations in adult basic education have been specified. Two extensive tables listing sources of most of the oral and silent reading evaluation instruments presently available and appropriate for adults were included in this chapter. However, some of the items listed in the tables are referred to in chapters 18 and 19.

One-half the earth's adults, totaling seven hundred million people, have never attended school and neither can they read nor write (Berg 1965, p. 47).

After initial reading levels have been established and instruction has begun with materials that are relevant to the learner and at the proper instructional level, then the adult basic education teacher will probably want to take a more intensive look at the specific problems involved. Each problem will be unique. No two reading problems will be caused by exactly the same combination of factors. Therefore, each individual will require special consideration.

Several things need investigation: the specifics of the reading performance itself; factors internal to the learner, such as physical and emotional problems; and the factors that are external to the learner, such as learning environment and types of assignments that can be handled—all require the teacher's attention.

Separating the Strands of the Reading Problem

To many illiterates, you represent the upper classes. If you are condescending in your manner toward them, they will be aware of it. They will resent it (E. H. Smith 1970, p. 6).

An analysis of a silent reading test and/or an oral inventory will still leave many questions in the teacher's mind regarding strengths, weaknesses, and inhibiting factors to the reading process. The qualitative data from these tests and inventories used as previously suggested will show the teacher which areas need further exploration and delineation.

Visual and Auditory Problems

Visual and auditory problems are the first thing that should be considered when exploring a severe reading problem. Certainly, if the learner cannot see the test clearly, he cannot read it. If he cannot hear properly, he cannot respond to phonetic elements correctly. The teacher has the responsibility of being alert to signs that these physical factors may be inhibiting the reading process. Beyond general screening for these problems, medical specialists are needed to determine the extent of the difficulty and prescribe any treatment or correction.

Of the many signs that a visual perception deficit may be a contributing factor to a reading problem, difficulty in copying forms and words, difficulty in maintaining writing on a straight line, a tendency to read in seemingly awkward physical positions in an effort to focus properly, and a tendency to skip lines during oral reading are the most generally observed performance deviations noted in adult readers. As far as test results are concerned, slow reading and a low vocabulary score with a low score on Huelsman's *Word Discrimination Test* (1955) would indicate a need for a more detailed examination.

Functioning on the *Keystone Visual Survey Tests* (1961) will indicate to the teacher whether or not acuity and binocularity problems exist. These are problems in the visual mechanism itself. Problems in the way the neurological system organizes visual information may be ascertained by functioning on the *Minnesota Percepto-Diagnostic Test* (Fuller 1969), or some of the Wold's screening tests (1970) may give further clues about the problem.

When a learner cocks one ear toward the speaker, leans forward as if to get closer to the sound, or fails to respond when he cannot see the speaker, there is a good chance that an auditory acuity problem may be involved in the reading difficulty. The public health nurse can quickly administer an audiometer test to verify your suspicions. She can also help make some arrangements for treatment or correction.

However, it is possible for a learner to have excellent auditory acuity—that is, the hearing mechanism is in good working order—yet he still experiences difficulty in interpreting and organizing the sounds of language. This is called auditory perception and is as much a learned neurological functioning as it is an acoustical one. Continual mispronunciation of particular phonemes, difficulty in learning to apply phonic generalizations, and a low score on any kind of a phonics test would be indicative of the possible existence of this kind of problem. The *Wepman Auditory Discrimination Test* (1959), which is found in appendix 23, and the *Roswell-Chall Auditory Blending Test* (1959) both explore this problem. Certainly these instruments will identify the phonemes that are giving difficulty so that these can be taught to the learner.

Problems with Reversals and Word Organization

An occasional reversal in an oral reading inventory or in daily reading performance may be atypical. However, if the learner does this very often, the teacher would be interested in exploring further. This would be particularly appropriate if the learner were ambidextrous, left-handed, or did not have right laterality established for the whole body. Experts are not certain just what the relationship is between laterality and reading problems, but most are certain that such a relationship does exist.

Laterality can be determined by a number of informal observations, such as the following:

1. Which ear does the individual use to answer a telephone?
2. Which eye does he use to sight a rifle or a telescope?
3. Which hand does he use to throw a ball? To catch a ball? To eat with? To write with? And for various other tasks?
4. Which foot does he use to kick a ball? To hop on? Step down first on?
5. Which side of his body would he say was the strongest?

These observations can determine whether laterality is clearly established down one side of the body, or whether it is mixed. If it is mixed or left dominant, there appears to be a tendency toward difficulty with language skills.

To determine whether any tendency toward right-to-left orientation is of sufficient magnitude to be a factor in a reading problem, look again at Huelsman's *Word Discrimination Test* (1955). By writing in the margin the kinds of errors the learner made—for example, inversion of *n* and *u*, reversal of *b* and *d*, reversal of whole word, or reversal of word parts— a pattern may become apparent. If there are more than a few reversals here, it would be well to ask the learner to read Zintz' *List of Easily Confused Words* (1977) found in appendix 24. If the lack of left-right orientation is sufficient to be a factor in the reading problem, it will be evident on these two instruments.

Word Analysis Problems

If the oral inventories or silent reading tests suggest weaknesses in word identification, then process instruments designed to gather further data about specific skills should be used.

General Weakness in Word Identification Skills

Difficulty in identifying unknown words in the daily reading experience, low scores on vocabulary subtests of silent reading tests, and slow, labored reading may all be indicators of difficulty in this area. Probably the most extensive diagnostic instrument that would be appropriate for adults is the *McCullough Word Analysis Test* (1963). The *Silent Reading Diag-*

nostic Test by Bond, Balow, and Hoyt (1970) also evaluates these skills, but the instrument is more child-oriented than McCullough's test. A quick, but not nearly so detailed, analysis of word skills can be gained through the *Roswell-Chall Reading Test of Word Analysis Skills* (1959). Performance on one of these instruments would indicate which word identification skills are particularly weak and need instruction.

Weakness in Phonic Analysis

There is nothing more deadly to the instructional process than insisting on teaching phonic generalizations that have already been learned or for which the learner has no present need. If the scores on the general reading tests indicate a weakness in relating the sound of the language to the printed symbols, or if such a difficulty is observed during everyday reading instruction, the administration of one of the phonic inventories would be useful. The *Boyd Phonics Test* (1968), which is found in appendix 26, or the *Botel Phonics Test,* which is a part of the larger *Botel Reading Inventory* (1961), will specifically identify those phonic elements that require instruction. The *California Phonics Test* (Brown and Cottrell 1962) elicits other types of data regarding the learner's understanding of the sound system of the language. This would be useful later on in the instructional process.

Weakness in Structural Analysis

When it is noted that the learner omits affixes, or does not differentiate compound words from other word structures, then it would be well to look again at the responses made on the *McCullough Word Analysis Test* (1963) or the *Roswell-Chall Reading Test of Word Analysis* (1959). There are sections in these tests dealing with most of the important structural features of words. This information will help to pinpoint the exact difficulty. Another informal means of securing data about the learner's understanding of compound words is through the Zintz *List of Compound Words* (1977), found in appendix 26. If the learner does not understand compound words, certainly these must be taught.

Emotional Problems As Related to Reading

Emotional problems and reading problems go hand-in-hand. For the adult learner, any emotional problem that might be a concomitant factor in the reading difficulty is probably so intertwined with other problems that it is very difficult for the teacher to identify it. Without prying and invading personal privacy, or without going beyond the usual expertise of a teacher, most of the needed information on this inhibiting factor will be gained through observation. Some hints regarding an emotional problem may possibly be given in an autobiography, or structured sentence completion exercise. One must be careful, however, not to read too much into these projective techniques. As the reading teacher gains in rapport with the learner and as he talks about himself, his life, and his needs, most of the data in this area that would relate to a reading problem will be forthcoming.

Evaluating Second Language or Dialectical Problems

The interference of a second language or a dialect may be the basic cause of many of the difficulties noted both in everyday reading performance and on both silent and oral reading tests. A few instruments are available that help to ascertain language functioning. These are listed and described in table 18.1, "Ability and Placement Tests Suitable for Speakers of English as a Second Language." The problem for the teacher is to determine the following:

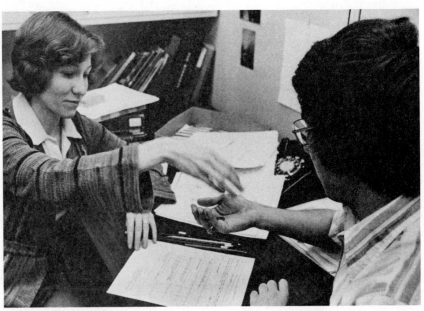

Teacher administering an oral English as a second language test. (Courtesy of William Rainey Harper College, Palatine, Illinois.)

1. What language does the learner think in? Sometimes the question, "When you are very angry, which language will you curse in?" gives the answer.
2. Does he read and/or write in a language other than English?
3. How does his level of oral language usage in English compare with his reading usage of English?
4. Can he learn to be comfortable functioning in both languages, using each when appropriate?
5. What are the interference points that are causing difficulty? These need to be identified on the phonemic (sound) level, the syntactical (sentence structure) level, and the semantic (meaning) level.

Unfortunately, most of this data cannot be gathered through test instruments. Most will be gathered informally through interview and by just listening to the learner as he uses oral language.

Learning Style Diagnosis

*In a literacy campaign we need faith, hope, and love—these three;
and the greatest of these is love. It has no substitutes. When it fails,
everything fails (Laubach 1960, p. 36).*

Kidd has cautioned that for an adult, learning implies a change in behavior, thus a change in self-concept. If he learns, he must change and become to some degree someone he was not before. This new person must be someone he can accept and defend. It is in the relationships with other learners and with the teacher that this new person does in actuality become defensible (Kidd 1959).

Creating a learning situation in which these changes can occur is a major task. Certainly as the teacher is involved in the assessment of other aspects of the task of learning to read, he will also be concerned with factors in the individual's learning style that will inhibit or promote this atmosphere. These are the factors that will merit consideration.

Learning Environment

Each person has different requirements as to an environment conducive to learning. Look for the answers to these questions:

1. Where does the learner appear to do his best work? At home? In the classroom? In the library or media center? In the outdoors?
2. What kind of physical environment seems to promote the best learning? Large room with open spaces? Or cubicle, office-type space?

TABLE 18.1 ABILITY AND PLACEMENT TESTS SUITABLE FOR SPEAKERS OF ENGLISH AS A SECOND LANGUAGE

Test Name and Author(s)	Description	Publisher
Barranquilla Rapid Survey Intelligence Test (1958) by Francisco Del Olmo.	Provides an index of learning potential by evaluating verbal intelligence and number reasoning through items covering general knowledge, vocabulary, verbal reasoning, logical reasoning, and numerical reasoning. Administered in Spanish. Ranges from grades 3 through adults.	The Psychological Corp. 304 E. 45 St. New York, N. Y. 10017
Bilingual Syntax Measure (BSM) (1975) by Marina K. Burt, Heid, C. Dulay and Eduardo Hernandez.	Test only gives norms for young children. However, an adult educator should consider this instrument. Content-wise, it would not be offensive to an adult. It is an inventory to assess the English and Spanish oral syntactic proficiency and/or the language dominance of the children in bilingual programs.	Harcourt, Brace Jovanovich, Inc. 757 Third Avenue New York, N. Y. 10017
Comprehensive English Language Test for Speakers of English As A Second Language (1970) by Dale P. Harris and Leslie A. Palmer.	Divided into three sections—listening, language structure, and vocabulary. Designed for grades 9-16 and adults. Listening test is concerned with comprehension of short statements, questions, and dialogues as spoken by native English speakers. Structure section is concerned with manipulation of English grammatical structures. Vocabulary section is difficult. Some reading is required. Test is administered in English.	McGraw-Hill Book Co. 1221 Ave. of the Americas New York, N. Y. 10036
Cooperative Inter-American Series (1967) by Herschel T. Manuel.	A series of tests in various areas available in parallel English and Spanish forms. Parts of the series are: tests of general ability; tests of language usage; tests of natural sciences: vocabulary and interpretation of reading materials; and tests of reading. The range is from grades 8-13. Tests developed for use in Puerto Rico and Mexico.	Guidance Testing Assoc. 6916 Shirley Ave. Austin, Tex. 78752
Escala de Inteligencia Wechsler para Adultos (1968) by David Wechsler; Translated and adapted by R. F. Green and J. N. Martinez.	A Spanish translation of the *Wechsler Intelligence Scale for Adults.* Adapted to the Spanish culture of Puerto Rico. Individually administered. Requires competent psychometric skills as well as good use of Spanish to administer and interpret.	The Psychological Corp. 304 E. 45 St. New York, N. Y. 10017

Oral Placement Test for Adults (1971) by Allen Ferrel.	Test employs a structured interview to assess the English oral production and aural comprehension of adult basic education learners. Emphasis of the test is on the use of English as a functional tool of communication. Proficiency levels identified are: elementary, intermediate, advanced and exempt.	Southwest Cooperative Educational Laboratory, Inc. 1404 San Mateo Blvd., S.E. Albuquerque, N. M. 87108
Structure Test-English Language (STEL) (1976) by Jeanette Best and Donna Ilyin.	Provides a quick placement or achievement measure of the learner's knowledge of the structure of the English language. Two forms are available on each of three levels. Appropriate for teenagers and adults.	Newbury House Publishers, Inc. 68 Middle Road Rowley, Mass. 01969

3. Does he learn better at a desk than he does sitting in an easy chair, with his feet up, or changing position frequently?
4. What type of lighting, temperature controls, and ventilation appear to be the most conducive to attention and learning?
5. What kind of sound can the learner tolerate and still be productive? A murmur? Distant sound? High level of conversation? Soft music? Laughter? The "buzz" of groups working? Or does he require absolute quiet?

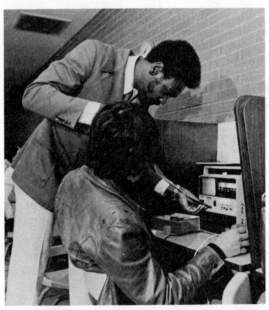

Learning hardware sometimes enhances the learning environment for some adults. (Courtesy of Albuquerque Technical-Vocational Institute, Albuquerque, N. M.)

Attention and Time Pressures

Each person has particular times during the day when it is difficult to be alert and pay attention to a learning task. Moreover, the length of attention span and the way it is utilized is different for each one. Some people attend to the task continuously until it is completed, while others work by irregular, short bursts of concentrated effort interrupted by forgetting periods. Consideration of these factors when planning instruction can make the difference between a successful and an unsuccessful experience.

Perceptual Styles and Strengths

How does the student learn most easily? In designing instructional experiences, the teacher must be aware of the modalities that the learner most easily utilizes for learning—visual experiences, such as books and pictures; auditory experiences, such as sound recordings; tactile and kinesthetic experiences of touching, feeling, and moving; or a combination of these.

Types of Structure and Assignments

Some individuals are self-activated, self-motivated learners who require little more than a guide to learning. Others are not, but require much structure, with short-term goals, deadlines, and strict schedules. Some learners need very little external pressure and motivation to succeed, while others need a continual pressure and constant reinforcement in order to be productive. Some individuals cannot learn unless each detail of the assignment is laid out for him. Others are more at ease with a contract, which they and the teacher have designed. Still others can produce through totally self-directed projects. The teacher will also want to consider whether or not the learner is comfortable working in groups.

    These are the most important aspects of individual learning style that must be assessed and taken into consideration when instruction in reading is planned.

Summary

For some disabled readers "silent reading is almost wholly divorced from oral reading. (They are) not only more advanced in silent reading, but treat oral reading as though it had nothing to do with silent reading. These are, to their minds, separate functions, requiring separate abilities. They can read a sentence silently without error yet ten seconds later be incapable of reading the same sentence aloud" (Hawkins 1972, p. 87).

This chapter has been concerned with the specific weaknesses that a teacher might note in reading performance. It has further been concerned with the physical, emotional, and dialectical difficulties that might be partially responsible for the problem. The adult's individual learning style and its effect on the reading performance was also discussed. These are all areas of functioning with the potential of limiting success in reading if the adult education teacher does not deal with them diagnostically.

19.
Assessment
of Reading and
Learning Potential

Is the teacher going to put pressure on me? Treat me like a child? Is he going to be an authoritarian 'know-it-all,' or a friendly guide? These are the concerns of the adult learner (Fellenz 1974, p. 97).

For most of the learners in adult basic education classes, the ability to learn to read can be assumed to be adequate. Some who return to school for learning later in life were classified as slow learners or borderline mental defectives during their public school experience. But this earlier classification may have been based on many dynamics in the individual's life that are no longer pertinent. The fact that the individual has survived in our society and is now a mature, job-oriented adult who is seeking assistance in learning to read is probably a sufficient indicator that the basic abilities to do so are existent.

But such an assumption is a subjective judgment. Unfortunately, it may not always be true. Therefore, the adult educator needs to develop some techniques for assessing reading and learning potential. This will probably only need to be undertaken when it appears that present efforts to learn to read are not succeeding.

Assessment Through Listening Comprehension

Reading waits on the reader, patiently, forever, if need be. This is not so in listening (Hillburn 1973, p. 30).

Assessing reading potential through listening comprehension appears to be one of the most logical avenues for the reading teacher to use. Listening and reading are both components of language. Usually a measurement of one will be indicative of potential for development of the other. The ability to process information and to utilize cognitive skills through oral language (listening and speaking), where reading of the printed page is not involved, has long been regarded as a general indicator of mental functioning as well as a predictor of achievement in reading.

Informal Procedures

Informally, a teacher may do this in the classroom, by simply being aware of how the learner functions cognitively in oral discussions and oral reports. Of course any judgment made would be subjective, since no normative or criterion standards would apply. When this kind of measurement is needed; however, this kind of judgment is seldom adequate.

Another informal procedure that may be employed is an extension of the oral reading inventory or the silent reading test. The method is simple. When in the process of an oral reading inventory the learner's reading skills have noticeably broken down and the frustrational reading level has been reached, the teacher then continues reading the paragraphs orally *to* the learner. Comprehension questions on each paragraph are given, to which the learner responds orally. This procedure is continued until the learner can no longer respond adequately to the comprehension questions. Of course, this extension of the inventory cannot be included in the reading score, but is scored separately as a capacity level for reading.

A silent reading test can be used for a listening test in a similar manner by allowing the learner to listen while the teacher reads the vocabulary and paragraph comprehension subtests orally to him. Responses may be given orally or recorded on an answer sheet. Such a test administration should be scored in the same manner in which the silent reading test is scored. But it must be remembered that the score will be somewhat inflated because the standardization of the test has been tampered with by using administration procedures that were not allowed for in the standardization process. The difference between this score and the reading score may be indicative of reading potential.

Standardized Procedures

Unfortunately, very few standardized listening comprehension tests are available on the market. None have been created specifically for adults with adult norms and test content. Some, however, may be useful in adult programs, provided the adult educator takes into account the youth-oriented norms rather than adult comparisons.

In each of these standardized listening comprehension tests, the learner has to respond on an answer sheet, which by necessity he must be able to read. In some cases, the words that he must choose from are on the answer sheet. Therefore, he is not only listening to receive information; he is also doing a minimal amount of reading. Because of this, some researchers have justly criticized the instruments, saying that the scores are really a composite of mostly listening ability, but also some reading.

The *Brown-Carlsen Listening Comprehension Test* (1955) appears to have the least amount of this contamination. It is also the one that would be the most meaningful and enjoyable for adults. The three levels of the *Durrell Listening-Reading Series* (1969) judge listening comprehension in a somewhat different manner. This test presents equal material through both listening and reading. Thus, two scores on equivalent material are available for comparison. The *New Zealand Listening Comprehension Test* (1972) utilizes material that would mostly be acceptable to adults, but does require answer sheets that must be read. All of these assessment instruments are briefly described in table 19.1.

Assessment Through Measurement of Learning Ability

In 1970, the Bell System estimated that its companies spent $25 million just on basic education for its employees; and the subsidiary of another large national company claimed that the cost of training new workers to meet basic literacy requirements would be $3.8 million over a four year period. . . . We cannot afford to ignore this national disease, or to treat it with "benign neglect" (Smith 1974, p. 2).

Measurement of learning ability goes beyond the specific concern regarding language development. Psychologists and neurologists are uncertain regarding the details of learning ability. Therefore, it becomes a very difficult entity to measure in any meaningful way. A detailed analysis of an individual's cognitive abilities can be pursued by a psychologist or a psychometrist who is trained in administering and interpreting the complex instruments required. In cases where educators are experiencing a great deal of confusion regarding curriculum specifications for a particular individual because of the severity of his learning problem, it is recommended that such services be sought.

However, for most needs in adult basic education the teacher can utilize a few of the simple individually administered tests without the assistance of a more highly trained person. That is, he can do so *if* he is willing to do the following things:

1. Study the test manual and the test itself thoroughly before using it, then follow the test directions *exactly*.
2. Practice with the instrument until you can accurately handle the materials with ease, keeping your mind on the learner rather than on the testing procedures.
3. Be objective, taking care not to either verbally or nonverbally influence the quality of the learner's responses in any way.
4. In interpreting the results, be careful not to generalize the findings too broadly or attempt to make the test results mean more than was intended by the testmaker.
5. Remember the limits of your expertise.

TABLE 19.1 LISTENING COMPREHENSION TESTS USEFUL IN ADULT BASIC EDUCATION

Test Name and Author(s)	Description	Publisher
Brown-Carlsen Listening Comprehension Test (1955) by James I. Brown and G. Robert Carlsen.	Test is normed for grades 9 through 12. Content is appropriate for adults, even if norms are not. Contains four parts: immediate recall, following directions, recognizing transitions, and lecture comprehension. Available in two forms. Scores are in grade levels and percentiles.	Harcourt Brace Jovanovich, Inc. 757 Third Ave. New York, N. Y. 10017
Durrell Listening-Reading Series (1969) by Donald D. Durrell and Mary T. Hayes.	Test is built for grades 1 through 9 of the public school. Test is constructed in three levels: primary (grades 1-3.5), intermediate (grades 3.5-6), and advanced (grades 7-9). Material presents a reading test with equal material to that of the listening test. Result is in the form of age equivalents (which are not applicable to adults), percentiles and stanines. Some of the content would be difficult to use with adults. Most of the advanced level utilizes content that is suitable.	Harcourt Brace Jovanovich, Inc. 757 Third Ave. New York, N. Y. 10017
Progressive Achievement Test: Listening Comprehension (1972) by Warwich B. Elley and Neil A. Reid.	Developed for use in New Zealand schools; therefore, norms may not be exactly applicable. Available in two forms. Content generally would be acceptable for adult populations, although norms are questionable. Yields percentile scores.	New Zealand Council for Educational Research Education House 178-182 Willis St. Wellington C, 2, New Zealand

If the teacher is willing to follow these specifications, the instruments that broadly assess intellectual abilities are available for use.

Individual Assessment

Closely akin to the concept of estimating potential for learning by assessing listening ability are the procedures that attempt to measure verbal-mental ability through an individual diagnostic technique. The evaluation is done in such a way that the learner never needs to read. In this way, his ability to function cognitively is demonstrated both through his ability to comprehend the oral language he hears and his ability to respond with oral language. Several standardized instruments that can be utilized in adult basic education are available to investigate both of these aspects of language functioning.

Probably the most useful one is the *Peabody Picture Vocabulary Test* (Dunn 1959). The task requirement for the learner is to point to the picture that has something to do with the word the teacher says to him. At no time does he have to become involved with the printed form of that word, only the oral concept. This is clearly a measurement of receptive vocabulary—that is, the words he can hear and perceive meaning from. Since general learning ability and oral language development are so closely related, the score on the PPVT is highly correlated to the Full Scale Score of a Wechsler test (1955).

A low PPVT score may not be indicative of low innate mental ability, but more correctly is indicative of insufficient language development. Such a finding would direct the teacher to spend more effort in the development of oral skills rather than to specifically work on reading.

Another individual measurement instrument that adult basic education teachers have found to be useful is the *Slosson Intelligence Test* (1963). This test is quite different from the PPVT and is tapping different abilities. The SIT is a developmental Binet-type scale that evaluates developmental tasks, reasoning ability, and the accumulation of prior knowledge. The items were adapted from both the Binet and the Wechsler tests. Scores on this tend to run somewhat low for persons with reading problems because, to an extent, it is measuring accumulated school learning. However, the score correlates well with the *Binet* and is a satisfactory measurement of general learning ability (Swanson 1970).

A low score on the SIT would have to be investigated by examining the items the learner missed and attempting to infer the reason for the error, rather than just assuming that he lacks innate mental ability.

Unless learning to read has really "hit a snag," making it necessary to look differently at the various facets of the individual's cognitive strengths

and weaknesses, measurement with either one of these instruments should
be adequate.

Group Measurements of Ability

Group measurements of ability have the same weaknesses and problems
as do group measurements of reading. Most are generally unfair to older
learners because they are heavily weighted for speed and are largely dependent on the individual's acquired and stored knowledge or memory.
They are heavily weighted with items depending on formal school information that adults may no longer be concerned with or that may have
been forgotten.

Kidd (1959), in investigating the utility of group intelligence tests with
adults points to these limitations:

1. They are based on tasks associated with school rather than with real
   life situations.
2. They rely on a motivation factor which is characteristic of youth, but
   not necessarily of adults.
3. They are based on experiences and performances of children and adolescents rather than adults.
4. They measure performance in units of time, which is an inevitable
   handicap for older persons (pp. 77-78).

An additional handicap should be added to this list when anticipating the
use of group ability tests with adults who are poor readers. They must
read the test to demonstrate their cognitive abilities.

In spite of all of these very serious limitations, many adult education
programs insist on evaluating mental ability with paper and pencil group-
administered tests. It might be added here that educational programs are
not the only agencies ignoring these limitations. Employment agencies
and many businesses and industries routinely administer these tests to
prospective employees under the guise of being "aptitude" tests. Because
of this, both the group and the individual tests that are available to adult
programs are listed and briefly described in table 19.2.

Implications for Reading Instruction from the
Wechsler Adult Intelligence Scale (1955)

This is a highly sophisticated instrument that should *only* be administered
and scored by a person with the proper psychometric credentials. However, each of the eleven subtests has implications for reading instruction.

Our purpose here is to show the teacher what to look for *after* the psychometrist has administered this instrument to the learner. A description of of the subtests and the thought functions that each purports to measure is given on the "Strength-Weakness Spectrum for Wechsler Tests," found in appendix 28. Consider some of these implications for reading instruction, which should be helpful.

Analysis of Subtests in Relation to Reading Ability

The information and vocabulary subtests are two good measures of general, or global, intelligence. An adult may score low in information because he has been away from the school learning situation, but he should score well on vocabulary regardless of how long he has been out of school. This appears to be one of the few abilities that hold and even expand throughout life. It appears to resist the deterioration of age, and is, therefore, useful in evaluating the learning ability of adult illiterates.

In the comprehension subtest the learner is presented with practical situations common to our society and asked what he would do. Quite often the person with a reading disability has a good grasp of the social situations and an understanding of society. Illiterates generally score well here because achievement does not depend on book learning.

The similarities subtest is a good one to assist in distinguishing between the slow learner and the handicapped reader, since it is so sensitive to intellectual impairment. Disabled readers generally score comparatively high here.

Barring the effects of transient anxiety, the arithmetic score may run higher than some of the others for the handicapped reader of average or better ability. This subtest only calls for arithmetical reasoning.

In the digit span subtest, the learner is presented with orally administered numerals that he has to repeat in proper sequence, first forward and later backward. This is an important help in analyzing reading difficulties that might have a neurological genesis. Learners with neurological deficits usually have extreme difficulty repeating the digits backwards.

The object assembly subtest involves the ability to see relationships of parts of the whole in a familiar configuration. Along with the block design, this task gives much insight into how the learner approaches a problem, his working habits, level of frustration, and persistence. Problem-solving techniques are apparent, such as logical, sequential, analytical, and trial and error. The manner in which the student tackles this task is often the manner in which he attacks unknown words. The confusion shown here is important in assessing reading disabilities.

The block design subtest is the opposite of object assembly. In this

TABLE 19.2 ABILITY TESTS USEFUL IN ADULT BASIC EDUCATION

Test Name and Author(s)	Description	Publisher
Arthur Point Scale of Performance Tests: Form I and Form II. Rev. (1947) by Grace Arthur.	An individually administered test appropriate for handicapped readers. Requires minimum use of language. Scale consists of performance tasks, such as the Knox Cube, various form boards, picture completion, mazes, etc. Form I was supposed to be superceded by Form II, although the earlier form is still reported in use by some evaluators. Form II ranges from 4.5 years to superior adults. May be suitable for second-language problems. Test requires a trained psychometrist for administration and interpretation.	Form I available from: Stoelting Company 1350 S. Kostner Chicago, Ill. 60623 Form II available from: Psychological Corp. 304 E. 45 St. New York, N.Y. 10017
Chicago Nonverbal Examination (1963) by Andrew W. Brown.	A group test designed to evaluate learning ability without the involvement of language. Suitable for those for whom English is a second language or for those with reading problems or other handicaps. Standardized for either verbal or pantomime administration. Ranges from 6 years through adults.	Psychological Corp. 304 E. 45 St. New York, N.Y., 10017
Fundamental Achievement Series (FAS) (1969) by George K. Bennett and Jerome D. Doppelt.	Designed to assess the knowledge and competencies that a job applicant may be expected to have acquired in the course of ordinary daily living and that will be relevant to actual job performance—generally termed *aptitude test.* FAS-Verbal Test consists of items measuring ability to read signs, menus, directories, recognize correct spelling, vocabulary, understand orally presented information and write legibly. Numerical test is concerned with telling time, recognizing numbers, using calendars, computing interest, and other arithmetic problems. Can be administered by tape recorder. Ranges from basic literacy level through 8th grade.	Psychological Corp. 304 E. 45 St. New York, N.Y. 10017
Gilliland Learning Potential Examination (1970) by Hap Gilliland.	Designed specifically for poor readers. Ranges from 6 years through adults. Measures visual memory, symbolic representation, symbolic identification, relationships, listening comprehension, picture completion and general information. Yields nonreading and noncultural IQ scores. Some subtests also useful in determining interests so that relevant instructional materials can be chosen.	Montana Reading Clinic Publications 517 Rimrock Rd. Billings, Mont. 59102

Test	Description	Publisher
gence Tests: Scales I, II, III (1963) by Raymond B. Cattell and A.K.S. Cattell	are series, classification, matrices and conditions. Perceptual and nonverbal measurements. Spanish edition available. Ranges are: scale I—ages 4-8 and mentally defective adults; scale II—ages 8-13 and average adults; scale III—grades 9-12 and superior adults.	Ability Testing 1602 Coronado Dr. Champaign, Ill. 61820
Kahn Intelligence Test: Experimental Form (1960) by Theodore C. Kahn.	Individually administered test requiring a minimum of verbalization and almost independent of differential educational and cultural learning factors. Requires psychometric training for administration and interpretation. Ranges from one month old through adults.	Psychological Test Specialists Box 1441 Missoula, Mont. 59801
Leiter International Performance Scale (1965) by Russell Grayton Leiter.	Individually administered, nonverbal test appropriate for illiterates, foreign born, disabled readers. Consists of subtests requiring matching, ranging from pairing of colors to the relationships of designs and analogies. Requires psychometric training for administration and interpretation. Ranges from age 2 through adulthood.	Stoelting Co. 1350 S. Kostner Chicago, Ill. 60623
Nonverbal Reasoning Test (1966) by Raymond J. Corsini.	Tests the ability to think logically through the medium of pictorial problems. Purported to be relatively culture-free and not influenced by language facility. Norms are reported only for adult male employees. Utilized by industry as an aptitude test.	Education-Industry Service 1225 E. 60 St. Chicago, Ill. 60637
Personnel Tests for Industry: Oral Directions Test, Form S (1954) by Charles R. Langmuir.	Wide-range measure of ability minimizing effects of reading, and writing. Measures the ability to understand what one is told to do. Ranges from adolescent to adult. Also available in a Spanish edition. Used by industry as a screening test.	The Psychological Corp. 304 E. 45 St. New York, N. Y. 10017
Peabody Picture Vocabulary Test (1959) by Lloyd M. Dunn.	Individual test designed to provide a well-standardized estimate of verbal intelligence through measuring his hearing vocabulary. Requires no language. Only requires student to point to a picture. Ranges from age 2 through 18. Suitable for adults.	American Guidance Services Publishers Bldg. Circle Pines, Minn. 53014
Purdue Nonlanguage Test (1969) by Joseph Tiffin.	A culture-free test designed for use in industry to measure mental ability. Items consist entirely of geometric forms. Normed for adults only.	University Book Store 360 State St. West Lafayette, Ind. 47906

TABLE 19.2 (Continued)

Test Name and Author(s)	Description	Publisher
Quick Word Test (1967) by Edgar F. Borgatta and Raymond J. Corsini.	Provides a quick, inexpensive and easily applied measure of general ability. Group administered. Measurement is verbal, based on extensiveness of vocabulary. Test range is grades 4-15. Available in two levels (elementary and high school) with parallel forms for each level. Norms are not specifically for adults, although this test is reported in use by some adult education centers.	Harcourt Brace Jovanovich, Inc. 757 Third Ave. New York, N. Y. 10017
RBH Industrial Questionnaire (1963).	Purported to be a measure of general ability designed for use in the screening of basic blue-collar employees, unskilled laborers, and routine factory workers, etc. Items cover reading comprehension, arithmetic reasoning, and chemical comprehension. Used by industry as an aptitude test.	Richardson, Bellows, Henry & Co., Inc. 1140 Connecticut Ave., N.W. Washington, D. C. 20036
RBH Nonverbal Reasoning Test (1963).	A nonverbal and nonlanguage test designed for use in screening employees. Examinee must be able to read numbers; identify illustrations, symbols and geometric design. Available in long form and in short form. Purports to use a minimum of language skills. Used by industry as an aptitude test.	Richardson, Bellows, Henry & Co., Inc. 1140 Connecticut Ave., N.W. Washington, D. C. 20036
RBH Test of Learning Ability, Forms DS-12 and DT-12 (1963).	Measures three components of intelligence: vocabulary comprehension, arithmetic reasoning, and ability to perceive spatial relationships. Purports to use a minimum of language. Used by industry as an aptitude test.	Richardson, Bellows, Henry & Co., Inc. 1140 Connecticut Ave., N.W. Washington, D. C. 20036
SRA Pictorial Reasoning Test (1967) by Robert N. McMurray and Phyllis D. Arnold.	A measure of reasoning and concept formation that is relatively independent of language and reading skills. Utilizes five drawings or pictures, four of which are related. Does not require language, but is not completely culture-free. Can be used for groups or individuals. Ranges from age 14 through adulthood.	Science Research Assoc. 259 E. Erie St. Chicago, Ill. 60624
Slosson Intelligence Test (1963) by Richard L. Slosson.	Brief, easily administered individual intelligence test based on Binet-type scale. Examinee does not have to read, but must respond in oral language. Ranges from age 4 through adulthood.	Slosson Educational Publications 140 Pine St. East Aurora, N. Y. 14052

Test	Description	Publisher
Test of General Ability (1960) by John C. Flanagan.	Measures basic learning ability independent of school-acquired skills. First part of test (information) measures ability to grasp meanings, recognize relationships, and understand basic concepts of the environment. Second part (reasoning) measures ability to understand relationships and form concepts. Fairly free of acculturation. All items are pictorial. Ranges from grades 9-12. Does not have adult norms, although in usage by some adult programs.	Science Research Assoc. 259 E. Erie St. Chicago, Ill. 60624
United States Training & Employment Service Nonreading Aptitude Test Battery (NATB) (1969).	The nine aptitudes measured are: intelligence, verbal aptitude, numerical aptitude, spatial aptitude, form perception, clerical perception, motor coordination, finger dexterity, and manual dexterity. Tests included in battery are: picture word matching, oral vocabulary, coin matching, design completion, tool matching, three-dimensional space, form matching, coin series and name comparison. The mark-making, place, turn, assemble, and disassemble tests from the *General Aptitude Test Battery* are also included. Not available to general public, but used by employment services.	United States Training & Employment Service 14 St. & Constitution Ave., N. W. Washington, D. C. 20210
WLW Culture Fair Inventory (1969) by Lynde C. Steckle, Robert W. Henderson, and Barbara O. Murray.	An untimed, nonverbal test for adults measuring intelligence with items that are not influenced by effects of environment and education. Test sections are: selection of figure in five that is most different, block counting, selection of fifth figure in a series, paper form board and selection of figure which completes pattern. Used by industry as an aptitude test.	William, Lynde & Williams. 113 E. Washington St. Painesville, Ohio 44077
Wechsler Adult Intelligence Scale (1955) by David Wechsler.	Probably the most efficient measurement of intelligence of adolescents from age 16 through adulthood, age 75. More thoroughly researched than other tests. Six verbal and five performance tests, individually administered; yield scores translate to IQs and percentiles. Requires highly trained psychometrist to adminster and interpret.	The Psychological Corp. 304 E. 45 St. New York, N. Y. 10017
Wesman Personnel Classification Test (1965) by Alexander G. Wesman.	Test of intelligence designed for use in industry. Verbal subtest requires use of reasoning through analogies and the perception of relationships in order to correctly respond to the item. Numerical subtest measures basic arithmetic skills and number concepts. Ranges from grade 8 through adulthood.	The Psychological Corp. 304 E. 45 St. New York, N. Y. 10017

task, the learner must be able to analyze the whole into its component parts. The test is helpful in noting disturbance of visual perception and motor coordination. It measures logical insight into space relationships and can show lack of synthesizing ability, which is the same ability a learner needs in order to blend sounds and to apply phonic generalizations and to put a word together as well as to integrate it successfully into a sentence.

The coding subtest involves speed and accuracy of learning and writing unfamiliar symbols. It indicates the quality of visual-motor coordination and immediate memory. Nonreaders who have spent years copying work from a chalkboard tend to do well on this test. The thing that is important here in reading diagnosis is the ability to remember symbols and the coordination between visual perception and motor coordination, as well as the ability to learn a new task.

The maze subtest involves planning ability and the ability to follow a visual pattern that is an important part of the reading task.

Picture completion demonstrates visual alertness for essential details and visual memory, as well as perception of the whole in relation to its parts. A lack of attention to detail may be indicative of the type of word-identification problem that the learner is having.

Picture arrangement measures the individual's ability to get the idea from a story, to size up a total situation, anticipate and plan, and to pick out essential clues that would be indicative of sequence. This ability is important to the reading task. Disabled readers tend to do better on this subtest than they do on comprehension because the use of words is not involved.

Analysis from Relationship of Subtest Scores

The last section of the "Strength-Weakness Spectrum for Wechsler Tests," found in appendix 28 suggests various groupings of scores and their relationships that might assist the teacher in deciding whether or not the learner's difficulties were caused by an overall weakness in learning ability, or by a specific reading disability.

In dealing with these analyses remember that each of the Wechsler subtest scores are converted from raw scores (the number of correct responses) to a weighted scaled score. Because of this the subtest scores can be compared to each other or averaged. Performance on any subtest could range from zero to twenty. Thus, an expected average score on any single subtest would be 10.

There are other criteria for evaluating performance on the *Wechsler Adult Intelligence Test*. The test is rich in clinical data as well as educational implications, and therefore, cannot be treated lightly. The implications given in this chapter appear to be the ones most pertinent for a reading teacher to be aware of (Glasser and Zimmerman 1972; Lutey 1966; Massey 1969; Searls 1975).

Summary

If we fail (to eradicate illiteracy), we condemn millions of the wordless—young and old—to half-lives of constant bafflement, bombarded from the media by signals and messages they cannot comprehend (Smith and Fay 1973, p. 7).

This chapter has discussed the problems associated with the evaluation of learning ability. Two approaches can be useful in adult basic education. The first is the use of measurements of listening ability as an estimate of reading potential. The second, more complex approach is the evaluation of mental ability through either group or individual tests. Undoubtedly the most reliable data in this area comes from the *Wechsler Adult Intelligence Scale.* Although the complexity of this instrument makes it mandatory that it be administered by a trained psychometrist, the adult basic education teacher can learn much about the adult learner by studying his responses on the test.

20.
Guiding
Adults
in Decision Making

The last twenty years have produced some important new additions to the content of adult learning projects. Through group and individual methods, many adults now set out to increase their self-insight, their awareness and sensitivity with other persons and their inter-personal competence. They learn to "listen to themselves," to free their body and their conversations from certain restrictions and tensions, to take a risk, to be open and congruent. Attempting to learn this sort of knowledge and skill seemed incredible to most people twenty years ago. Great changes in our conception of what people can and should set out to learn have been created by T-groups, the human potential movement, humanistic psychology, and transpersonal psychology (Tough 1973, p. 31).

Education is a process that goes on as long as an individual is actively responding to the stimuli around him and making new decisions in his environment. Any mature adult that works with the undereducated adult population at any level has a responsibility to help each one find a place in modern social living, interacting with those that affect his work-a-day life and that of his family. The traditional objectives of education have been (1) to acquire the cultural heritage; (2) to learn the necessary skills for earning a livelihood; and (3) to learn how to live in an "open" society that is the national ideal.

The Educational Ladder Is Accessible

Illiteracy often breeds illiteracy and we must find a way to interrupt and reverse these perpetuating processes of failure and helplessness (Curriculum Guide to Adult Basic Education: Intermediate Level (1966, p. 2).

Some of the adults currently enrolling in adult basic education programs have *never* had any formal schooling. This may be difficult for most teachers to really understand, since formal schooling for most of these teachers was "*the* way of life" when they were children. The number of years one has attended school is not, of course, a valid measure of what wisdom has been gained through those years or what concepts in casual conversation are readily understood. The teachers' responsibilities, then, become those of helping the learner to start wherever he is in the learning process, accept himself at "face" value, and proceed to build the skills he needs to become the person he feels he is capable of becoming.

A few adults come to the basic education class because there is one specific skill they need at that time. This bit of learning is crucial, but the teacher must understand that once his immediate need has been satisfied, the learner may not attend any further classes until he has defined a further need.

One young man enrolled in an adult basic education class said he wanted to learn to figure interest on money. His only explanation was that *if* he had some he could invest it to earn interest. As soon as he learned how to compute simple interest to his satisfaction, he stopped attending the class.

On the Navajo Indian Reservation, many Navajos have studied diligently until they passed the test for a driver's license so that they might legally drive their cars either on or off the reservation. Once they acquired the coveted license, they had satisfied their learning need for the time being. This experience, with its shortcomings, is described by the adult-education workers.

Jackson and Polacca (Zintz 1965) described adult Navajos who wished to learn all the information about being safe drivers on the highway and

Each learner must accept the responsibility for completing assignments. (Courtesy of Albuquerque Technical-Vocational Institute, Albuquerque, N. M.)

to obtain a driver's license of their state of residence. However, many of these people know very little English and rely on all the information being imparted to them in Navajo. They may even pass the written test in Navajo. Therefore, their only concern in learning written English is to identify correctly all the written road signs that they will encounter. For example, some Navajos indicated that before they were instructed, they believed the sign that read "Yield—right-of-way" meant that the driver *had* the right-of-way. They did not know the word "Yield" so they ignored it and assumed they could go when, in reality, they must STOP.

It is possible that these people are not motivated at this time to learn more than just the few sight words that they need for driving on the highway. In truth, many know too little English language to learn to read in it. What they do learn could hardly be called "reading." Perhaps there are many adults who will be motivated only to read such labels and signs and, for them, this is the only level of recognition of the printed words to which we should aspire to teach. Or perhaps we should be satisfied to start with that and see if a little bit of success will generate a higher level of motivation in them.

As has been expressed throughout the text, for those who enroll in adult basic education classes without knowledge of English, the *first* requisite is intensive practice in the audio-lingual method of learning English as a foreign language. Of course, this cannot be unmotivated, monotonous, meaningless repetition of sentence patterns, but must be a habituated, automatic response to the commonest speech utterances needed in everyday life at home and on the street.

The second level of readiness is that demonstrated in the traditional readiness for reading programs: (1) understanding spoken language to follow directions; (2) retelling stories with ideas in the proper sequence; (3) hearing likenesses and differences in both beginning and ending sounds of words; (4) seeing likenesses and differences in word forms; and (5) developing motor control in writing one's name, in manuscript, following the lines. The extent of vocabulary, ability to express oneself lucidly in clear, concise sentences, and a desire to read are the most important elements in reading success.

At the third level, the teacher will introduce "formal" aspects of reading through many, many experiences of writing what the student says and showing it to him written down. This occurs over and over in recorded sentences on the chalkboard, in all the experience stories recorded both on the chalkboard and on large sheets of newsprint, in directions written clearly and uniformly from session to session, and in continued reference to *the date,* the *teacher's name,* the *announcements* written on the chalkboard, and *brief messages* to be remembered. This is the level of primary reading and in addition to shifting from language experience reading to more formal reading, the teacher should teach crucial vocabulary for adults, such as that included in appendixes 14 and 15. Writing and spelling elementary concepts and utilizing them in originally constructed sentences is a further aspect of primary education.

For those adults who progress beyond this point, there is need for highly individualized programs to provide the work-type reading skills, the spelling and writing practice, the arithmetic, and the social and general science concepts that provide the usual education of the elementary school.

Motivating adults to adjust their levels of aspiration upward as opportunities present themselves may make possible attending an Manpower Development Training Act training program, entering specialized trade skills, technical-vocational schools, apprenticing to more highly skilled types of jobs, or earning the GED certificate.

The use of the General Educational Development Tests to equate with a high school diploma has become sufficiently widespread so that most adults are aware of the possibility, even though they may never have thought of it for themselves.

Counselors in universities should be consulted by teachers teaching adults whenever there is the possibility that, with a stipend, an individual might be able to attend a university and obtain a degree. It is much easier for the typical university graduates to think or cry, "He'd never make it," but that is being disproved by many of the adult education programs operating today.

Guideposts Magazine, A Practical Guide to Successful Living, July 1966, carries the "success story" of a Negro girl, Dorothy Brown. Born illegitimate, she was reared in an orphanage. When she had her tonsils removed at age five, she liked the sights, sounds, and smells of the hospital and decided to be a doctor when she grew up. By age eight, she wondered why she didn't have visitors as many other children did. A Presbyterian family did arrange to visit her at the suggestion of the superintendent. At age thirteen, her mother took her to a slum area of the city. At fourteen, she left school to work. Her employer helped her budget her income and she saved five hundred dollars in two years. She lived with an old Negro couple and went four years to high school. A Methodist group gave her a scholarship and she went four years to college. She worked as an inspector in an ordnance depot for two years and saved two thousand dollars and went off to a medical school in Nashville. She got a medical degree in 1948 and stayed on five years to specialize in surgery.

Decision Making Can Change Behavior

*Studies show that level of aspiration does not begin to operate before
some ego formation has been achieved. . . . Since adult ego formation
is highly advanced and complex, the setting of levels of aspiration
would seem to be clearly significant for adult choices of goals (Kirchner
1966, pp. 95-96).*

While one might correctly conclude the success story of Dorothy Brown
in the previous section is an exceptional case and one difficult to generalize from, there have been many organized programs in the past fifteen
years that demonstrate that many adults can radically change the course
of their lives if given the opportunity. In 1963, Hilliard reported that the
size of welfare payments in the urban Chicago area had reached 16 million dollars a month and was increasing. Hilliard wrote:

> Negroes in Chicago . . . have been relegated to live in another world
> . . . a city of segregated housing and unemployment, a city of no hope,
> where lack of education prevails, where many-faceted discrimination
> blocks even the efforts of the brave ones who try to break out . . .
> denied communication with society in general . . . no opportunity to
> become urbanized and acquire the mores and culture of the middle class
> . . . they live on the bleak grey level of subsistence . . . (p. 1034).

Yet, Hilliard reports that when these people were offered literacy education, the response was eager and enthusiastic, attendance was excellent,

Group interaction is helpful to adults in developing
decision-making ability. (Courtesy of Venice-Lincoln
Technical Center, Venice, Illinois.)

their personal appearance indicated real interest in "looking their best," and discipline was no problem. The success of the story is borne out by the statement that after approximately two years, the urban Chicago area had reduced its total welfare payments in half.

In 1965, Brazziel et al. report retraining of hard-core unemployed. Under a special grant from the U.S. Office of Education and the Office of Manpower, Automation, and Training, Virginia State College provided both literacy training and job-skill training for a hundred men who had been unemployed for a specified length of time. The program included a great deal of personal counseling for these men who were "studying" on subsistence allowances, and special group counseling for their wives who were trying to care for large families. Ninety of the men learned a technical skill (auto mechanics, electronics, etc.) and the average literacy scores were raised about three years. Their interpersonal relations improved and almost all of the ninety found good jobs (Brazziel, et al. 1965).

In 1968, 184 adults who had successfully completed literacy training at Adult High School, Flint, Michigan, between 1962 and 1966 were interviewed and retested for reading ability to determine the follow-up effectiveness of the literacy training program.

1. Holding power had been low; these 184 represented only 10 percent of the total who had entered the program.
2. Social aspects of the literacy classes had been an important factor in keeping participants.
3. They could still read at least as well as they could when they finished the program two to six years earlier.
4. A large number had continued to improve and gave evidence that they *do* read.
5. Attitudes toward school, vocations, and community responsibility had expanded. Over 80 percent of these 184 adults were engaged in organized adult activities, while less than 10 percent indicated such participation prior to training.
6. Their voting habits had changed. A higher percentage of these 184 adults had voted in the most recent local and national election than was true of all the registered voters of Flint (Warsh 1970).

Smith and Martin (1974) report from the National Advisory Committee on Adult Basic Education the following figures for programs in ABE for 1967.

62,000 adults learned to read and write for the first time.
28,000 registered and voted for the first time.

37,000 found jobs, received raises, or were promoted.

48,000 entered job training programs.

27,000 became subscribers to newspapers or magazines.

Career Opportunity Programs funded across the nation from 1970 until the middle 1970s made possible school attendance while on the job so that many adults were able to move all the way through a university degree program while they were already utilizing many of the skills they were learning by being employed at a "lower" level in the hierarchy in which they hoped to be later permanently employed. It seems clear, then, that adult educators have a responsibility to interact with the adult learner so that he begins to see himself as he is, and, through the help of teacher and counselor, what he has the capacity to become (Mocker 1975).

In terms of learning decision making, adult basic education teachers should be concerned with:

1. Helping the adult move from being a dependent personality toward one of being a self-directed human being.
2. Guiding the adult toward the accumulation of a growing storehouse of experiences that become an increasing resource for learning.
3. Providing purposes or motivation oriented more and more to the everyday tasks of his social roles.
4. Encouraging learning for the immediate application of knowledge to his life situations.

The will to learn is an intrinsic motive, one that finds its source and its reward in its own exercise (Houle 1964). The adult who dropped out, who experienced only failure, or who never had an opportunity to experience this will to learn, needs to be encouraged to *believe* that he can change. No learning takes place without a motive. With adults, the motivation is dependent upon getting the students to interact with each other and begin early to place a portion of the responsibility for learning on the adult. Mocker (1975) expressed it this way.

> As we begin to involve the adult in the selection of what is to be learned and why it is to be learned, and as we reinforce student-student interaction throughout the reading lesson, concluding by helping the adult see the application to his life, then the cooperative reading process can be a potent technique in adult basic education (p. 444).

The Learner and the Decision-Making Process

Below are four statements about the adult as a learner and what he must do in the learning process. Paired with each of these four statements are four statements that may help teachers and counselors to be the best possible facilitators in getting the learning process to work.

1. The learner must feel a need to learn.

   Teachers can, through group involvement, help individuals to see where they are and where they might be, and what the gap is in between.

2. The learner must feel that the facilitator of learning *wants* him to feel good about himself, have trust in his leader, and be willing to express and accept differences.

   Teachers who, themselves, feel confident can accent comfort, interaction, tolerance of differences, personal worth, and encouragement.

3. The learner must accept responsibility for behavioral change when he is committed to a new goal.

   Teachers can remain neutral, nondirective, think of options, ask questions that reflect feelings, and encourage students *not* to be hasty in making new decisions.

4. Adult learners would like to see fairly immediate rewards for their efforts.

   Teachers can be careful to sift the essentials and be able to add details to the skeleton outline after an effort has been rewarding or has "begun to pay off." The teacher knows that the best time to learn anything is when whatever is to be learned is immediately useful to us.

McClusky (1973), in an article "An Approach to a Differential Psychology of the Adult Potential," concludes:

> ... We have attempted to build a case for a differential psychology of the adult years, and in so doing have also proposed a post hoc interpretive hypothesis that the trend of both empirical and theoretical evidence is supportive of the view that adults have a potential for continuing learning and inquiry which historic conventional wisdom has failed to recognize. Ours, then, is a stance of unrealized potential and not one of *de facto* limitation. It will be interesting to note in years ahead which of these two views the thinking and research of the future will tend to confirm (p. 156).

Houle (1964) lists seven keys to effective learning:

1. Act as though you are certain you can learn.

   ... For most things adults want to know, their maturity, their wealth of association, their breadth of awareness, and their disciplined use of their powers make them able to learn even more effectively than they did when they were children.

2. Set realistic goals—and measure their accomplishment.
3. Remember the strengths of your point of view.
4. Actively fit new ideas and new facts into context.
5. Seek help and support when you need it.
6. Learn beyond the point necessary for immediate recall. (If you want to remember something permanently, you must overlearn it, you must keep reviewing it. Without this reinforcement, it will be forgotten.)
7. Use psychological as well as logical practices (pp. 18-36).

The adult learner must believe in these principles if he is to be successful in his new learning venture.

Common Types of Family Problems About Which Teachers Can Offer Understanding and Counsel

The most important key to the resources for learning is you, yourself. Through the centuries, students have been won by the magic of the teacher's smile, the strength of his encouragement, and the wisdom of his advice (Hunter 1966, p. 545).

Problems that seem extremely difficult to the family in poverty, or to the family without English language abilities, may not seem so insurmountable to the mature adult who is willing to reason about them. Six such problems have been selected to discuss briefly here. These may not be the most important, but they have been common problems for some undereducated adults.

Installment Buying

Salesmen are apt to be completely convincing about the small amount of cost each week or each month, about the desirability of possessing the article, and about the ease and convenience of paying for something on the installment plan. Yet, they never explain how long it will take, how much interest is really being charged for the use of the money, or whether or not the article will be worth the cost when there is so little money to buy such artifacts. A wise counselor may be able to reason with the individual and help arrive at a logical solution to certain problems. A woman with few conveniences may need a sewing machine very badly if she is to try to keep her family neatly dressed. It may well be worth a long period of installment buying.

Helping adults understand the forms and contracts they sign is an important part of an adult basic education program. (Courtesy of Venice-Lincoln Technical Center, Venice, Illinois.)

Buying a Car

Buying a car is sure to require installment buying, but because the need for transportation for the family is keenly felt and the avarice of the salesman is apt to put the buyer at a disadvantage, this item deserves special emphasis.

Sales of cars to any buyers who may not be wise to the shrewd antics of high-pressure salesmen cause many of these adults to buy a car that looks new and shiny but has a motor that is already worn out or in *need of new piston rings*. Many times the *term payment plan* is immediately turned over to a *finance company* that writes contracts with "catch" clauses that can cheat the buyer out of his monthly payment if it is "made a few days too late each month." The buyer may not appreciate the seriousness of buying a car that looks very satisfactory but has *already been in an accident*. If the *brakes* are in need of overhauling, this may cost the new buyer a sizeable sum of money that he does not have.

If the person buying a second-hand car can take a friend with him who knows something about motors or who has worked as a mechanic, his friend may be able to keep him from making a serious mistake.

Exchanging, Borrowing, and Cooperating

In a few situations today in the United States, there still exists the possibility of the members of an extended family helping each other. Brothers, and brothers-in-law, can exchange work jobs in rural areas, so they join forces when extra hands are needed. Before the advent of the combine, farmers in the Middle West joined forces to operate large threshing crews in the summer. The grandfather, the patriarch, in the large Spanish-American families in New Mexico held his extended family together in many places almost until the present time.

If families can work amicably together, they may be able to help each other a great deal.

Joining the Cooperative

The cooperative, once established, affords each participant the opportunity to borrow money at lower short-term rates than he could obtain elsewhere. Establishing a cooperative and operating it effectively is important enough that it must be done by a competent person. Once it is established, it is easily possible that one of its own members will learn how to operate it and be the manager of the cooperative.

While its most important function is to provide loans to members to help them in any time of need, it serves another very valuable function in permitting members to increase their investment by very small amounts. Once some families get a few dollars saved in the cooperative, saving then becomes a *value* for them and a dollar that might easily be spent on wine or beer may make its way to additional shares in the cooperative.

"Your Children Can Go To College"

It is possible for a bright boy or girl with an excellent high school record to go to college without financial assistance from the parents. Of course, it requires that counselors know what funds are available, how to apply for them, and how to encourage the young people to take advantage of them.

Social Agencies in the Community That Can Help

Teachers working with undereducated adults should be prepared to help them find services that are available in the community. There are many such public agencies that can "advise" families about various problems in everyday life.

1. The *County Public Health Nurse* can provide information about vaccinations needed by the children, problems of diet and nutrition, where to obtain birth-control information.

2. The *county social workers* can evaluate the economic needs of the family, determine minimum levels of subsistence, and make recommendations about children's problems with vision, hearing, or other health needs.
3. The *school principal* may be able to provide information about children's lack of success in school and make recommendations to the parents. Most important, he can sit with the parents and discuss problems and frustrations they may feel and try to help them to arrive at a clear understanding of the problems.
4. Many agencies that receive funds through the United Fund (Community Chest, Red Feather Agency) may have information about the specific problem in a given family. In many cities, such agencies as The Hearing Center, The Association for Retarded Children, The Mental Health Association, The Cerebral Palsy Association, The Family Service League, and Homes for Unwed Mothers, Neglected and Dependent Children are able to help in the solution of specific problems.

Benjamin: An Illustrative Case Study

Readin. . . . That the beginnin of every thing. . . . When you can read and write why you can do anything. Do any thing. Be any thing (Miller 1959, p. 1).

Hawkin's (1972) story of Benjamin illustrates the myriad of problems presented by the adult with family responsibilities who wants to learn reading and writing skills in a sincere, motivated way but is blocked at almost every turn to concentrate on learning when he is continuously anxious and threatened about meeting his day-to-day needs for himself and his family. Although Benjamin was only nineteen years old, he was already a married man with two tiny children. His wife was a staunch supporter in his effort, and his tutor allowed none of the many interferences to completely break off their tutoring sessions.

Benjamin is uncomfortable about being on welfare and is under a great deal of tension to get some kind of employment.

He badly needs help with formulating an organized plan of budgeting his meager amount of money so that rent, food, and utilities all are provided for throughout the month.

How does one keep appointments with the tutor without bus fare, with sudden baby-sitting problems, without a wristwatch, or with an inability to keep a written calendar of appointments?

The problems of being *black*, of having grown up in a chaotic world, of having the two people who expressed the most love for him both die by the time he was seven, of trying to respond to the demands of a white society for his existence, all of these greatly complicate the process of trying to learn to read. An extremely innovative tutor, patient counseling, and great flexibility in keeping the reading program continuing, do seem to work miracles in keeping Benjamin's strong ego thriving and enable him to demonstrate continuous progress.

Summary

Benjamin: "I know we kine-a been playing a game, an sometimes you my friend an other times you my teacher. But I go long with it cause I know it important, an I need someone who gonna do more than just be a buddy. I could tell how you expected me to come through, sooner or later, with some hard work, an that's the main reason I did (Hawkins 1972, p. 132).

One of the purposes of education of adults in basic education classes is that they will learn how to be thinking, participating citizens in the community where they live. Teachers will help them achieve this objective by making them aware of community activities, community services, and business practices that will help insure making wise decisions.

The number of years of formal education a person has attained need not determine how well he has learned to be a useful citizen in his community. Nevertheless, the uneducated or the newcomer must have some means of becoming informed about health insurance and that, in most cases, is one of the benefits of having a steady job; about unemployment compensation; about worker's disability compensation; about employment offices and the differences between the private ones and those operated by the state.

The skillful teacher will soon learn many ways to present much of this information to his students so that, through an experience story with a very practical lesson, this knowledge about everyday living can become the basis for the reading lesson to teach the elementary skills in reading.

Appendix 1

The Fernald Kinesthetic Tracing Technique

The Fernald method begins by asking the learner what words he would like to learn how to read. His initial words may build such a sentence as "I live in Albuquerque." He is encouraged to compose his own stories and the vocabulary is not controlled. He learns to write from memory each word used in his story. He reads his written copy and then within twenty-four hours is presented with a typewritten copy to insure learning to read print. Either manuscript or cursive writing may be used. The kinesthetic method develops through four stages:

Stage I: Tracing. The teacher writes the word in large print for the learner. The learner traces with the third and index fingers over the teacher's writing and pronounces the word in syllables as he traces. He then writes it in his story. If he misspells the word, he goes back to tracing. In this stage, finger contact is important, writing from memory to put the word in the story is significant, and the learner pronounces the word by syllables as he writes it. The teacher writes the words on large uniform strips of paper and they can be filed alphabetically as learned. The learner, then, learns alphabetical order through practice from the beginning.

Stage II: Writing without tracing. Depending on the individual, after an individual has learned about one hundred words he looks at the new word, pronounces it in syllables, and writes it from memory without tracing. (This is similar to the visual-motor method described by Harris.[2]) The individual's stock of sight words can now be filed alphabetically on 3″ by 5″ cards.

Stage III: Recognition in print. The person becomes able to study the word in print, is told what it says, pronounces it in syllables, and writes it from memory. It is no longer necessary to keep a file of every new word. He may now be introduced to book reading. He may know 150 words and can begin to read in a more difficult book than a preprimer.

1. Grace M. Fernald, *Remedial Techniques in Basic School Subjects*, (New York: McGraw-Hill Book Company, Inc., 1943, 1971).
2. Albert J. Harris, *How to Increase Reading Ability*, 6th ed. (New York: Longmans, Green and Company, 1975), pp. 320-21.

Stage IV: Word Analysis. Word attack skills are developed through techniques that teach the learner to decipher new words through parts of "old" ones and through learning structural analysis.

By this method, tracing, writing, saying, and hearing are all sensory impressions that supplement the visual memory that plays a large part in usual reading-teaching methods (Adult Education Council of Greater Chicago 1965; Geeslin 1971; Geeslin and Geeslin 1971; Grabouski and Glenn 1974; Wilson and Barnes 1974).

Appendix 2 · Selected Sources of Materials for Teaching Reading in Adult Basic Education

This is a representative list of publishers and materials that have been found to be useful in teaching reading in adult basic education. Titles that are illustrative of their offerings have been included.

The fact that an entry is included in this list should not be construed to be a value judgment as to the quality of the material. Certainly, materials need to be selected with the individual learner in mind. It is a good policy to request publishers to send you their catalogs that offer further description of the material. It is also advantageous before purchase to preview and study the material to determine if it will meet the particular needs of the individual.

Addison-Wesley Publishing Co.
2725 Sand Hill Rd.
Menlo Park, Calif. 94025

Reading Development Kits, Levels A,B,C, by Edwin H. Smith et al.

Allied Education Council
P. O. Box 78
Galien, Mich. 49113

The Mott Basic Language Program, by Byron Chapman et al. Consists of many levels of materials, mostly phonic-oriented, some programmed. Also publishes useful instructional material oriented toward vocations.

American Book Co.
450 W. 33 St.
New York, N.Y. 10010

Writing for Adults. Teaches cursive writing for adults.

American Southern Publishing Co.
Northport, Ala.

Handwriting for Adults and *Advanced Handwriting for Adults; Manuscript for Adults* and *Advanced Manuscript for Adults.*

Ann Arbor Publishers
P. O. Box 1446
Ann Arbor, Mich. 48105

Michigan Tracking Program and *Michigan Successive Writing Program,* useful in the development of visual perception, rate, handwriting, and other skills.

Arco Publishing Co., Inc.
219 Park Ave., S.
New York, N. Y. 10003

Preliminary Practice in the High School Equivalency Diploma Test. Also offers other such materials.

Barnell-Loft
Rockville Centre, N. Y.

Specific Skills Series, useful in the teaching of comprehension skills.

Barron's Educational Series, Inc.
113 Crossways Park Dr.
Woodbury, N. Y. 11797

Publishes materials for the preparation of the GED Examination and other materials useful particularly on the intermediate level.

Behavioral Research Laboratories
Box 577
Palo Alto, Calif. 94302

Reading Series I-V, and *Why Work.* Self-directed and programmed materials.

California Test Bureau
Del Monte Research Park
Monterey, Calif. 93940

Reading Skill Series: Comprehension, Following Directions, Reading-Interpretations, Reference Skills, etc. Each programmed booklet is useful for specific skill development.

Cambridge Book Co.
488 Madison Ave.
New York, N. Y. 10022

Television Study Guide: Reading; Television Study Guide: English Grammar, and numerous other materials directed toward basic reading and toward GED preparation. *Cambridge Adult Basic Education* Series and other materials particularly for new readers and new citizens. Also publishes GED preparatory materials.

Clearinghouse for Offender Literacy
Programs
1705 DeSales St., N. W.
Washington, D. C. 20036

UNIPAK Instructional Modules offers lessons in filling out job applications and other practical needs.

Continental Press, Inc.
Elizabethtown, Pa. 17022

Ditto masters of numerous drill materials for skill development and for visual perception that could be adapted for adults.

Cowles Education Corp.
Look Building
488 Madison Ave.
New York, N. Y. 10022

How to Pass the High School Equivalency Examination. Also offers other materials for GED preparation classes.

Educational Development Laboratories,
Inc.
Huntington, N. Y.

Learning 100 System consists of both hardware and software for adult basic reading. Utilizes the controlled reader, tachistoscope, and audio equipment.

Educators Publishing Service, Inc.
75 Moulton St.
Cambridge, Massachusetts 02138

Reading Improvement for Men and Women in Industry. Intermediate level material.

Fearon Publishers
Lear Siegler, Inc. Educational Division
6 Davis Dr.
Belmont, Calif. 94002

Vocational and practical everyday living problems form the content for this reading instructional material. Some titles are *Using Dollars and Sense* and *Jerry Works in a Service Station.*

Follett Educational Opportunities
Corp.
1010 W. Washington Blvd.
Chicago, Ill. 60607

This company publishes several basic reading systems such as *Getting Started—Communications I, On Your Way—Communications II, Full Speed Ahead—Communications III: Systems for Success;* and *Reading for a Purpose* and *Reading for a Viewpoint.* It also offers extensive supplementary material for adult basic education in the areas of vocations, family management, personal adjustment, communication, social problems, etc.

Frank E. Richards Publishing Co.
215 Church St.
Phoenix, N. Y. 13135

Some of the titles suitable for adult basic education from this company are *Getting Ready for Pay Day, Finding Ourselves,* and *Unemployed Uglies.*

Ginn and Co.
Educational Development Corp.
2550 Hanover St.
Anaheim, Calif. 92801

Help Yourself to Read, Write and Spell, a skill development series.

Globe Book Co., Inc.
175 Fifth Ave.
New York, N. Y. 10010

English on the Job and *Vocational English* are among the offerings that are useful to adults from this company.

Harcourt Brace and Jovanovich, Inc.
757 Third Ave.
New York, N. Y. 10017

English Lessons for Adults offers help with langauge and grammar.

Hobbs-Dorman Publishers
441 Lexington Ave.
New York, N. Y. 10017

How to Fill Out Application Forms.

Holt, Rinehart and Winston, Inc.
383 Madison Ave.
New York, N. Y. 10017

Learning to Read and Write furnishes information on the sounds of letters. Also offers materials for preparation for GED, such as *High School Certification Through GED Tests.*

Interpretive Education
400 Bryant St.
Kalamazoo, Mich. 49001

Applications and Forms Workbook and *Driver Education Workbook* offer resources for the teacher of adult basic reading.

Koinonia Foundation Press
Box 5744
Baltimore, Md. 21200

Among the materials available from this source is *Going to Have a Baby?, We are Chosen,* and charts on the *Principle Sounds of the English Letters.*

Learning Trends
175 Fifth Ave.
New York, N. Y. 10010

Forms in Your Future is a workbook of vocational and everyday forms that are useful in adult basic education.

Macmillan, Inc.
866 Third Ave.
New York, N. Y. 10022

English This Way, English 900 Series, and *Key to English Vocabulary* all offer good sources of drill material. *The Special English Series—Medicine, Hotel Personnel, Engineering,* etc. also offer good ideas. *No Hot Water Tonight* (1975) provides excellent relevant reading practice.

McGraw-Hill Book Co., Inc.
1221 Ave. of the Americas
New York, N. Y. 10020

Sullivan's Programmed Reading for Adults, a complete phonic-oriented beginning reading program is the basic adult reading series from this company. Supplementary vocational reading materials, such as *Charley: The TV Repairman, Judy, the Waitress* and *What Job for Me,* are all useful.

National Tutoring Institute
P. O. Box 2112
Kansas City, Mo. 64142

The *Tutor-Student System* by John George was developed for adults. It purports to be a complete eclectic approach.

New Readers Press
Box 131
Syracuse, N. Y. 13210

New Streamlined English is a complete basic reading program utilizing mostly phonics. This nonprofit organization publishes exclusively for adult literacy programs. Supplementary materials for reading instruction in the areas of vocations, health, family management and living, social problems, and biblical themes are offered. Some of the better known titles are the *Be Informed Series, News for You,* and *Everyday Reading and Writing.*

Noble & Noble Publishers, Inc.
523 N. Hanover St.
Anaheim, Calif. 92801

Operation Alphabet is the reading system published by this company. Other adult materials are also offered, such as *We Want You, How We Live,* and *From Words to Stories.*

Oddo Publishing, Inc.
Storybook Acres Beauregard Blvd.
Fayetteville, Ga. 30214

Photo Phonics and *Photocabulary* are two vocationally oriented reading instructional materials that are somewhat different.

Oxford Book Co., Inc.
11 Park Pl.
New York, N. Y. 10007

Materials for new citizens and concerning everyday living problems, such as *How to be a Wise Consumer,* form the content for most of these reading instructional publications. Instructional materials for GED preparation is also offered.

P.A.R.
Abbott Place
Providence, R. I. 02900

Programs for Reading Achievement is a series of workbooks on basic reading and preparation for the GED.

Portal Press, Inc.
369 Lexington Ave.
New York, N. Y. 10000

Springboards, series of pamphlets on relevant discussion topics that would interest adults as well as develop reading skills on intermediate levels.

Prentice-Hall, Inc.
Englewood Cliffs, N. J. 07632

Be A Better Reader Series. Paragraph comprehension and content area development. Can be adapted for adults.

Psychotechnics, Inc.
105 W. Adams St.
Chicago, Ill. 60600

Both hardware and software for reading development, utilizing tachistoscopic and pacing devices.

Reader's Digest Services, Inc.
Educational Division
Pleasantville, N. Y. 10570

Adult Readers, Skill Builders, Second Language Series, and other materials on various levels. Most are rewrites of *Reader's Digest* articles.

Regents Publishing Co., Inc.
2 Park Ave.
New York, N. Y. 10016

Sounds and Syllables, The Signs of Life, and *A Handful of Letters* offer basic reading resources. *The Food We Eat* is another title that has been useful. Besides offering titles that are attractive to new citizens and new readers, this company publishes much GED preparation material.

Scholastic Book Services
50 W. 44 St.
New York, N. Y. 10036

Scope Visuals 13: Getting Applications Right, a collection of useful ditto masters and overhead transparencies. Other collections in this series are also useful. Publishes other skill development material, magazines, and paperback books that can be utilized in adult reading instruction.

Science Research Associates, Inc.
259 E. Erie St.
Chicago, Ill. 60611

The familiar *SRA Reading Laboratories, SRA Reading for Understanding,* etc. are multilevel materials that can be adapted for adult basic education. Vocational materials such as the *Rochester Occupational Reading Series* and *Our Working World* are also useful.

Steck-Vaughn Co.
Box 2028
Austin, Tex. 78767

Numerous workbook type adult basal reading materials are offered, such as *I Want to Read and Write, How to Read Better, The Family Development Series,* and *Activities for Reading Improvement.* Supplementary vocational and family management topics are also used as reading instructional materials, such as *Where Does the Money Go?* and *We Are What We Eat.*

U.S. Government Printing Office
Division of Documents
Washington, D. C. 20000

Materials for new citizens, as well as vocational titles, such as *Joe Wheeler Finds a Job and Learns About Social Security* are available. The chart of *Standard Traffic Control Signs* is especially useful.

University of Illinois
Home Extension Service
Champaign, Ill. 61820

How the Johnsons Face a Money Emergency and *How the Johnsons Compare the Cost of Credit* are two of the pamphlets that are useful for reading instruction.

Zaner-Bloser Co.
612 N. Park St.
Columbus, Ohio 43200

Handwriting filmstrips and "Peek Thru" alphabets are helps for developing cursive and manuscript writing.

Appendix 3

A Selected List of Tesol Text Materials

American English Series: English As a Second Language. Four volumes. Boston: D. C. Heath & Co., 1965-1967.

Boggs, Ralph S., and Dixon, Robert J. *English Step by Step with Pictures.* Rev. ed. New York: Regents Publishing Co., 1971.

Bumpass, Faye L. *We Speak English.* New York: American Book Co., 1967.

Dixon, Robert J. *Complete Course in English.* Rev. ed. Four volumes. New York: Regents Publishing Co., 1972.

———. *English As a Foreign Languge Series.* New York: Regents Publishing Co., 1950.

———. *Modern American English.* New York: Regents Publishing Co., 1962.

English Language Services, Inc. *English 900.* New York: Macmillan, 1964.

———. *English This Way.* Twelve volumes. New York: Macmillan, 1964.

Finocchiaro, Mary. *Learning to Use English, Books I-II.* New York: Simon & Schuster, 1966-1968.

Hall, Eugene J. *Practical Conversation in English for Beginning Students.* New York: Regents Publishing Co., 1972.

The Institute of Modern Languages, Inc. *Contemporary Spoken English.* Six volumes. New York: Thomas Y. Crowell Co., 1967-1968.

Lado, Robert. *English Series: A Complete Course in English as a Second Language.* Six volumes. New York: Regents Publishing Co., 1970-1973.

Mackin, Ronald. *Exercises in English Patterns and Usage.* Five volumes. London: Oxford University Press, 1969.

———. *A Short Course in Spoken English.* London: Oxford University Press, 1975.

Mellgren, Lars, and Walker, Michael. *New Horizons in English.* Three volumes. Reading, Mass.: Addison-Wesley Publishing Co., 1973.

National Council of Teachers of English. *English for Today.* New York: McGraw-Hill, 1973.

Rand, Earl. *Constructing Dialogs.* New York: Holt, Rinehart and Winston, 1969.

———. *Constructing Sentences.* New York: Holt, Rinehart and Winston, 1969.

Reader's Digest Services. *English as a Second Language Series.* New York: Reader's Digest Services, 1963.

Richards, I. A., and Gibson, Christine. *English Through Picture Series.* New York: Washington Square Press, 1969.

———. *A First Workbook of English.* New York: Washington Square Press, 1969.

Taylor, Grant. *Learning American English.* New York: McGraw-Hill, 1956.

U.S. Department of Agriculture. *Como Comprar Los Comestibles* (*How to Buy Food*), A Bilingual Teaching Aid. Washington: Information Division of Agricultural Marketing Service, 1971.

Wheeler, Gonzales. *Let's Speak English.* Six volumes. New York: McGraw-Hill, 1967.

Wright, Audrey L. *Practice Your English.* Kinderhook, New York: American Book Co. 1960.

Appendix 4

Evaluation Form: A Scale for Evaluation of Adult Basic Education Instructional Materials

Evaluator: _____

Material(s): _____

My position in ABE is: Administrator, Supervisor, Full-time teacher, Part-time teacher, other: _____

Directions: Please put the symbol for the material you are rating in the space you feel represents the quality of the material for the attribute mentioned in the question. A rating of 10 would be for a perfect material; and a rating of one would be for a completely inadequate material.

1. Have you taught students using this material? Yes_____ No_____

2. How familiar do you feel you are with this material?

   ‾‾ ‾‾ ‾‾ ‾‾ ‾‾ ‾‾ ‾‾ ‾‾ ‾‾ ‾‾
   1   2   3   4   5   6   7   8   9   10

3. Do the materials contribute to the teaching of those values necessary for the ABE student's becoming a productive member of society?

   ‾‾ ‾‾ ‾‾ ‾‾ ‾‾ ‾‾ ‾‾ ‾‾ ‾‾ ‾‾
   1   2   3   4   5   6   7   8   9   10

4. Does the content of the material contribute to the teaching of those *general concepts* necessary for the ABE student's becoming a productive members of society?

   ‾‾ ‾‾ ‾‾ ‾‾ ‾‾ ‾‾ ‾‾ ‾‾ ‾‾ ‾‾
   1   2   3   4   5   6   7   8   9   10

5. Does the content of the material conform to the areas in which your experience has shown the ABE student to have an *interest*?

   ‾‾ ‾‾ ‾‾ ‾‾ ‾‾ ‾‾ ‾‾ ‾‾ ‾‾ ‾‾
   1   2   3   4   5   6   7   8   9   10

From *Teacher Training Syllabus: Unit 4 Materials*, pp. 27-28, by Carol M. Geeslin and Robert H. Geeslin. Morehead, Ky.: Morehead State University, 1971. Used by permission.

6. Is the *format* of the material adult in appearance?

$$\overline{1} \quad \overline{2} \quad \overline{3} \quad \overline{4} \quad \overline{5} \quad \overline{6} \quad \overline{7} \quad \overline{8} \quad \overline{9} \quad \overline{10}$$

7. Does the material provide for the teaching of *word attack skills*?

$$\overline{1} \quad \overline{2} \quad \overline{3} \quad \overline{4} \quad \overline{5} \quad \overline{6} \quad \overline{7} \quad \overline{8} \quad \overline{9} \quad \overline{10}$$

8. Does the material provide for the teaching of *comprehension skills*?

$$\overline{1} \quad \overline{2} \quad \overline{3} \quad \overline{4} \quad \overline{5} \quad \overline{6} \quad \overline{7} \quad \overline{8} \quad \overline{9} \quad \overline{10}$$

9. Does the material provide for the teaching of *critical reading skills*?

$$\overline{1} \quad \overline{2} \quad \overline{3} \quad \overline{4} \quad \overline{5} \quad \overline{6} \quad \overline{7} \quad \overline{8} \quad \overline{9} \quad \overline{10}$$

10. Does the material adequately take into account *individual differences* in learning rates?

$$\overline{1} \quad \overline{2} \quad \overline{3} \quad \overline{4} \quad \overline{5} \quad \overline{6} \quad \overline{7} \quad \overline{8} \quad \overline{9} \quad \overline{10}$$

11. How easy do you feel it would be to use the material?

$$\overline{1} \quad \overline{2} \quad \overline{3} \quad \overline{4} \quad \overline{5} \quad \overline{6} \quad \overline{7} \quad \overline{8} \quad \overline{9} \quad \overline{10}$$

12. If the material were modestly priced, would you recommend that it be bought for your ABE program?

$$\overline{1} \quad \overline{2} \quad \overline{3} \quad \overline{4} \quad \overline{5} \quad \overline{6} \quad \overline{7} \quad \overline{8} \quad \overline{9} \quad \overline{10}$$

Feel free to make additional comments:

Appendix 5

Common Prefixes and Suffixes

Prefixes

A prefix may be defined as a syllable, group of syllables, or word united with or joined to the beginning of another word to alter its meaning or create another word, as in *un*happy, *nondis*appear*ing* or *under*develop. The meaning of a prefix is often dependent upon the word with which it is joined as *subordinate*, meaning lower in rank; *subhuman*, meaning to a lesser degree than; *subcarbonate*, meaning less than the normal amount of; *subdivision*, meaning forming a division; *subsoil*, meaning under. Some prefixes are:

pre	- preschool	arch	- archbishop
re	- reappear	post	- postbellum
per	- perceive	ante	- antebellum
mis	- misplace	semi	- semiannually
dis	- dishonest	under	- underdevelop
non	- nonresident	super	- supersede
un	- unhappy	anti	- antiaircraft
in	- insignificant	dia	- diameter
en	- endanger	demi	- demitasse
hypo	- hypothermal	circum	- circumnavigate
de	- descend	ultra	- ultramodern
be	- bereave	extra	- extrapolated
bi	- bimonthly	hypo	- hypodermic
di	- diacid	hyper	- hypercritical
ad	- admit	super	- superstructure
ab	- abdicate	contra	- contradict
ob	- obsolete	amphi	- amphibiotic
en	- enlarge	cata	- catabolism
ex	- expel	para	- parallel
sub	- submerge	epi	- epidemic
sur	- surplus	hemi	- hemisphere
syn	- synapse	peri	- perimeter
mal	- maladjusted	mono	- monolayer
com	- combine	vice	- vice-president
trans	- transatlantic	eo	- eolithic
dys	- dysgenic	al	- alchemy

Suffixes

A suffix is a sound, syllable, or syllables added to the end of a word or word base to change its meaning, give it grammatical function, or form a new word as *ish* in *smallish*, or *opia* in *diplopia*. Some suffixes are:

s - looks		most - foremost	
ing - looking		ate - chlorinate	
ed - looked		hood - childhood	
er - richer		ous - nitrous	
est - richest		ious - mysterious	
less - toothless		tious - cautious	
ful - hopeful		itious - nutritious	
ness - happiness		ulous - populous	
ish - childish		ferous - coniferous	
ist - receptionist		aceous - herbaceous	
ment - amusement		anthous - monanthous	
th - growth		ive - objective	
age - leakage		ative - talkative	
en - woolen		ac - cardiac	
y - rainy		ic - photographic	
ly - friendly		ics - statistics	
fy - glorify		ice - justice	
ty - cruelty		ia - pneumonia	
ity - abnormality		ial - dictatorial	
ility - sensibility		ical - economical	
osity - generosity		al - terminal	
cy - bankruptcy		ese - Japanese	
acy - piracy		ose - cellulose	
ary - boundary		osis - osmosis	
ory - auditory		ol - alcohol	
ery - bravery		oid - celluloid	
ably - comfortably		id - pyramid	
mony - sanctimony		ide - sulfide	
ency - dependency		esque - picturesque	
ence - persistence		ina - ballerina	
ance - appearance		ine - medicine	
ent - correspondent		itis - arthritis	
ant - inhabitant		et - rivulet	
ion - selection		arch - matriarch	
tion - creation		ulent - fraudulent	
ation - affectation		ize - democratize	
ition - nutrition		le - prattle	
ee - employee		cle - particle	
eer - engineer		able - impenetrable	
or - inventor		tude - solitude	
ster - trickster		ure - composure	
ism - heroism		hood - childhood	
some - lonesome		ana - Americana	

Appendix 6

Generalizations About Consonants and Vowels

1. For the most part, consonant sounds are regular. Exceptions to this generalization are "hard" and "soft" *c*, "hard" and "soft" *g*, *s*, and *x*.
2. When two consonants are combined to create a new sound, they are called a digraph. The consonant digraphs are: *ch, ck, gh, ng, nk, sh, th, wh*.
3. When two or three consonants are blended together but each retains its own sound, they are called consonant blends. The consonant blends are *bl, cl, fl, gl, br, cr, dr, fr, sc, sk, sm, sn, tw, scr, spr, str, pl, sl, dw, gr, pr, tr, wr, sp, st, sw, shr, spl, sch, thr*.
4. The consonant *r* is a clue to the vowel sound. If *r* follows a vowel at the end of a word or syllable, the sound of the vowel is changed: *farm, term, fir, horn, fur*.
5. The letter *c* has the sound of *k* except when followed by *e, i,* or *y*. Then *c* has the sound of *s*.
6. The letter *g* has the sound of *g* as in *goat* except when it is followed by *e, i,* or *y*. It then has the sound of *j* as in *giraffe*. The *g* in *girl, get,* and *geisha* are some exceptions to this generalization.
7. The letter *g* is always followed by *u* to make a *kw* sound.
8. The letter *x* has the *ks* sound in *box*, the *gs* sound in *exhibit*, and the *z* sound in *xylophone*.
9. The *gh* in words like *light* and *night* makes no sound but it causes the vowel to have its long sound.
10. Many words have double consonants, although we hear only one consonant sound: *balloon, cabbage, ladder, grasshopper*.
11. The letters *ph* usually have the *f* sound in *photograph*.
12. The blend *ck* is used to make a *k* sound at the end of a word or syllable.
13. *Sh, ch, th,* and *wh* are consonant digraphs that have two letters, but one sound.
14. The final consonant is usually doubled when a short vowel precedes the final consonant, as in *hop, hopped, hopping*.
15. The schwa is the unaccented vowel sound in a syllable, as in *about, pencil, beckon, latent*.
16. Vowel sounds are extremely irregular. Vowel letters may represent more than one sound. For instance, the *a* is used in all of these words: *ape, laid, gauge, pay, break, vein, eight, they, mat, late, card, hair, prayer, any, ago, laugh*.

VOWELS

CONSONANTS

Single Consonants	Consonant Combinations	Single Vowels	Vowel Combinations	Vowel-Consonant Combinations	The Schwa
Single consonants (one phoneme):	Consonant blends:	Single vowels (May be long or short):	Vowel digraphs:	Vowels A followed by "l" or "w":	(e)
b d f h	bl br sc tw	a e i	ai in sail	"aw" in bawl	pencil
i k l m	cl cr sk scr	o u	ay day	"al" in wall	*about*
n w y z	fl dr sm spr	y (sometimes)	ea beat		beckon
	gl fr sn str		ea head	Vowels followed by "r":	latent
Single consonants with two or more common sounds:	pl gr sp shr		ea tea	a in arm	
	sl pr st spl		ee sleep	e fern	
"c" as "k"	dw tr sw sch		ei receive	i dirt	
"c" as "s"	wr thr		ie believe	o word	
			ey key	u hurt	
"g" as "g"	Consonant digraphs:		ey they	y martyr	
"g" as "j"			oa boat		
	One sound:		oe toe	q and u	
"s" in hiss			ow show		
rose	gh, ph, sh, ck, ng, nk		ou though	qu in quick	
sugar				squ squirrel	
	Two or more sounds:		Vowel blends (diphthongs):		
"x" in six			oi in soil		
xylophone	th: this, thin		oy boy		
exact	wh: what, who		ue true		
	ch: chin,				
	chalet		ew in new		
	choir		ow now		
			ou though		
			oa goal		

Note: The phonic elements above need not be taught in any sequence. If the teacher is aware of what phonic elements need to be discriminated, the learner should learn them as he needs them in reading to meet his purposes. No formal phonics lessons or workbooks need to be relied upon to master this ability.

17. The position of the vowel is a clue to its sound in a word.
18. When two vowels appear together in a one-syllable word, the reader needs to use clues with caution: Many times the sound of the first vowel is long and the second is not pronounced: *goat, cream, board, pain, heap;* however, there are many exceptions: *field, break, brief, George, piece, great;* or, *bread, head, death;* or, *said, eight, neigh.*
19. In a one-syllable word with a VCV ending, the first vowel usually has its long sound and the *e* at the end is silent.
20. The vowel is usually long if there is one vowel in the word and it is at the end of the word: *so, we, by, hi.*
21. The vowel is usually short if there is one vowel and it comes at the beginning of a one-syllable word: *am, end, odd.*
22. The vowel is usually short if there is one vowel between two consonants in a syllable or in a one-syllable word: *bad, men, bit, top, cut.*
23. The diphthongs *ou* and *ow* usually make the sound we hear in *south* and *crowd,* but sometimes *ow* has the sound of *o* in *show.*
24. The diphthong sound *oi* or *oy* is spelled *oy* if it is at the end of a word, such as *boy* and *toy;* but it is spelled *oi* if it is not at the end of the word as in *toil* and *boil.*

Appendix 7   Syllabication Generalizations

1. Syllables often follow the same patterns as monosyllabic words.
2. Each syllable contains only one vowel sound, although this may be two vowel letters.
3. Identify syllables orally before identifying them in written form.
4. Divide words into syllables by first checking the vowels, and then looking to see what is between the two vowels. The configuration of vowels and consonants generally determines the division.
5. When two or more consonants occur together, syllables separate between them, unless the consonants form a blend. *Examples: pad·dock, hy·dro·gen*, and *cash·ier.*
6. Single consonants usually go with the following vowel if they can be pronounced with it.
7. Prefixes and suffixes are syllables by themselves.
8. Usually a vowel followed by a consonant in the same syllable has a short accent. *Examples: fan, nit, madly*, and *cat.*
9. A vowel on the end of an accented syllable is usually long. *Examples: may·be, do·nate*, and *re·late.*
10. A vowel-consonant-vowel syllable usually has a short medial vowel.
11. A consonant-vowel syllable usually has a long ending vowel.
12. A vowel-consonant syllable usually has a short initial vowel.
13. In words ending with *le*, the consonant before *le* usually begins the last syllable and the *e* is silent. *Examples: sham·ble, cat·tle, puz·zle, cod·dle* and *sim·ple.*
14. The suffix *-ture* is pronounced much like *chur* and is a separate syllable. *Example: fu·ture.*
15. When the letters *v* or "*x*" are in a word of more than one syllable, the letters *v* or "*x*" usually goes with the preceding vowel to form a syllable.
16. In dividing a word into syllables, when there is one consonant between two vowels, the consonant usually goes with the next syllable. *Example: to·ma·to.*
17. When there are two consonants between the two vowels, divide the word between the two consonants. One consonant will go with one syllable and the other will go with the next syllable. *Examples: pep·per*, and *let·ter.*
18. The letters *ck* go with the preceding vowel to form a syllable. *Examples: chick·en* and *pick·le.*

Appendix 8
Word Accent (Stress) Generalizations

1. Unaccented syllables yield the schwa sound.

    Examples:
    caper (kap·ər)
    deity (dē·əotē)
    concern (kan·sern)

2. Accent is sometimes determined only by the context.

    Examples:
    The farmer used a *combine* (käm´bīn) to do the work in the fields.
    When you *combine* (kəm·bin) the ingredients correctly the cake
    will turn out well.

3. In compound words, the primary accent falls on the first part of the word.

    Examples:
    sídewalk
    flóormat

4. Accent tends to shorten the vowels of the syllables preceeding it.

    Example:
    combination (käm·bə·nā´shən)

5. In derived forms, the accent shifts toward the end of the word.

    Examples:
    cómment - commentáry
    catástrophe - catastróphic

6. Suffixes tend to be unaccented.

    Examples:
    informátion
    delícious

7. In words of more than one syllable that begin with *ex-*, *be-*, *de-*, *re-*, or *in-*, the second syllable is usually accented.

    Examples:
    ex-pire
    be-long
    de-tract

re-turn
in-fect

8. In two syllable words beginning with *a*, the *a* is usually unaccented. Some exceptions are *apron* (á·prən), and *able* (á·bəl), in which case there are consonant blends.

   Examples:
   around
   aloud
   applaud
   about

9. In most two syllable words that end with *y* which is preceded by a consonant, the first syllable is usually accented.

   Examples:
   buggy
   tiny
   fifty

10. Two like-consonant letters following the first vowel are usually a clue to an accented first syllable.

    Examples:
    puppet
    letter

11. In such words as *pickle, socket, jackal,* the letters *ck* are usually a clue to an accented first syllable.

12. When the final syllable of a word ends in *le* preceded by a consonant, that syllable is usually unaccented.

    Examples:
    table
    scramble
    coddle

13. In a multisyllabic word ending in the suffix *-ate,* the primary accent usually falls on the third syllable from the end.

    Example:
    eliminate (ə·lím·ə·nāt)

14. In multisyllabic words ending in the suffixes *-ion, -ic, -ical, -ity, -ian, -ial,* and *-ious,* the primary accent usually falls on the syllable preceding the suffix.

    Examples:
    information
    economic
    political

profanity
beautician
jovial
delicious

15. If *-tion* or *-ture* is the final syllable of a word, it is usually unaccented.

    Examples:
    election
    mixture

Appendix 9

List of Important Prepositional Phrases

Common Phrases

IN PHRASES
in the house
in the box
in the street
in the store
in the tree
in the morning
in the forest

OFF PHRASES
off the hill
off the table
off the ice
off the boat
off the train
off the air
off the floor

AGAINST PHRASES
against the wall
against my wishes
against the rules
against playing
against the law
against tradition
against reason

ON PHRASES
on the table
on the road
on TV
on the Christmas tree
on my dress
on the way

OF PHRASES
of the house
of the story
of my coat
of my hand
of the game
of a lesson
of the city

OVER PHRASES
over the hill
over the fence
over the house
over the trees
over the fields
over the flu
over the city

FOR PHRASES
for my mother
for my friends
for a red dress
for a haircut
for a dime
for a friend
for a little girl

WITH PHRASES
with the teacher
with a ribbon
with a stick
with a penny
with a friend
with sugar and
cream

UP PHRASES
up the hill
up the stairs
up the street
up the river
up my arm
up in the sky
up the road

FROM PHRASES
from the teacher
from the lesson
from a story
from my friends
from my children
from the store
from your mother

WITHOUT PHRASES
without any supper
without the zipper
without a friend
without any money
without trying
without sugar and
cream

DOWN PHRASES
down the stairs
down the basement
down the road
down the river
down the street
down the hatch
down the hole

BETWEEN Phrases   *BENEATH* Phrases

between the books   beneath the stars
between the games   beneath the papers
between the stories   beneath the table
between the lessons   beneath the desk
between the posts   beneath the chair
between you and me   beneath the bed
between us   beneath me

BY Phrases   *UNDER* Phrases

by the river   under the book
by the house   under the tree
by my side   under the clouds
by the rules   under the water
by the law   under the law
by the school   under the flag
by the street   under the agreement

Combination Phrases

to me for the lesson
on Monday at 9:00 o'clock in the morning
off the street into the yard
up the street to the store for the candy
in the yard for the game
to bed without any supper
in the sky over the city
to the game with the men from the office
for a haircut at the barbers
with a ribbon in her hair
at home on TV
on the horse for a ride to the lake in the mountains
at the end of the story
with my friends at her house
in a box on the table at home
down the stairs to the street
to play by the rules of the game
down the river in a boat for him
off the pocket of my coat
in the tree in the morning for a song

Appendix 10

The Fry Readability Graph

GRAPH FOR ESTIMATING READABILITY
by Edward Fry, Rutgers University Reading Center, New Jersey
Average number of syllables per 100 words

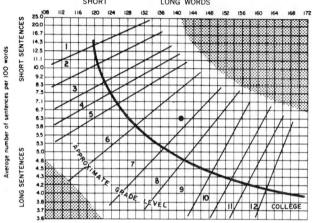

Directions: Randomly select 3 one-hundred-word passages from a book or an article. Plot average number of syllables and average number of sentences per 100 words on graph to determine the grade level of the material. Choose more passages per book if great variability is observed and conclude that the book has uneven readability. Few books will fall in gray area but when they do grade level scores are invalid.

Example:

	SYLLABLES	SENTENCES
1st Hundred Words	124	6.6
2nd Hundred Words	141	5.5
3rd Hundred Words	158	6.8
AVERAGE	141	6.3

READABILITY 7th GRADE (see dot plotted on graph)

References:

Fry, Edward. A readability formula that saves time. *Journal of Reading* 11 (1968): 513-16, 575-77.

Fry, Edward. Addendum: The readability graph. *The Reading Teacher* 22 (1969): 750.

Fry, Edward. The readability graph validated at primary levels. *The Reading Teacher* 22 (1969):534-38.

Maginnis, George H. The readability graph and informal reading inventories. *The Reading Teacher* 22 (1969):516-18, 559.

From "A Readability Formula That Saves Time," by Edward Fry. *Journal of Reading*, April 1968, pp. 513-16.

Appendix 11   The Flesch Readability Formula

Purposes of the Formula

To provide information along two dimensions.

1. "Reading ease" or difficulty of the material (in terms of word length and sentence length).
2. Human interest (as reflected in personal words and sentences, direct address to the reader, questions to the reader, and other devices that contribute to the appeal of reading matter).

Assumptions Made in Connection with the Formula

1. Sentences containing many words are, in general, harder to read and comprehend than sentences containing fewer words.
2. Words containing many syllables tend to be harder to read and comprehend than words containing fewer syllables.
3. Personal references in a passage contribute to ease of comprehending the material and to human interest. Personal references include pronouns referring to people, names of people, and other words that refer to people; for example, *girl, boy, woman, man,* etc., used to refer to a particular person (but not to man, etc., in the collective). Other devices like direct questions to the reader contribute to interest.

Comment

According to Flesch, an analysis of a sufficient number of sample passages in a book to ascertain the average word length (in syllables), the average sentence length, and the percentage of "human-interest" words and sentences can be helpful to us in estimating the difficulty level and interest level of material we are considering for use or are now using with our students.

Adapted from pp. 1-10 in *How to Test Readability* by Rudolf Flesch. Copyright © 1951 by Rudolf Flesch. Reprinted by permission of Harper & Row, Publishers, Inc.

Coding

WL = Average number of syllables per 100 words.
SL = Average sentence length in words.
PW = Average number of personal words in the 100-word passages analyzed.
PS = Percentage of personal sentences.

Formulas were computed on the basis of sample 100-word sections taken at regular intervals throughout the entire book.

The formula for "reading ease" is based on WL and SL above.
The formula for "human interest" is based on PW and PS above.

Formula for Reading Ease

RE = 206.835 − .846 WL − 1.015 SL

Formula for Human Interest

HI = 3.635 PW + .314 PS

Table for Reading Ease

Circled scores indicate where this particular book is classified, according to Flesch.

Reading-Ease Score	Description of Style	Average Syllables per 100 Words	Average Number of Words per Sentence	Public School Grade Level
0-30	Very difficult	192+	29+	The difficulty of very difficult technical material—may require professional training to read
30-50	Difficult	167	25	College level
50-60	Fairly difficult	155	21	Sophomore, junior, or senior in high school
60-70	Standard	147	17	8th grade, or high school freshman
70-80	Fairly easy	139	14	7th grade
80-90	Easy	131	11	6th grade

Readability Formulas

Flesch (high school and college)

1. Count
   a. 100-word sample starting at the beginning of the first complete paragraph on every tenth page. Count contractions and hyphenated words as one word; count as word numbers separated by space.
   b. The number of syllables in each 100-word sample (if in doubt consult dictionary). Will be *WL* in formula.
   c. Figure the average sentence length for all your samples combined. In each 100-word sample find the sentence ending nearest the 100-word mark, e.g., 94th or 109th word. Count sentences to that point and divide words in those sentences by number of sentences. Will be *SL* in formula.
   d. Figure number of "personal words" per 100 in all your samples combined. Personal words—
      1) All first, second, and third person pronouns except the neuters (it, its, itself, and they, them, their, theirs, themselves) if referring to things.
      2) All words having masculine or feminine natural gender, e.g., Jane, Mary, father, sister, iceman, actress. Do not count common gender words like teacher, employee, assistant, spouse. Will be *PW* in formula.
   e. Figure number of personal sentences per 100 sentences in all your samples combined. Personal sentences—
      1) Spoken sentences marked by ". . . ." or otherwise, often including so-called speech tags like he said.
      2) Questions, commands, requests, and other sentences directly addressed to the reader.
      3) Exclamations.
      4) Grammatically incomplete sentences whose full meaning has to be inferred from the text, e.g., "Doesn't know a word of English—" "Handsome, though—well he wasn't!", etc.
      5) Divide number of "personal sentences" by total number of sentences found in c above. Will be PS in formula.

Appendix 12

The Fog Index— A Quick Estimate of Readability

The Fog Index was developed by Robert Gunning. The following are the steps in its application.

1. Take several samples of one hundred words each, spaced evenly through the article or book.

   Count the number of sentences in each sample. (Stop the sentence count with the sentence ending nearest the one-hundred-word limit).

   Divide the total number of words in the passage (100) by the number of sentences.

   This gives you the average number of words in a sentence. Jot down this number.

2. Count the number of words of three syllables or more per one hundred using the same samples.

   Do *not* count these words:

   a. Words that are capitalized.
   b. Compound words that are the combination of short, easy words (Ex. bookkeeper).
   c. Words that are verb forms made from three syllables by adding -ed, or -es (Ex. created).

   This gives you the percentage of hard words in the passage. Jot this figure directly under the figure obtained in step one.

3. To determine the Fog Index, total the two figures just counted and multiply that total by .4 (four-tenths). This gives you the approximate grade placement of the writing, but tends to run somewhat high with more difficult materials.

From *Reading Institute Extension Services,* Unit 8, (May 15, 1966) by Lawrence Carrillo. Chicago: Science Research Associates, Inc., 1966), p. 11. Used with permission.

Appendix 13

Wilson's Essential Vocabulary List

There is a *need* (crucial) for *everyone* who is mobile to know a minimum vocabulary of words found on signs everywhere in everyday life. Such a list should be useful to a teacher of educable mentally retarded teenagers, of remedial reading cases, or of adult literacy programs at elementary achievement levels.

Adults only
All cars (trucks) stop
Antidote
Ask attendant for key
Beware
Beware of cross winds
Beware of the dog
Bridge out
Bus only
Bus station
Bus stop
Caution
Closed
Combustible
Condemned
Construction zone
Contaminated
Curve
Danger
Dangerous curve
Dead end
Deep water
Deer (cattle) crossing
Dentist
Detour
Dim lights
Dip
Doctor (Dr.)
Do not block walk
   (driveway)
Do not cross, use tunnel
Do not crowd
Do not enter

Do not inhale fumes
Do not push
Do not refreeze
Do not shove
Do not stand up
Do not use near heat
Do not use near open flame
Don't walk
Down
Drifting sand
Drive slow
Dynamite
Elevator
Emergency exit
Emergency vehicles only
Employees only
End 45
End construction
Entrance
Exit
Exit only
Exit speed 30
Explosives
External use only
Falling rocks
Fall out shelter
Fire escape
Fire extinguisher
First aid
Flammable
Flooded
Floods when raining
Found

Four-way stop
Fragile
Freeway
Garage
Gasoline
Gate
Gentlemen
Go slow
Handle with care
Hands off
Help
High voltage
Hospital zone
In
Inflammable
Information
Inspection station
Instructions
Junction 101A
Keep away
Keep closed at all times
Keep off (the grass)
Keep out
Keep to the left
Keep to the right
Ladies
Lane ends
Last chance for gas
Left lane must turn left
Left turn O.K.
Left turn on this signal only
Left turn only
Listen

From "An Essential Vocabulary," by Corlette T. Wilson. *Reading Teacher* 17 (November 1963):94-96. Reprinted by permission of the author and the International Reading Association.

Live wires
Loading zone
Look!
Look out for the cars
Look out for the trucks
Lost
Mechanic on duty
Men
Men working
Merge left
Merge Right
Merging traffic
Military reservation
M.P.H.
Next
Next (window, gate)
No admittance
No checks cashed
No credit
No diving
No dogs allowed
No dumping
No fires
No fishing
No hunting
No left turn
No loitering
No minors
No parking
No passing
No right turn
No right turn on red light
No smoking
No smoking area
No spitting
No standing
No stopping
No swimming
No touching
No trespassing
No turns
No U turn
Not a through street

Not for internal use
Noxious
Nurse
Office
One way—Do not enter
One way street
Open
Out
Out of order
Pavement ends
Pedestrians prohibited
Ped-Xing
Playground
Proceed at your own risk
Poison
Poisonous
Police (station)
Post no bills
Post office
Posted
Private
Private property
Private road
Pull
Push
Put on chains
Railroad crossing
Restrooms
Resume speed
Right lane must turn right
Right turn only
R.R.
Road closed
Road ends
Safety first
School stop
School zone
Shallow water
Shelter
Slide area
Slippery when frosty
Slippery when wet
Slow down

Slower traffic keep right
Smoking prohibited
Speed checked by radar
Steep grade
Step down (up)
Stop
Stop ahead
Stop for pedestrians
Stop motor
Stop when occupied
Taxi stand
Terms cash
Thin ice
This end up
This side up
This lane may turn left
This road patrolled by
aircraft
Three-way light
Traffic circle
Truck route
Turn off
Turn off 1/2 mile
(1/4 mile)
Unloading zone
Up
Use before (date)
Use in open air
Use low gear
Use other door
Violators will be prosecuted
Walk
Wanted
Warning
Watch for flagman
Watch for low flying
aircraft
Watch your step
Wet paint
Winding road
Women
Yield
Yield right of way

Appendix 14

Adult Basic Education Curriculum Guide Vocabulary List

A partial list of practical signs with which students might become familiar:

Addressing	Dispose of trash properly	Railroad crossing
Airport	Emergency	Repairs
Avoid damage to your	Entrance	Restroom
parcel post	Exit	Road curves ahead
Baggage	Express	Road under construction
Bus station	First aid	Sale
Bus stop	Food, lodging, gas	School
Check packing, wrapping	Fruit	School crossing
Children at play	Furniture	Separate and bundle
Civic center	Gate 1	your mail
Closed Saturday and	Gentlemen	Shop and mail early
Sunday	Guests	Single lane traffic
Closed today	Ivy Road	Slippery when wet
Clothing	Information	Slow
Danger	Keep off the grass	Slow construction ahead
Dead end	Keep left	Speed limit
No hunting	Keep out	Stamps
No loitering	Keep right	Stop
No parking	Ladies	Stop here for signal
No skating	Legal holiday	Taxi stand
No smoking	Local	Thin ice
No swimming	Local traffic	Tickets
No U turn	Mail early for Christmas	Today's special (meat,
Not for deposit of mail	Mail early in the day	veg., etc.)
Obey anti-litter laws	Meat	Train station
One way	Men	U.S. Mail
Out of town	Merging traffic	U.S. Mail collection box
Parking	No driving	Women
Passengers	No fishing	Yield right of way
Ped-X	Penalty for throwing trash	
Detour	Playground	

From *Curriculum Guide to Adult Basic Education: Beginning Level*, pp. 121-22. Washington, D. C.: U.S. Government Printing Office, 1966.

Appendix 15

A List of Basic Sight Words for Older Disabled Readers

1. more	24. might	47. war
2. than	25. great	48. until
3. other	26. year	49. something
4. such	27. since	50. fact
5. even	28. against	51. though
6. most	29. used	52. less
7. also	30. states	53. public
8. through	31. himself	54. almost
9. years	32. few	55. enough
10. should	33. during	56. took
11. each	34. without	57. yet
12. people	35. place	58. government
13. Mr.	36. American	59. system
14. state	37. however	60. set
15. world	38. Mrs.	61. told
16. still	39. thought	62. nothing
17. between	40. part	63. end
18. life	41. general	64. called
19. being	42. high	65. didn't
20. same	43. united	66. eyes
21. another	44. left	67. asked
22. white	45. number	68. later
23. last	46. course	69. knew

From "A Supplement to the Dolch Word Lists," by Jerry L. Johns. *Reading Improvement* 7 (Winter 1971-1972):91. Used by permission.

Appendix 16

Slosson Oral Reading Test (SORT)

The Slosson Oral Reading Test is a valuable resource for every adult educator. The sample presented here will demonstrate the range of the test. One of its important features is the ease with which it can be administered and scored.

LIST P (20)

1. see
2. look
3. mother
4. little
5. here
15. is
16. up
17. make
18. ball
19. help
20. play

LIST 1 (40)

1. with
2. friends
3. came
4. horse
5. ride
6. under
16. basket
17. food
18. road
19. hill
20. along

LIST 2 (60)

1. game
2. hide
3. grass
4. across
5. around
6. breakfast
7. field
17. forest
18. stars
19. heavy
20. station

LIST 3 (80)

1. safe
2. against
3. smash
4. reward
5. evening
6. stream
7. empty
8. stone
18. hunger
19. excuse
20. understood

LIST 4 (100)

1. harness
2. price
3. flakes
4. silence
5. develop
6. promptly
7. serious
17. future
18. claimed
19. common
20. dainty

LIST 5 (120)

1. cushion
2. generally
3. extended
4. custom
5. tailor
6. haze
7. gracious
8. dignity
18. ambition
19. presence
20. merchant

LIST 6 (140)

1. installed
2. importance
3. medicine
4. rebellion
5. infected
6. responsible
7. liquid
8. tremendous
9. customary
13. yearning
20. compliments

LIST 7 (160)

1. administer
2. tremor
3. environment
4. counterfeit
5. crisis
6. industrious
7. approximate
8. society
9. architecture
10. malignant
14. reminiscence

From Slosson Educational Publications, 140 Pine Street, East Aurora, New York, 1963. Used by permission.

344

List 8 (180)	High School (200)	Score
1. prairies	1. traverse	List P
2. evident	2. affable	List 1
3. nucleus	3. compressible	List 2
4. antique	4. excruciating	List 3
5. twilight	5. pandemonium	List 4
6. memorandum	6. scrupulous	List 5
7. ~~whimsical~~	7. primordial	List 6
	~~advertisement~~	List 7
		List 8
10. formulated		
11. articulate	11. facsimile	
12. deprecate	12. auspicious	

SAMPLE

This *Oral Reading Test* is to be given individually and is based on the ability to pronounce words at different levels of difficulty. The words have been taken from standardized school readers and the *Reading Level* obtained from testing represents median or standardized school achievement. A correlation of .96 (variability on a group of 108 children from first grade thru high school: Gray Mean = 5.0, SORT Mean = 5.0, Gray S.D. = 2.0, SORT S.D. = 2.3) was obtained with the *Standardized Oral Reading Paragraphs* by William S. Gray, published by The Bobbs-Merrill Company, Inc., Indianapolis, Indiana. Permission to use this test by Gray for purposes of validation is deeply appreciated.

A reliability coefficient of .99 (test-retest interval of one week) shows that this Oral Reading Test can be used at frequent intervals to measure a child's progress in reading, providing no specific coaching with these particular words has been given. Such periodic testing can be highly motivating.

Directions

1. Allow the individual to read from one sheet while you keep score on another. At the start, say the following: *"I want to see how many of these words you can read. Please begin here and read each word aloud as carefully as you can."* (Indicate at what list to start.) *"When you come to a difficult word, do the best you can and if you can't read it, say 'blank' and go on to the next one."*

2. Start with a list where you think he can pronounce all 20 words in that one list correctly. Note that each list of words is graded. List P (primer) is for the first few months of first grade, List 1 is for the balance of first grade, List 2 is for second grade, etc. If the *starting list* is too difficult and the learner makes even one mistake, go back until you reach an easier list where he can pronounce all 20 words correctly.

3. After you have found the *starting list*, go on into more advanced lists until you find the *stopping list*, where he mispronounces or is unable

to read all 20 words. When you reach a point where the words become very difficult, say: *"Look quickly down this list and read the words you think you know."*

4. When the learner reads very slowly and takes more than 5 seconds on each and every word, move him along by saying the "blank" for him. Or call out the number of the word at a rate of about 5 seconds each. Still another plan is to use a small card or piece of paper, covering up a word after a 5 second exposure, forcing him on to the next word.

5. Count as an error each mispronounced or omitted word as well as a word which takes more than about 5 seconds to pronounce. (If a child has a speech defect such as a stutter, disregard the 5 second interval and allow as much time as necessary.) Count it an error when a child is uncertain about a word and gives more than one pronunciation, even though one of them may have been correct. Be particularly careful about scoring the word endings as they must be absolutely correct. Keep score by putting a check mark ($\checkmark$) after each error or a plus sign ($+$) after each correct word. Enter the number of correct words at the bottom of each list as you go along. An analysis of scatter on the test, as well as an analysis of the types of errors made, will indicate areas of weakness.

6. To find a *raw score* for reading, count the total number of words he was able to pronounce correctly in all lists and add the words below the starting list for which he automatically receives credit. To obtain the *Reading Level*, look up the value of this raw score in the table below. A simple way to determine the *Reading Level* is to take half the raw score. For example, if the raw score were 46, half of this number would be 23 and the Reading Level would be 2.3 or the 3rd month of 2nd grade.

Changing the Raw Score to Reading Level

(Reading grade level is given in years and months. For example, 5.2 means the 2nd month of 5th grade.)

SCORE	GRADE	SCORE	GRADE	SCORE	GRADE
0-1	0.0	62-63	3.1	124-125	6.2
2-3	0.1	64-65	3.2	126-127	6.3
4-5	0.2	66-67	3.3	128-129	6.4
6-7	0.3	68-69	3.4	130-131	6.5
8-9	0.4	70-71	3.5	132-133	6.6
10-11	0.5	72-73	3.6	134-135	6.7
12-13	0.6	74-75	3.7	136-137	6.8
14-15	0.7	76-77	3.8	138-139	6.9
16-17	0.8	78-79	3.9	140-141	7.0
18-19	0.9	80-81	4.0	142-143	7.1
20-21	1.0	82-83	4.1	144-145	7.2

Score	Grade	Score	Grade	Score	Grade
22-23	1.1	84-85	4.2	146-147	7.3
24-25	1.2	86-87	4.3	148-149	7.4
26-27	1.3	88-89	4.4	150-151	7.5
28-29	1.4	90-91	4.5	152-153	7.6
30-31	1.5	92-93	4.6	154-155	7.7
32-33	1.6	94-95	4.7	156-157	7.8
34-35	1.7	96-97	4.8	158-159	7.9
36-37	1.8	98-99	4.9	160-161	8.0
38-39	1.9	100-101	5.0	162-163	8.1
40-41	2.0	102-103	5.1	164-165	8.2
42-43	2.1	104-105	5.2	166-167	8.3
44-45	2.2	106-107	5.3	168-169	8.4
46-47	2.3	108-109	5.4	170-171	8.5
48-49	2.4	110-111	5.5	172-173	8.6
50-51	2.5	112-113	5.6	174-175	8.7
52-53	2.6	114-115	5.7	176-177	8.8
54-55	2.7	116-117	5.8	178-179	8.9
56-57	2.8	118-119	5.9	180-200	H.S.
58-59	2.9	120-121	6.0		
60-61	3.0	122-123	6.1		

Appendix 17

The Graded Word List: Quick Gauge of Reading Ability

The San Diego Quick Assessment is a quick way to gauge a student's reading ability. It is a graded word list, formed by drawing words randomly from basal reader glossaries, and from the Thorndike list. Words initially were assigned levels according to these sources, with some shifting on the basis of students' responses.

The graded word list has two uses: (1) to determine a reading level, and (2) to detect errors in word analysis. One can use the test information to group students for corrective practice or to select appropriate reading materials for those students.

The list is remarkably accurate when used for these purposes. During the last two years we have had students in our undergraduate reading classes give this test to children in our campus laboratory school. Following testing, we asked them to recommend appropriate reading levels for these children. In all but four cases out of more than one hundred, their recommendations coincided with those of the classroom teachers who had been working with these children for a large portion of the year.

The list, like other instruments, is not appropriate for all students. Among high school and adult groups, we find it most effective for those who have poor decoding skills. Junior high students need not be so disabled for this to be an effective instrument.

Administration

1. Type out each list of ten words on an index card.
2. Begin with a card that is at least two years below the student's grade-level assignment.
3. Ask the student to read the words aloud to you. If he misreads any on the list, drop to easier lists until he makes no errors. This indicates the base level.
4. Write down all incorrect responses, or use diacritical marks on your copy of the test. For example, *lonely* might be read and recorded as *lovely*. *Apparatus* might be recorded as *a·per'·a·tus*.

From "The Graded Word List: Quick Gauge of Reading Ability," by Margaret LaPray and Ramon Ross. *Journal of Reading* 12 (January 1969):305-7. Reprinted by permission of the authors and the International Reading Association.

5. Encourage the student to read words he does not know so that you can identify the techniques he uses for word identification.
6. Have the student read from increasingly difficult lists until he misses at least three words.

PP	Primer	1	2	3
see	you	road	our	city
play	come	live	please	middle
me	not	thank	myself	moment
at	with	when	town	frightened
run	jump	bigger	early	exclaimed
go	help	how	send	several
and	is	always	wide	lonely
look	work	night	believe	drew
can	are	spring	quietly	since
here	this	today	carefully	straight

4	5	6	7	8
decided	scanty	bridge	amber	capacious
served	business	commercial	dominion	limitation
amazed	develop	abolish	sundry	pretext
silent	considered	trucker	capillary	intrigue
wrecked	discusses	apparatus	impetuous	delusion
improved	behaved	elementary	blight	immaculate
certainly	splendid	comment	wrest	ascent
entered	acquainted	necessity	enumerate	acrid
realized	escaped	gallery	daunted	binocular
interrupted	grim	relativity	condescend	embankment

9	10	11
conscientious	zany	galore
isolation	jerkin	rotunda
molecule	nausea	capitalism
ritual	gratuitous	prevaricate
momentous	linear	risible
vulnerable	inept	exonerate
kinship	legality	superannuate
conservatism	aspen	luxuriate
jaunty	amnesty	piebald
inventive	barometer	crunch

Analysis

1. The list in which a student misses no more than one of the ten words is the level at which he can read independently. Two errors indicate his instructional level. Three or more errors identify the level at which reading material will be too difficult for him.
2. An analysis of a student's errors is useful. Among those that occur with greatest frequency are the following:

ERROR	EXAMPLE
reversal	ton for not
consonant	now for how
consonant clusters	state for straight
short vowel	came for can
long vowel	wid for wide
prefix	inproved for improved
suffix	improve for improved
miscellaneous	(accent, omission of syllables, etc.)

3. As with other reading tasks, teacher observation of student behavior is essential. Such things as posture, facial expression, and voice quality may signal restlessness, lack of assurance, or frustration while reading.

Botel
Reading
Inventory

A—Word Recognition

This sample will demonstrate the range of this important evaluation tool.

A (PREPRIMER)	B (PRIMER)	C (FIRST)	D (SECOND—1)
Word	*Word*	*Word*	*Word*
1. a	all	about	across
2. ball	at	as	balloon
3. blue	boat	be	best
4. come	but	by	burn
5. father	do	could	care
6. get	duck	fast	coat

SAMPLE

15. play	saw	party	
16. ride	stop	sat	six
17. see	thank	some	table
18. to	there	tell	together
19. want	three	tree	turn
20. will	train	walk	wood

E (SECOND—2)	F (THIRD—1)	G (THIRD—2)	H (FOURTH)
Word	*Word*	*Word*	*Word*
1. above	able	act	abandon
2. bakery	block	beach	armor
3. broke	child	bounce	borrow
4. clown	daddy	chance	chimney
5. done	edge	cottage	costly
6. face	fix	distance	digest

SAMPLE

15. rode	secret	scared	
16. sell	silver	shoot	release
17. sorry	squirrel	spill	security
18. strong	teeth	stupid	speaker
19. third	trap	ticket	telegram
20. wet	watch	wire	underneath

Word Opposites Test (Reading)

Botel's Word Opposite Test used in conjunction with the Word Recognition Test is a valuable tool in the testing repertoire of adult basic education teachers. The samples presented on these pages indicate the wide range of the instrument.

Directions: Pick a word in each line which means the opposite or nearly the opposite of the numbered word. Draw a line under it.

Name _____

Date _____

Teacher _____

Example:
1. no   oh   yes   not

A	a	b	c
1. white	yellow	black	back
2. work	funny	happy	play
3. day	play	red	night
4. take	away	give	find
	the	them	then
		over	out
			new

B	a	b	c
1. front	under		
2. always	never	every	
3. last	run	fast	high
4. before	near	prize	laugh	next
	far	in	hungry	better
		big	cry	funny
			fish	friend
				on

C	a	b	c
1. left	above		
2. dark	black	sing	
3. happy	loud	silly	supper
4. hard	soft	cold	story	right
	change	began	old	teacher
		sister	sorry	laugh
			picnic	straight
				sure

D	a	b	c
1. easy	light		
2. right	again	poor	
3. against	tree	almost	full
4. rich	plenty	follow	important	begin
	cabbage	pass	part	quiet
		shout	enter	slide
			clever	black

Score____%

E	a	b	c
1. often	now		
2. swiftly	slowly	look	
3. discover	arrive	pair	sorry
4. daughter	brother	sick	tall	short
	wise	thick	stupid	empty
		sting	pleasant	full
		son	wife	
			bottom	

F	a	b	c	d
1. absent				
2. wake	morning			
3. careful	angel	devil		
4. gather	scatter	since	rich	
	chance	cheap	special	laundry
		succeed	sure	freedom
			punish	answer

G	a	b	c	d
1. ugly	children			joy
2. noisy	dazzle	lower		
3. moisture	party	unhappy	weak	
4. merry	weary	mountain	yard	overflow
	injure	inner	free	journey
		wander	width	southward
			deny	agree
				loose

H	a	b	c	d
1. strengthen	stronger			
2. advance	retreat	release		
3. include	angle	shelter	omit	
4. positive	needless	accept	worthwhile	scandal
	scarce	rarely	insist	ugly
		hero	crisis	usual
			seldom	simple
				barren

I	a	b	c	d
1. accidental	agreeable			
2. usually	readiness	normal		
3. tardy	strict	frequently	seldom	
4. idiot	genius	average	vulgar	stupid
	implement	enthusiastic	negative	indifferent
		modern	president	co-operate
			incorrect	apply
				confess

J	a	b	c	d
1. colorless	jovial			
2. chastise	antique	glamor		
3. restrained	small	sympathize	expansive	
4. illegal	lawyer	refined	illusion	admonish
	irresistible	lawful	pertinent	festive
		fragile	citadel	prohibit
			imitation	conceal
				obvious

Interpreting the Reading Placement Tests

The Table of Standards (below) will help you find the Instructional and Frustration Levels for pupils. For most pupils, the Instructional Level is not a single level but rather a range of levels at which they can read with profit.

Also indicated in the table is the Free Reading Level, at which a pupil can read easily, without help or hesitation. A pupil's library books should generally be at the Free Reading Level. However, the pupil should never be restricted from selecting more difficult books. Frequently, a pupil will read a library book that is apparently at his Instructional or Frustration

Level with pleasure and real understanding and with no help from the teacher. This may happen with an abler reader.

Table of Standards

READING LEVELS	WORD RECOGNITION TEST		WORD OPPOSITES TEST	
	No of words correct out of 20	*% of accuracy*	*No. of words correct out of 10*	*% of accuracy*
Free Reading Levels (Easy: Pupil can read with profit without any teacher help.)	20 19	100% 95%	10 9	100% 90%
Instructional Levels (Suitable: Pupil usually needs teacher guidance for comprehension and interpretation.)	18 17 16 15 14	90% 85% 80% 75% 70%	8 7	80% 70%
Frustration Levels (Too difficult: Pupil cannot read with profit even with teacher help.)	13–0	65%–0	6–0	60%–0

Appendix 19

Brief Individual Instant Word Oral Reading Test

How to Use

Ask the student to read each word aloud. Mark each word read incorrectly with an X on the word. Stop the test when the student misses two complete lines.

Scoring

Count the total number of words read correctly and write the number correct in the space provided. This test does not yield a grade level but rather aids the instructor in selecting curriculum materials and planning lessons. The letters in parentheses indicate the group of Instant Words. "1a" means first 100 word group "a," "2c" means second 100 word group "c," etc. Students should know nearly all of these words when they have obtained the upper fourth-grade reading ability level. Do not use this test for teaching; use the complete list of Instant Words.

1.	(1a)	the	is	of
2.	(1b)	they	if	would
3.	(1c)	by	our	which
4.	(1d)	who	their	other
5.	(2a)	upon	because	say
6.	(2b)	where	year	found
7.	(2c)	right	leave	another
8.	(2d)	five	shall	also
9.	(3a)	don't	does	ask
10.	(3b)	myself	eight	write
11.	(3c)	off	start	close
12.	(3d)	early	eyes	though
13.	(4a)	country	tired	brought
14.	(4e)	believe	month	whole
15.	(4i)	die	minute	fourth

Total number of words read correctly (maximum 45) _____

From *Reading Instruction for Classroom and Clinic*, pp. 65-69, by Edward Fry. Copyright © 1972 by McGraw-Hill Inc. Used by permission of McGraw-Hill, Inc.

This is a test for individual or group administration in primary grades and remedial reading situations for:

1. Determining the starting point in teaching the Instant Words, which is a graded high-frequency reading vocabulary.
2. Measuring general reading achievement, which is useful for such purposes as placing children in reading groups.

Directions for the Instant Word Recognition Test

This test may be given to one child or to a whole class. However, with first graders or slow students or older remedial children the test is more valid if it is administered to small groups of ten or fewer pupils so that the teacher can observe each student and see that he follows directions properly and does not look at another child's paper—separation of seats is desirable.

Instruct the students to fill in the data at the top of their test sheets. Writing the teacher's name or group, date, and Form 1 or Form 2 on the chalkboard is helpful. For Form 1 of the test the teacher reads the directions for Form 1, and for Form 2 the teacher reads from the directions for Form 2. The child marks the same test blank. The only difference in Form 1 and Form 2 is the difference in directions.

Next, copy the example on the chalkboard:

A   it   have   can   a   with   and say:

"In this test we want to find out how many words you can read. I am going to call out one word for each line and you are to place an X on top of the word I call out.

"Now look at the first line of words, line A. If I call out the word *can,* you place an X on top of the word *can* like this (illustrate on chalkboard). You should all mark an X on *can."*

Check to see if all the students have the examples marked correctly.

Next read off the list of words from either Form 1 column or Form 2 column (not both). Read the line number, the word, the word used in a simple sentence or phrase, and the word once more. Do not give additional repetitions of the word or any additional hints, examples, or other help.

For example:

"Line 1, *and,* Bill *and* Mary went to town, *and."*

Interpretation

This test measures the sight recognition of the Instant Words (which is a little easier than the skill of reading them aloud).

The test is in serial order progressing from easy to hard. The column at the far right tells from which group of Instant Words the line was selected. There are two lines for each group of twenty-five Instant Words. The first line for each group is a random selection of words, while the second line of each group chooses groups of words which have similar beginning sounds. Hence, if a student gets the first line for each group correct and not the second the teacher may well suspect that the student knows begining word *sounds* but not the Instant Words at this level.

The main value of this test is that it will suggest to the teacher which groups of Instant Words can most profitably be taught to individuals or groups.

Though this test does not have a large standardization group, it has been administered to 153 first graders in December and their mean score was 11.1.

It also has some value in predicting success in reading or when compared with the paragraph meaning subtest of the Stanford Achievement Test given in May. The correlation was 0.77. This also indicates that the Instant Word Recognition Test can also profitably be used for ranking students within the class as one of the criteria for placing them in reading groups.

Note that the same Students Test Sheet is used for both Form 1 and Form 2; the only difference is in the teacher's directions.

For an individually administered oral reading test the student may be asked to read aloud from the Student Test Sheet.

Teacher's Directions for Instant Word Recognition Test

Form 1. Lower Level

1.	and	Bill *and* Mary went to the store.
2.	that	Is *that* your pencil?
3.	up	Look *up* at the airplane.
4.	so	John took his ball *so* the children could play.
5.	go	Did you *go* to school?
6.	was	He *was* the tallest boy in the class.
7.	she	Did *she* help you?
8.	were	The children *were* skating.
9.	could	Bill *could* not find his pencil.
10.	saw	We *saw* the helicopter land.
11.	eat	What shall we *eat* for lunch?
12.	white	Betty wore a *white* sweater.
13.	each	*Each* boy did his best.
14.	next	The *next* boy was named Henry.
15.	must	You *must* use a sharpened pencil.
16.	such	It was *such* a lovely day we went for a walk.
17.	buy	Please *buy* a loaf of bread.
18.	green	Janie wore a *green* dress.
19.	seven	There were *seven* boys on one team.
20.	sit	Billy wanted to *sit* in the big chair.

21. bed   Linda went to *bed* at eight o'clock.
22. set   Do you help Mother *set* the table?
23. through We went *through* a dark tunnel.
24. town   The little *town* had pretty houses.

Form 2. Lower Level

1.   be   I will *be* at home.
2.   as   Run *as* fast as you can.
3.   out   We went *out* to play.
4.   had   They *had* a new ball.
5.   come   Please *come* here.
6.   what   *What* time is it?
7.   give   Please *give* the book to John.
8.   their   Lucky is *their* dog.
9.   could   We *could* see everyone.
10. back   Bill played in the *back* yard.
11. found   Jane *found* a nickel.
12. bring   Did he *bring* the fruit?
13. why   *Why* did Betty stay home?
14. never   We *never* went to that zoo.
15. shall   I *shall* go home.
16. sure   Tom was *sure* he had a pencil.
17. every   *Every* house had a porch.
18. goes   Jack *goes* to the store for his mother.
19. write   Can you *write* your name?
20. hot   The stove was *hot*.
21. wash   Did you *wash* your hands?
22. along   Ride *along* the sidewalk.
23. fat   She held a *fat* little puppy.
24. took   We *took* a lunch with us.

Form 1. Upper Level

25. garden   Mother likes her *garden*.
26. told   She *told* me a secret.
27. cover   *Cover* your mouth when you sneeze.
28. street   Which *street* do you live on?
29. mean   I *mean* what I say.
30. fight   Girls don't like to *fight*.
31. side   Which *side* are you on?
32. wind   The *wind* howled through the trees.
33. follow   Let's play "*Follow* the Leader."
34. short   We will only stay a *short* time.
35. note   He took a *note* home.
36. cost   How much does that *cost*?
37. dinner   It's time for *dinner*.
38. feed   May we *feed* the monkeys?
39. sick   Some people make me *sick!*
40. farm   Grandpa lived on a *farm*.
41. kept   Grandma *kept* cookies in a jar.
42. ring   She wore a gold *ring*.
43. idea   Whose *idea* was this?

44. strong   How *strong* are you?
45. result   What is the *result* of striking a match?
46. court   The *court* fined him $15 for speeding.
47. twelve   *Twelve* things make a dozen.
48. perhaps   *Perhaps* you can help me.

Form 2. Upper Level

25. story   This is a good *story*.
26. table   Put the dishes on the *table*.
27. number   What *number* comes after nine?
28. still   Hold your hand *still!*
29. need   How many do you *need?*
30. feel   How do you *feel?*
31. front   Put the smaller children in *front*.
32. wear   You should *wear* your sweater when it is cold.
33. pass   *Pass* the ketchup, please.
34. ship   They painted their *ship* black.
35. less   Three is *less* than five.
36. cow   A *cow* eats grass.
37. egg   She had an *egg* for breakfast.
38. fell   Jack *fell* down the stairs.
39. great   The President is a *great* man.
40. finish   When you *finish* the book, put it back on the shelf.
41. well   They went to the *well* for water.
42. wrote   I *wrote* a letter to my friend yesterday.
43. herself   She cut *herself* on the nail.
44. study   You need a quiet place to *study*.
45. enjoy   Most boys *enjoy* playing football.
46. continue   *Continue* to practice until I tell you to stop.
47. aunt   My *aunt* is very nice.
48. possible   We can only do something if it is *possible*.

Student Test Sheet Instant Word Recognition Test

Lower Level

STUDENT'S NAME _____

DATE_____

TEACHER OR GROUP_____

A. it have can a with   (Example)
1. you the is and be   (1a)
2. at this as that are   (1a)
3. I about me out up   (1b)
4. he so had been some   (1b)
5. go by or some us   (1c)
6. what his which has was   (1c)
7. she take give again down   (1d)
8. three who their were work   (1d)
9. could because into think night   (2a)
10. box book saw say back   (2a)

11. eat   want   four   found   last   (2b)
12. bring white black where   ball   (2b)
13. use   why   each   these   let   (2c)
14. tree   next   tall   never   name   (2c)
15. shall thing kind   call   must   (2d)
16. over   such   own   only   sure   (2d)
17. buy   every fly   clean   thank   (3a)
18. gave   sleep green goes   small   (3a)
19. write those myself seven   eight   (3b)
20. hat   hot   sing   hold   sit   (3b)
21. hard   bed   wash   fail   dress   (3c)
22. always sat   set   along   ground   (3c)
23. keep   fat   eyes   only   through   (3d)
24. town   ten   took   pair   part   (3d)

Upper Level

A. it   have   can   a   with   (Example)
25. garden father across story   brought   (4a)
26. done   told   different table tried   (4a)
27. number matter together cover   hit   (4b)
28. still   sun   city   state   street   (4b)
29. need   mean   send   thought half   (4c)
30. enough during feel   hundred fight   (4c)
31. side   front   young   kill   air   (4d)
32. wear   wind   world   won't   built   (4d)
33. follow company pass   begin   reason   (4e)
34. certain ship   sent   fair   short   (4e)
35. Bird   wait   note   less   ever   (4f)
36. past   cow   cost   charge milk   (4f)
37. egg   dinner return ground hair   (4g)
38. hill   feed   fell   alone   sir   (4g)
39. became cry   great   whom   sick   (4h)
40. finish bread   farm   floor   snow   (4h)
41. well   fourth step   kept   act   (4i)
42. heart   real   swim   ring   wrote   (4i)
43. herself idea   themselves wonder twenty   (rj)
44. smile   stood   study   strong whose   (4j)
45. demand figure enjoy   human   result   (rk)
46. court   case   increase continue price   (4k)
47. aunt   lie   rode   twelve mark   (4l)
48. public president perhaps pen   possible   (4l)

Appendix 20

Model for an Informal Reading Inventory

Directions

When the signal is given, read pages 1-4, stopping at, "How Does the Carburetor Work." Read this information in a similar manner to that which you usually use in reading information-type material. As soon as you have finished reading, look at the chalkboard and write the figure you see on the board in the blank marked *Time*. Once you have finished reading, turn the reading material in. You *are not* allowed to read any section of the manual once you have begun to answer the questions, so read carefully.

● ● ● ●

TIME _____

Questions Based on the Reading Selection

I.
    A. What is the basic difference between the strokes of a four-cycle engine and a two-cycle engine?
    B. What obvious difference could you conclude between fuel intake of the two-cycle and four-cycle engine?

II.
    A. It is important that you recognize and remember important details when reading. Below are statements found in the reading you just finished. If the statement is true, put *T* on the line before the statement, and if it false put *F* on the line.
    __ 1. Because the crankcase of the two-cycle engine acts as a transfer pump for the air-fuel mixture, lubrication of the engine depends on the addition of oil to the gasoline.
    __ 2. The exhaust valve in a two-cycle engine is larger than the intake valve.
    __ 3. The two-cycle engine has to do in two strokes what the four-cycle engine does in four.

This reading selection is taken from *The Two-Cycle Engine*, pp. 1-4. Urbana, Ill.: Vocational Agriculture Service. The informal inventory was prepared by Rodney Lee Winter, Illinois State University, 1975. Used by permission.

B. It is important that you retain the main concepts of the material that you read. Check statements below that are main ideas in this article.

___1. The easiest way to understand two-cycle operation is to compare it with four-cycle operation.

___2. Reed valves act as an exhaust in the two-cycle engine.

___3. Intake and compression occur during the upward movement of the two-cycle engine.

___4. The reed valve is open when the two-cycle piston is at Top Dead Center.

C. It is important for you to draw conclusions from what you have read. Which of the following generalizations can be drawn from this article?

___1. Both four-cycle and two-cycle engines have similar types of valve operations.

___2. Four-cycle and two-cycle engines have similar strokes, but they are done in different ways.

___3. Vacuums are created in both engines with similar piston movement.

D. It is necessary to know the exact meaning of words you read. Below are sentences with a word italicized in each. Under each sentence are four choices; check the one that best relates to the italicized word.

1. *Reed valves* are thin pieces of spring steel located on the crankcase side of the engine.

___a. Allows fuel mixture intake.

___b. Allows exhaust outlet from the cylinder.

___c. Acts as a very quiet muffler.

2. A *fuel-mixture* is required in two-cycle operation.

___a. Combination of gasoline, oil, and air.

___b. Combination of air and gas only.

___c. Relates to mixing of liquids.

3. A two-cycle engine has two basic *strokes*.

___a. A combination of all working parts in the engine moving once.

___b. Either a downward or upward movement of the piston.

___c. A combination of both a downward and upward movement of the piston.

III.

A. What method or process did you use in reading this information on two-cycle engines? Tell just how you went about reading it.

1. What did you do to get the main idea?

2. What did you do to get the details?

3. What did you do when you met a word you did not know?

Appendix 21

Cloze Exercise

Directions

The passage that you are to read discusses the relationship between you and your child. As you read, fill in the blanks with the words that are missing.

Most people believe that praise builds up a child's confidence and makes him feel secure. In actuality,_____may result in tension _____misbehavior. Why? Many children_____, from time to time,_____wishes about members of_____ family. When parents tell_____child, "You are such_____ good boy," he may_____be able to accept_____because his own picture_____himself is quite different._____ his own eyes, he_____be "goo" when only_____he wished that his_____had a zipper on_____mouth or that his _____would spend next weekend_____the hospital. In fact,_____more he is praised,_____more he misbehaves in_____to show his "true_____." Parents frequently report that _____after praising a child_____ good deportment, he starts_____go wild, as though_____ disprove their compliment. It _____possible that "acting up" is _____child's way of communicating_____private reservations about his_____image.

Does this mean _____praise is now "out?"_____ at all. It does_____however, that praise, like_____, must not be administered_____. There are rules and_____ that govern the handling _____potent medicines, rules about _____ and dosage, cautions about _____allergic reactions. There are_____regulations about the administration _____emotional medicine. The single _____important rule is that_____deal only with the_____efforts and accomplishments, not _____his character and personality. when a boy cleans up_____yard, it is only_____to com-

Exercise prepared by Lauren Majerczyk, Illinois State University, 1975. Used by permission. Materials from *Between Parent and Child*, pp. 44-45, by Haim G. Ginott. New York: Avon Publishers, 1965.

ment on how_____ he has worked and _____ how good the
yard_____ . It is highly unrelated, and inappropriate to tell him
how good he is.

List of Deleted Words

1. praise	18. the	35. cautions
2. and	19. the	36. of
3. have	20. order	37. timing
4. destructive	21. self	38. possible
5. their	22. just	39. similar
6. a	23. for	40. of
7. a	24. to	41. most
8. not	25. to	42. praise
9. it	26. is	43. child's
10. of	27. the	44. with
11. In	28. his	45. When
12. cannot	29. public	46. the
13. recently	30. that	47. natural
14. mother	31. Not	48. hard
15. her	32. mean	49. on
16. brother	33. penicillin	50. looks
17. in	34. haphazardly	

Evaluation of Test Results

To the teacher: Multiply the number of correct responses that are the
same as the author's words by two. This gives you a percentage score.
Rank the scores on the chart below.

FRUSTRATIONAL LEVEL *(Below 40%)*	INSTRUCTIONAL LEVEL *(40 to 60%)*	INDEPENDENT LEVEL *(Above 60%)*

Appendix 22   Reading Diagnosis Sheet

TEACHER _____
SCHOOL _____
NAME _____
GRADE _____

Category	Item	1st Check	2nd Check	3rd Check	No.
OTHER RELATED ABILITIES	Inability to locate information				27
	Undeveloped dictionary skill				26
	Written recall limited by spelling ability				25
SILENT READING	Inability to adjust reading rate to difficulty of material				24
	Inability to skim				23
	Voicing-lip movement				22
	High rate at expense of accuracy				21
	Low rate of speed				20
ORAL SILENT DIFFICULTIES	Response poorly organized				19
	Unaided recall scanty				18
	Fails to comprehend				17
ORAL READING	Unable to use context clues				16
	Lacks desirable structural analysis				15
	Blends, digraphs or dipthongs not known				14
	Vowel sounds not known				13
	Consonant sounds not known				12
	Guesses at words				11
	Sight vocabulary not up to grade level				10
	Basic sight words not known				9
	Substitutions				8
	Insertions				7
	Inversions or reversals				6
	Repetitions				5
	Omissions				4
	Poor pronunciation				3
	Incorrect phrasing				2
	Word-by-word reading				1

D–Difficulty recognized
P–Pupil progressing
N–No longer has difficulty

The items listed above represent the most common difficulties encountered by pupils in the reading program. Following each numbered item are spaces for notation of that specific difficulty. This may be done at intervals of several months. One might use a check to indicate difficulty recognized or the following letters to represent an even more accurate appraisal:

From *Locating and Correcting Reading Difficulties*, p. 5, by Eldon E. Ekwall. Columbus, Ohio: Charles E. Merrill Publishing Co., 1970.

Appendix 23

Wepman Auditory Discrimination Test

Form I

	No	Yes
1. tub - tug		■
2. lack - lack	■	
3. web - wed		■
4. leg - led		■
5. chap - chap	■	
6. gum - dumb		■
7. bale - gale		■
8. sought - fought		■
9. vow - thou		■
10. shake - shape		■
11. zest - zest	■	
12. wretch - wretch	■	
13. thread - shred		■
14. jam - jam	■	
15. bass - bath		■
16. tin - pin		■
17. pat - pack		■
18. dim - din		■
19. coast - toast		■
20. thimble - symbol		■

Form II

	No	Yes
1. gear - beer		■
2. cad - cab		■
3. led - lad		■
4. thief - sheaf		■
5. sake - shake		■
6. jail - jail	■	
7. ball - ball	■	
8. lake - lake	■	
9. bead - deed		■
10. rub - rug		■
11. wing - wing	■	
12. gall - goal		■
13. pet - pit		■
14. lit - lick		■
15. bug - bud		■
16. lass - lath		■
17. cope - coke		■
18. pool - tool		■
19. zone - zone	■	
20. fret - threat		■

Form I   Form II

Form I	No	Yes	Form II	No	Yes
21. cap - cat		■	21. bar - bar	■	
22. din - bin		■	22. bum - bun		■
23. lath - lash		■	23. lave - lathe		■
24. bum - bomb		■	24. shot - shop		■
25. clothe - clove		■	25. wedge - wedge	■	
26. moon - noon		■	26. suck - sock		■
27. shack - sack		■	27. vie - thy		■
28. sheaf - sheath		■	28. rich - rich	■	
29. king - king	■		29. pit - kit		■
30. badge - badge	■		30. guile - dial		■
31. pork - cork		■	31. rash - wrath		■
32. fie - thigh		■	32. chew - chew	■	
33. shoal - shawl		■	33. fag - sag		■
34. tall - tall	■		34. phase - phase	■	
35. par - par	■		35. sick - thick		■
36. pat - pet		■	36. wreath - reef		■
37. muff - muss		■	37. map - nap		■
38. pose - pose	■		38. muss - mush		■
39. lease - leash		■	39. cart - tart		■
40. pen - pin		■	40. cuff - cuss		■

Directions for Test Administration and Scoring

Administration of the test to older five-year-old children and to younger six-year-olds permits the selection of those who are likely to be able to utilize phonics in learning to read and those who will encounter difficulty with the sound-symbol relationships. For older children and adults, the test is useful in the differential diagnosis of reading and speech difficulties.

With the subject facing the examiner while receiving the instructions, say:

I am going to read some words to you—two words at a time. I want you to tell me, or let me know in some way, whether I read the same word twice or two different words. Remember, if the two words are exactly the same, you say "Yes" or "Same"; if they are not exactly the same, you say "No" or "Different." Let's try a few pairs for practice.

"Man (pause) Man—Did I say the same word twice or two different ones?"

When he has completed a correct discrimination, go on to the next pair, saying,

Let's try another pair. Hat (pause) Pat—What about that pair, were they the same or different?

After instructions have been given and you feel that the subject understands what he is being asked to do, he should be so seated that he cannot see the examiner's mouth or the words on the test form, as the test is given. The word pairs should be read clearly, but not overarticulated. The voice should not drop at the end of either word, nor should either word receive a different emphasis.

On the test form are two response columns, one headed *different* and the other headed *same*. Mark a mark ($+$) or ($-$) in the response column corresponding to each word pair as the subject responds. Do not repeat word pairs. If the subject indicates that he has not heard, go on after noting the pair not answered and return to those pairs after completing the rest of the test.

The score is obtained by counting the correct responses (number of $+$s in the *different* column only. Built into the test are two checks against patterning responses; failure to understand instructions or failure to pay attention. (1) a score of *less* than 10 in the *different* column and/or (2) a score of *less* than 7 in the *same* column invalidates the test. If either or both of these conditions exist, the test score should not be considered a true measure of discrimination ability. Frequently, retesting using the alternate form of the test at a later time will produce a more accurate measure.

The table on the following page presents an interpretation of the scores. Children at the five- and six-year-age level whose scores are low at those ages may be slow in developing the discriminatory ability and develop adequate ability in the next two years. Older children at the 7- or 8-year levels as the table shows are less likely to show extensive improvement. Above the age of eight almost no change is found in auditory discrimination ability. These subjects are most likely to have a specific auditory learning disability, especially if they show similar low scores in auditory memory and sequential ability.

Standardization and Interpretation Table—Forms IA and IIA

RATING SCALE*	AGE			
	5	6	7	8
+2	30 29	30 29	30 29	30
+1	28 27	28 27	28	29
0	26 25 24	26 25 24	27 26	28 27
−1 Adequacy	23 22 21 20 19	23 22 21	25	26
Threshold −2	18 17 16 15 14 13 12 11 10	20 19 18 17 16 15 14 13 12 11 10	24 23 22 21 20 19 18 17 16 15 14 13 12 11 10	25 24 23 22 21 20 19 18 17 16 15 14 13 12 11 10
Scores below 10 invalidate the test. NOTE: Scores in the SAME column below 7 also invalidate the test.	9 8 7 6 5 4 3 2 1 0	9 8 7 6 5 4 3 2 1 0	9 8 7 6 5 4 3 2 1 0	9 8 7 6 5 4 3 2 1 0

I N V A L I D

*Rating Scale Legend for Interpretation based on cumulative frequencies.

15%	+2	indicates a very good development
20%	+1	above average ability
30%	0	average ability
20%	−1	below average discrimination ability
15%	−2	below the level of the threshold of adequacy

Appendix 24

List of Easily Confused Words

NAME _____ GRADE ____ AGE ____ DATE ____
SCHOOL _____ READING TEACHER _____

stop	pots	tops
who	how	now
and	said	new
star	rats	tars
was	saw	on
no	not	ton
or	our	off
for	of	tap
tap	pat	apt
tub	but	put
team	meat	yes
eyes	say	net
dab	bad	add
pal	lap	alp
God	ma	nap

Score: _____
Number wrong: _____
Number right: _____
Percent right: _____
Diagnosis of Problem:

From *Corrective Reading*, 2d ed., pp. 65, 66-67, by Miles V. Zintz. Dubuque, Ia.: Wm. C. Brown Co. Publishers, 1972. Used by permission.

Appendix 25

Boyd Test
of Phonetic
Skills

Directions of Administration

Each adult should be tested individually. It is suggested that the examiner introduce the test in the following manner: Say, "*I have some cards here which have words on them. They are not real words, but words which have been made up. We call them nonsense words because they do not mean anything. I want you to read them to me out loud.*" (Present the first card.) "*Read this one for me.*" Present only one card at a time. Once the card has been presented and removed, do not allow the adult to look at it again.

You may encourage the adult by saying: "*You are trying very hard,*" or "*Yes, go on.*" It is correct at any time to encourage the adult. It is not, however, permissible to tell him how he is achieving. Do not give him any indication concerning his score. The administrator may repeat the sounds which the child gives only for the purpose of clarification. It is recommended that the examiner be certain after a definite pause on the part of the adult that the last sounds he made were his final answer to the item. Say: "*Is this what you said . . . ?*" If the adult responds negatively, ask him to repeat his answer.

Do not rush the adult. This is not a timed test. As far as possible make him feel comfortable. The test may be given in two sittings if you feel the individual is anxious or is tiring.

The record sheet should be as inconspicuous as possible. The adult's attention should be directed solely to the cards. If the adult is very curious about what the examiner is doing with the record sheet, he may say, "*I am writing your answers here to help me remember them later.*" The sole purpose of such a comment is to set the adult at ease.

Syllabication section. Cut out or fold over the record sheet so the adult can concentrate on words. Say: "*These are not real words, they are nonsense words. I want you to divide them into their sound parts of syllables, just as you would do with real words. Use this mark (draw a / to illustrate) where one syllable ends and the next one begins.*" Do not do any for him; this is a test and not a learning situation. If he fails to understand

From *Clinical Studies in Reading III,* by Robert D. Boyd. Edited by Helen M. Robinson and Helen K. Smith. Sem #97 (1968) Boyd Phonics Test, pp. 161-64. Used by permission. Chicago: University of Chicago Press, 1968.

you, repeat the instructions. If it is a case of the student's not knowing how to syllabicate words, then he fails the test, and you have found out what you wanted to know.

The response given by the adult to each item should be recorded immediately. If the answer is correct, a check should be made in the appropriate column. If the answer varies in any way from the accepted response, it should be recorded phonetically.

Directions for Scoring

One point is given for each of the tested phonetic elements recognized and pronounced correctly. Thus, where *cl* as a phonetic element is tested, the adult is given one point if he recognizes and pronounces this even though the remainder of the item is incorrect. For example, he may pronounce the item "clup" as clop or clap, etc. Emphasis in evaluation is placed on qualitative interpretation of performance.

The test is not standardized; therefore it cannot be assumed that passing a particular level, say 2G, means that the individual can do all the steps up to this one. It is suggested that the test be given from the beginning. The last selection, *Selection and Application*, should not be given to those who appear to be almost completely illiterate.

NAME_____ DATE_____ EXAMINER _____

Directions: Record incorrect responses phonetically. Check error classification (✔)

LEVEL I   KEY

Consonants—Vowels

	Record	B	E	V	B = Beginning
					E = Ending
					V = Vowel
1. bem					Bl = Blend
2. dor					D = Digraph
3. fet					C = Consonant
4. hus					P = Phonogram
5. kon					
6. vip					
7. wos					TOTAL RIGHT
8. yeb					
9. nem					I _____ II-G _____
10. cul					II-A _____ III _____
11. jeg					II-B _____ III-A _____
12. mid					II-C _____ III-B _____
13. gud					II-D _____ IV _____
14. rip					II-E _____ IV-A _____
15. sab					II-F _____ V _____

LEVEL II-A

Consonant Blends

	Record	Bl	V	E
1. clup				
2. fron				
3. gris				
4. tran				
5. swed				
6. cron				
7. bret				
8. glit				
9. stris				

LEVEL II-B

Consonant Digraphs

	Record	D	V	E
1. chas				
2. shan				
3. thob				
4. whes				
5. seck				
6. quin				

LEVEL II-C

Vowel Controllers

	Record	Bl	V	C
1. blar (far)				
2. scur (fur)				
3. flir (stir)				
4. smaw (saw)				
5. skow (cow)				
(know)				
6. sler (her)				
7. snal (pal)				
(all)				
8. stor (for)				

LEVEL II-D

Open Syllables

	Record	B	V
1. po (ŏ)			
2. mu (ū)			
3. ri (ī)			
4. te (ē)			
5. fa (ā)			
6. ky (ī)			
7. or (ē)			

LEVEL II-E

Beginning Vowels

	Record	B	V
1. et (ĕ)			
2. ab (ă)			
3. ut (ŭ)			
4. ig (ĭ)			
5. os (ŏ)			

LEVEL II-F

C and G Sounds

	Record	B	V	E
1. gen (j)				
2. cof (k)				
3. gam (g)				
4. cil (s)				
5. ces (s)				

LEVEL II-G

Final E

	Record	B	V	E
1. nobe (nōb)				
2. rafe (rāf)				
3. sebe (sēb)				
4. tife (tīf)				
5. hute (hūt)				

LEVEL III   LEVEL III-A

Vowel Digraphs   *Phonograms*

	Record	B	E	D
1. meid (ē)	___	___	___	___
2. woit (oi)	___	___	___	___
3. noaf (ō)	___	___	___	___
4. luet (ū)	___	___	___	___
5. fain (ā)	___	___	___	___
6. hius (ī)	___	___	___	___
7. dieb (ī)	___	___	___	___
8. keat (ē)	___	___	___	___
9. toen (ō)	___	___	___	___
10. moy (oi)	___	___	___	___
11. kay (ā)	___	___	___	___
12. doot (oo)[1]	___	___	___	___
13. soun (ow)[2]	___	___	___	___

	Record	B	P
1. hing	___	___	___
2. mang	___	___	___
3. fink	___	___	___
4. nill	___	___	___
5. dank	___	___	___
6. pell	___	___	___
7. desion	___	___	___
8. lamous	___	___	___
9. mought	___	___	___

LEVEL III-B

Silent Letters

	Record	B	E	V
1. knet (net)	___	___	___	___
2. pnan (nan)	___	___	___	___
3. wrat (rat)	___	___	___	___

1. "oo" can be pronounced as in noon or as in book.
2. "ou" can be pronounced as in noun or as in soul.

LEVEL IV   LEVEL IV-A

Open Syllables   *Closed Syllables*

1. tapod _____   1. dabbet _____
2. setin _____   2. delrim _____
3. himut _____   3. fumdol _____
4. hogim _____   4. higtat _____
5. nusig _____   5. posrud _____

LEVEL V

Selection and Application   *Syllabication*

1. rutemub (rūtmŭb)   nubinto
              (rū te mub)   limmobe
2. goreato (gō rē to)   allomut
3. fawlote (faw lōt)   frintonna
4. thaldar   iniptir
5. stitemeid (stī te mēd)   hapter
              (stĭt mēd)   cluppas
6. pnum (num)   illummas
7. panciate (panshēāt)   teepmot
8. stilo (stīlō)   utasmir
9. vaiper (vāpur)   halooner
10. sublogue (sublog)   eallimot

Level V (continued)

11. ubidge (ūbij)
12. ruker (rōōkur)
13. bicture (bikchur)
14. dacial (dāshul)
15. juve (jōōv)
16. aption (apshun)
17. rhambuf (rambuf)
18. kough (kuf, kof)
19. gudge (guj)
20. ackbility (akbiluti)
21. pactuate (pakchōōat)
22. nace (nās)
23. baccum (bākum)
           (baccum)
24. cymtur (simtur)
25. teigh (tā)
26. taysen (tāsun)
27. bential (benshul)
28. callion (kalyun)
29. canberize (canberīz)
30. vapdow (vapdō)
           (vapdow)

Appendix 26

Compound Words Test

Somebody	Something	Tonight
Daytime	Peanut	Workbag
Another	Grandmother	Farmhouses
Birthday	Lonesome	Anyone
Himself	Everywhere	Haystack
Firemen	Schoolhouse	Boxcar
Railroad	Package	Waterfall
Runway	Lemonade	Maybe
Downtown	Popcorn	Blueberries
Watchman	Policeman	Watchdog
Postman	Sandwiches	Tablecloth
Whoever	Campfire	Bedroom
Popover	Sometimes	Housekeeper
Schoolbook	Grandfather	Without
Snowbank	Everything	Indeed
Schoolroom	Pullman	Fireplace
Gatepost	Jackknife	Anything
Buttermilk	Scarecrow	Whatever
Blackboard	Thanksgiving	Somewhere
Airplane	Grandma	Grandchildren

*Score:*_____
Number missed:_____
Number correct:_____
Percent correct:_____

From *Corrective Reading*, 2d ed., pp. 65, 66-67, by Miles V. Zintz. Dubuque, Ia.: Wm. C. Brown Co. Publishers, 1972. Used by permission.

Appendix 27

Strength-Weakness Spectrum for Wechsler Tests— Implications for Reading Instruction

NAME_____ SCHOOL_____ GRADE_____

EXAMINER_____ AGE_____

REPORT TO_____ BIRTHDATE_____

DATE TESTED_____

Test Given   *Score*

___WWPSI ___WAIS   ___ Performance IQ

___WISC ___W-B II   ___Verbal IQ   ___ Performance Median

___WISC-R   ___Verbal Median ___ Scaled Score

                     ___Scaled Score ___ Full Scale IQ

(Interpretation Note: The normative medium-scaled score of each subtest for the pupil's peer group is 10. Performance in each area should be assessed as *strong, average,* or *weak* in terms of this normative median score, as well as in terms of ipsative scaling, that is, rating a response of only the individual's own characteristic strengths and weaknesses without regard to a normative group.)

Verbal Subtests

Scaled Score	Ratings Normative	Ipsative	Subtest	Thought Functions Measured	Practical Descriptions
			Information (I)	Intellectual effort—integration of words, objects, facts and relationships; intellectual ambitiousness; memory development.	Knowledge of facts gained from experience, culture, and education; effectiveness of listening skills.
			Comprehension (C)	Social judgment—practical knowledge; drawing conclusions and predicting outcomes.	Common sense; social responsibility; ability to evaluate past experience; moral codes.
			Arithmetic (A)	Abstract reasoning; ability to relate objects in space; concentration and active focusing of attention.	Concentrating to solve reasoning problems within a time limit.
			Similarities (S)	Verbal concept formation at the concrete, functional and abstract levels; ability to categorize and describe relationships between objects; ability to generalize and to use context.	Logical thinking ability; ability to see common factors.
			Vocabulary (V)	General intelligence; learning ability; cultural environment; memory; concept formation; reflection of early educational environment.	Word knowledge from experience and education; verbal fluency and richness.
			Digit span (DS)	Mental control; effortless attention and auditory memory; auditory organization.	Attention and rote memory.

Performance Subtests

SCALED SCORE	RATINGS		SUBTEST	THOUGHT FUNCTIONS MEASURED	PRACTICAL DESCRIPTIONS
	Normative	Ipsative			
			Picture Completion (PC)	Visual organization; perception of the whole in relation to its essential parts; attention to details.	Visual alertness and visual memory.
			Picture Arrangement (PA)	Nonverbal anticipation and planning; sensitivity to social outcomes; visual organization.	Interpretation of social situations and interpersonal relationships; ability to get the "idea" of a story.
			Block Design (BD)	Ability to analyze a whole in relation to its parts; visual analysis and synthesis; logical insight into space relationships; visual-motor perception and organization.	Abstract reasoning. Learning through practice; use of planning or trial-and-error work method and persistence; logical use of clues.
			Object Assembly (OA)	Ability to analyze the parts in relation to the whole; seeing relationships of parts to the whole in a familar configuration; critical appraisal of small details; visual-motor coordination and organization; anticipation.	Putting together concrete forms; approach to working habits; logical use of clues; use of planning or trial-and-error work method.
			Coding (Cod)	Short-term memory; visual-motor co-ordination; association of symbols in an unfamiliar task.	Speed of learning and writing symbols; ability to memorize symbols without confusion.
			Mazes (M)	Foresight; planning; visual-motor co-ordination.	Planning and following a visual pattern.

Implications from Subtest Grouping Scores

SCHOLASTIC ACHIEVEMENT = A + I
Expected Average Score = 20
Pupil's Score: _____
Rating: _____

CONCEPTUALIZING ABILITY = C + S + V
Expected Average Score = 30
Pupil's Score: _____
Rating: _____

RIGHT HEMISPHERE FUNCTIONING = PA + BD + OA (Spatial Organization)
Expected Average Score = 30
Pupil's Score: _____
Rating: _____

LEVEL OF ANXIETY = DS + A + Cod
Expected Average Score = 30
Pupil's Score: _____
Rating: _____

SEQUENCING ABILITY = DS + (PA or A) + Cod
Expected Average Score = 30
Pupil's Score: _____
Rating: _____

INDICATIONS THAT THE PUPIL IS PROBABLY A REMEDIAL:
___ Right Hemisphere Functioning Scored Higher than Left Hemisphere Functioning
___ Spatial Score Higher Than Conceptualizing Score
___ Conceptualizing Score Higher than Sequencing Score
___ Spatial Score Higher than Sequencing Score
___ Performance Score Higher than Verbal Score

SPATIAL ABILITY = PC + BD + OA
Expected Average Score = 30
Pupil's Score: _____
Rating: _____

LEFT HEMISPHERIC FUNCTION = I + A + DS (Symbol Manipulation)
Expected Average Score = 30
Pupil's Score: _____
Rating: _____

Examiner's Comments

Bibliography

Adult Education Council of Greater Chicago. *An Investigation of Materials and Methods for the Introductory Stage of Adult Literacy Education.* Springfield: Illinois Office of Education, 1965.

Alcock, Dorothea. *Grab.* Covina, Calif.: Dorothea Alcock, 1953.

Alesi, Gladys, and Pantell, Dora. *New American English: Books I and II.* New York: Oxford Book Co., 1972.

Allen, Harold B., and Campbell, Russell N. *Teaching English as a Second Language, A Book of Readings.* New York: McGraw-Hill Books Co., 1972.

Allen, James E. "James E. Allen in Memorial." *Reading Newsreport* 6 (Nov.-Dec. 1971):53.

Allen, Virginia, and Forman, Sidney. *English as a Second Language: A Comprehensive Bibliography.* New York: Teacher's College Press, 1970.

American Bar Association. *A Reading Needs Assessment Handbook for Correctional Educators.* Washington, D. C.: American Bar Association, 1974.

Applications and Forms Workbook. Kalamazoo, Mich.: Interpretive Education Co., 1974.

Associated Press. "Americans Short in IQ Category." *Daily Pantagraph*, Bloomington, Ill., 8 June 1975, p. 2.

Athey, Irene. "Affective Factors in Reading." In *Theoretical Processes and Models of Reading*, edited by Harry Singer and Robert Ruddell. Newark, Del.: International Reading Association, 1970.

Aukerman, Robert D. *Approaches to Beginning Reading.* New York: John Wiley & Sons, 1971.

———. "Some Spicy Commentary on Beginning Reading." *Reading Newsreport* 7 (October 1972):20-25.

Bailey, C. J.; Hayes, Ann; Rose, Harold; and Stamper, Robert, comp. *Morehead Adult Basic Education Teacher Trainer Reading Workshop: Final Report.* Morehead, Ky.: Morehead State University, 1971.

Bailey, Mildred Hart. "The Utility of Phonic Generalizations in Grades One Through Six." In *Teaching Word Recognition Skills*, edited by Mildred Dawson, pp. 90-95. Newark, Del.: International Reading Association, 1971.

Baltes, Paul B., and Labouvie, G. V. "Adult Development of Intellectual Performance: Description, Explanation and Modification." In *The Psychology of Adult Development and Aging*, edited by Carl Eisdorfer and M. P. Lawton. New York: American Psychological Association, 1973.

Baltes, Paul B., and Shaie, K. W. "Aging and IQ: The Myth of the Twilight Years." *Psychology Today* 7 (March 1974):35-40.

———. *Life-Span Developmental Psychology: Personality and Socialization.* New York: Academic Press, 1975.

Banks, Olivia E. "I Just Want to Learn to Read." *School and Community* 52 (November 1965):23-24.

Baratz, Joan C. "Teaching Reading in an Urban Negro School System." In *Language and Poverty*, edited by Frederick Williams, p. 11. Chicago: Markham Publishing Co., 1970.

Barbe, Walter. *Basic Skills List*. Englewood Cliffs, N. J.: Prentice-Hall, 1970.

Barnes, Robert F. "Problems Facing Teachers and Administrators in Adult Basic Education Today." A speech delivered to an assembly of adult basic education teachers in Chicago, April 3, 1965. In *Teaching Adults to Read: Guidelines*, edited by Byron Chapman, pp. 15-26. Galien, Mich.: Allied Education Council, 1966.

Bauer, Josephine. *Communications I: Getting Started*. Rev. ed. Chicago: Follett Publishing Co., 1966.

Bayley, N. "Research in Child Development: A Longitudinal Perspective." *Merrill Palmer Quarterly* 11 (1965):183-208.

Be Informed Series. Syracuse, N. Y.: New Reader's Press, 1970.

Berdrow, John. *Teaching Adults*. Adult Education Circular Series A-174, pp. 2-4. Springfield, Illinois: Office of Education, 1965.

Berg, Paul Conrad. "Illiteracy at the Crossroads." In *Basic Education for the Disadvantaged Adult*, edited by Frank W. Lanning and Wesley A. Many, p. 47. New York: Houghton Mifflin Co., 1965.

Betts, Emmett. *Foundations of Reading Instruction*. New York: American Book Co., 1954.

Birren, J. E. *The Psychology of Aging*. Englewood Cliffs: N. J.: Prentice-Hall, 1964.

Bischof, L. J. *Adult Psychology*. New York: Harper & Row, 1969.

Bloom, Benjamin, ed. *Taxonomy of Educational Objectives, Handbook I: Cognitive Domain*. New York: David McKay Co., 1956.

Board of Education of the City of New York. *Teaching English as a New Language to Adults*, pp. 7-9. Curriculum Bulletin, no. 5, 1963-1964 Series. Brooklyn: Board of Education of the City of New York Publications Sales Office, 1964.

Bodman, Jean, and Michael, Lanzaro. *No Hot Water Tonight*. New York: Collier Macmillan International, 1975.

Bond, Guy; Balow, Bruce; and Hoyt, Cyril J. *Silent Reading Diagnostic Test*. Chicago: Lyons & Carnahan, 1970.

Boning, Ricard A. *We Study Word Shapes*. Rockville Centre, New York: Dexter & Westbrook, Ltd., 1970.

Boone, Edgar J., and Quinn, Emily H. *Curriculum Development in Adult Basic Education*. Chicago: Follett Publishing Co., 1967.

Bormuth, John R. "Factor Validity of Cloze Tests as Measures of Reading Comprehension." *Reading Research Quarterly* 14 (Spring 1969):358-67.

Botel, Morton. *Botel Reading Inventory*. Chicago: Follett Publishing Co., 1961.

Botwinick, Jack and Qazilbash, Husain. *Teacher Training Reading Syllabus: Monograph One—Too Old to Learn?* Morehead, Ky.: Morehead State University, 1971.

Boyd, Robert D. "Boyd Phonics Test." In *Clinical Studies in Reading, III*, edited by Helen M. Robinson and Helen K. Smith. Chicago: University of Chicago Press, 1968.

Brazziel, William F. "Behavioral Analysis and Support in Programs for the Undereducated Adult: Psychology of the Undereducated." In *Trainers of Teachers of Undereducated Adults*, edited by Miles Zintz, pp. 39-52. Albuquerque: University of New Mexico Press, 1965.

——. *Retraining the Hard Core Unemployed.* Public Document, no. FS 5-213: 13027. Washington, D. C.: U.S. Government Printing Office, 1965.

Brown, Don A. *Test That's Not A Test.* Greeley, Colo.: Basic Education Trade House, 1974.

Brown, Grace M., and Cottrell, Alice. *California Phonics Test.* Monterery, Calif.: CTB/McGraw Hill Division, 1962.

Brown, J. I. *Brown-Carlsen Listening Comprehension Test.* New York: Harcourt Brace Jovanovich, 1955.

Brown, LeRoy, and Blair, J. C. *Gift: Good Ideas for Teaching Reading.* Mobile, Ala.: Mobile County Public Schools, 1972.

Bruner, J. S. *Toward a Theory of Instruction,* p. 40. Cambridge, Mass.: Harvard University Press, 1966.

Buchanan, Cynthia Dee. *Sullivan Programmed Reading for Adults.* New York: McGraw Hill Book Co., 1967.

Bureau of Vocational, Technical, and Adult Education. *ABC's: Introducing the Alphabet to the Adult Student.* Mimeographed. Charleston, W. V.: Bureau of Vocational, Technical, and Adult Education, 1965.

Burie, Audrey Ann, and Heltshe, Mary Ann. *Reading With a Smile: 90 Reading Games That Work.* Washington, D. C.: Acropolis Books Ltd., 1975.

Burmeister, Lou E. "Usefulness of Phonic Generalizations." In *Teaching Word Recognition Skills,* edited by Mildred Dawson, pp. 103-11. Newark, Del.: International Reading Association, 1971.

——. *Words—From Print to Meaning.* Reading, Mass.: Addison-Wesley Publishing Co., 1975.

Burnet, Mary. *The ABC's of Literacy.* Paris, France: UNESCO [United Nations Educational, Scientific, and Cultural Organization], 1965.

Buros, Oscar. *Mental Measurements Yearbooks.* Highland Park, N. J.: Gryphon Press, 1972.

——. *Reading Tests and Reviews.* Highland Park, N. J.: Gryphon Press, 1968.

——. *Reading Tests and Reviews—II.* Highland Park, N. J.: Gryphon Press, 1975.

Butcher, H. J. *Human Intelligence: Its Nature and Assessment,* pp. 172-78. New York: Harper & Row, 1973.

Caffarella, Rosemary. "The Counseling Process and Continuing Education." *Adult Leadership* 23 (December 1974):181-83.

Carlton, Lessie. "Teaching Word Recognition Skills." Lectures, Illinois State University, 1970.

Carrillo, Lawrence. *The Chandler Reading Program.* New York: Noble & Noble Publishers, 1970.

Cass, Angelica. *Adult Elementary Education,* pp. 30-40, 139-50. New York: Noble & Noble Publishers, 1956.

Chall, Jeanne. *Learning to Read: The Great Debate.* New York: McGraw Hill Book Co., 1967.

Chapman, Byron. *Teaching Adults to Read: Guidelines.* Galien, Mich.: Allied Education Council, 1965.

Chilman, Catherine, and Sussman, Marvin. "Poverty in the United States in the mid-Sixties." In *Basic Education for the Disadvantaged Adult: Theory and Practice,* edited by Frank Lanning and Wesley Many. Boston: Houghton Mifflin Co., 1966.

Cleugh, M. F. *Educating Older People.* 2d ed. New York: Tavistock Publications (Barnes & Noble), 1970.

Clymer, Theodore. "The Utility of Phonic Generalizations in the Primary Grades." In *Teaching Word Recognition Skills,* edited by Mildred Dawson, pp. 82-89. Newark, Del.: International Reading Association, 1971.

Coates, Robert H. "Preparing Adults for Rapid Change." *NEA Journal* 23 (December 1966):30-33.

Criscuolo, Nicholas P. *A Tutor's Guidebook for Remedial Reading.* Midland, Mich.: Pendell Publishing Co., 1972.

Curriculum Guide to Adult Basic Education: Beginning Level. Public Document no. FS 5-213:13032. Washington, D. C.: U.S. Government Printing Office, 1966.

Curriculum Guide to Adult Basic Education: Intermediate Level. Public Document no. FS 5-213:13031. Washington, D. C.: U.S. Government Printing Office, 1966.

Dale, Edgar, and Chall, Jeanne. "A Formula for Predicting Readability," *Educational Research Bulletin,* Ohio State University, 27 (1948):11-20, 28, 37-54.

Davis, Frederick B. "Criterion Referenced Tests: A Critique." In *Measuring Reading Performance,* edited by William E. Blanton et al., pp. 44-50. Newark, Del.: International Reading Association, 1974.

Del'Apa, Frank. *Educational Programs in Adult Correctional Institutions: A Survey.* Boulder, Colo.: Western Interstate Commission for Higher Education, 1973.

Desmond, T. C. "America's Unknown Middle-agers." *The New York Times,* 29 July 1956.

DeStafano, Johanna S. *Language, Society, and Education: A Profile of Black English.* Worthington, Ohio: Charles A. Jones Publishing Co., 1973.

Dillard, J. L. *Black English.* New York: Random House, 1973.

Dolch, Edward W. *Basic Sight Word List.* Champaign, Ill.: Garrard Publishing Co., 1952.

———. *Dolch Word Games and Phrase Cards.* Champaign, Ill.: Garrard Publishing Co., 1952.

Dunn, Lloyd M. *Peabody Picture Vocabulary Test.* Circle Pines, Minn.: American Guidance Services, 1959.

Durrell, Donald. *Word Analysis Cards.* New York: Harcourt Brace Jovanovich, 1960.

Durrell, Donald, and Hayes, Mary T. *Durrell Listening-Reading Series.* New York: Harcourt Brace Jovanovich, 1969.

Elley, Warwich B., and Reid, Neil A. *Progressive Achievement Test: Listening Comprehension.* Wellington C., 2, New Zealand: New Zealand Council for Educational Research, 1972.

Eisdorfer, C., and M. P. Lawton, eds. *The Psychology of Adult Development and Aging.* Washington: American Psychological Association, 1973.

Ellis, Henry C. *The Transfer of Learning.* New York: Macmillan, 1965.

Emans, Robert. "The Usefulness of Phonic Generalizations Above the Primary Grades." In *Teaching Word Recognition Skills,* edited by Mildred Dawson, pp. 96-102. Newark, Del.: International Reading Association, 1971.

Emery, Donald G. "Interview," *Reading Newsreport* 6 (March 1972):6.

English 900: Book 2. New York: Macmillan, 1965.

English Language Services, Inc. *English Pronunciation: A Manual for Teachers.* New York: Macmillan, 1968.

Ephrom, Beulah Kantor. *Emotional Difficulties in Reading.* New York: Julian Press, 1953.

Fader, Daniel. "Hooked on Books." A speech made to a convention of book publishers, Puerto Rico, 1965.

Farquhar, William W.; Krimboltz, John D; and Wren, C. Gilbert. *Learning to Study.* New York: Roland Press, 1960.

Fay, Jean B. "Psychological Characteristics Affecting Adult Learning." In *Basic Education for the Disadvantaged Adult,* edited by Frank Lanning and Wesley Many. New York: Houghton Mifflin Co., 1966.

Fellenz, Robert A. "How to Teach What You Know." *You Can Be a Successful Teacher of Adults.* Washington: National Association of Public School Adult Educators, 1974.

Ferndale Adult Basic Education Curriculum. Ferndale, Mich.: Ferndale High School, 1971.

Fernald, Grace. *Remedial Techniques in Basic School Subjects.* New York: McGraw-Hill, 1943.

Fersh, Seymour. "Studying Other Cultures: Looking Outward Is 'In'." Chapter 8. In *International Dimensions in the Social Studies,* edited by James Becker and Howard Mehlinger. Washington, D. C.: National Council for the Social Studies, 38th Yearbook, 1968, pp. 126, 129, 132, 134. Citing Felix C. Robb, "International Education: the Prospect," White House Conference on International Cooperation, Washington, D. C., 30 November 1965.

Finocchiaro, Mary. *English as a Second Language: From Theory to Practice.* New York: Simon & Schuster, 1967.

————. *Teaching English as a Second Language.* New York: Harper & Row, 1969.

Flesch, Rudolph. *How to Test Readability.* New York: Harper & Row, 1951.

————. "A New Readability Yardstick," *Journal of Applied Psychology* 32 (June 1948):221-33.

Fox, C. "Vocabulary Ability in Later Maturity," *Journal of Educational Psychology* 38 (1947):41-46.

Froese, Victor. "Cloze Readability versus the Dale Chall Formula." In *Teachers, Tangibles, Techniques: Comprehension of Content in Reading,* edited by Bonnie Smith Schulwitz, pp. 31-36. Newark, Del.: International Reading Association, 1975.

Frostig, Marianne. "Visual Modality: Research and Practice." In *Perception and Reading,* edited by H. K. Smith. Proceedings of the 12th Annual Convention of the International Reading Association 12 (1968):25-31.

Fry, Edward. *The Emergency Reading Teacher's Manual.* Highland Park, N. J.: Dreier Educational Systems, 1964.

————. *Instant Word Recognition Test.* Highland Park, N. J.: Dreier Educational Systems, 1971.

————. *Oral Reading Paragraphs.* Highland Park, N. J.: Dreier Educational Systems, 1971.

————. "A Readability Formula That Saves Time," *Journal of Reading* 11 (1968): 513-16, 575-77.

————. *Reading Instruction for Classroom and Clinic,* pp. 64-70. New York: McGraw-Hill Book Co., 1972.

Fuller, G. B. *Minnesota Percepto-Diagnostic Test.* Brandon, Vermont: Clinical Psychology Publishing Co., 1969.

Gates, Arthur I. *Gates Reading Survey, Form 3*. New York: Teachers College Press, 1958.

————. *The Improvement of Reading*, 3d ed. New York: Macmillan, 1947.

Gattengo, Caleb. *Words in Color*. Cooper Station, New York: Schools for the Future, 1962.

Geeslin, Carol M., and Geeslin, Robert H. *Teacher Training Reading Syllabus: Unit Four—Materials*. Morehead, Ky.: Morehead State University, 1971.

Geeslin, Robert H. *Teacher Training Reading Syllabus: Monograph Two—Teaching Reading in Adult Basic Education: Materials and Sources*. Morehead, Ky.: Morehead State University, 1971.

Geyer, John. "Models of Perceptual Processes in Reading." In *Theoretical Processes and Models of Reading*, edited by Harry Singer and Robert Ruddell, pp. 47-94. Newark, Del.: International Reading Association, 1970.

Gibson, Eleanor J., and Levin, Harry. *The Psychology of Reading*. Cambridge, Mass.: The Massachusetts Institute of Technology Press, 1975.

Gilmore, John V., and Gilmore, Eunice C. *Gilmore Oral Reading Test*. New York: Harcourt Brace Jovanovich, 1968.

Glasser, Alan J., and Zimmerman, Irla Lee. *Clinical Interpretations of the WISC*. New York: Grune & Stratton, 1972.

Goldberg, Herman K., and Schiffman, Gilbert B. *Dyslexia: Problems of Reading Disabilities*. New York: Grune & Stratton, 1973.

Goltry, M. *Forms in Your Future*. New York: Learning Trends Company, 1973.

Goodman, Kenneth. "Analysis of Oral Reading Miscues: Applied Psycholinguistics." *Reading Research Quarterly*, Autumn 1969, pp. 9-30.

Grabowski, Stanley M. and Glenn, Ann C. *Directory of Resources in Adult Education*. DeKalb, Ill.: Educational Resources Information Center (ERIC) University, 1974.

Gray, William S. *On Their Own in Reading*, rev. ed. Chicago: Scott, Foresman and Co., 1960.

————. "Teaching Adults to Read," In *Basic Education for the Disadvantaged Adult*, edited by Frank Lanning and Wesley Many. New York: Houghton Mifflin Co., 1966.

Greenlee Associates. *An Evaluation of the Basic Educaton Program of the State of Illinois*, appendix. New York: Greenlee Associates, 1965, pp. ii-v.

Griffin, Bobbie L., and Blankenship, A. Ray. *Training and Use of Volunteer Recruiters in Adult Basic Education Programs: Final Report*. Morehead, Ky.: Morehead State University, 1971.

Grindstaff, Colletta. *Teacher Training Reading Syllabus: Unit 3—Comprehension Skills*. Morehead, Ky.: Morehead State University, 1971.

Guide for Trainers of Teachers of Undereducated Adults. Washington, D. C.: United States Office of Education, 1967.

Gunning, Robert. "The Fog Index." In *Reading Institute Extension Service, Grades 7-12: Unit 8—Getting Ready for Next Year*, edited by Lawrence Carrillo, p. 11. Chicago: Science Research Associates, 1963.

Guszak, Frank. *Diagnostic Reading Instruction in the Elementary School*, pp. 139-60. New York: Harper & Row, 1972.

Haffner, Lawrence E. "Improving Grade Point Averages Through Reading-Study Skills Instruction." In *New Frontiers in College-Adult Reading*, edited by G. B. Schick and M. M. May. Yearbook of the National Reading Conference 15 (1965):46-50.

Haggstrom, Warren C. "Poverty and Adult Education," *Adult Education*, Spring 1965, pp. 145-60.

Hall, Eugene J. *Sounds and Syllables: A Reading Improvement Text for Adults.*
New York: Regents Publishing Co., 1967.

Hardy, Madeline I. "Follow-up of Four Who Failed," *Journal of Reading* 12
(February 1969):379-83, 416-19.

Harman, D. "Illiteracy: An Overview," *Harvard Educational Review* 40 (1970):
226-43.

Harrington, Michael. *The Other America: Poverty in the United States,* p. 22.
Baltimore: Penguin Books, 1963.

Harris, Louis. *The 1971 National Reading Difficulty Index: A Study of Functional Reading Ability in the U.S. for the National Reading Center.* Washington, D. C.: Louis Harris and Associates, Inc., 1971.

———. "Survival Literacy Study." Conducted for the National Reading Council,
September, 1970; discussed by the Hon. Margaret M. Heckler of Massa-
chusetts in the House of Representatives, as reported in the *Congressional
Record,* E9719-#9723, 18 November 1970.

Havighurst, Robert J. "Social Backgrounds: Their Impact on School Children."
In *Reading for the Disadvantaged: Problems of Linguistically Different
Learners,* edited by Thomas Horn, pp. 11-20. New York: Harcourt Brace
Jovanovich, 1970.

Hawkins, Thom. *Benjamin: Reading and Beyond.* Columbus, Ohio: Charles E.
Merrill Publishing Co., 1972.

Henney, R. L. *Systems for Success: Book I,* rev. ed. Chicago: Follett Publishing
Co., 1965.

Herber, Harold. *Teaching Reading in the Content Areas.* Englewood Cliffs,
N. J.: Prentice-Hall, 1970.

Herr, Selma E. *Learning Activities for Reading.* Dubuque, Ia.: Wm. C. Brown
Co., 1969.

Hertert, Patricia. "Problem Areas in School Attendance of Undereducated
Adults." In *Trainers of Teachers of Undereducated Adults,* edited by Miles
Zintz, p. 74. Albuquerque: University of New Mexico Press, 1965.

Hiemstra, Roger. *The Teaching of Reading in Adult Basic Education.* Lincoln:
Nebraska State Department of Education, 1973.

Hill, Mary Anne. *The Language Experience Approach for the Culturally Disadvantaged.* Reading Information Series: Where Do We Go? Newark, Del.:
International Reading Association, 1972.

Hillburn, Nancy. "At Least Listen!" *Reading Newsreport* 7 (January 1973):30.

Hilliard, Raymond M. "Massive Attack on Illiteracy." *American Library Association Bulletin* 57 (1963):1034-38.

Houle, Cyril O. *Continuing Your Education,* pp. 18-36. New York: McGraw-
Hill Book Co., 1964.

Houston, Susan H. "Black English." *Psychology Today* 6 (March 1973):45-48.

Huelsman, Charles. *Word Discrimination Test.* Oxford, Ohio: Miami University
Alumni Association, 1955.

Hunter, Madeline. "Project Linkage: Where Teachers Are Accountable." *Reading Newsreport* 6 (March 1972):25-27.

———. "When the Teacher Diagnoses Learning." *Educational Leadership,* April
1966, p. 545.

Hurlock, Elizabeth B. *Developmental Psychology,* 4th ed. New York: McGraw-
Hill Book Co., 1975.

Isenberg, I., ed. *The Drive Against Illiteracy.* New York: The H. W. Wilson
Co., 1964.

Jackard, Charles R., Jr. "The American Adult Male Rejects Counseling." *Adult Leadership,* May 1974, pp. 9-10.

Jenkinson, Marion D. "Increasing Reading Power in the Social Studies." In *Corrective Reading in the High School Curriculum,* edited by Alan Robinson and Sidney Rauch, p. 76. Newark, Del.: International Reading Association, 1966.

Job Corps Conference on "The Underachiever in Reading." Sponsored by the American Association of Colleges of Teacher Education, Dallas, Texas, May 1972.

Joffe, Irwin L. *Developing Outlining Skills.* Belmont, Calif.: Wadsworth Publishing Co., 1972.

Johns, Jerry. "A List of Basic Sight Words for Older Disabled Readers." *English Journal* 61 (October 1972):1059.

———, ed. *Literacy for Diverse Learners.* Newark, Del.: International Reading Association, 1974.

———. "A Supplement to the Dolch Word Lists." *Reading Improvement* 8 (Winter 1971-72):90-91, 94.

Johnson, Henry Sioux, and Hernandez, William J. *Educating The Mexican American.* Valley Forge, Pa.: Judson Press, 1970.

Johnson, Robert D. "Reading: A Case Study." In *Reading and Revolution: The Role of Reading in Today's Society,* edited by Dorothy M. Dietrich and Virginia H. Matthews. Perspectives in Reading Series, no. 13, pp. 38-44. Newark, Del.: International Reading Association, 1970.

Johnson, Samuel. *The Rambler,* 28 May 1751.

Jolly, Constance, and Jolly, Robert. *When You Teach English as a Second Language.* Brooklyn: Book Lab, 1974.

Jonas, William. *A Teacher's Guide to Teaching Adult Basic Reading.* Albany: The University of the State of New York: The State Education Department Bureau of Continuing Education Curriculum Development, 1968.

Jones, H. E., and Conrad, H. S. "The Growth and Decline of Intelligence." *General Psychological Monographs* 13, 1933. Quoted in J. R. Kidd's *How Adults Learn.* New York: Association Press, 1959.

Jones, Lewis Wade. "The Social Unreadiness of Negro Youth." *Saturday Review* 45 (October 20 1962):83.

Kangas, J., and Bradway, K. "Intelligence at Middle Age: A 38 Year Follow-up Study." *Developmental Psychology* 5 (1971):333-37.

Kauffman, Adrienne. Case Study. Albuquerque: The University of New Mexico, 1975.

Kaulfers, Walter V. "Gift of Tonges or Tower of Babel." *Educational Forum,* November 1954, p. 82.

Kent, W. P. *Job-Related Adult Basic Education: Vol. II.* Falls Church, Va.: System Development Corporation, 1971.

Keystone Visual Survey Tests. Meadville, Pa.: Keystone View Company, 1961.

Kidd, J. R. *How Adults Learn.* New York: Association Press, 1959.

Kincaid, J. Peter. *Use of the Automated Readability Index for Evaluating Peer-prepared Material for Use in Adult Reading Instruction.* Sponsored by USOE, Grant no. OEG-4-71-0069. Statesboro: Georgia Southern College, 1972.

Kincaid, J. Peter; Van Deusen, John; Thomas, Georgelle; Lewis, Robert; Anderson, Patricia T.; and Moody, Linda. *Big Red and Other Stories,* USOE Grant No. OEG-4-71-0069. Statesboro: Georgia Southern College, 1972: 12-14.

Kirchner, Corinne. "Motivation to Learn." In *Basic Education for the Disadvantaged Adult*, edited by Frank Lanning and Wesley Many, pp. 97-99. New York: Houghton Mifflin Co., 1966.

Klevins, Chester. *Materials and Methods in Adult Education*. New York: Klevins Publications, 1972.

Knowles, Malcolm S. *The Adult Education Movement in the United States*. New York: Holt, Rinehart and Winston, 1962.

———. *The Adult Learner: A Neglected Species*. Houston, Tex.: Gulf Publishing Company, 1973.

Koehler, Lawrence J. *Handbook for Teachers of Adults*. Sacramnto: Bureau of Adult Education, Division of Instruction, California State Department of Education, 1968.

Kucera, Henry, and Francis, W. Nelson. *Computational Analysis of Present-day American English*. Providence, R. I.: Brown University Press, 1967.

Labouvie-Vief, G.; Hoyer, W. J.; Baltes, P. B.; and Baltes, M. M. "Operant Analysis of Intellectual Behavior in Old Age." From "Age and IQ: Myth of the Twilight Zone." *Psychology Today* 7 (March 1974):38.

Lambert, William, and Lambert, Wallace. *Social Psychology*. Englewood Cliffs, N. J.: Prentice-Hall, 1964.

Labov, William. "Logic of Nonstandard English." In *Language, Society and Education: A Profile of Black English*, edited by Johanna S. DeStafano, p. 43. Worthington, Ohio: Charles A. Jones Publishing Co., 1973.

Langerman, Philip D., ed. *You Can Be a Successful Teacher of Adults*. Washington, D. C.: National Association of Public Continuing Adult Education, 1974.

LaPray, Margaret, and Ross, Ramon. "The San Diego Word List: Quick Gauge of Reading Ability." *Journal of Reading*, January 1969.

Laubach, Frank C., and Laubach, Robert. *Toward World Literacy*. Syracuse, N. Y.: Syracuse University Press, 1960.

Laubach, Frank C. and Kirk, Elizabeth Mooney. *City Living*. Syracuse, N. Y.: New Reader's Press, 1969.

———. *Everyday Reading and Writing*. Syracuse, N. Y.: New Reader's Press, 1970.

———. *In the Valley*. Syracuse, N. Y.: New Reader's Press, 1969.

———. *The New Streamlined English Series*. Syracuse, N. Y.: New Reader's Press, 1968.

Lee, Doris, and Allen, R. V. *The Language Experience Approach to the Teaching of Reading*. New York: Harper & Row, 1970.

Leibert, Robert. *Adult Informal Reading Inventory*. Kansas City, Mo.: University of Missouri, 1972.

Levey, Sylvia. "The New Hot Potato." *Reading Newsreport* 5 (November-December 1970):49.

Levin, Beatrice J. "Reading Requirements for Satisfactory Careers." In *Reading and Career Education*, edited by Duane M. Mielsen and Howard F. Hjelm. Perspectives in Reading Series, No. 19, pp. 77-83. Newark, Del.: International Reading Association, 1975.

Liddle, William. *Reading for Concepts*. New York: Webster Division of McGraw-Hill Book Company, 1970.

Lindsay, Peter H., and Norman, Donald A. *Human Information Processing*. New York: Academic Press, 1972.

Litchman, Marilyn. *Reading/Everyday Activities in Life.* New York: Cal Press, 1972.

Lorge, Irving. "Confusion as an Aspect of the Learning of the Older Adults." *Psychological Bulletin* 32 (1936):559.

————. "Gerontology—Later Maturity." *Annual Review of Psychology* 7 (1956): 349-94.

————. Articles in *Review of Educational Research* Vol. 11, December 1941; Vol. 14, December 1944; Vol. 17, December 1947; and Vol. 20, June 1950. Quoted in J. R. Kidd, *How Adults Learn.* New York: Association Press, 1959.

————. "Thorndike's Contribution to the Psychology of Learning of Adults." *Teacher's College Record,* May 1940, pp. 778-89.

Lutey, Carol. *Individual Intelligence Testing: A Manual.* Greeley, Colo.: Executary, Inc., 1966.

Mace, David. "Marriage by Arrangement." *McCalls* 86 (August 1959):50-51. Cited by Seymour H. Fersh, "Semantics and the Study of Culture." *Social Education,* May 1963.

Mager, Robert F. *Preparing Instructional Objectives.* Belmont, Calif.: Fearon Publishers, 1965.

Maryland State Department of Education. *Basic Education: Teaching the Adult.* Owings Mills: Maryland State Department of Education, 1975.

Massey, James O. *WISC Scoring Criteria,* 4th ed. Palo Alto, Calif.: Consulting Psychologists Press, 1969.

Matthews, Virginia H. "Adult Reading Studies: Their Implications for Private, Professional, and Public Policy." *Library Trends,* October 1973, p. 172.

Miles, W. R. "Psychological Aspects of Aging." *Problems of Aging,* p. 86. Baltimore: The Williams & Wilkins Co., 1952.

Miller, Harry G.; Beasley, John B.; and Swick, Kevin J. "Drill Re-examined: A Taxonomy for Drill Exercises." Mimeographed. Carbondale: Southern Illinois University, 1974.

Miller, Harry L. *Teaching and Learning in Adult Education.* New York: Macmillan, 1964.

Miller, Warren. *Cool World.* New York: Fawcett, 1959.

Miner, John B. *Adult Intelligence.* New York: Springer Publishing Co., 1957.

Mitzell, Adele. "Adult Basic Word List." *Adult Education* 16 (Winter 1966): 67-69.

Mocker, Donald W. "Cooperative Learning Process: Shared Learning Experience in Teaching Adults to Read." *Journal of Reading* 18 (March 1975): 440-44.

————. *A Report on the Identification, Classification, and Ranking of Competencies Appropriate for Adult Basic Education Teachers.* Kansas City: University of Missouri, 1974.

Murphy, Richard T. "Assessment of Adult Reading Competence." In *Reading and Career Education,* edited by Duane M. Nielsen and Howard F. Hjelm. Perspectives in Reading Series, no. 19, pp. 50-61. Newark, Del.: International Reading Association, 1975.

Mystery of the Mountains and Other Stories. Pleasantville, N. Y.: Reader's Digest Services, 1964.

McClusky, Howard Y. Cited in *The Adult Learner: A Neglected Species,* by Malcolm Knowles, p. 156. Houston, Tex.: Gulf Publishing Co., 1973.

McCreary, Eugene. "Pawns or Players?" *Phi Delta Kappan* 49 (November 1967): 138-42.

McCullough, Constance. *McCullough Word Analysis Tests.* Princeton, N. J.: Personnel Press, Inc., 1963.

McGarry, Florence A. "The Right to Read: Be Wary." *Reading Newsreport* 5 (March 1971):30-32.

National Association of Public Continuing Adult Educators. *Adult Basic Education: A Guide for Teachers and Teacher Trainers,* part II, pp. 3-25. Washington, D. C.: National Association of Public Continuing Adult Education, 1969.

———. *Counseling and Interviewing Adult Students.* Washington, D. C.: National Association of Public Continuing Adult Education, 1969.

———. "Everybody Has a Message: Do You Read Me?" In *Tested Techniques for Teachers of Adults,* pp. 6, 43. Washington, D. C.: National Association of Public Continuing Adult Education, 1972.

———. *When You're Teaching Adults,* p. 9. Washington, D. C.: National Association of Public Continuing Adult Education, 1969.

Nephew, Ervin. "The Oral Reading Mystique." *Reading Newsreport* 5 (April 1971):32.

Newman, Loretta M. "Community Clinic: Rx for Reading Ills." *Reading Newsreport* 6 (October 1971):43.

Nilsen, Don L. F., and Nilsen, Aileen Pace. *Pronunciation Contrasts in English.* New York: Simon & Schuster, 1971.

Northcutt, Norvell W. "Functional Literacy for Adults." In *Reading and Career Education,* edited by Duane M. Nielsen and Howard F. Hjelm. Perspectives in Reading Series, no. 19, pp. 43-49. Newark, Del.: International Reading Association, 1975.

O'Donnell, Michael P. *Teaching Reading to the Untaught.* New York: Multimedia Education, Inc., 1972.

Oettinger, D. "Physical Concomittants of Reading." *Yearbook of the Claremont Reading Conference.* Claremont, California: Claremont College, 1963.

Ohnmacht, Fred W. and Fleming, James T. "Further Effects of Selected Deletion Strategies and Varying Contextual Constraints on Cloze Performance." In *Interaction: Research and Practice for College-Adult Reading,* edited by Phil L. Nacke, pp. 163-71. 23d Yearbook of the National Reading Conference. Clemson, S. C.: National Reading Conference, 1974.

Olsen, James. "Instructional Materials for Functionally Illiterate Adults." *Phi Delta Kappan* 46 (May 1965):458.

Oppenheimer, Jess. "All About Me." *Journal of Learning Disabilities* 5 (August-September 1972):33-48.

Orata, Pedro T. "The Paradox of Ignorance." In *Basic Education for the Disadvantaged Adult,* edited by Frank Lanning and Wesley A. Many, p. 66. New York: Houghton Mifflin Co., 1966.

Otto, Wayne, and Ford, David. *Teaching Adults to Read.* New York: Houghton Mifflin Co., 1967.

Otto, Wayne; McMenemy, Richard; and Smith, Richard J. *Corrective and Remedial Teaching.* New York: Houghton Mifflin Co., 1966.

Owens, W. A. "Age and Mental Abilities: A Longitudinal Study." In *Readings in Psychological Development Through Life,* edited by D. C. Charles and W. R. Looft, pp. 243-54. New York: Holt, Rinehart and Winston, 1973.

Parker, Don. *Reading Comprehension Laboratory.* Chicago: Science Research Associates, 1961.

Patterson, Robert E. *Lesson Guide for English as a Second Language: Phase I.* Treasure Valley Migrant Education Program. Ontario, Ore.: Treasure Valley Education Program, 1968.

Patterson, Robert E., and Larsen, Lawrence H. *Treasure Valley Migrant Program: Administration of the OEO Migrant Program at Treasure Valley Community College and Administration of the Adult Migrant Basic Education Program.* Ontario, Oregon: Treasure Valley Migrant Education Program. County Action Memorandum no. 23, 1967. Ditto.

Paulson, Christina Bratt, and Bruder, Mary Newton. *Teaching English as a Second Language: Techniques and Procedures,* p. 4. Cambridge, Mass.: Winthrop Publishers, Inc., 1976.

Peterson, Joe, and Carroll, Martha. "The Cloze Procedure as an Indicator of the Instructional Level for Disabled Readers." In *Interaction: Research and Practice for College-Adult Reading,* edited by Phil L. Nacke, pp. 153-57. 23d Yearbook of the National Reading Conference. Clemson, S. C.: National Reading Conference, 1974.

Pitman, Sir James. *Initial Teaching Alphabet.* New York: Initial Teaching Alphabet Publications, 1960.

Platts, Mary E. *Spice.* Stevensville, Mich.: Educational Service, Inc., 1972.

———. *Rescue.* Stevensville, Mich.: Educational Service, Inc., 1972.

Powell, Walter. *Our World Is Small.* Syracuse, N. Y.: New Reader's Press, 1964.

Preston, Dennis R. "English as a Second Language in Adult Basic Education Programs." *TESOL Quarterly* 5 (September 1971):181-82.

Puckett, Patricia A. "When Business and Education Wed." *Reading Newsreport* 7 (October 1972):8, 10, 11, 48.

Ramanauskas, Sigita. "The Responsiveness of Cloze Readability Measures to Linguistic Variables Operating Over Segments of Text Longer Than a Sentence." *Reading Research Quarterly* 8 (Fall 1972):72-91.

Rauch, David B. "New Priorities for Adult Education." In *New Priorities for Adult Education,* edited by David Rauch, p. 22. New York: Macmillan, 1972.

Rauch, Sidney J., ed. *Handbook for the Volunteer Tutor.* Newark, Del.: International Reading Association, 1969.

Reading Curriculum Guide for Adult Basic Education. Sacramento: California State Department of Education, 1972.

Reissman, Frank. *The Culturally Deprived Child.* New York: Harper's Magazine Press, 1962.

Riegel, K. F. and Riegel, R. M. "Development Drop and Death." *Developmental Psychology* 6 (March 1972):306-19.

Rivers, Wilga. *The Psychologist and the Foreign Language Teacher.* Chicago: University of Chicago Press, 1964.

Robeck, Mildred C., and Wilson, John A. R. *Psychology of Reading.* New York: John Wiley and Sons, Inc., 1974.

Robb, Felix C. "International Education: The Prospect." Address delivered at the White House Conference on International Cooperation, Washington, D. C., 30 November 1965.

Roberts, Paul. *English Sentences.* New York: Harcourt Brace Jovanovich, 1962.

Robinson, Helen M. "The Major Aspects of Reading." In *Reading: Seventy-five Years of Progress,* edited by H. Alan Robinson. Chicago: University of Chicago Press, 1966.

Rodale, J. I. ed. *Quinto Lingo* 6 (February 1969):2. Emmaus, Pa.: Rodale Press.

Roswell, Florence G., and Chall, Jeanne S. *Roswell-Chall Auditory Blending Test*. New York: Essay Press, 1959.

————. *Roswell-Chall Reading Test of Word Analysis Skills*. New York: Essay Press, 1959.

Ruchlis, Hy. *Guidelines to Education of Nonreaders*. Brooklyn: Book Lab, Inc., 1973.

Ruddell, Robert. "Psycholinguistic Implications for a Systems of Communication Model of Reading." In *Theoretical Processes and Models of Reading*, edited by Harry Singer and Robert Ruddell, pp. 239-58. Newark, Del.: International Reading Association, 1970.

Russell, David H., and Karp, Etta E. *Reading Aids Through the Grades*. New York: Bureau of Publications, Teachers College, Columbia University, 1963.

Samuda, Ronald J. *Psychological Testing of American Minorities: Issues and Consequences*. New York: Dodd-Mead Company, 1975.

Sanders, Norris. *Classroom Questions: What Kinds*. New York: Harper & Row, 1966.

Savage, John F., ed. *Linguistics for Teachers, Selected Materials*. Chicago: Science Research Associates, 1973.

Schapiro, Jeri. *Scope Visuals 13: Getting Applications Right*. New York: Scholastic Book Services, 1973.

Schrank, R., and Stein, S. "Basic Education: What are the Realistic Possibilities?" *Training in Business and Industry* 12 (June 1970):4-6.

Seymour, Dorothy Z. "Black Children, Black Speech." *Commonweal* 19 November 1971, pp. 175-77.

————. "Interview." *Reading Newsreport* 6 (February 1972):6, 7, 48, 49.

Seaman, Don F. *Preventing Dropouts in Adult Basic Education*. Tallahassee: Florida State University, 1971.

————. *Starting Students Successfully in Adult Basic Education*. Tallahassee: Florida State University, 1971.

Searls, Evelyn F. *How to Use WISC Scores in Reading Diagnosis*. Newark, Del.: International Reading Association, 1975.

Shaie, K. W. "Age Changes and Age Differences." In *Developmental Psychology: A Book of Readings*, edited by W. R. Looft, pp. 60-67. Hinsdale, Ill.: Dryden Press, 1972.

————. "A General Model for the Study of Developmental Problems." *Psychological Bulletin* 64 (1973):92-107.

————. "A Reinterpretation of Age-Related Changes in Cognitive Structure and Functioning." In *Life-Span Developmental Psychology: Research and Theory*, edited by L. R. Guolet and P. B. Baltes. New York: Academic Press, 1970.

Shaie, K. W., and Strother, C. R. "The Effect of Time and Cohort Differences on the Interpretation of Age Changes in Cognitive Behavior." Abstract. *American Psychologist* 19 (1973):10.

Shaie, K. W.; Labouvie, G. W.; and Buech, B. U. "Generational and Cohort-Specific Differences in Adult Cognitive Functioning: A Fourteen Year Study of Independent Samples." *Developmental Psychology* 9 (1973):151-61.

Shen, Yao, and Crymes, Ruth H. *Teaching English as a Second Language: A Classified Bibliography*. Honolulu: East-West Center Press, 1965.

Sherk, John K., Jr. "Psychological Principles in a Strategy for Teaching the Reading of a Standard Dialect." In *Reading: Process and Pedagogy*, edited by George B. Schick and Merrill M. May, p. 291. 19th Yearbook. Milwaukee, Wis.: National Reading Conference, 1970.

Sherman, Mark A., and Klare, George R. *The Cloze Procedure in Adult Basic Education,* Technical Report, no. 4, ABE Project CREATES, Title III, USEA Contract, no. o-8-03183-4369 (039), 1 July, 1970, pp. 18-22. Computing Center, Graduate School of Education, Harvard University.

Singer, David A., Jr., and Fuller, James W. "The Sleeping Giant," *Adult Leadership* 23 (June 1974):41-43.

Singer, Harry, and Ruddell, Robert B. *Theoretical Models and Processes of Reading.* Newark, Del.: International Reading Association, 1970.

Sleisenger, Lenore. *Guidebook for the Volunteer Reading Teacher.* New York: Teachers College Press, 1965.

Slosson, Richard L. *Slosson Intelligence Test.* East Aurora, New York: Slosson Educational Publications, 1963.

———. *Slosson Oral Reading Test.* East Aurora, New York: Slosson Educational Publications, 1963.

Smith, Carl B., and Fay, Leo C. *Getting People to Read,* pp. 3, 7. New York: Dell Publishing Co., 1973.

Smith, D. E., and Carrigan, P. M. *The Nature of Reading Disability.* New York: Harcourt Brace Jovanovich, 1959.

Smith, E. Brooks; Goodman, Kenneth; and Meredith, Robert. *Language and Thinking in the Elementary School.* 2d ed. New York: Holt, Rinehart and Winston, 1976.

Smith, Edwin H. *Literacy Education for Adolescents and Adults,* pp. 3-6. San Francisco: Boyd & Fraser Publishing Co., 1970.

———. *Teaching Reading in Adult Basic Education,* Bulletin 71H-4, p. 6. Reprint. Tallahassee, Florida: Department of Education, 1968.

Smith, Edwin H., and Bradtmueller, Weldon G. *Follett Individual Reading Placement Inventory.* Chicago: Follett Publishing Co., 1970.

Smith, Edwin H., and Martin, McKinley. "Do Adult Literacy Programs Make a Difference?" In *Literacy for Diverse Learners,* edited by Jerry L. Johns, p. 88. Newark, Del.: International Reading Association, 1974.

Smith, Frank. *Comprehension and Learning: A Conceptual Framework for Teachers,* p. 176. New York: Holt, Rinehart and Winston, 1975.

———. *Understanding Reading.* pp. 35, 83. New York: Holt, Rinehart and Winston, 1970.

Smith, Helen K. "The Responses of Good and Poor Readers When Asked to Read for Different Purposes." *Reading Research Quarterly* 3 (Fall 1967): 53-83.

Smith, Nila Banton. *Reading Instruction for Today's Children,* p. 364. Englewood Cliffs, N. J.: Prentice-Hall, 1963.

Speer, George. *Adult Basic Education National Teacher Training Study—Part I: Review of the Literature.* Kansas City: University of Missouri Press, 1972.

———. *Adult Basic Education National Teacher Training Study: State of the Art.* Kansas City: University of Missouri Press, 1972.

———. *Adult Basic Education National Teacher Training Study—Part III: Survey of Needs.* Kansas City: University of Missouri Press, 1972.

———. *Adult Basic Education National Teacher Training Study—Part IV: Final Report.* Kansas City: University of Missouri Press, 1972.

Staton, Thomas F. *How to Instruct Successfully.* New York: McGraw-Hill Book Co., 1960.

Stauffer, Russell G. *The Language Experience Approach to the Teaching of Reading.* New York: Harper & Row, 1970.

Stauffer, Russell G., and Cramer, Ronald L. "Reading Specialist in an Occupational Training Program." *The Reading Teacher* 20 (March 1967):525-31.

Stevick, Earl W. *Helping People Learn English: A Manual for Teachers of English as a Second Language.* Nashville: Abingdon Press, 1967.

Stewart, William C. *The Dialect of the Black American.* A recording. New York: Western Electric Company, 1972.

Sticht, Thomas G., ed. *Reading for Working: A Functional Literacy Anthology.* Alexandria, Va.: Human Resources Research Organization, 1974.

Sticht, Thomas G.; Beck, Lawrence J.; Haune, Robert; Kleiman, Glenn M.; and James, James H. *Auding and Reading: A Developmental Model.* Alexandria, Va.: Human Resources Research Organization, 1974.

———. "Project REALISTIC: Determination of Adult Functional Literacy Skill Levels." *Reading Research Quarterly* 7 (1972):424-65.

Sticht, Thomas G., and McFann, Howard H. "Reading Requirement for Career Entry." In *Reading and Career Education,* edited by Duane M. Neilsen and Howard F. Hjelm, pp. 62-76. Newark, Del.: International Reading Association, 1975.

Stories for Adult Readers. Tallahassee: Florida Department of Education, 1973.

Stone, Clarence. *Progress in Primary Reading.* St. Louis: Webster Publishing Company, 1950.

SWAP Newsletters. Washington, D. C.: National Association of Public Continuing Adult Education. Published monthly.

Swanson, Merlyn S., and Jacobson, Anita. "Evaluation of the S.I.T. for Screening Children with Learning Disabilities." *Journal of Learning Disabilities* 3 (June 1970):22-24.

Taylor, Grant. *Practicing American English.* Drill 153. New York: McGraw-Hill Book Co., 1962.

Taylor, Wilson. "Cloze Procedure: A New Tool for Measuring Readability," *Journalism Quarterly* 30 (1953):415-33.

Terman, L. M., and Oden, M. H. *The Gifted Group at Mid-Life: Thirty-five Years Follow-up Study of the Superior Child,* vol. 5. Stanford, Calif.: Stanford University Press, 1959.

Thatcher, John H. *Public School Adult Education: A Guide for Administrators,* rev. ed., p. 180. Washington, D. C.: National Association of Public Continuing Adult Education, 1963.

Thompson, Frank, Jr. "Adult Undereducation." In *Basic Education for the Disadvantaged Adult,* edited by Frank Lanning and Wesley Many, p. 46. New York: Houghton Mifflin Co., 1966.

Thompson, Richard A. *Energizers for Reading Instruction.* West Nyack, N. Y.: Parker Publishing Co., 1973.

Thorndike, Edward. *Adult Learning.* New York: Teachers College Press, 1928.

———. *The Teacher's Word Book of 30,000 Words.* New York: Teachers College Press, 1944.

Toolgood, James L. *Adult Population Distribution with Regard to Social, Economic, and Ethnic Characteristics.* Sacramento: California State Department of Education, 1969.

Tough, A. *The Adult's Learning Projects,* p. 42. Toronto, Ontario: Institute for Studies in Education, 1971. Cited by Malcolm Knowles, *The Adult Learner: A Neglected Species,* p. 39. Houston, Tex.: Gulf Publishing Co., 1973.

Ulmer, Curtis. *Teaching the Disadvantaged Adult.* Washington, D. C.: National Association of Public Continuing Adult Education, 1969.

U.S. News and World Report 21 (May 26, 1975):4.

Vonderhaar, Kathleen; Mocker, Donald W.; Leibert, Robert E; Maass, Vera. *Tests for Adult Basic Education Teachers.* Kansas City: University of Missouri, 1975.

Valencia, Atilano A., and Olivero, James L. *Innovative and Dynamic Instructional Approaches to Adult Basic Education.* Albuquerque, N. M.: Southwestern Cooperative Educational Laboratory, Inc., 1969.

Van Allen, Roach. *Language Experiences in Communication.* Boston: Houghton-Mifflin Company, 1976.

Van Allen, Roach and Van Allen, Claryce. *Language Experience Activities.* Boston: Houghton-Mifflin Company, 1976. Associates, 1972.

Verner, Coolie, and Davison, Catherine V. *Physiological Factors in Adult Learning and Instruction.* Tallahassee: Florida State University, 1971.

———. *Psychological Factors in Adult Learning.* Tallahassee: Florida State University, 1971.

Wagner, Guy, and Hosier, Max. *Reading Games: Strengthening Reading Skills with Instructional Games.* Darien, Conn.: Educational Publishing Corporation, 1961.

Wallace, Mary. *Literacy Instructor's Handbook,* pp. 6, 7. Chicago: Follett Publishing Co., 1965.

Wallen, Carl J. *Competency in Teaching Reading.* Chicago: Science Research Associaes, 1972.

Warsh, Herman E. "Behavior Modification of Adult Illiterates and Functional Illiterates Who Learned to Read." Dissertation, Wayne State University. *Dissertation Abstracts International* 31 (1970):1002-A. (Xerox, University Microfilms, Ann Arbor, Mich.)

Wardhaugh, Ronald. *Reading: A Linguistic Perspective.* New York: Harcourt Brace Jovanovich, 1969.

Warren, Virginia B. *Techniques for Teachers of Adults.* Washington, D. C.: National Association of Public Continuing Adult Education 5 (November 1964):2.

———. *Techniques for Teachers of Adults.* Washington, D. C.: National Association of Public Continuing Adult Education 1 (October 1970):1.

———. *Techniques for Teachers of Adults.* Washington, D. C.: National Association of Public Continuing Adult Education 13 (December 1970):2.

———. "Psychology of Learning." *Techniques for Teachers of Adults,* special ed., p. 3. Washington, D. C.: National Association of Public Adult Continuing Education, n.d.

———. *A Treasury of Techniques for Teaching Adults.* Washington, D. C.: National Association of Public Continuing Education, 1968.

———. *A Second Treasury of Techniques for Teaching Adults.* Washington, D. C.: National Association of Public Continuing Education, 1970.

Wayne State University. "Adult Learning." *Adult Basic Education Pre-Institute Seminar Proceedings.* Detroit, Mich.: Wayne State University Press, 1967.

Weber, Robert E. "A Dollars and Cents Look at Reading Failure." *Reading News report* 7 (May-June 1971):27.

Webster's Selected Stories. Champaign, Ill.: Garrard Publishing Co.

Wechsler, David. *Wechsler Adult Intelligence Scale.* New York: Psychological Corporation, 1955.

———. *WISC-R Manual.* New York: Psychological Corp., 1974.

——. *The Measurement of Adult Intelligence*, rev. ed. Baltimore: Williams & Wilkins Co., 1955.

Weiskopf, E. A. "Intelligent Malfunctioning and Personality." *Journal of Abnormal and Social Psychology* 3 (1951):410-23.

Welford, A. T. *Skill and Age: An Experimental Approach*. London: Oxford University Press, 1951.

Wepman, Joseph. "The Modality Concept—Including a Statement of the Perceptual and Conceptual Levels of Learning." In *Perception and Reading*, edited by H. K. Smith. Proceedings of the 12th Annual Convention of the International Reading Association 12 (1968):1-7.

——. *Wepman Auditory Discrimination Test*. Chicago: Language Research Associates, 1958.

Whipple, James E. *Especially for Adults*, p. 10-23. Chicago: Center for the Study of Liberal Education for Adults, 1957. Reprint. Syracuse, N. Y.: Syracuse University Press, 1968.

Wills, Vernon L. "A Study of Leadership." *Adult Leadership*, October 1974, pp. 116-18.

Wilson, Corlette T. "An Essential Vocabulary." *The Reading Teacher* 17 (November 1963):94-96.

Wilson, Robert M., and Barnes, Marcia M. *Survival Learning Materials: Suggestions for Developing*. College Reading Association Publication. York, Pa.: Strine Publishing Co., 1974.

Wilkie, F., and Eisdorfer, C. "Intelligence and Blood Pressure in the Aged." *Science* 172 (1971):959-62.

Winter, Gerald D. and Nuss, Eugene M. *The Young Adult: Identity and Awareness*. Chicago, Ill.: Scott, Foresman and Co., 1969.

Witty, Paul A. "Campaign Against Illiteracy—A War We Must Win." In *Basic Education for the Disadvantaged Adult*, edited by Frank Lanning and Wesley Many, p. 61. New York: Houghton Mifflin Co., 1966.

Wold, Robert. *Screening Tests to be Used by the Classroom Teacher*. Chula Vista, Calif.: Academic Therapy Publications, 1970.

Womer, Frank B. "What is Criterion Referenced Measurement?" In *Measuring Reading Performance*, edited by William E. Blanton, *et. al*, pp. 34-43. Newark Del.: International Reading Association, 1974.

Woodcock, Richard W. *Peabody Rebus Reading Program*. Circle Pines, Minn.: American Guidance Services, Inc., 1968.

Yaz, William (pseudonym). "Teachers and Administrators in American Indian Education." *The Indian Historian* 6 (Summer 1973):18-22.

Young, Robert. "Culture." In *Language and Cultural Diversity in American Education*, edited by Roger D. Abrahams and Rudolph C. Troike, pp. 40-41. Englewood Cliffs, N. J.: Prentice-Hall, 1972.

Zintz, Miles V. *Corrective Reading*, 3d ed. Dubuque, Ia.: Wm. C. Brown Co., 1972.

——. *The Reading Process: The Teacher and the Learner*, 2d ed. Dubuque, Ia.: Wm C. Brown Co., 1975.

——. comp. 2nd ed. *Trainers of Teachers of Undereducated Adults*, p. 242. Albuquerque, N. M.: College of Education, University of New Mexico, 1965.

Index

Ability tests, 234, 294-97
Absenteeism, 39
Abstraction, 79
Accent, word, 128, 330-32
Acceptance, need for, 34
Achievement tests, 235
Adult Basic Education, 16, 46, 52
Adult Basic Education Curriculum Guide
 Vocabulary List, 342
Adult Basic Education Student Survey,
 268
Adult Basic Learning Examination
 (ABLE), 268
Adult Basic Reading Inventory, 268
Adult Education Council of Greater Chi-
 cago, 14, 314
Adult Informal Reading Inventory, 246,
 255
Adult learner, different than child, 9
Adult Performance Level Test (APL),
 16
Affixes, 126-27, 173-74
Age group, needs, 11, 12
Aggression, 71
Aging, 12, 43
Alcock, Dorothea, 119, 132
Alesi, Gladys, 210
Alexander, Grace C., 269
Allen, Harold B., 20, 208
Allen, James E., 131
Allen, R. V., 117
Allen, Virginia, 208
Allred, Ruel A., 261
Alphabet, 119-20
American Bar Association, 39, 62
American Literacy Test, 268
Analysis of
 abilities, 250-51
 subtests, 293, 299
 word structure, 173-74
Antecedents, 148, 164
Antonyms, 148, 171-72
Anxiety, 41-42
 adjustments to, 43-44
 antisocial adjustments, 45

maturity and aging, 43
 withdrawal adjustments, 44
Approach, selection of, 96-100
Arnold, Phyllis D., 296
Arrow Book of Brain Teasers, 166
Arrow Book of Word Games, 166
Arthur, Grace, 294
Arthur Point Scale of Performance Tests:
 Form I and II, 294
Assessment instruments
 See individual titles and subjects
 selection of, 267
Assessment plan, 237
Assessment of reading needs
 case study, 230
 group, 229
 individual, 229
 informal, 229
 observation, 230
 oral language, 231-32
 standardized, 228
Assessment Survey—Multilevel Achieve-
 ment Series, 269
Assimilation, 72-74, 75
Associated Press, 183
Associating, 76
Athey, Irene, 76
Attendance, 233
Attention span, 50, 130, 284
Attitude, change in, 50
Auditory
 acuity, 25, 57
 defects, 22
 discrimination, 26, 79, 80, 121-22
 factors, 25
 perception, 26, 277
 problems, 276-77
Auditory-motor level, 78-79
 sequential development of, 80
Aukerman, Robert D., 96, 98

Bailey, Mildred Hart, 134
Balow, Bruce, 273, 279
Baltes, M. M., 57
Baltes, Paul B., 56, 57, 58

Banks, Olivia E., 197
Baratz, Joan C., 204
Barbe, Walter, 130
Barnes, Marcia M., 314
Barnes, Robert F., 9, 13, 14, 15, 16, 20,
    31, 41
*Barranquilla Rapid Survey Intelligence
    Test,* 282
Basal approach, 98
Basic Reading and Rate Scale, 269
Basic Reading and Word List, 269
Basic Sight Word List, 194, 196, 242-43
Basic Studies Inventory, 269
Bauer, Josephine, 181
Bayley, N., 57
Be Informed Series, 134, 187
Beasley, John B., 84
Behavior change, 304-8
Behavioral objectives, 94
Bennett Cerf's Book of Laughs, 166
Bennett, George K., 294
Berdrow, John, 29, 43
Berg, Paul Conrad, 276
Best, Jeanette, 283
Betts, Emmett, 240
Bible reading, 16
Bijou, Sidney, 262
Bilingual Syntax Measure (BSM), 282
Birren, J. E., 43
Bischof, L. J., 43
Black English, 205-8
Blending principles, 123-24
Bloom, Benjamin, 84
Board of Education of the City of New
    York, 215
Bond, Guy L., 273, 279
Boning, Richard A., 100
Book passages, 245
Boone, Edgar J., 96
Borgatta, Edgar F., 296
Botel, Martin, 255
Botel Reading Inventory, 244, 255, 351-
    54
  Word Opposites Test, 352
  Word Recognition Test, 351
Botwinick, Jack, 53
Boyd Phonics Test, 255, 279, 371-75
Boyd, Robert D., 255
Bradtmueller, Weldon G., 256-57
Bradway, K., 57
Brazziel, William F., 31, 38
Brief Test of Literacy, 269
Brown, Andrew W., 294
*Brown-Carlsen Listening Comprehension
    Test,* 288, 290
Brown, Claude, 7

Brown, Don A., 246, 261
Brown, Grace M., 256, 279
Brown, James I., 272, 290
Brown, Leroy, 100-101
Bruce, Dana, 166
Bruder, Mary Newton, 223
Buchanan, Cynthia Dee, 181
Bureau of Vocational, Technical and
    Adult Education, 121
Burie, Audrey Ann, 119, 132
Burket, George R., 272
Burmeister, Lou E., 125-26, 134
Burnet, Mary, 38, 112, 237
Burnett, Richard W., 268
Buros, Oscar, 249, 275
Burt, Marina K., 282
Butcher, H. J., 54

California Achievement Tests, 270
California Phonics Test, 256, 279
Campbell, Russell N., 208
Car purchase, 309
Career Opportunity Programs, 306
Carlsen, G. Robert, 290
Carlton, Lessie, 125-26
Carrigan, P. M., 70
Carrillo, Lawrencĕ, 100, 130
Carter, Joseph B., 271
Cartoons, 152, 154
Carver, Ronald P., 269
Case studies, 3-6, 7, 230-31, 311
Cass, Angelica, 11, 25, 29, 39
Categorization, 79
Cattell, A. K. S., 295
Cattell, Raymond B., 295
Cerf, Bennett, 166
Chall, Jeanne S., 178, 260, 277, 279
Chapman, Byron, 16, 80, 92, 118, 121,
    131, 181
Chicago Nonverbal Examination, 294
Clark, Willis W., 273
Classifying, 166-67
Cleugh, M. F., 43
Cloze exercises, 246-47, 363-64
Cloze procedure, 148, 168-69
Clymer, Theodore, 134, 228
Coates, Robert H., 39
Coding subtest, 298
Coffee breaks, 29
Cognitive flexibility, 58
Comparison of scores, 265-66
Composition skills, 86, 87
Compound Words Test, 279, 376
Comprehension, 72, 74
  applied, 86

exercises, 148, 156
interpretive, 74, 86, 148
literal, 74, 84, 86, 147
paragraph, 265
skills, 84, 85, 147-67
Comprehensive English Language Test for Speakers of English as a Second Language, 282
Comprehensive Test of Basic Skills (CTBS), 270
Concept formation, 63, 79
Confidence, 66
Configuration systems, 100
Conrad, H. S., 55
Consonants, 127-28, 326-28
Context skills, 83
Cooperative, 310
Cooperative Inter-American Series, 282
Corsini, Raymond J., 295, 296
Cottrell, Alice B., 256, 279
Counseling, by teacher, 49
County Public Health Nurse, 310
County Social Workers, 311
Courage, 19-21
Cramer, Ronald L., 117
Criscuolo, Nicholas P., 112
Critical reading, 86
Crymes, Ruth H., 208
Crystallized intelligence, 57
Cultural
awareness, 199-203
differences, 104
experience, 63, 71
Culture Fair Intelligence Tests: Scales I, II, III, 295
Curriculum Guide to Adult Basic Education, 23, 29, 40, 69, 77, 80, 94, 116, 124, 242, 342

DNA, 70
Dale, Edgar, 178
Dale-Chall Formula, 179
Davison, Catherine V., 22, 59
Daydreaming, 45
Decision-making, 300-312
Decoding, 112, 127, 130, 232
process, 74, 75, 79, 83-84
synthesis approach, 97
tools for reading, 83
Defense mechanism, 71
Del Olmo, Francisco, 282
Dell 'Apa, Frank, 96, 101
Denny, E. C., 272
Derived forms, 126-27
Detail finding, 148, 156-59

Diagnosis sheet, 365
Diagnostic data, 227
Diagnostic Reading Scales, 256
Dialect, 199, 232
language, 61
problems, 280-81
Dictation exercises, 194-97
Dictionary
exercises, 148, 174-75
usage, 84
Dillard, J. L., 205
Distractions, from learning, 48
Disuse, dangers of, 93
Dolch Basic Sight Word List, 119
Dolch, Edward, 119, 132, 256
Dolch Sight Word Lists, 256
Dolch Word Games and Phrase Cards, 132
Donlon, Thomas F., 269
Doppelt, Jerome D., 294
Doren Diagnostic Reading Test of Word Recognition Skills, 270
Doren, Margaret, 270
Drop-out, 50
Dulay, Heidi C., 282
Dunn, Lloyd M., 259, 291, 295
Durrell, Donald D., 132, 231-32, 290
Durrell Listening-Reading Series, 288, 290

Economic factors, 35
Educational potential, steps to improve, 9
Educational reasons, 19
Effective learning, 307-8
Eisdorfer, C., 43, 57
Elley, Warwich B., 290
Ellis, Henry C., 93
Emans, Robert, 134
Emery, Donald G., 96
Emotional problems, 279-80
Empathy, 40-41, 48
Encoding, 72, 76, 79
Encouragement, need for, 46
Energizers for Reading Instruction, 132
English as a second language, 209-23, 280-81, 282-83
substitution, 212
transformations, 217-23
vocabulary, 215
English-Spanish structures, 215
Environmental conditions, 29
Ephrom, Beulah Kantor, 71
Epilepsy, 22
Escala de Inteligencia Wechsler para Adultos, 282

Ethnic background, 10
Evaluation
    of instructional materials, 322-23
    of reading status, 228
Everyday Reading and Writing, 187
Experience repertoire, 62-63

Fader, Daniel, 33
Familial factors, 35
Family problems, 308
Fantasy, 45
Farquhar, William W., 59
Fatigue, 29
Fay, Jean B., 42-43, 49
Fay, Leo C., 177, 299
Fear, 41-42, 65
    of failure, 57
Fear-anxiety level, 48
Feldt, Leonard S., 271
Fellenz, Robert A., 287
Fernald, Grace, 131, 313
Fernald Kinesthetic Tracing Technique,
    122, 313-14
Ferndale Adult Basic Education Curric-
    ulum, 97, 121
Ferrel, Allen, 283
Fersh, Seymour, 199-200
Finocchiaro, Mary, 222-23
Flanagan, John C., 297
Flesch Readability Formula, 179, 245,
    336-38
FOG Index, 179, 245, 339
Follett Individual Reading Placement In-
    ventory, 246, 256-57
Ford, David, 45-46, 133
Forman, Sidney, 208
Forms
    application, 64
    filling in, 181, 183-94
Forms in Your Future, 187
Foster, Casters B., 269
Fox, C., 28, 61
Francis, W. Nelson, 243
Frostig, Marianne, 28
Fry, Edward, 112, 257
Fry Instant Word Recognition Test, 244,
    257, 355-60
Fry Phonics Criterion Test, 257
Fry Readability Formula, 245
Fry Readability Graph, 178, 335
Fuller, G. B., 259, 277
Function words, 167
Functional illiterates, case studies, 3-6
Fundamental Achievement Series (FAS),
    294

GED tests, 16, 303
Gardner, Eric F., 268, 273
Gardner, Martin, 166
Gates, Arthur I., 257, 270
Gates-MacGinitie Reading Survey Tests,
    270
Gates-McKillop Reading Diagnostic Test,
    257
Gates Primary Word List, 196
Gates Reading Survey Test, 5
Gattegno, Caleb, 100
Geeslin, Carol M., 314
Geeslin, Robert H., 100-101, 314
General concept, 148, 159
General Educational Development
    (GED), 16, 303
Genetic deficiencies, 22
Geyer, John, 75, 76
Gibson, Eleanor J., 76
Gilliland, Hap, 258, 294
Gilliland Learning Potential Examination,
    294
Gilliland Test of Individual Needs in
    Reading, 258
Gilmore, Eunice C., 258
Gilmore, John V., 258
Gilmore Oral Reading Test, 5, 258
Glasser, Alan J., 299
Glenn, Ann C., 314
Goldberg, Herman K., 70
Goltry, M., 187
Goodman, Kenneth, 76, 208
Grabowski, Stanley M., 314
Graphic symbols, interpretation of, 24
Gray Oral Reading Test, 258
Gray, William S., 71, 72, 126, 133, 250,
    258
Green, R. F., 282
Greenlee Associates, 31, 33, 34
Grindstaff, Colletta, 147
Group
    dynamics, 49
    interaction, 82
    testing, 229
Groupings, 91-92
Guide for Trainers of Teachers of Under-
    educated Adults, 130
Gunning's FOG Formula, 179, 245, 339
Guszak, Frank, 130

Habits, 65
Haffner, Lawrence E., 60
Haggstrom, Warren C., 32
Hall, Eugene J., 181
Handwriting, 86, 181-98

integrating, 197
Hardy, Madeline, 7
Harrington, Michael, 34-35
Harris, Albert J., 313
Harris, Dale P., 282
Havighurst, Robert J., 26, 80
Hawkins, Thom, 238, 239, 246, 275, 285, 311, 312
Hayes, Mary T., 231-32, 290
Health factors, 21
Heltshe, Mary Ann, 119, 132
Henderson, Robert W., 297
Henney, R. L., 181
Herber, Harold, 84
Hernandez, Eduardo, 282
Herr, Selma E., 119, 132
Hertert, Patricia, 11, 12
Hiemstra, Roger, 97
Hill, Mary Anne, 117
Hillburn, Nancy, 76, 287
Hodges, Raymond J., 269
Homonyms, 148, 172-73
Hosier, Max, 119, 132
Hostility, 45
Houle, Cyril, 147, 306, 307
Houston, Susan H., 205
Hoyer, W. J., 57
Hoyt, Cyril J., 273, 279
Hubbard, Elbert, 59
Huelsman, Charles B., 264, 271
Huelsman Word Discrimination Test, 271
Humiliation, 38, 39
Hunter, Madeline, 87
Hypomentia, 22
Hurlock, Elizabeth B., 53, 55, 56
Hysterical reactions, 44

Idaho State Penitentiary Informal Reading Inventory, 259
Ilyin, Donna, 283
Individual testing, 229
Individualized Criterion-Referenced Testing, 271
Inflectional forms, 126
Informal
   assessment, 228, 287-88
   reading inventories, 244-46
   Reading Inventory model, 361-62
Information finding, 147, 148-50
Inherited
   dominance defects, 22
   dysrhythmias, 22
   metabolic diseases, 22
   speech and hearing defects, 22
   visual defects, 22

Inhibition, 71
Installment buying, 308-9
Intelligence
   of adults, 52
   cross-sectional studies, 53-54
   longitudinal research, 53-54
   measurement limitations, 53
   measurement of, 52, 54
Interaction, 91
Interests, 33, 65, 107
International Reading Association, 167
Involvement, 90
Iowa Test of Educational Development, 271
Isenburg, I., 38

Jastak, J. R., 262
Jenkinson, Marion D., 167
Job Corps Centers, 100
Johns, Jerry, 119, 243
Johnson, Robert D., 7
Johnson, Samuel, 169
Jonas, William, 97
Jones, H. E., 55
Jones, Lewis Wade, 9, 80
Juncture, 129

Kahn Intelligence Test: Experimental Form, 295
Kahn, Theodore C., 295
Kangas, J., 57
Karlsen, Bjorn, 268, 273
Karp, Etta E., 132
Kauffman, Adrienne, 236-37
Kaulfers, Walter V., 132, 133, 201
Kent, W. P., 39
Keystone Visual Survey Tests, 277
Kidd, J. R., 25, 28, 52, 54, 55, 56, 57, 281, 292
Kincaid, J. Peter, 206
Kirchner, Corinne, 17, 18, 304
Kirkland, William, 259
Klare, George R., 169
Klevins, Chester, 97
Kline, William E., 272
Koehler, Lawrence J., 11, 29, 48
Krimboltz, John D., 59
Kucera, Henry, 119, 243

Labouvie-Vief, G., 57
Labov, William, 204
Lambert, Wallace, 50
Lambert, William, 50

Langerman, Philip D., 97, 227
Langmuir, Charles R., 295
Language, 231-32
  development sequence, 78-80
  experiences, 116-17, 134-35
  facility, 60-61
LaPray, Margaret, 244, 261, 348-49
Larsen, Lawrence H., 119
Laterality, 24, 278
Laubach, Frank C., 51, 112, 130, 187,
    227, 239, 281
Learning
  ability, 52
    decline of, 56
    group measurement, 292
    individual, 291
    measurement of, 289
  environment, 281
  laws of Thorndike, 56
  potential, 11
  style, 281
  theory, 89
Learning Activities for Reading, 132
*Learning Lab Reading Placement In-
    ventory,* 271
Lee, Doris, 117
Lefever, D. Welty, 269
Leibert, Robert, 246, 255
Leiter International Performance Scale,
    295
Leiter, Russell Grayton, 295
Letterwriting, 64
Levey, Sylvia, 209
Levin, Harry, 76
Lichtman, Marilyn, 260
Liddle, William, 134
Life experience, 62
Lindquist, E. F., 271
Lindsay, Peter H., 76
*Linguistic Blocks Series, The First Rolling
    Reader,* 196
Linguistic facets, 72
List of Easily Confused Words, 278, 279,
    370
Listening,
  abilities, 79, 80-81
  assessment,
    informal, 287-88
    standardized, 288-89
  comprehension, 287-89
  comprehension tests, 290
Litchman, Marilyn, 246
Literal comprehension, 74, 84, 86, 147
Lorge, Irving, 56, 57
Lutey, Carol, 299

McCarty, John J., 268
McClusky, Howard Y., 307
McCreary, Eugene, 88
McCullough, Constance M., 272
McCullough Word Analysis Test, 272,
    278, 279
McFann, Howard H., 39
McGarry, Florence A., 148
MacGinitie, Walter M., 270
McGovern, Ann, 166
McKillop, Ann S., 257
McMeaney, Richard, 134
McMurray, Robert N., 296
McPeek, W. Miles, 269
Madden, Richard, 268
Mager, Robert F., 90
Manuel, Herschel T., 282
Mark Twain, 30
Markwart, Frederick C. Jr., 259
Martin, McKinley, 305
Martinez, J. N., 282
Massey, James O., 299
Matthews, Virginia, 7
Maturity, 43
Maze subtest, 298
Meaning, anticipating, 148, 167-69
Memory, 59, 179-80
  principles, 123
Mental
  deterioration, 53-58
  retardation, 22
  rigidity, 64, 65
Mental Measurements Yearbooks, 249,
    275
Meredith, Robert, 208
Merwin, Jack C., 273
Miles, W. R., 60
Miller, Harry G., 84
Miller, Warren, 311
Minnesota Percepto-Diagnostic Test, 259,
    277
Minority group status, 32
Mitzell Adult Basic Word List, 119
Mocker, Donald W., 306
Motivation, 63, 117, 202-3, 284
  parent image, 14-15
  social status, 15
  strength of, 16
  vocational, 13-14
Motor factors, 28
Multiple meanings, 148, 170-71
Murphy, Barbara O., 297

NAPCAE. *See* National Association of
    Public Continuing Adult Edu-
    cators

Naslund, Robert A., 269
National Association of Public Continuing Adult Educators, 16, 34, 43, 45, 46, 49, 52, 134, 230, 241, 300
Navajo culture, 201-3
Needs
specific, 108
Neff, Monroe C., 268
Nelson-Denny Reading Test, 272
Nelson, M. J., 272
Nephew, Erwin, 249
Neurological
development, 70
factors, 23-25
sex differences, 24
Neurophysiological deterioration, 58
New Hampshire Informal Reading Inventory for Adult Basic Education, 259
Newman, Loretta M., 94
New Streamlined English Series, 6, 61, 113, 114-15, 120, 121
Nilsen, Aileen Pace, 214
Nilsen, Don L. F., 214
Non-English backgrounds, 199
Nonstandard English, 203-5
Nonverbal
reinforcement, 46
test, 234-35
Nonverbal Reasoning Test, 295
Norman, Donald A., 76
Northcutt, Norvell W., 16, 39
Nuss, Eugene M., 11

Objectivity, 64
Oden, M. H., 57
Oettinger, D., 22, 44
Olsen, James, 97, 121
Oppenheimer, Jess, 28
Oral language, 231-32
practice, 223
Oral Placement Test for Adults, 283
Oral reading
inventory of, 252-54
testing instruments, 255-63
testing procedure, 249-50
Orata, Pedro T., 72, 116
Organic health factors, 22
Organizing ideas, 148, 160-64
Orientation, 33, 117
Otto, Wayne, 45-46, 133, 134
Owens, W. A., 57

Palmer, Leslie A., 282
Pantell, Dora, 210

Paragraph comprehension, 265
Parent image, 14-15
Parker, Don, 124, 134
Patterson, Robert E., 46, 119
Paulson, Christina Bratt, 223
Peabody Individual Achievement Test, 259
Peabody Picture Vocabulary Test, 291, 295
Peer-prepared materials, 206
Perceptual styles, 285
Persistence rate, 17
Personal problems, 47-48
Personnel Tests for Industry: Oral Directions Test, Form S, 295
Phonemic approach, 98
Phonic
analysis, 74, 83-84, 133, 279
analysis skills, 127
approaches, 97
Physical
factors, 28
needs, 29
Pictures
arrangement of, 298
completion of, 298
meaning from, 152-56
Pitch, 128
Pitman, Sir James, 100
Platts, Mary E., 119, 132
Pope Inventory of Basic Reading Skills, 260
Pope, Lillie, 260
Positive assets, 11
Potential, 9, 307
Poverty-related factors, 32
Practice, 92
Pragmatism, 32
Prefixes, 173-74, 324
Prepositional phrases, 333-34
Prescriptive Reading Inventory, 272
Preston, Dennis R., 209
PRI Interim Tests, 259
Primacy, 92
Principles of learning, 88-89
Problem solving, 79
Programmed instruction, 98-100
Progressive Achievement Test: Listening Comprehension, 290
Projection, 71
Psychological
consequences, 38
defenses, 39-40
evaluation, 234
strengths, 50
supports, 49-50

variables, 58
Psychosomatic illnesses, 44
Puckett, Patricia A., 88, 94
Purdue Nonlanguage Test, 295

Quick Gauge of Reading Ability, 244, 261, 348-50
Quick Word Test, 296
Quinn, Emily H., 96

RBH Industrial Questionnaire, 296
RBH Nonverbal Reasoning Test, 296
RBH Test of Learning Ability, Forms DS-12 and DT-12, 296
RNA, 70
Rapport, 236-37, 239
Rate scores, 251
Rates of reading, 75
Rationalization, 44-45, 71
Rauch, David B., 61, 112, 128, 131
Reaction, 72, 75
Reaction time, 57
Readability, 148, 177-79
Reading Aids Through the Grades, 132
Reading for Concepts, Levels A-H, 134
Reading Curriculum Guide for Adult Basic Education, 129
Reading/Everyday Activities in Life: R/EAL, 246, 260
Reading Games: Strengthening Reading Skills, 132
Reading inventories, 235
  commercially prepared, 246
  informal, 245-46
  for listening comprehension, 288
  oral, 230, 249-50
  silent, 230, 250-51
Reading levels
  frustration, 241
  hearing-capacity, 241
  independent, 240
  instructional, 240
Reading problem
  origin of, 233
Reading process, 69, 72-73
Reading readiness, 77
Reading Tests and Reviews, 249, 275
Reading with a Smile: 90 Reading Games That Work, 132
Reality, 64
Reid, Neil A., 290
Reinforcement, 93
Reissman, Frank, 29, 32, 50

Relevancy, 63, 64
Remembering, 148, 179-80. *See also* Memory
Repetition, 134
Repression, 71
Rescue, 132
Resistance to change, 42
Reversal, 277-78
Riddles, 148, 165
Riegel, K. F., 58
Rivers, Wilga, 223
Robeck, Mildred C., 76
Roberts' English Series, 218
Roberts, Paul, 218
Robinson, Helen M., 72, 258
Rockowitz, Murray, 166
Rodale, J. I., 201
Rogers, Arnold R., 269
Rosof, Elvin, 268
Ross, Ramon, 244, 261, 348-49
Roswell-Chall Auditory Blending Test, 260
Roswell-Chall Reading Test of Word Analysis Skills, 260, 277, 279
Roswell, Florence G., 260, 277 279
Ruddell, Robert, 70, 76
Rudman, Herbert C., 273
Russell, David H., 119, 132

SRA Pictorial Reasoning Test, 296
SRA Reading Comprehension Laboratory, 134
SRA Reading Index, 273
San Diego Graded Word List: Quick Gauge of Reading Ability, 244, 261, 348-50
Sanders, Norris, 84
Savage, John F., 208
Scanning, 150
Schiffman, Gilbert B., 70
Scholastic Scopevisuals 13: Getting Applications Right, 187
School
  principal, 311
  records, 233
Schrank, R., 39
Seaman, Don F., 18
Searls, Evelyn F., 299
Second language
  ability-placement tests, 282-83
  problems, 280
Self-acceptance, 42
Self-concept, 20, 42, 66, 76, 82, 281
Self-confidence, 46-47
Self-importance, 46

Self-improvement, 14
Sensory modalities, 23, 70
Sentence
    completion, 148, 168
    structure, 210-211
Service words, 118-19
Seymour, Dorothy, 199, 207
Shaie, K. W., 54, 56, 57, 58
Shen, Yao, 208
Sherk, John K., 204
Sherman, Mark, 169
Sight-configuration skills, 83
Sight vocabulary, 118
    for older readers, 343
Significance, finding, 159-60
Silent Reading Diagnostic Test, 273,
    278-79
Silent reading tests, 250-51, 267, 268-74,
    276
Skimming, 150-51
Sleisenger, Lenore, 112
Slosson Intelligence Test, 291, 296
Slosson Oral Reading Test (SORT), 243,
    261, 343-47
Slosson, Richard L., 261, 296
Slow maturation, 22
Smith, Barry M., 269
Smith, Carl B., 177, 299
Smith, D. E., 70
Smith, E. Brooke, 208
Smith, Edwin H., 26, 37, 52, 129, 256-57,
    276, 289, 305
Smith, Frank, 76, 100, 131, 156, 167,
    264
Smith, Helen K., 60
Smith, Nila Banton, 150, 179, 180
Smith, Richard J., 134
Social
    agencies, 310
    outlets, 15
    promotion, 19
    worker, 51, 311
Socioeconomic levels, 10, 15
Sociopathic-type behavior, 45
Sociopsychological forces, 10-18
Sources of materials, 315-19
Spache, George W., 256, 274
Special alphabets, 100
Specific skill, 301-3
Speed of learning, 56-57
Speer, George, 93
Spice, 132
Standardized evaluations, 228, 235, 249,
    267, 288-89
Stanford Achievement Test, 273
Stauffer, Russell G., 116, 117, 121

Steckle, Lynde C., 297
Stein, S., 39
Stereotyping, 8
Stevick, Earl W., 210
Stewart, William C., 205
Sticht, Thomas G., 39, 76
Stipends, 50-51
Stone List, 119
*Strength-Weakness Spectrum for Wech-
    sler Tests*
    implications, 380
    performance subtests, 379
    verbal subtests, 378
Stress, 128, 330-32
Strother, C. R., 54
Structural analysis, 83, 124, 133, 279
    derived forms, 126-27
    inflected forms, 126
Structure Test-English Language
    (STEL), 283
Student personalities, 10
Study skills, 59-60
Substitution, 212
Success, 46-47
Successful teachers, 129
*Sucher-Allred Reading Placement In-
    ventory*, 261
Sucher, Floyd, 261
Suffixes, 173-74, 325
Summer Daze, 166
Suspicion, 65
Swanson, Merlyn S., 291
SWAP newsletters, 66
Swick, Kevin J., 84
Syllabication, 128-29, 329
Synonyms, 148, 172

Taylor, Grant, 213
Teacher-made inventories, 244
Television, 152, 155
Tell Me A Joke, 166
Tell Me A Riddle, 166
Terman, L. M., 57
Tesol text materials, 320-21
Test of Adult Basic Education, 273-74
Test of General Ability, 297
Test scores, comparisons of, 265-66
Test structure, 264
Test-taking techniques, 266
Test That's Not a Test, (T-NAT), 246,
    261
Thatcher, John H., 244
Thompson, Frank Jr., 246
Thompson, Richard A., 119, 132
Thorndike, Edward, 56, 92, 93

Thorndike word list, 251
Thorpe, Lois P., 269
Tiegs, Ernest W., 273
Tiffin, Joseph, 295
Time pressure, 264, 284
Tinker, Miles, 269
Topic sentences, 151-52
Tough, A., 300
Townsend, Agatha, 274
Tradition, 42-43
Transfer, of learning, 50, 93
Transformations, 217-23
Traumatic brain injuries, 22
*Triggs Diagnostic Reading Test, Survey
    Section,* 274
Triggs, Frances, 274
Tutorial instruction, 100-101

Ulmer, Curtis, 31, 62, 71-72
Understanding, 47
*United States Training and Employment
    Service Nonreading Aptitude Test
    Battery,* 297
Unstructured approach, 116

Value
    judgement, 34
    structure, 31
Van Allen, Roach, 117
Verbal
    ability, 60
    language facility, 60-61
    tests, 234-35
    vocabulary, 61
Verner, Coolie, 22, 59
Visual
    acuity, 27, 57
    defects, 22
    discrimination, 121-22
    factors, 26
    perception, 28
    performance, 27-28
    problems, 276-77
Visualization, 58
Visual-motor development, 78-79
Visuo-motor flexibility, 58
Vocabulary, 61, 215
    extension, 148, 169
    lists, 175-77
    scores, 251, 264
Vocational
    frustration, 39
    motivation, 13-14
Vowels, 127-28, 326-28

WLW Culture Fair Inventory, 297
Wagner, Guy, 119, 132
Wallace, Mary, 9, 21, 40, 47, 66, 77, 88,
    145, 236
Wallen, Carl J., 121, 123, 124
Wardhaugh, Ronald, 181
Warren, Virginia B., 8, 16, 18, 33, 49, 63,
    134, 228, 248
Wayne State University, 59
Weber, Robert E., 49, 194
Wechsler Adult Intelligence Scale, 5, 56,
    235, 292, 297, 298, 299. *See also
    Escala de Inteligencia Wechsler
    para Adultos*
Wechsler, David, 282, 297, 378-80
Weiskopf, E. A., 22
Welford, A. T., 57
Wepman Auditory Discrimination Test,
    261, 277, 366-69
Wepman, Joseph M., 26, 28, 97, 261
Wesman, Alexander G., 297
Wesman Personnel Classification Test,
    297
Whipple, James E., 62
White, Ernie, 259
Wide Range Achievement Test (WRAT),
    262
Wilkie, F., 57
Wilson, Corlett T., 262
Wilson, John, 76
Wilson, Robert M., 314
Wilson's Essential Vocabulary List, 242,
    340-41
Wilson's Essential Word List, 262
Winter, Gerald D., 11
Withdrawal adjustments, 44
Witty, Paul, 76, 78, 134, 223
Wold, Robert M., 262
*Wold Screening Tests to Be Used by the
    Classroom Teacher,* 262, 277
Woodcock Reading Mastery Test, 262
Woodcock, Richard W., 100, 262
Word
    analysis problems, 278
    games, 119, 132, 166
    identification, 121, 131-34, 138-42
    identification skills, 278
    lists, 119, 241-44, 256
        functional, 242
        grade-level, 242-44
    organization, 278
    perception, 72, 74
    wheels, 132
Word Analysis Cards, 134
Word Discrimination Test, 264, 277, 278
Wren, C. Gilbert, 59

Writing
  experience, 181-98
  skills, 86
Yaz, William, 203
Young, Robert, 201

Zimmerman, Irla Lee, 299
Zintz Compound Words, 263
Zintz List of Easily Confused Words,
  263
Zintz, Miles V., 71, 72, 76, 263, 278, 301